N

Plandome

LIRR
Little Neck
Great Neck
Auburndale
Bayside
Douglaston
Broadway

Flushing
Main St
Flushing
ets Point
Hollis
Shea Stadium
111 St
LIRR
103 St-Corona Plaza
FLUSHING MEADOWS
CORONA PARK
nction Blvd
169 St
mhurst Ave
Parsons Blvd
ood Ave
Woodhaven Blvd
63 Dr-Rego Park
65 Ave
Forest Hills
71 Ave
75 Ave
Kew Gardens
Union Tpke
Briarwood
Van Wyck Blvd
Sutphin Blvd
Jamaica Center
Parsons/Archer
E·J·Z
R
Forest
Hills
Kew
Gardens
Briarwood
Van Wyck
Sutphin Blvd
Archer Ave
JFK Airport
E·J·Z·LIRR
Laurelton
FOREST
PARK
121 St
J·Z
111 St
J
Ozone Park
Lefferts Blvd
A
Middle Village
Metropolitan Ave
M
104 St
J·Z
Woodhaven Blvd
85 St-Forest Pkwy
111 St
A
Fresh Pond Rd
M
Forest Ave
M
Rockaway Blvd
104 St
A
75 St
Cypress Hills
88 St
Seneca Ave
M
EVERGREEN
CEMETERY
80 St
Dekalb Ave
Crescent St
J·Z
Aqueduct Racetrack
Halsey St
Wilson Ave
Norwood Ave
J·Z
Grant Ave
Aqueduct
North Conduit Ave
A
Myrtle
Wyckoff Aves
L·M
Bushwick Ave
Aberdeen St
Cleveland St
J·Z
Euclid Ave
A·C
cker Ave
Chauncey St
Broadway
Junction
J·L·Z
Van Siclen Ave
Shepherd Ave
Howard Beach
JFK Airport
A
al Ave
J
Alabama Ave
J
AIRTRAIN
JFK
INTERNATIONAL
AIRPORT
Woodm
Gates Ave
J·Z
Atlantic
Ave
C
Liberty
Ave
C
Vab Siclen Ave
C
Kosciuszko St
J
East NY
New Lots Ave
3
Sutter Ave
C
Van Siclen Ave
3
Lawrence
A·C
Halsey St
L
Ralph Ave
C
Rockaway Ave
C
Pennsylvania Ave
3
Inwood
A·C
Utica Ave
A·C
Junius St
3
Livonia Ave
3
Far Rockaway
Mott Ave
A
ington
Throop Aves
LIRR
Rockaway Ave
3
New Lots Ave
3
Beach 25 St
A
Nostrand Aves
Saratoga Ave
3
East 105 St
Beach 36 St
A
A
Crown Hts
Utica Ave
3·4
4
Sutter Ave-Rutland Rd
Beach 40 St
A
Franklin Ave
2·3
Kingston Ave
3
Canarsie
Rockaway Pkwy
L
Beach 60 St
A
Nostrand Ave
Broad Channel
A·S
President St
Beach 67 St
A
Botanic
Garden
Sterling St
St
Prospect
Park
2·3
Winthrop St
Church Ave
2·5
Church Ave
Beach 90

inside **NEW YORK 2011**

inside NEW YORK

PUBLISHER Alessandra Gotbaum
EDITOR-IN-CHIEF Yin Yin Lu

DINING EDITOR Adam May
FEATURES EDITOR Elaine Wang
NEIGHBORHOODS EDITOR Anna Feuer
NIGHTLIFE EDITOR Trevor Vaz

ASSOCIATE EDITORS Chloe Eichler
Austin Moukattaf
Natalie Schachar

LAYOUT & GRAPHIC DESIGN Beatrix Carroll
MAPS Jed Dore

STAFF EDITORS Nina Lukina
Mila Rusafova
Cody Zupnick

WEB EDITORS Kyla Cheung
Deaton Jones
José Stephan Perez

STAFF WRITERS
Lauren Bishop, Reuben Blum, Ashton Cooper, Frances Corry, Dan Flatley, Sarah Fox, Katherine Freedman, Ahiza Garcia, Shane Galante, Alexis Nedd, Tomasz Otlowski, Anthony Patterson, Zander Padget, Maya Popa, Shruti Sehgal, Zack Sheppard, Juliana Stebbins, Sara Weber, Evan Wilson

CONTRIBUTORS
Daniel Bachrach, Helen Bao, Nishant Batsha, Mpho Brown, Rose Donlon, Shane Ferro, Morgan Fletcher, Helen Goodman, Ariel Hudes, Evan Johnston, Tim Moran, Ilya Okunev, Sheila Palmer, Justine Rosenthal, Ian Scheffler, Michael Snyder, John Speyer

PHOTOGRAPHERS
Michelle Andujar, Lauren Bishop, Shirin Borthwick, Cara Buchanan, Kyla Cheung, Maurice Decaul, Chloe Eichler, Dan Flatley, Alice Gao, Vladimir Lukin, Nina Lukina, Zander Padget, Serena Piol, Tomasz Otlowski, Justine Rosenthal, Mila Rusafova, Natalie Schachar, Julienne Schaer, Elaine Wang, Cody Zupnick.
Back page spread and InsideNewYork.com ads: Julienne Schaer

SALES ASSOCIATE
Adrian Soghoian

Inside New York
2960 Broadway, MC 5727
New York, NY 10027
212-854-2804
www.insidenewyork.com

Printed by:
Ripon Printers
656 S. Douglas Street
Ripon, WI 54971

Special thanks to Syeda Lewis, Sam Reisman, Beth Vanderputten, Bernadette Maxwell, Jared Hecht, Heather Perceval, Al Spuler, and the whole Columbia CCE staff.

If you are interested in purchasing advertising space in Inside New York or on insidenewyork.com, e-mail ads@insidenewyork.com or call 212-854-2804.

For bulk sales, university sales, corporate sales, or customized editions, e-mail info@insidenewyork.com or call 212-854-280.

If your bookstore would like to carry Inside New York, contact Columbia University Press at 800-944-8648.

Inside New York is a publication of the Student Enterprises Division of Columbia University.

New York is a city that resists definition. Or, rather, it resists one definition—it can be defined in many different ways, all of which are extreme. It's the city that never sleeps. The financial, cultural, culinary, media, fashion, and entertainment capital of the world. The metropolis of America, and America's leading tourist resort. The city of light, towers, orchestras, skyscrapers, islands, and friendly people. New York City doesn't just have everything: it is everything.

Yes, it's overwhelming, discombobulating, and impossible to completely understand. But it can also feel as familiar as home. As Alistair Cooke once proclaimed, "New York is the biggest collection of villages in the world." And indeed, this city of cities has been called the crossroads of the globe, the ultimate melting pot. Think of it not as a sprawling metropolis, but as an amalgamation of small neighborhoods, each with its own distinct identity and ethnic enclaves. This is the way we've presented New York—not as a place to visit, but as a place to live. Within each neighborhood, we've highlighted the faces behind the storefronts, the people who own them, who frequent them every day. It is these people who define the city, who literally make it what it is: a magnificent cosmopolitan microcosm, from Greenpoint's Little Poland to West Harlem's Little Senegal.

But this book is not complete. We've featured what we think are the quirkiest, most unconventional local haunts, as well as the best of the conventional mainstays the city has to offer. Go to these places, but don't limit yourself to them—for the only way to become a true Inside New Yorker is to make the city your own. We've only given you where to begin. The rest is up to circumstance, your sharpest instincts, and your most reliable pair of walking shoes.

Alessandra Gotbaum, Publisher
Yin Yin Lu, Editor-in-Chief

SYMBOLS KEY

 Vegetarian

 Vegan

 Wifi

 Outdoor Seating

 Kosher

 Delivery / Take out

 BYOB

 All Ages Allowed

 Dancing

 18+

 Live Music

 Cash Only

TABLE OF CONTENTS

ESSENTIALS

Casual sightseeing is one thing, but spending quality time in New York City is quite another. To distinguish yourself from the swarms of camera-clicking, fanny pack-toting tourists, you'll need to immerse yourself in the day-to-day essentials of city life. Whether you're on an extended stay or have begun to call the city "home," these sections will give you the scoop on basic metropolitan operations.

The typical tourist unfolds an unwieldy subway map, but fret not—you can maneuver the city's labyrinthine streets without looking like a total tenderfoot. Prep yourself on the metro system, city buses, commuter rails, taxis, and more in **Transportation**. Read **Settling In** for tips and tricks on finding the right housing for your needs, as well as how to install all-important amenities such as Wi-Fi, phone service, and cable.

    Government & Safety and **City Commerce** will give you the lowdown on important branches of city government, staying safe, banking, business hours, taxes, and tipping. To truly become an informed New Yorker, you'll need to keep up with some of the cardinal periodicals, television channels, radio stations, and blogs listed under **Media**.

Though real estate prices are as outrageous as ever, you don't have to be a Rockefeller to roost in New York City. By renting instead of buying, or checking into a hostel instead of a Marriott, there are ways to save big bucks. Just be willing to compromise, plan ahead, and keep in mind that the more luxurious your new pad, the less you'll want to venture out to explore the city (that's not to say you should downgrade to a closet, of course).

HOSTELS

For the frugal traveler passing through for a few days, a hostel provides all the essential amenities of a hotel at only a fraction of the cost. Besides saving a few bucks, the upside of sharing cramped quarters is getting discounted tours and the chance to meet travelers from around the world. Although naysayers cite safety and cleanliness as primary concerns, the city offers plenty of reputable choices with spaces in hot demand. Here are some, with rates listed per person, per night:

As the largest independent hostel in the city, **Chelsea International** gets high ratings for its cleanliness and unbeatable location within walking distance of all that downtown has to offer in eating, shopping, and bar-carousing. *251 W 20th St. 212-647-0010. $40.*

Tried-and-true with tours, bar crawls, and summer BBQs to boot, the Upper West Side's **Jazz on the Park** offers a restful lull from the downtown hubbub. *36 W 106th St. 212-932-1600. $27-85.*

Clean and spacious, **The New York Loft Hostel** occupies a former warehouse in gentrifying East Williamsburg, conveniently two blocks off the Morgan Avenue stop on the L Train. *249 Varet St. 718-366-1351. $45-65.*

SUBLETS

If you plan on staying in New York for several weeks or months, you will most likely want to find a sublet. A sublet is an agreement in which the tenant allows a subtenant to share his lodgings for a certain length of time in return for a rental fee. Essentially, the tenant pays the landlord and you pay the tenant.

This form of housing is flexible and convenient, but be warned—many sublets in New York are illegal (that is, offered without the consent of the landlord). Plenty of renters and their subtenants choose to take the risk, but if a dispute arises or the boarder stops paying rent to the landlord, the subtenant could be evicted and the tenant lose his or her security deposit. Unless you sign a sublease provided by the landlord, you are probably violating the tenant's lease and have little legal recourse.

The best place to look for sublets is online or through word-of-mouth. Many people find sublets through **craigslist.org**, **newyorkcity.sublet.com**, or **subletinthecity.com**. Of these three, Craigslist is the most popular, but watch out for scams. Be wary if someone asks you to wire money or send a copy of your passport.

SETTLING IN

FINDING AN APARTMENT

Finding an apartment to rent in New York City is a juggling act between your budget and your needs and desires. Many people get a shock the first time they see an apartment in Manhattan ("*This* costs $3,000 a month? At home, that would get me a mansion!"). So adjust your expectations accordingly, and be ready to compromise on either space (size and amenities), neighborhood, or price.

When to Start

Planning ahead is always advisable, but don't expect to find an apartment two months in advance. Housing turns over quickly in New York, and landlords often put up apartments only two weeks before the expected date of signing a lease. Begin your search about one month or three weeks prior to your anticipated move-in date. This gives you time to do armchair research, tour the neighborhoods on your list, and inspect a few viable spaces.

Searching

Most people use the internet for apartment hunting. Hands down the most popular website, **craigslist.org** updates listings every minute and has one of the largest inventories of available apartments. Other user-friendly sites include the *Village Voice* online (**villagevoice. com**), **rapidnyc.com**, and **hotpads.com**.

On all of these sites, watch out for realtors' exaggerations and distortions. Some will use a photo from a different but "similar" apartment in the same building, while others might substitute "East Williamsburg" for Bushwick or the "The Upper West Side" for Harlem Only follow up on ads that give the exact address of the apartment.

Brokers

They can be helpful in expediting your search, but avoid the ones who charge a broker's fee. Look for the words "no fee" in listings, and con-

firm this with the person showing you the apartment—either the owner, usually an employee from a large real estate company or the broker himself. If you choose to go with a broker, let the agent amaze you by showing you apartments that fit your needs.

Viewing

Now comes the exciting day when you have arranged to visit a select handful of apartments. If you're looking at several in the same area, it makes sense to schedule viewings about 45 minutes apart. This gives you time to ask questions about each, walk to the next, and not be overwhelmed in the process.

Bring a water bottle, a tape measure, a camera, a notebook, a checkbook, and a friend. Don't be afraid to get down and measure rooms, ask questions, take pictures, and make notes. If you find a place that you like, the agent or broker will take you back to their office to fill out an application. Many students use guarantors (often parents) who guarantee that the tenant will pay rent on time by showing proof of income. Be ready to fax the appropriate application to your guarantor, who should have his or her financial documents ready.

Finding Roommates

If you don't know anyone that you want to live with, or the timing isn't working out, publicize your search in every way you can. Ask friends, post on Facebook, put up signs at work, and advertise on **craigslist.org**, **easyroommate. com**, or **newyork.backpage.com**. If you don't know the person who responds, interview them about their background, current activities, and means of paying rent. If you're set on getting a roommate for your new apartment, consider finding one before you sign the lease so that you are both legally bound to pay.

Buying
The price of purchasing real estate varies widely throughout the city. As with leasing an apartment, the trade-off is between location and size. Brooklyn wows with plenty of chic condos starting from about $400k or $500k, while prime ground in Manhattan hikes up the sum to $800k or $900k.

AMENITIES

The city offers more activities than one can complete in a lifetime, but sometimes all you want to do is keep your laptop company and stay home, surfing the web, watching TV, or chatting with a friend over the phone. These well-established providers will install whatever service you need when you pick up the phone and call. Carefully consider which packages suit your needs and compare prices before making a final purchasing decision.

Wireless Internet
While free Wi-Fi, internet cafés, and work stations in public libraries and schools provide convenient access to the web, having 24/7 wireless at your fingertips is indispensable these days. All of these providers offer low introductory rates, but after a period of about six months, prices will increase to roughly $40-50. If you're determined, you can negotiate a lower price by threatening to switch to a different provider.

Comcast (1-866-937-1750). $19.99/month for first six months, then $42.99/month.
Optimum Online (1-866-552-2048). Starts at $29.95/month.
Time Warner (1-866-924-7257). Starts at $34.95/month.

Phone Services
Cell phones are ubiquitous, but it's useful to have another set of digits in case you're unreachable via cell. Plus, there's nothing like having your own landline to feel completely settled in at your new address. These national providers can hook you up with a plan that meets your needs:

AT&T (1-888-333-6651). From $39.99/month.
Verizon (800-256-4646). From $39.99/month.

Cable and Satellite TV
Unless you're planning to glue your eyes to Youtube or Hulu on your laptop screen, you'll want cable to catch all your must-see shows and stay up-to-date on breaking developments. These providers deliver your favorite programs live, offering prices that depend on how many add-on channels you'd like:

DirecTV (1-877-265-9218). From $24.99/month.
Optimum (1-866-747-3455). From $29.99/month.
Time Warner (1-866-924-7257). $49.99/month.

13

A whopping population of over eight million makes parking in the city an ordeal, so it's hardly surprising that some New Yorkers have never sat behind a wheel—nor wish to. Fortunately, a sprawling 24-hour subway system and extensive bus lines (both local and interstate) make travel both convenient and affordable. There's a cab, bus, train, or boat for every occasion, as public transit options range from the speedy to the scenic, the economic to the luxurious.

WALKING

New York may have a plethora of public transportation options, but traveling al fresco is sometimes the most convenient way to get around, especially when trains are delayed. With a few helpful pointers in mind, navigating Manhattan's rectangular **grid system** is a cinch. Streets north of Houston stretch horizontally across the island and increase in number from 1st (right above Houston St) north to 220th. Avenues run vertically and increase from 1st Ave by the East River west to 12th Ave on the shores of the Hudson. Lengths of blocks vary, however—an avenue is usually two to four times longer than the average street block. Here are some **deviations** from the grid system:

- East of 1st Ave between Houston and 14th St lie four additional avenues collectively known as Alphabet City. From west to east, these are lettered A, B, C, and D.
- North of 14th St, between 3rd Ave and 5th are Lexington, Park, and Madison Ave from east to west.
- Between 59th and 110th St, the avenues west of 7th are Central Park West, Columbus, Amsterdam, and West End.
- The West Village, which predates the 1811 grid plan of Manhattan, seems to be turned 30 degrees counterclockwise, lying on a true east-west axis.
- Broadway cuts across Manhattan at an angle from northwest to southeast.
- 6th Ave is also known as Avenue of the Americas.
- South of Houston St and in most of the outer boroughs, streets have names rather than numbers.

SUBWAYS

New York City's crisscrossing webwork of underground trains is the fundamental mode of everyday transit: it carries an average of 7 million straphangers to 468 stations every day. Although service slows overnight, most lines operate 24/7 along their main routes. Each of the 24 lines is designated by either a number or a letter. Lines grouped under a single color share the same track for part of their run, in which case one or more will be express, stopping at certain stations only, and the others local, making all stops.

When looking for the right platform to board your train, follow the "Uptown" or "Downtown" signs. Trains are referred to by their number or letter and either their final stop or destination borough (a downtown N train, for example, might be called "Brooklyn-bound N"). For up-to-the-minute updates on service delays, maps, schedules, and route changes, visit **mta.info**. You can also use **HopStop.com** to find the fastest course by train, bus, or foot.

Popular Stops

Several major stations transfer an influx of riders from one line to another. If you're lost, it helps to get off at one of these gateways to

TRANSPORTATION

reorient yourself:
Times Sq-42nd St: ❶❷❸❼ⓃⓆⓇ Ⓢ
connection to Port Authority Bus Terminal
Grand Central-42nd St: ❹❺❻❼Ⓢ
connection to Metro-North
34th St-Herald Sq: ⒷⒹ❻ⒻⓂ Ⓝ Ⓡ
connection to PATH
34th St-Penn Station: ❶❷❸ⒶⒸⒺ
connection to Amtrak, LIRR, NJ Transit
14th St-Union Sq: ❹❺❻ⓁⓃ Ⓠ Ⓡ
In Brooklyn, **Atlantic Ave-Pacific St** ❷❸
❹❺ⒷⒹⓇⓇ is second only to Times Square
in the number of lines it serves.

CITY BUSES

MTA compensates for the limitations of its
subway system: hop on a bus to go crosstown
above 59th St or to get around in the outer
boroughs, where subway stations are often
spread far apart. Some New Yorkers prefer
the bus to traveling underground simply for
the leisurely street gazing it affords. The 200+
routes are named by a letter designating their
primary borough (B=Brooklyn, Bx=Bronx,
M=Manhattan, Q=Queens, S=Staten Island),
followed by a number. Any bus route beginning
with a "BM," "QM," "BxM," or "X" is express,
meaning that it runs through an outer borough
and Manhattan, skipping some stops along the
way. A "limited" bus is one that runs on a local
route but skips certain stops. For a complete
listing of routes and hours check **mta.info**,
especially since most buses don't run between
midnight and 5am, and some halt service over
the weekends.

METROCARDS

MetroCards can be purchased from
vending machines located in every
subway station. Avoid ferreting for exact
change by using your card to board
MTA buses as well. A single ride on a
subway or local bus costs $2.25, while a
ride on an express bus is $5. The vending
machine adds a 15% bonus for refillable
cards with over $8 in purchases.

Frequent travelers can buy a MetroCard
with unlimited rides for a day or over a
period of 7, 14, or 30 days. But unlike
regular MetroCards, these are not
accepted on express buses or the PATH
train. Unlimited-ride cards always allow
free transfers from bus to subway (and
vice versa), while pay-per-ride cards
allow free transfers within two hours
of the initial swipe. The new EasyPay
Xpress program allows customers to
turn their debit or credit card into a
MetroCard that automatically refills
every month.

You can also get discounts at
participating museums, restaurants, and
stores with the purchase of your card.
Visit **mta.info** for details.

TAXIS

Over 13,000 cabbies roam Manhattan on the lookout for potential fares. Although more expensive than the subway or bus, taxis are faster and more comfortable.

Standard City Cab Rate:

- $2.50 base fee.
- $0.40 for each additional unit (1/5 mile or minute spent idle/traveling at less than 12 mph).
- Night surcharge of $0.50 between 8pm and 6am.
- Weekday peak hours (Mon-Fri 4-8pm) surcharge of $1.
- New York State tax surcharge of $0.50 per ride.
- Varying bridge and tunnel tolls.
- A flat fee of $45, plus applicable tolls, from JFK to Manhattan. Newark airport rides to Manhattan are metered, with a $15 surcharge.
- It is customary to tip 10-15% for short rides and 15-20% for longer distances.

You can pay the driver with cash or credit card. To estimate the cost and time of your cab ride in advance, visit **nyc.taxiwiz.com**. Keep your receipt in case you leave something behind in the car. If this happens, submit a report online at **nyc.gov**.

If you're in an outer borough and need a ride, call a livery cab service (aka car service) such as **Court Express Car Service** (*718-237-8888*), **Elite Car and Limousine Services** (*718-937-6336*), and **Arecibo Car Service** (*718-783-6465*). These companies can only take customers who call ahead, and the dispatcher will quote a fare on the phone. Make sure that the car that comes to pick you up has a base name and number on its side and an ID behind the driver's seat. To file a complaint, call 311 or go to **nyc.gov/tlc**. Although rare, a seedy car

how to... **HAIL A CAB**

Whether you're running late for a meeting or caught in a sudden downpour, flagging down a cab can be a desperate challenge at times. But like all survival skills, it can be taught and honed with experience.

1 Stand on the curb with your hand outstretched and look for a yellow taxi with a lit-up number on its roof.

2 If others are waiting, cab drivers will pick up the closest person on the sidewalk. Either wait your turn or discreetly edge your way in the direction of oncoming traffic.

3 Tell the driver right away where you're headed. Cabbies are obligated to take you anywhere in the five boroughs.

might try to solicit your business on the street. These chauffeurs operate illegal "gypsy cabs," and their passengers commonly complain of being ripped off.

COMMUTER TRAINS

New York City is connected to a far-flung network of local and long-distance rail lines that shepherd droves of regular commuters, vacationers, and business travelers into the city every day.

Amtrak
- National rail operator with service to all 50 states.
- Three lines from Penn Station: Northeast Regional local service to Springfield, MA ($30), Philadelphia ($35), and Boston ($40), Acela Express for faster but more expensive service to the same cities, and Empire Service to Albany ($37).
- Amtrak.com, 1-800-USA-RAIL

Long Island Rail Road (LIRR)
- Service to Long Island from Penn Station, Atlantic Terminal (Brooklyn), Hunterspoint Ave (Queens), and Jamaica (Queens).
- Rates vary by destination, direction, and time of day ($14.25-29 to the Hamptons).
- mta.info/lirr

New Jersey Transit
- Routes to northern and central New Jersey from Penn Station.
- Rates vary by destination ($15 to Newark Airport).
- njtransit.com

PATH
- Rapid-transit railroad with service from 34th St-Herald Sq and WTC to stations in New Jersey (Hoboken, Journal Square, and Newark).
- Flat fare for one trip is $1.75. Accepts pay-

essentials.transportation

per-ride MetroCard swipes.

- panynj.gov/path

Metro-North Railroad

- Service to upstate New York, Connecticut, and parts of northern New Jersey.
- All trains depart from Grand Central Terminal and Harlem-125th St (*125th St & Park Ave*), but trains to Pascack Valley and Port Jervis depart from Hoboken, NJ.
- Rates vary by destination, direction, and time of day ($7.25-9.75 one way from GCT to White Plains).
- mta.info/mnr

INTERSTATE BUSES

Slower but less expensive than their choo-chugging counterparts, national buses are a viable option for any destination within five hours of the city. Most interstate bus companies operate from the **Port Authority**

Bus Terminal (*42nd St & 8th Ave*), while the cheaper but less regulated **Chinatown buses** have their own pick-up locations. For any bus line, it's best to arrive early. Greyhound sometimes lets customers with later departure times grab a spot on an earlier bus, but may turn away ticketed passengers who arrive once the bus is full.

Greyhound

- Largest national bus company; has over 2,400 stops nationwide, many in small towns.
- Departs from Port Authority with prices varying by destination; discounts available online ($12 to Philadelphia, $20 to Boston).
- Book at greyhound.com or call 1-800-231-2222.

Megabus

- Service to Boston, Philadelphia, Washington, Baltimore, Albany, Buffalo, Toronto, and other cities in the area.
- Departs from outside of Penn Station (*31st

St and 8th Ave).
- Book in advance for tickets as low as $1.
- Tickets can only be bought online at megabus.com or at the ticketing counter across from the pick-up location.

Popular Chinatown Bus Lines
- Fung Wah Bus (*139 Canal St, fungwahbus.com*): $15 hourly buses to Boston.
- New Century Travel (*20 Allen St, www.2000coach.com*): $12 hourly buses to Philadelphia, $20 to Washington DC.
- Bus lines pick up and drop off passengers at their respective addresses in Chinatown.
- Tickets can be bought online or at the station.

AIRPORTS

John F. Kennedy (JFK)
- Located in Jamaica, Queens.
- Services all major domestic and international airlines.
- Directions: **Ⓐ Ⓔ Ⓙ Ⓩ** or LIRR from Penn Station to Jamaica Station, then AirTrain ($5 to and between terminals); B15 bus ($2.25); Super Shuttle ($20-25, 800-BLUE-VAN); taxi ($45 plus tolls and tip).

LaGuardia Airport (LGA)
- Located in Flushing, Queens.
- Services domestic flights.
- Directions: New York Airport Service Express Bus from Grand Central, Port Authority Air Trans Center, or Penn Station ($12); M60 bus from 106th St & Broadway ($2.25); Super Shuttle ($15-20); metered taxi ($20-30 plus tolls and tip).

Newark Liberty International Airport (EWR)
- Located in Newark, NJ.
- Services international and domestic flights.
- Directions: NJ Transit from Penn Station ($15); express bus from Port Authority or Grand Central ($15); Super Shuttle ($25-30); metered taxi ($50-60 plus tolls and tip).

ALTERNATIVES

ZipCar
This car rental service lets you reserve cars online for an hourly fee of $8 with 180 free miles, as long as you're willing to pay $50 a year and a $25 application fee.

Staten Island Ferry
Now free, this famous ferry takes passengers to Staten Island 24 hours a day.

NY Waterway
For a scenic Hudson cruise to parts of New Jersey, board a ferry at Battery Park, Pier 11-Wall Street, or W 39th St.

essentials.government & safety

Ah, bureaucracy, that soulless system despised by the masses. As much as ordinary folks would like to keep the red tape of government at arm's length from day-to-day life, the first time you receive a parking ticket, it helps to know which part of the beast you'll be dealing with. Becoming acquainted with the various branches of officialdom empowers New Yorkers to take charge on issues close to home. And it's nice to know which eyes and ears are looking out for your safety and well-being.

CITY OFFICIALS

In a city of over 8 million residents, the well-oiled government can seem exhaustively complex. The mayor oversees the affairs of the entire city, which is divided into five boroughs: the Bronx, Manhattan, Queens, Brooklyn, and Staten Island. The boroughs are organized into 51 districts, each of which appoints a representative for City Council. The 59 community boards tend to local matters concerning residents within their respective zones.

New Yorkers get to elect the following top public officials (names current as of print):

Mayor: Michael Bloomberg
Comptroller: John C. Liu
Public Advocate: Bill de Blasio
City Council Speaker: Christine C. Quinn
Bronx BP: Ruben Diaz Jr.
Brooklyn BP: Marty Markowitz
Manhattan BP: Scott Stringer
Queens BP: Helen M. Marshall
Staten Island BP: James P. Molinaro

BEAUROCRACY

There's no simple way of breaking down the metropolis's labyrinthine bureaucracy. But it pays to know some of the major organs through which your tax dollars are flowing.
* **The Board of Elections** oversees voter registration, city council elections, and the selection of the mayor.
* **Department of Correction** is responsible for the city's inmates, most of whom are housed on Riker's Island and Roosevelt Island.
* **Department of Health and Mental Hygiene** operates free mental health clinics, distributes condoms, and shuts down your favorite restaurant.
* **Department of Sanitation** dumps your trash and handles recycling.
* **Department of Transportation** manages the road system and renames streets.
* **Taxi and Limousine Commission** regulates official cabs and determines the rate.
* **Office of the Mayor** has the final word on just about anything.

PANHANDLING

A stroll down Park Avenue will bring you past luxurious apartment buildings and vagrants sleeping on street corners. Although homelessness has fallen over the years, disparity in wealth remains conspicuous and widespread. While some of the less fortunate don't seek or accept money, others will entreat passerby for spare change. If you choose to give directly to panhandlers, be sure to carry coins in easily accessible pockets. Concerned that monetary donations would assist drug addiction, some New Yorkers choose to donate canned foods or send their cash through organizations such as **Picture the Homeless, Coalition for the Homeless, and City Harvest.**

GOVERNMENT & SAFETY

SAFETY

New York City real estate prices have gone through the roof—in part because of the dramatic reduction in crime over the last 20 years. The rampant violence that plagued the city in the 70s and 80s was unprecedented. Wealthy residents left in droves as impoverished neighborhoods fell into states of disrepute. In the 1990s, Mayor Giuliani's administration launched a series of crime prevention initiatives including Comp-Stat and Broken Window Policing. These measures, along with a beefed up police force, helped transform areas like Times Square from a seedy red light district into the family-friendly, touristy destination it has since become.

Although New York City now ranks among the safest major cities in the country, it's still important to take basic precautions against the realities of urban life. Criminals prey on those who are vulnerable, unaware of their surroundings, or unable to get help, so keep your guard up and use common sense to steer out of trouble. To ward off persistent panhandlers, walk confidently and don't make eye contact. Always store your valuables in the inner compartments of your backpack or purse, and keep a good grip on your bags. Be extra vigilant of pickpockets or purse snatchers when milling in crowds.

Some neighborhoods are less safe than others, so talk to people, do some research, and know where to go and when. According to recent FBI statistics, the area around 125th St and St. Nicholas Ave ranks among the most dangerous neighborhoods in the country.

When venturing out at dusk, it's best to stick to well-lit, populated streets. Save the iPod for later—distracted pedestrians wearing headphones are often targets of theft. If you are approached in a way that makes you uncomfortable, politely demand your space, but don't overreact to any provocations. You can also take refuge in the nearest store and ask the shopkeeper for assistance. If worst comes to worst, don't hesitate to call 911.

EMERGENCY numbers

911 Emergency Services
311 Government Information and Services
646-610-5000 Police Switchboard
800-577-8477 Police Tip Line
212-577-7777 Crime Victims Hotline
212-267-7273 Rape Hotline
800-621-4673 Domestic Violence Report Hotline
800-543-3638 Crisis Intervention
212-340-4494 Poison Control
718-722-3600 Arson Hotline

essentials.city commerce

Pundits and Europeans declare that Wall Street is in a state of decline, but Times Square's LED screens insist otherwise. Proudly brandishing the names of corporate giants, this greenback-rolling metropolis dares naysayers to sully its sensational CNBC rap as "the financial capital of the world." With 42 Fortune 500 companies and a gross metropolitan product of over $1 trillion, it's clear that when it comes to dollar signs and numbers, this city means business.

CHOOSING A BANK

With over 200 banks in the city, there's no shortage of competition for your financial investments, but figuring out which is the best fit for your banking needs can be a challenge. To start, decide what kind of account—checking, savings, money market, etc.—you're looking to open.

The last thing you want is to sign up with an institution whose branches are few and far between. It can be a nuisance to get charged for having to use a different bank's ATM. If you're the globetrotting type, you might also want to

consider which banks have the greatest presence overseas so that you can easily withdraw funds from your account while abroad.

Visit your local branches to speak to customer service representatives in person. Ask if they offer **special student packages** or other plans such as **joint accounts** that suit your needs. Compare **annual maintenance fees** and **interest rates** if you're planning to apply for a credit card. Consider any **limitations** such as minimum deposit, a quota on the number of withdrawals you can make per month, or hidden fees associated with the account.

OPERATING HOURS

While the city doesn't need the help of the energizer bunny to run 24/7, not every business is open all day and night: even public parks have their downtime. Every office and venue has its own hours, but here are some approximations:

- **Banks:** 9am-5pm during the week; many are open Saturdays from 9am-noon.
- **Bars:** Open anywhere between 2-5pm for happy hour and close by 4am.
- **Clubs:** Open anywhere from 8-10pm and close anytime between 4-7am.
- **Parks:** Many close after nightfall, although some stay open until midnight.
- **Pharmacies and drugstores:** Most are 24/7 but others have regular business hours.
- **Post offices:** 8:30 or 9am-5pm on weekdays; 9am-noon on Saturdays.

CITY COMMERCE

TIPPING POINTS

Since gratuity comprises a significant portion of a worker's income, leaving an adequate tip is not just recommended but necessary for the following services:

Bartenders
Tipping is crucial if you're hoping to expedite your order at the counter: $1 for a beer, $2-3 for a mixed drink, 15-20% on the total tab.

Hairdressers or barbers
In general, the more time a stylist devotes to your mane, the more generously you should tip: 15-20% of the base cost. To thank the assistants who shampoo or blow-dry your locks, leave $3-5.

Maids and housekeepers
Since hotel staff must be careful not to take items that belong to you, leave your tip in an unsealed envelop in your room: $1-2 at a motel, $3-5 at a hotel.

Porters and bellhops
For heavier luggage, tip $3 per item, otherwise $1-2 per bag.

Sommeliers
Depending on the classiness of the venue, $2-3 for a glass of wine and 15-20% for a bottle.

Taxi drivers
10-15% in general, 15-20% for longer distanc-

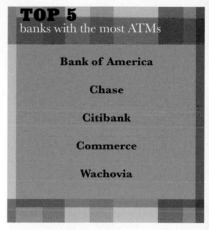

TOP 5
banks with the most ATMs

Bank of America

Chase

Citibank

Commerce

Wachovia

es. Always tip a limo driver 15-20%.

Waiters and waitresses
15-20% of the pretax bill is standard. 20-25% for luxurious fine dining.

SALES TAX

New York's **8.375%** sales and use tax comprises a 4% sales tax, a 4% state sales and use tax, and a 0.375% surcharge for the MTA. Most tangible personal property, gas, telephone, electricity, cleaning, maintenance services, hotel and motel occupancy, food and beverages sold at restaurants, and admission prices to amusement sites are among the goods and services subject to this tax.

Anything can change in a New York minute, so it's no wonder some of the most prestigious news outlets in the world are headquartered here. From Pulitzer prize-amassing juggernauts to riveting tabloids, papers and magazines circulate all the talk that's buzz-worthy and more, while local tube stations zero in on neighborhood-specific stories. Radio talk shows and the robust blogosphere cover the rest, chewing over every development from economics to juicy hearsay in this "age of interconnectedness."

NEWSPAPERS

New York Times (*nytimes.com*)
Heralded as "the newspaper of record" since its inception in 1851, the *Times* is the shining paragon of investigative journalism. Besides publishing all the international and national news "that's fit to print," it features a left-leaning editorial page and various lifestyle sections.

Wall Street Journal (*online.wsj.com*)
This finance and biz-focused broadsheet is the most widely circulated of all newspapers, on par with the prestige of the *Times*, but with a conservative swing.

Daily News (*nydailynews.com*)
The layperson's newsfeed, New York's leading tabloid distinguishes itself in its reportage of the city's crime-busting operations as well as another kind of investigative work—digging the dirt on famous names.

New York Observer (*observer.com*)
The cream of the tabloid crop, the *Observer's* slick salmon sheets can be spotted on Upper East Side stoops. Most famous for publishing Candace Bushnell's column on Manhattan social life, which became the basis for *Sex and the City*, there's no denying that the *Observer's* influence and its coverage of culture, media, and real estate is nothing short of "fabulous."

Village Voice (*villagevoice.com*)
A weekly outlet with eclectic content, the *Voice* hails from the Bohemian cradle of Greenwich Village with arts reviews, current affairs, event listings, and "Best Of's."

MAGAZINES

New Yorker (*newyorker.com*)
When it comes to the art of good writing, *The New Yorker's* iconic dandy Eustace Tilley sets the gold standard. With sharp "Talk of the Town" commentaries, short fiction, and titillating cartoons, Condé Nast's weekly publication is not just your typical coffee table essential.

New York Magazine (*nymag.com*)
Devoted to lifestyle pleasures, the weekly *New York Magazine* is the authoritative silver tongue on food and drink.

Time Out New York (*newyork.timeout.com*)
A staple in every major city, this daily calendar of sorts provides the lowdown on the Big Apple's juiciest offerings in fine arts, books, music, theater, dance, restaurants, and shopping. For a feel-good spending spree, consult the shopping section for the week's sample sales.

El Diario la Prensa (*eldiariony.com*)
The city's most-read Spanish-language daily, *El Diario* broadcasts local, national, and global affairs with special attention on Latin America.

Next Magazine (*nextmagazine.com*)
Considered the premier guide to New York's gay scene, *Next* features weekly LGBT-specific reviews of dining, theater, shopping, and nightlife.

TELEVISION

NY1 (*ny1.com*)
As New York's 24-hour cable news station, New York One certainly has the time to spare for ridiculous segments such as "In the Papers"—a rundown of top ink-and-paper headlines. But the channel does deliver more serious news stories, especially in the outer boroughs.

Manhattan Neighborhood Network (*mnn.org*)
Nothing says it better than the slogan "You're What's On!" when it comes to the company that provides programming for four public access channels. The country's oldest network includes news, shows, documentaries, and even sketch comedy by up-and-comers.

RADIO

WNYC (*93.9 FM or 820 AM, wnyc.org*)
National Public Radio's home in New York gathers the largest radio audience in the country. All of the traditional NPR shows are broadcasted, as well as some WNYC specials such as Soundcheck Showcase and Studio 360, the station's pop culture guide.

WFAN (*660 AM, wfan.com*)
"The Fan" is America's first 24/7 sports talk station.

Commercial Stations
Tune in to **WXRK** for alternative (*92.3 FM; krockradio.com*), **WQXR** for classical (*96.3 FM; wqxr.com*), **WQHT** for hip-hop (*97.1 FM; hot97. com*), **WCBS** for classic rock (*101.1 FM; wcbsfm. com*), **WHTZ** for all the recent hits (*100.3 FM;*

z100.com), and **WSKQ** for Spanish-language tunes (*97.9 FM; lamega.com*).

INTERNET

Gothamist.com
This popular blog provides updates on city personalities, news, and entertainment, with a map marking the locations of the latest incidents in all five boroughs.

Gawker.com
Your 411 for celebrity buzz, with deliberately snarky commentary.

HuffingtonPost.com/New-York
The startup web community by Arianna Huffington has become a prominent left-leaning editorial voice on national politics.

CityRoom.blogs.nytimes.com
An online extension of the *Times*'s Metro section, with topics running the gamut from politics and crime to transportation and human-interest stories.

NewYork.GrubStreet.com
A fulfilling meal is only a click away on NYMag's food blog. Complete with a "grub map," this handy guide gives diners the inside scoop on restaurant openings, closings, and places you absolutely can't miss.

NewYorkDailyPhoto.blogspot.com
Photo blog creator Brian Dubé has an eye for capturing tender, unexpected, and downright hilarious moments on the streets of New York.

LIFESTYLE

This metropolis is bursting with thousands of restaurants, shops, galleries, shows, bars, and leisurely pursuits. That's why you'll need this guidebook to help you find the cream of the bountiful crop. But before delving into a neighborhood, read through these Lifestyle sections for overviews of the following themes:

Digest the skinny on **Dining & Food**—from reservations, best street vendors, and dining out deals to the whereabouts of the freshest greenmarkets and compendious grocery chains. Dive into the **Shopping** world of fitting rooms and bartering, once you've perused the overviews on malls, department stores, boutiques, thrift stores, and flea markets.

Challenge and treat your senses to the best of the Big Apple's **Arts and Entertainment**—museums, galleries, musicals, plays, films, concerts, readings, and ball games are all at your fingertips. Save big on green by consulting **Student Discounts** for staggering deals on the city's immortal arts fest.

While there's much to see and do in daylight, the **Nightlife** section offers just as many exciting exploits of your own choosing, while **LGBT** provides recommendations on gay and lesbian-themed bars, lounges, and dance clubs, as well as information on nontraditional neighborhoods, resources, shopping, dining, and pride events.

Do your homework before you sign up for a useful class to pick up a new hobby or career skill. Under **Classes & Volunteering**, you'll find a breakdown of the different kinds of instruction offered in the city as well as opportunities to put your hobbies or skills to use by helping those in need.

*From glossy magazines, the **Times** lifestyle sections, and unending streams of blog posts, it's apparent that being a critic in New York City is everyone's part-time occupation. The glorified stages and exalted gallery halls of these streets have enraptured generations of artists and audiences. Eagerly flocking to both the most heartily applauded and the most unsparingly lambasted shows, New Yorkers love the provocative and controversial, which explains the bold artistic ingenuity that this bona fide cradle of creative arts continues to produce.*

FINE ARTS

Fueled by city government, Wall Street, and philanthropist dollars, New York's arts machine is a subject of national pride and global allure. Household names like "The Met" and "MoMA" roll smoothly off foreign tongues for a reason: these high-powered museums have an eye for international patronage and a magnetic draw on unsung artists and Old World artifacts alike.

A true tourist knows that a trip to the Big Apple is incomplete without a stop at **The Metropolitan Museum of Art** *(5th Ave at 82nd St)*. Time-traveling and globe-trotting through its colossal exhibits of world art require only a sturdy pair of legs. Somewhat overshadowed by The Met, **The Brooklyn Museum** *(200 Eastern Parkway)* is renowned for its extensive African and Native American collections.

Back in Manhattan, there's never a dull moment for students, art critics, or tourists at **The Museum of Modern Art** *(11 W 53rd St)*, where blank canvases and unusual shows within its compendium of contemporary works raise eyebrows and stir wonder. On the east side of town, the monolithic white spiral structure of the **Guggenheim Museum** *(1071 5th Ave)* looms as impressively as the post-20th century exhibitions displayed within architect Frank Lloyd Wright's temple to modernism. Celebrat-

ing the mélange of contemporary American art, **The Whitney** *(945 Madison Ave)* spotlights exciting newcomers, and, unlike its peers, favors the creative toil of living artists over their dead predecessors.

Straying from the hype of mainstream giants, the myriad **Chelsea galleries** *(14th St to 26th St btwn 10th & 11th Ave)* showcase ever-changing installations that bring bankable sculptors and emerging photographers to the fore of the downtown art scene. Legions of the uninitiated join snobby collectors on their Saturday afternoon gallery-hopping jaunts.

Meanwhile, some of the most innovative art in recent years has been budding out of warehouses under the Brooklyn Bridge. The **DUMBO Arts Center** *(30 Washington St)* presides over this blossoming creative neighborhood, hosting the annual **DUMBO Art Under the Bridge Festival**, in which neighbors and growing ranks of outsiders congregate by the waterfront to study the bold visual ideas of avant-garde artists.

DANCE

As the birthplace of modern dance, New York is home to some of the world's most prestigious troupes, including the acclaimed African-American modern dance company, **The Alvin Ailey**

ARTS & ENTERTAINMENT

American Dance Theater *(405 W 55th St at 9th Ave)*. Other performances choreographed and presented by various New York companies are showcased year round at **The Joyce Theater** *(175 8th Ave, at 19th St)*, **City Center** *(131 W 55th St, btwn 6th & 7th Ave)*, and **Dance Theater Workshop** *(219 W 19th St, off 7th Ave)*.

Admirers of the pirouette, on the other hand, side leap to Lincoln Center to watch classical ballet performances by the **American Ballet Theatre** *(890 Broadway, btwn 19th & 20th St)* and the **New York City Ballet** *(20 Lincoln Center Plaza)*, co-founded by George Balanchine.

OPERA

Skeptical neophytes think of blond-haired Viking women, but those who have donned their finest garb and watched a full three-hour production know better. Crooning sopranos, altos, tenors, and basses weave together a story with passion, while captivated audiences sit on the edges of their seats. New York's most eulogized companies, **The Metropolitan Opera** *(Lincoln Center)* and **The New York City Opera** *(20 Lincoln Center)*, transform several classical works a year into modern masterpieces. Prices are as steep as the ascending rows of seats, and performances are often patronized by Italian and French-speaking out-of-towners. As can be expected, bespectacled devotees and music

students with notepads often discuss arias and chromaticism within their respective circles during intermission.

THEATER

The proverbial razzle-dazzle of the stage has captivated audiences for over a hundred years. From 41st to 53rd St, the beckoning lights of 40 theaters bestrew fabled Broadway, home to some of the most buzzed-about productions including *Mama Mia, Wicked,* and other perennial favorites, and the longest-running Broadway musical, *The Phantom of the Opera*. Traditionally, musicals have fared better than plays at the ticket booth, although both receive a respectably ample audience. Recognizable screen ac-

lifestyle.arts & entertainment

tors and actresses are sometimes cast in leading roles to attract more fanfare.

Off-Broadway shows receive a smaller crowd (less than 500 seats), and some, such as *Spring Awakening* and *Rent*, are later moved onto Broadway. The term "Off-Off Broadway" has been adopted to refer to shows with fewer than 100 seats, where more experimental or amateur performances are held. Most Broadway shows have open-ended runs, and when the tide turns, they either close down or tour another city.

READINGS

Playwrights, poets, and novelists frequently gather at cafés, bookstores, bars, and other cozy joints to read their recent works to a group of devoted readers and fellow writers. These events can range from intimate storytelling to open mic poetry slams. Many are free, but some cost anywhere from $3 to $12. The *New Yorker*

publishes lists of weekly readings, but check out these venues and organizations for scheduled events:

- Housing Works Used Book Café *(126 Crosby St. Free. 212-334-3324. housingworks. org/usedbookcafe)*
- The Poetry Project *(131 E 10th St. Students: $7. 212-674-0910. poetryproject.com)*
- KGB Bar *(85 E 4th St. Free. 212-505-3360. kgbbar.com)*
- Bowery Poetry Club *(308 Bowery. Free-$12. 212-614-0505. bowerypoetry.com)*

CONCERTS

Whether you enjoy concerts at huge venues or jazz at a local pub, the nooks and open streets of the city thrive on the sound of live music. Big venues where you might see Lady Gaga or the Dave Matthews Band include **Madison Square Garden** *(4 Penn Plaza)*, **Radio City Music Hall** *(1260 6th Ave)*, and **The Nokia**

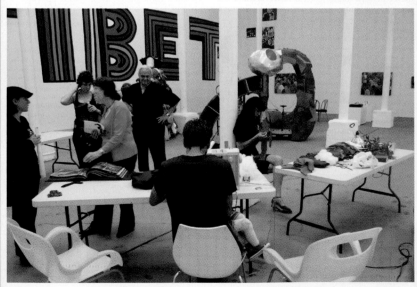

Theatre *(1515 Broadway)*. Large tours tend to hit up those spots, but hole-in-the-wall jazz clubs and underground indie rock spaces are cheaper, dominating the downtown music scene.

Rising indie artists frequent places such as **The Bowery Ballroom** *(6 Delancey St)*, **The Mercury Lounge** *(217 E Houston St)*, and **Webster Hall** *(125 E 11th St)*. Jazz afficionados haunt the West Village, where bars such as the historic **Village Vanguard** *(178 7th Ave)* host local musicians and open jam sessions. Meanwhile, uptown's famous **Carnegie Hall** *(57th St at 7th Ave)* and **Lincoln Center** *(62nd-66th St at Broadway)* have presented concerts featuring some of the most renowned classical orchestras and singers.

PROFESSIONAL SPORTS

New York City may be known as a nexus for the arts, but on any given day, you can be sure that there's a sporting event going on. The city has enjoyed a distinguished history in professional sports, hosting such national events as the U.S. Open. With a sizable market of high-energy fans, New York is the only metropolitan city that's home to multiple baseball, football, hockey, and men's basketball teams. Fans wear their team's jerseys with pride on the subways, but you don't need to follow a Yankees cap to find the new stadium—here's the low-down on locations and where to buy tickets online:

New York Yankees (MLB) - Yankee Stadium *(161st St at River Ave, Bronx)* mlb.com/nyy/ballpark

New York Mets (MLB) - Citi Field *(126th St at Roosevelt Ave, Flushing, Queens)* newyork.mets.mlb.com/nym/ballpark

New York Giants (NFL) - Meadowlands Stadium *(50 State Highway 120, East Rutherford, NJ)* newmeadowlandsstadium.com

New York Jets (NFL) - Meadowlands Stadium *(50 State Highway 120, East Rutherford, NJ)* new-meadowlandsstadium.com

New York Knicks (NBA) - Madison Square Garden *(4 Penn Plaza at 33rd St & 8th Ave)* the-garden.com

New York Liberty (WNBA) - Madison Square Garden *(4 Penn Plaza at 33rd St & 8th Ave)* thegarden.com

New York Rangers (NHL) - Madison Square Garden *(4 Penn Plaza at 33rd St & 8th Ave)* the-garden.com

New York Islanders (NHL) - Nassau Veterans Memorial Coliseum *(1255 Hempstead Turnpike, Uniondale, Long Island)* nassaucoliseum.com New York Red Bulls (MLS) - Red Bull Arena *(600 Cape May St, Harrison, NJ)* redbullarena.us

lifestyle.classes & volunteering

Even if your dormitory days are behind you, it pays to think of New York as one big school of continuing education. With everything from en pointe intensives and linoleum printmakers' master courses to language partnerships and conservancy projects, there's always an opportunity to rub elbows and learn a little something new. Rolling up your sleeves and pitching in isn't a pesky high school requirement anymore—not when you can chat, dance, run, and garden while making a resounding difference in the community.

CLASSES

Plenty of New Yorkers these days are taking classes to pursue new hobbies or hone skills in a particular field. There are enough writing courses and culinary workshops to keep you in school for the rest of your life. Only this time around, it's the kind of stuff you might actually want to learn.

ACTING

Every conceivable skill is taught at **HB Studio**, where classes include such peculiar offerings as Stage Combat and Chekhov Performing Lab.
120 Bank St (btwn Washington & Greenwich St). 212-675-2370. 9-week class $180. hbstudio.org.

Beginner improv performers and seasoned sketch writers come together for classes at **Upright Citizens Brigade**, where they hang around afterwards for one of its sweaty, innuendo-laden shows.
307 W 26th St (Theatre), 145 W 30th St 4th floor (Training Center). 212-366-9176 (Theatre), 212-929-8107 (Training Center). 1 session $10, 4-week course $175, 8-week course $325. ucbtheatre.com.

ART

Offering a genuine art school experience complete with high-ceiling studios and lockers with poetry inked on the inner doors, **The Art Students League of New York** caters to painters, sculptors, metalworkers, and printers of all ages.
215 W 57th St (btwn 7th Ave & Broadway/8th Ave). 212-247-4510. Monthly tuition $200. theartstudentsleague.org

Classes at **3rd Ward** range from fashion design to silkscreening to woodworking, with everything in between. Instructors are hired on a rotating basis, so the schedule is constantly evolving.
195 Morgan Ave, Brooklyn & 573 Metropolitan Ave, Brooklyn. 718-715-4961. Prices vary. 3rdward.com.

MUSIC

A downtown center for music, pottery, children's education, and social services outreach, **Greenwich House** also offers chamber classes and private instruction in various instruments.
44-46 Barrow St (btwn Bedford & Bleecker St). 212-242-4770. 1-hour private lesson $64, prices vary for group classes. greenwichhouse.org

Bloomingdale School of Music's gritty musical instrument basics is for beginners and aspiring songwriters, not those hunting for golden technique.
323 W 108th St (btwn Broadway St & Riverside Dr). 212-663-6021. 1-hour private lesson $68, 17-week group class $505, most ensembles $250. bsmny.org.

CLASSES & VOLUNTEERING

CREATIVE WRITING

Finishing the first draft and selling the final product are equally important at **Gotham Writers' Workshop**, where you can sign up for group courses or one-on-one sessions.
555 8th Ave (7 Manhattan locations & online). 212-974-8377. 1-day intensive $125, 10-week group course $395, 3-hour private session $195, 6-week private class $995. writingclasses.com.

Based out of the founder's apartment, the **Writers Studio** eschews genre instruction for technique—learn the writer's tools before attempting a screenplay or sonnet.
78 Charles St, #2R (btwn Bleecker & W 4th St). *212-255-7075. 10-week class $440. writerstudio. com.*

LANGUAGES

If the selection of over 20 languages isn't enough, **ABC Language Exchange** allows you to request a new dialect for either group or private instruction, or simply start your own class.
146 W 29th St, Suite 6E (btwn 6th & 7th Ave). 212-563-7580. 6 group evening classes $225. abclang.com.

The city's most comprehensive ESL school, **New York Language Center** offers every-

lifestyle.classes & volunteering

thing from part-time courses to a Super Intensive track and TOEFL training (available at any of the Center's five locations).

2637 Broadway (5 locations in NY). 212-678-5800. 48 evening hours $210, 10-week intensive language program $1,255. nylanguagecenter.com.

DANCE

Offering everything from beginners' ballet to belly dancing, **Steps on Broadway** is known for balancing a casual atmosphere with a distinguished faculty.

2121 Broadway (at W 74th St). 212-874-2410. 1 class $17, 10 classes $155. stepsnyc.com.

If you don't mind being watched by tourists filtering out of Columbus Circle several stories below, the **Ailey Extension of the Alvin Ailey American Dance Theater** features interesting alternatives to tap and jazz, including lessons in Capoeira and the Horton technique.

405 W 55th St (at 9th Ave). 212-405-9056. 1 class $16.50, 10 classes $145.50. alvinailey.org

Broadway Dance Center is a premier New York dance studio that has served professional and recreational students since 1984. BDC offers quality dance education from master facul-

ty and a nurturing environment for all dancers.

322 W. 45th St. (between 8th and 9th Avenues). 212-582-9304. www.BroadwayDanceCenter.com

FITNESS

A focus on vinyasa and live musicians sets the **Laughing Lotus Yoga Center** apart. Most classes in the refreshingly spacious studio are open to all levels.

59 W 19th St (at 6th Ave). 212-414-2903. Hour class $11, 1 week unlimited yoga first timer pass $20, 10 classes $145, 6 months unlimited $750. laughinglotus.com.

With a diverse selection of class sizes and workouts, **Core Pilates** welcomes longtime enthusiasts and newbies alike.

99 University Pl, 9th floor (at E 12th St). 212-260-5464. 1 mat class $17, 10 apparatus sessions $290, 10 private sessions $750. corepilatesnyc.com.

COOKING

At **Camaje** (that's "kuh-MAHJ"), novices get hands-on cooking experience in the bistro's kitchen. Class offerings include "One Night Stands," which allow amateur hosts to entertain family and friends with their own culinary creations in Camaje's private dining room.

85 MacDougal St (btwn Bleecker & Houston St). 212-673-8184. One Night Stand $275 for 1 cook. Prices vary. camaje.com.

Housing the French Culinary Institute and the Italian Culinary Academy, the **International Culinary Center** provides the opportunity to learn knife skills from the pros who taught Bobby Flay and David Chang. Perfect your pasta, indulge in a lesson on French classics, or digest the know-how's on cocktail concoctions.

462 Broadway St (at Grand St). 888-908-2783. Prices vary. internationalculinarycenter.com.

BARTENDING

Land a lucrative gig or impress friends and family by mixing the perfect mint julep. Certified graduates of the **Columbia Bartending Agency** provide instruction on how to craft hundreds of drinks, score a job offer, and bartend with flair. Fledgling bartenders who pass the agency's tough final exam have gone on to find success in bars, clubs, and private catering. Perfect for both aspiring professionals and dilettantes, the course costs a mere $200 in a city where most schools charge upwards of $500.
212-854-4537. 5-week 10-hour course $200. 18+ to sign up. columbiabartending. com.

VOLUNTEERING

While there are plenty of mammoth-size organizations like **New York Cares** with mission statements as broad as their alphabetical listing of programs, some centers focus on aiding just one demographic or area of the city. Whether you seek to invest time in the larger juggernauts or find an agency for a specific cause, here are some organizations with meaningful and fun activities that are sure to catch your interest.

TEACHING

Learn about another part of the world while helping someone get acclimated to the city. At the **International Center**, you can sign up for one-on-one conversation, pronunciation, or writing partnerships with an immigrant, refugee, or foreign student.

7th fl, 50 W 23rd St (btwn 5th & 6th Ave). intlcenter. org.

Put the spring in someone's step by teaching a free dance class at **Groove with Me**, which seeks passionate dancers devoted to helping girls and young women deal with the problems of crime, teen pregnancy, and substance abuse in disadvantaged neighborhoods.
2nd fl, 186 E 123rd St (btwn Lexington & 3rd Ave). 212-987-5910. groovewithme.org.

MENTORING

Based in Harlem, **Project LIVE** recruits volunteers to help kids and junior high students in programs that range from after-school tutorship to juvenile justice and legal advocacy.
105 E 22nd St (at Park Ave). 212-901-1954. childrensaidsociety.org.

Work out with disabled runners weekly or bi-weekly at the **Achilles Kids Program**, where volunteer trainers help children with disabilities succeed on the track.
4th fl, 42 W 38th St (btwn 5th & 6th Ave). 212-354-0300. achillestrackclub.org.

PLANTING

The **Central Park Conservancy** provides the opportunity to plant shrubs, rake leaves, pick up trash, and maintain gardens with a team of fellow horticulturists.
14 E 60th St. 212-360-2751. centralparknyc.org/volunteer.

Those with green thumbs can cultivate Brooklyn's 585 acres of woodland with **The Prospect Park Volunteer Corps**, but photographers, carpenters, and charismatic teachers can all contribute their skills.
95 Prospect Park W (btwn 4th & 5th St). 718-965-8960. prospectpark.org/support.

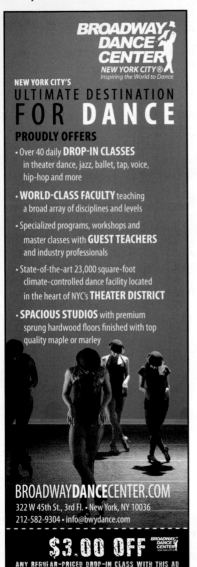

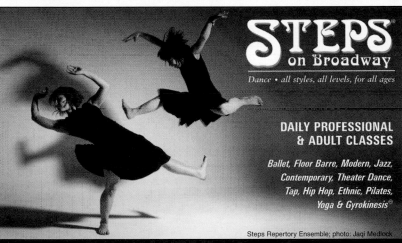

lifestyle.dining & food

In a city with restaurants serving consummately-prepared delicacies from the four corners of the earth, the unspoken philosophy could best be captured by George Bernard Shaw—"There's no love sincerer than the love of food." From royal sterling caviar to Ethiopian euphoria to dollar dumplings, there's something to gratify every budget and appetite. Many of the hottest Michelin-rated kitchens rely on the quality and variety of New York's local greenmarkets, which carry every conceivable ingredient for the freshest salami sandwiches and the creamiest yolk flans.

DINING OUT

With flavorful aromas wafting from brick ovens and every restaurant one-upping the previous with more tantalizing menus on display, making an impromptu decision for your palate can be a real ordeal. For a satisfying meal, do some research to figure out exactly where to go and what to expect. Consult these indispensable sites for user reviews and food critics' recommendations:

- Grub Street (*New York Magazine*'s food blog: newyork.grubstreet.com)
- Yelp.com
- Chow.com

Some of the more acclaimed resources publish dining guides and "Best Of" picks:

- *Time Out New York* (newyork.timeout.com)
- *New York Magazine* (nymag.com)
- *The New York Times* (nytimes.com)

DINING & FOOD

FINDING A DEAL

Lunch Specials. Minimize the damage to your wallet without settling for less quality. Restaurants often offer the same dishes at reduced prices during lunch hours, which vary from place to place (but generally, 11am-3pm). They are also less crowded at noon, which sometimes translates into more attentive service.

Prix Fixes. If you hesitate to pay the full fare, but crave a full course to get a wider tasting of the chef's cooking, opt for the prix fixe menu. Generally, higher-end restaurants will give you this option of choosing from a set list of appetizers, entrées, and desserts at a fixed price that's almost always well worth it.

Restaurant Week. Twice a year, in January and during the summer, you can enjoy 3-course prix fixe meals in some of the finest dining rooms New York has to offer. With over 275 participating restaurants, some helmed by celebrity chefs, the selections are abundant, and meals are alluringly affordable at about $24 for lunch and $35 for dinner (beverages, tax, and gratuity not included). Before making a reservation, scan the restaurant's regular menu to gauge the value of the deal you're getting. Visit *nycgo.com/restaurantweek* for more details and to book online.

Reservations

Many New Yorkers dine out on weekend and weekday nights, so reserving a table—particu-

TOP 8
street vendors

53rd and 6th Halal Cart
The chicken and rice, 'nuff said.

Big Gay Ice Cream Truck
Soft-serve with flamboyant toppings (elderflower syrup, anybody?).
Various locations, biggayicecreamtruck.com

El Rey Del Taco
Tacos, burritos, and quesadillas.
30th Ave near 33rd St, Astoria

Mia Dona Gelato Cart
Gelato drizzled with honey in a toasted brioche sandwich.
206 E 58th St, btwn 2nd & 3rd Ave

N.Y. Dosas
South Indian vegetarian crêpes.
Washington Square Park, Sullivan & W 4th St

Schnitzel & Things
Austrian chicken, pork, or cod cutlet with potato salad.
Various locations, schnitzelandthings.com

Wafels & Dinges Truck
Belgian waffles with a motley of sweet toppings.
Various locations, wafelsanddinges.com

Yvonne Yvonne
Jamaican braised oxtail and jerk pork, expertly done.
71st St & York Ave

lifestyle.dining & food

larly at a popular joint or an upscale venue—is the best way to avoid the hassle of waiting in long lines. While not every restaurant takes reservations, it pays to give it a try if you're uncertain. Even the places that don't will sometimes accommodate large parties. Most take reservations 30 days in advance, and some venues even require them. Call or go to **opentable.com**, a site that links to the databases of a large network of restaurants. If you're going to be late, it's best to call and let the reservationist know. There's usually a 15-minute grace period before your table will be given to other customers.

Dress

While the choice of outfit is yours alone, it's advisable to check whether an establishment is casual or more formal and to groom yourself accordingly. Generally, the more expensive the venue, the fancier the unwritten dress code. Business casual is the safe way to go for most mid to higher-end places. So leave your midriff tops and flip-flops at home and have fun dressing up for an exquisite dining experience.

Gratuity

10% is the bare minimum and should only be given for abominable service. Otherwise, 15-20% of the pretax bill is standard and 20-25% should be reserved for excellent fine dining. You can calculate an approximate 18% gratuity by doubling the tax. But before you calculate anything, make sure you know whether gratuity is already included in the bill. Sometimes parties of six or more are automatically charged an 18% tip.

Street Vendors

While savoring the bijou creations of New York's culinary masters, don't overlook the selection of cheap and yummy meals on wheels. Over the last decade, the nose-wrinkling notion of the dirty water hotdog stand has undergone

significant cleansing, and today's street eats bedazzle with their sheer number, ethnic variety, and surprising quality.

Some mobile trucks have garnered such a passionate following, that owners have started their own Twitter accounts to inform customers of their whereabouts and exclusive discounts. Many have gorged on or at least heard of the more trumpeted grub, namely the 53rd and 6th Halal Cart and Thiru Kumar's famous dosas in Washington Square Park. But plenty of traveling trucks and tucked away carts serve unfailingly mouthwatering bites of exotic and familiar cuisines to busy local professionals, students, and shoppers. And in an overworked city where time is money, street fare saves on both.

GREENMARKETS

Take a leaf out of your favorite chef's book. Growing numbers of restaurants in the city are buying ingredients from local farmers who sell over 600 varieties of fruits, vegetables, and other farm produce at greenmarkets all over the city. Go early in the morning for the freshest selections available.

The city's largest and most heralded fair, **Union Square Greenmarket** boasts a bounty of fruits, vegetables, meats, cheeses, and much more.
E 17th St & Broadway. ❹ ❺ ❻ ❻ *to 14th St-Union Square. Mon, Wed, Fri, Sat 8am-6pm year round.*

Rub elbows with the folks behind your food at **TriBeCa Green Market.** Professional cooks from the district's innumerable fine dining rooms shop at this bustling market, which incidentally sells some of the best jelly donuts in the tri-state area.
51 Chambers St, btwn Broadway and Centre St. ❶ ❷ ❸ *to Chambers St. Sat 8am-3pm year round, Wed 8am-3pm Apr-Dec.*

A social gathering, the **Brooklyn Borough Hall Greenmarket** provides grass-fed meat and lush veggies, but delights shoppers with free events including cooking demonstrations.
Court & Remsen St. Ⓜ Ⓡ to Court St, ❷❸❹❺ to Borough Hall, Ⓐ Ⓒ Ⓕ to Jay St. Tues, Sat 8am-4pm year round. Thurs 8am-6pm Apr-Dec.

SUPERMARKETS

Not everyone can find time to drop by their nearest greenmarket. Luckily, there's a wide range of options from fragrant corner bodegas to air-conditioned chains, open daily to help every shopper check items off their grocery lists.

Upper West Siders can't subsist without **Fairway**'s encyclopedic emporium of foodstuffs, superb deals, and upstairs café (turned steakhouse at night). The Harlem location draws distant shoppers eager to test their arctic endurance in the Cold Room, which houses plentiful stocks of meats, seafoods, and dairy products.
74th St & Broadway, ❶❷❸ to 72nd St. 132nd St & 12th Ave, ❶ to 125th St.

The gourmet chain **Whole Foods** carries organic goods and prepared offerings of sushi, salad, tacos, and pizza, all with little or no additives for a guilt-free meal on-the-fly.
Time Warner Center, ❶ Ⓐ Ⓑ Ⓒ Ⓓ to 59th St-Columbus Circle. 4 Union Square Ⓢ ❹❺❻ Ⓛ Ⓝ Ⓠ Ⓡ to 14th St-Union Square.

A true New York establishment, **Zabar**'s wows with its olives, but don't leave without a trip upstairs to browse the unbeatable collection of kitchen cookware.
2245 Broadway (at 80th St), ❶ to 79th St.

lifestyle.dining & food

TOP 4
discount wine

Whether cooking for two or entertaining a party of guests, no dinner seems complete without the clinking of glasses. Here are some stores that will help you find the perfect pairing at intoxicatingly low prices.

Not just a grocery store comparable to Whole Foods but with better prices, **Trader Joe**'s keeps a wine store that seduces with its "Three Buck Chuck"— sold at $3 a bottle. Now that's a steal. *142 E 14th St, btwn 3rd Ave & Irving Pl. 212-529-4612.*

Best Cellars groups its wine under eight categories—fizzy, fresh, soft, luscious, juicy, smooth, big, and sweet— all priced at $15 or less, and seduces customers with free afternoon tastings. *1291 Lexington Ave, btwn 86th & 87th St. 212-426-4200.*

Bottlerocket Wine and Spirit houses a selection of value bottles from $7-14 with in-store signs—"for a boss," "for an old friend," "unsure"—to help greenhorns navigate its exhaustive shelves. Subscribe to their mailing list and get a 10% discount. *5 W 19th St, btwn 5th & 6th Ave. 212-929-2323.*

With its $10-a-bottle collection that rotates every month and free tastings, **Astor Wines and Spirits** goes the extra mile with its lip-smacking staff picks and "Mr. Popular" bottles at discounted prices. *399 Lafayette St, btwn 4th St & Astor Pl. 212-674-7500.*

With 4am last calls, New York truly is the city that never sleeps—or at least the city that sleeps in. Whether you're searching for a high-heeled binge you won't remember, a pub for cheap rounds and wings, a knee-slapping black box performance, or a night of electrifying jazz riffs without the firewater, this city has it all covered. And with subways running 24/7, there's no excuse to turn in early.

BEFORE YOU GO

The drinking age in New York is 21, and most bars, clubs, and lounges will ask to scan a government-issued ID at the door. Snobbier places may prohibit those sporting jeans and tees from entering, so dress accordingly. You don't want to be cash-strapped while you're out on the town, especially since some clubs have a cover charge, and most bars require a minimum drink purchase before accepting cards.

TYPES OF VENUES

Dive Bar

Everyone at these casual haunts seems to know each other's names. The hole-in-the-wall variety survives on the charm of cheap booze while providing old neighbors and barflies with cozy company.

Beer Bar

If the refrigerated aisle disappoints, try a bar with dozens of beer on tap and over a hundred bottled brews. Browse the selection of American ales and foreign imports, but don't let the easy flow of liquor turn your swag on—lest you challenge a heavyweight to a drinking fest.

Wine Bar

Whether you prefer full-bodied or fruity, suave waiters can recommend a glass that suits your taste. Novices and aficionados mingle in a candle-lit setting to taste and learn about different grapes before purchasing. Some places will also pair your choice of vintage with a cheese or dessert.

Cocktail Lounge

Beyond cranberry vodka, these swanky saloons concoct experimental drinks while siphoning the pennies from your pocket. Revel in the ritz and order that mix you've never heard of, because you might not find it anywhere else.

Outdoor Bars and Lounges

You don't have to be stuck in a sweaty bar to enjoy the city's nightlife. Take advantage of balmy nights and people-watch from a sidewalk table or chill with friends in a rooftop lounge. You can also hit up a beer garden to swig your bottle in the lush outdoors.

Jazz Clubs

Home of the Blue Note and Billie Holiday, jazz clubs center on soulfully sober music. Well-known venues may charge a steep cover fee, but try a smaller club or an early set to minimize expenditure. Whether you choose a cozy underground bar or an exalted velvet-trimmed hall, the beats are bound to lift your spirits—cocktails or not.

Dance Clubs

Maneuver the crowds and show off your two-step on a riverside rooftop or in a leafy downtown space. There's a venue for everyone, whether you bop, twirl, or boogie.

NIGHTLIFE

Comedy Clubs

For an evening of titters, enjoy a few stand-up routines at a comedy club, where cover charge ranges from zilch to $20. Notable venues may feature Comedy Central regulars, while smaller stages are cheaper but can require a minimum drink purchase. Keeping the night as spontaneous as the improv, some clubs lend the stage to unannounced guests for surprise acts.

Live Music

With hundreds of would-be musicians flocking to the Big Apple, you might discover the next Bob Dylan strumming a strain in a cluttered bar with open mic. But you can also shell out twenties for tickets to see your favorite band's concert in Madison Square Garden. Live shows offer anything from avant-garde metal to bluegrass to hip-hop and Lady Gaga.

Art and Performance Space

Showcasing music, theater, film, visual art and everything in between, these venues are off the beaten Broadway path. From converted warehouses hosting nightly cabarets to cafés featuring poetry slams, it is the art that defines the space in a city with little space to spare.

Games and Bowling

Glow in the dark alleys and restaurants with lane side service keep the fun rolling well past midnight. Some bars even offer trivia nights, arcade games, dart boards, and karaoke, as well as beer pong for those looking to reclaim their collegiate title.

BAR HOPPING
hot spots

Don't feel compelled to warm one stool the whole night. With so many watering holes clustered within blocks of each other, you can sample the vibe at various venues in one epic, crapulous night. The best part of the experience is stumbling upon an unexpected new favorite.

As the sun sets, these streets burst to life with enough bars to keep you hopping until dawn:

- Bleecker St, Greenwich Village
- E 7th St *(2nd Ave to Ave A)*, East Village
- Ludlow St, Lower East Side
- Amsterdam Ave *(80th to 86th St)*, Upper West Side
- Hudson St, SoHo/TriBeCa
- Bedford Ave, Williamsburg
- Franklin St, Greenpoint
- 5th Ave, Park Slope

lifestyle.LGBT

New York City may seem nontraditional in many respects, but it has traditionally and proudly been an LGBT stronghold since the 1969 Stonewall Riots that kindled the Gay Rights Movement. As the East Coast counterpart to San Francisco, this metro hub is home to a number of LGBT trend spots, where gay and straight residents shop, dine, and get their groove on to exuberant beats.

NEIGHBORHOODS

All of New York City is gay-friendly, but for those looking to maximize their LGBT experience, a few specific neighborhoods present more concentrated selections of venues and possibilities:

- Sandwiched between the cobblestoned Garment District and the Village, it's no wonder that **Chelsea**'s streets are practically festooned with rainbow flags. This artsy niche isn't afraid to show its flamboyant side when a drag queen performs in one of its sleek nightclubs.

- Once a rough-and-tumble place of gang violence, **Hell's Kitchen** has quickly become a trendsetter in the LGBT community, attracting new residents with low rents and ethnic restaurants. A young crowd prowls the dance-all-night clubs and chill lounges.

- With fewer big clubs than other neighborhoods, the **Lower East Side** nevertheless flaunts gay bars on every corner of some intersections.

- Once New York's LGBT capital, the **West Village** has burgeoned to accommodate free spirits of every ilk. Still, historic sites such as Sheridan Square, where the Stonewall Riots took place, are remnants of a past of fervent activism not wholly forgotten.

- West of Prospect Park lies the Brooklyn lesbian community of **Park Slope**. With roots dating back to the 1960's feminist movement, this neighborhood is known today for its irresistible street fairs, free concerts, and clothing boutiques for the low-key bohemian.

RESOURCES

Providing guidance and insight into LGBT-specific issues, these resources will help you build a network of useful personal support:

- Headquartered in the West Village, the **LGBT Community Center** *(208 W 13th St, 212-620-7310)* is the perfect place to meet other individuals who care about the same issues, engage in volunteer work, and become better informed on current affairs. With over 6,000 visitors swinging by every week, this epicenter is a launching pad for social change activism.

- A free weekly lifestyle publication, **Next Magazine** is the premier guide on LGBT dining, theater, shopping, and nightlife.

SHOPPING & DINING

Visiting gay-themed shops and restaurants is a fun way to directly immerse yourself in this thriving community and support its small businesses.

- In the West Village, **Lips** *(2 Bank St and 227 E 56th St, 212-675-7710)* offers quite the entertaining cabaret experience. If you're on a date with an amateur food critic, don't expect to impress, but the waiters in drag certainly do their part to provide hysterical nightly performances.

- As suggested by its whimsical name, **Rainbows and Triangles** *(192 8th Ave, 212-627-2166)* runs the gamut with gifts, greeting cards, books, and swim gear.

- **Wear Me Out** *(358 W 47th St, 212-333-3047)* in Hell's Kitchen houses a vast selection of sassy menswear à la mode and sells tickets for upcoming Pride events.

LGBT

NIGHTLIFE

With their friendly reputation, LGBT night venues charm a mixed gay and straight clientele with everything from frisky dancing to mellow mingling.

Dance Clubs

Rampant fun awaits all who enter **Rush** *(579 6th Ave, 212-243-6100)*, where B-list celebrities from reality TV and *American Idol* have frequently been sighted. The larger and older **Splash Bar** *(50 W 17th St, 212-691-0073)* thrills with flashing lights and blaring top 40 hits. Latin beats keep the ladies swinging their hips at the lesbian **Bum Bum Bar** *(6314 Roosevelt Ave, Queens, 718-651-4145)*. In Brooklyn, **Sugarland** *(221 N 9th St, Brooklyn, 718-599-4044)* keeps its crowds happy with a sweaty dance floor, heart-throbbing go-go dancers, and a rooftop perfect for a breath of fresh air.

Lounges

Hell's Kitchen woos with swanky lounges and delicious cocktails. **Therapy** *(348 W 52nd St, 212-397-1700)*, a bi-level, modern, and down-to-earth casual haunt, titillates taste buds with popular concoctions like "Oral Fixation." The once little-known **Bar-Tini Ultra Lounge** *(642 10th Ave, 917-388-2897)* provides a relaxed atmosphere removed from the competitively trendy clichés of the Meatpacking District.

Bars

The steamiest of guilty pleasures, **The Cock** *(29 2nd Ave, 212-777-6254)* entices regulars and newbies with its grungy ambiance, cheap drinks, and a friendly crowd that only gets friendlier through the night. Featuring a pool table and outdoor seating, **Metropolitan** *(559 Lorimer St, 718-599-4444)* is a Brooklyn hangout spot for the conversational sort. On the Upper West Side, **Suite** *(992 Amsterdam Ave, 212-222-4600)* brings together a wide variety of people for good drinks and weekly karaoke. Skyrocketing off the popularity radar, **Cubbyhole** *(281 W 12th St, 212-243-9041)* is a favorite among the ladies, who recommend this packed hole-in-the-wall for a true girls' night out.

pride
EVENTS

June is the month to wave your rainbow flags in unison with whole throngs of passionate supporters. Since its inception in 1970, **NYC Pride** *(nycpride.org)* has been at the helm of an array of pride events, including its massive march, which organizers will refuse to call a parade until they believe equality has been achieved for the LGBT community. A street fair of epic proportions, **PrideFest** takes place on Hudson St, usually on the same day of the march. **Dance on the Pier** is yet another boisterous celebration, with live music performances that occur later in the night on Chelsea Piers.

lifestyle.shopping

While the typical New Yorker might not be quite as shopaholic as Rebecca Bloomwood, this fashion mecca has enough glitz to break even the toughest self-restraint. Whisperings of sweet deals draw swarms of local and wayfaring shoppers, who are more than eager to roll up their sleeves and rummage for the perfect ensemble. Getting one's paws on that one-of-a-kind silk scarf without breaking the bank requires some good-natured scuffling, but few cities boast such an abundance of affordable glamor.

MALLS

There are rashes of them in the suburbs, but only a few are scattered through Manhattan. The multipurpose **Manhattan Mall** (*100 W 33rd St, 212-465-0500*), conveniently located just half a block from the Empire State Building, Penn Station, and Madison Square Garden, houses a variety of low to mid-range clothing and specialty stores. On the higher end, **The Shops at Columbus Circle** (*10 Columbus Circle, 212-823-6300*) in the slickly polished Time Warner Center offers an impressive collection of brand names and Michelin-rated eateries. After ogling the displays at Armani Exchange and Coach, pick up an éclair at Bouchon Bakery or some gourmet groceries from Whole Foods.

Quaintly nestled in the Catskills, **Woodbury Commons** is an outdoor mall only an hour bus ride from Manhattan. Its 220 outlets specialize in jaw-dropping discounts on designer labels that include Ralph Lauren, Calvin Klein, Chanel, and Gucci. Accessories and home furnishings as well as comparatively run-of-the-mill sportswear stores provide the variety for a full day's spending extravaganza.
498 Red Apple Court, Central Valley, N.Y. 845-928-4000. Gray Line New York bus from Port Authority.

DEPARTMENT STORES

Attracting budgets of every shape, New York's superstores are perpetually bulging with shoppers, especially during the holiday season. Weekday mornings are the best time to visit to avoid congestion. While the following are four of the more popular stops, the city is strewn with others that come in more sizes than Bloomies' signature brown bags.

Hailed as the largest department store in the world, the **Macy's flagship store** (*34th St btwn 7th Ave & Broadway St, 212-695-4400*) in Herald Square is fondly known for its Thanksgiving Day Parade and holiday window displays. This retail giant's old-fashioned wooden escalators transport shoppers up and down ten expansive floors. For a first-timer, navigating the crowds

SHOPPING

can be overwhelming, so snag a floor plan from the visitor's center on the second floor, where international shoppers can also pick up the added perk of a discount card with 11% off most purchases.

A dress menagerie, **Bloomingdale's** (*Lexington Ave btwn 59th & 60th St, 212-705-2000*) rewards its stylish clientele with signature gifts for $200 same-day receipts. Paradoxically known as "New York's best kept secret," **Century 21** (*22 Cortlandt St near the WTC site, 212-227-9092*) is the place to hit for enticing 40-70% discounts. On the other end of the spectrum, Gossip Girl devotees or those with Swiss bank accounts will want to check out the trendy merchandise at

Barney's (*660 Madison Ave btwn 60th & 61st St, 212-826-8900*).

BOUTIQUES

Giving certain quarters of the city their pricey rep, boutiques offer unique couture for those with generous funds. Bedecked in diamonds, **5th Avenue**'s jewelers—Saks, Bergdorf Goodman, Tiffany's, Bulgari—bedazzle locals and tourists alike, and the trendsetting **Henri Bendel** (*712 5th Ave, 1-800-HBENDEL*) flagship store is something of a New York icon, amply stocked with handbags, jewelry, fragrances, and other gifts.

lifestyle.shopping

Besides its art galleries, **SoHo** also boasts the shop-ateliers of designers Kate Spade (*454 Broome St, 212-274-1991*), Anna Sui (*113 Greene St, 212-941-8406*), and Marc Jacobs (*163 Mercer St, 212-343-1490*). Weekends are the busiest time, with shoppers scanning both the fancier boutiques and the likes of American Eagle and Banana Republic.

Lesser-known **NoLIta** ("North of Little Italy"—*Canal to Houston St, Bowery to Lafayette St*) resembles a mini SoHo, as it features similarly exorbitant shops in a neighborhood populated by young professionals.

THRIFT & VINTAGE

Thrifting is not just the cheap way to buy clothes, but also a resourceful way to make a fashion statement à la Julia Roberts or Nicole Kidman.

At **Buffalo Exchange** (*504 Driggs Ave, 718-384-6901 & 332 E 11th St, 212-260-9340*), garments and accessories are bought, sold, and traded on the spot between customers. Staff members at the charitable **Angel Street Thrift Shop** (*118 W 17th St, 212-229-0546*) spotlight fashionable duds at the store's entrance. The one-of-a-kind **What Goes Around Comes Around** (*351 W Broadway btwn Broome & Grand St, 212-343-1225*) sells vintage clothes and contemporary brands, fusing a bohemian and 1960s Moroccan style with Native American flourishes. **Chelsea Girl** (*63 Thompson St, 212-343-1658*) offers designer day and evening dresses, suits, coats, and accessories primarily from the 50s through 80s.

No one shop in Manhattan beats Brooklyn's **Williamsburg** for a day of thrifting galore. Its edgy stores are often more affordable and include the beloved **Beacon's Closet** (*88th N 11th St btwn Berry & Wythe St, 718-486-0816*).

how to... HAGGLE

You won't be able to pass up a haggling opportunity at one of New York City's flea markets, as too many goodies come with ridiculously high sticker prices. Some frequent shoppers are natural negotiators, but most can use a few quick pointers:

1 Act casual—don't let the seller see you eyeballing that must-have trinket.

2 Decide how much you're willing to pay (or know how much it's genuinely worth) before asking for the vendor's price.

3 Demand a better price, and then offer one that's a few notches below what you're willing to pay.

4 If the seller doesn't budge, say that you'll pass and start walking away.

5 If the seller calls you back, you know you're close to striking an agreement. If not, try your luck at another stall.

6 Don't set your sights on an even lower price after you've decided to buy the item.

FLEA MARKETS

Moseying through open-air markets can be entertaining for observers, who get to witness the back-and-forth duels between shoppers and merchants. To avoid the pushing and shoving, arrive early, but to win the best deals, show up right before closing time when weary vendors are more likely to succumb to hagglers' demands.

Situated on an elementary school playground, **Park Slope P.S. 321 Flea** specializes in clothes and furniture but displays all sorts of interesting odds-and-ends for moms pushing strollers and casual passerby.
180 7th Ave btwn 1st & 2nd St, Brooklyn. 718-421-6763. Sat-Sun 9am-5pm.

The indoor and outdoor vendors at **Greenflea** (named for the farmers selling fresh produce) offer handmade crafts and books, among other merchandise.
Columbus Ave btwn 76th and 77th St. 212-239-3025. Sun 10am-5:30pm (Nov-Mar), 10am-6pm (Apr-Oct).

The over one hundred vendors at the ever-popular **Brooklyn Flea** feature an eclectic mix of products: repurposed furniture, vintage clothing, collectibles and antiques, new jewelry, as well as crafts by local artisans.
The Fort Greene Flea: 176 Lafayette Ave (btwn Clermont & Vanderbilt Ave), Sat 10am-5pm. The Flea at One Hanson: 1 Hanson Pl (at Flatbush Ave), Sun 10am-5pm.

Hell's Kitchen Flea Market hosts about 170 dealers in antiques, collectibles, vintage clothing, jewelry, and modern mid-century home decorations.
W 39th St btwn 9th & 10th Ave. 212-243-5343. Sat-Sun 10am-6pm.

TOP 5
haircut deals

Hair might have recently left Broadway, but New Yorkers take their coifs as seriously as ever. The city has no shortage of A-list salons, but if you're looking to lose some locks while keeping some cash, pay a visit to one of these top-notch stylists:

Any regular haircut at **Sei Tomoko** comes with shampooing, blowdrying, and a massage for the stress-beaten New Yorker.
142 W 4th St, 212-477-5475, Sun 11am-6pm, Mon-Sat 11am-8pm, $35–60, student discount with ID

At **Astor Place Hair Designers** customers can get a traditional cut or dress up their tresses with extensions, Japanese straightening, braiding, weaves, and more.
2 Astor Pl, 212-475-9854, Sun 9am-6pm, Mon 8am-8pm, Tue-Fri 8am-10:30pm, Sat 8am-8pm, $14+

Treat yourself to a hairdo from one of the junior stylists at star-studded **Sam Brocato Salon**, where you just might find yourself sitting next to Angelina Jolie.
42 Wooster St (near Grand St), 212-334-3777, Tue-Fri 9am-9pm, Sat 9am-7pm, $45+ "new talent" stylists, $45+

Gents can sip an espresso while they wait for a mane treatment at **Barbiere**, a classic barbershop fashioned in the Italian tradition.
246 E 5th St, 646-649-2640, Mon-Sat 11am-7pm, Sun 12-6pm, $20+

Chinatown's sleekly modern **Cutting Edge Salon** is staffed by a team of stylists who meticulously cater to customers' desires—if you want two inches off, they will actually cut off two inches.
181 Hester St, 212-625-2826, Mon-Fri 10am-7:30pm, Sat-Sun 10am-7pm, $26 short hair, $31 long hair

Art is a luxury, but fortunately many organizations offer exclusive discounts for college students to take advantage of New York City's goldmine of musicals, plays, exhibitions, film festivals, and concerts. Scrimp while you still can, but take comfort in knowing that anyone can enjoy free concerts, matinee deals, and half-off second sets.

THEATER

Telecharge.com offers discounts for students attending NYU, Columbia, and Baruch. Most other discounts are student rush tickets, which can be found online at **nytix.com** or **Playbill.com**. **The Lincoln Center Theatre** *(50 Lincoln Center Plaza, 212-239-6277)* also sells student rush and sometimes advance tickets for $20.

Broadway
The cheapest and hottest tickets on Broadway

can be obtained through student rush, standing room only, and the lottery. While it varies by show, **student rush** usually begins when the box office opens on the day of the performance, and theater fanatics have been known to line the block as early as 6am. These tickets can cost as little as $20, but are cash only, require a valid student ID, and are given on a first come, first served basis.

Standing room only tickets are offered only when a show is sold out, and yes, you must stand for the entire performance. The **lottery** began as a way to ensure that only die-hard fans of a show are sitting in the first two rows, reserving those 20 seats for a few lucky winners each night. Anyone can enter the lottery approximately two and a half hours prior to the show, and names are drawn two hours before the curtains rise. Winners get to sit at the very front for a mere $25 per ticket. For a full list of participating venues and box office hours check playbill.com.

Free and Cheap
During the summer months check out the ever-popular **Shakespeare in the Park** *(Delacorte Theater in Central Park, shakespeareinthepark.org)*, a series of free performances put on by The Public Theatre. If you're seeking something unique, try **Gorilla Repertory** *(Summit Park in Central Park near 83rd St & Central Park W, 212-252-5258)*, which stages classic plays in alternative

STUDENT DISCOUNTS

styles for free at various parks around the city.

Soho Rep *(46 Walker St, 212-941-8632)* and Red Tie Mafia are theatre studios that put on shows for cheap fees year around. On Sunday, Soho Rep tickets are 99 cents, and **Red Tie Mafia** *(21 Clinton St, 718-300-2440)* tickets range from $5 to $10.

Discount Sites

For information on countless on and off Broadway discounts, go to **CUarts.com**, and for information on indie theatre events log onto **indietheatre.org**.

FILM

Cinema Deals

- **Cinema Village** *(22 East 12th St, 212-924-3363)*. Students: $8.
- **Cobble Hill Theatre** *(265 Court St, Brooklyn, 718-596-9113)*. Matinee: $7 before 5pm on weekdays and before 2pm on weekends. Tuesdays and Thursdays, all shows $7.
- **Loews Lincoln Center** *(1998 Broadway, 212-336-5020)*. Students: $6 regular showing before noon and $10 IMAX before noon.
- **Village East Cinema** *(181-189 2nd Ave, 212-529-6799)*. Students: $7 on Tuesdays with free popcorn.

Film Festival Discounts

- **HBO Bryant Park Film 2010** *(212-512-5700)*. Students: Free. June-Aug, Monday evenings (usually btwn 8-9pm), but get there early. Lawn opens at 5pm.
- **Outdoor Cinema in Socrates Sculpture Park** *(32-01 Vernon Blvd at Broadway, Long Island City in Queens, 718-956-1819)*. Students: Free on Wed in July & Aug.
- **River Flicks** *(Hudson River Piers, 353 West St, 212-627-2121)*. Students: Free on Wed & Fri in July & Aug (8:30pm).
- **Rooftop Film Festival** *(Various Locations, 718-417-7362)*. Students: $10 (regular

51

price) May-Sept.

- **Japan Cuts: Film Festival** *(Japan Society 333 E 47th St, 212-832-1155)*. Students: $8 July 1st-16th.
- **Movies with a View** *(Brooklyn Bridge Park, Pier 1, 718-802-0603)*. Students: Free from July to Sept (at sunset)
- **Tribeca Film Festival** *(Various Locations, 212-941-2400)*. Students: $13-15 April-May.
- **Film Society of Lincoln Center** *(W 65th St btwn Broadway & Amsterdam Ave, 212-875-5600)*. Students: $8, $6 Mon-Fri before 6pm.

FINE ARTS

Museums

- **Museum of Modern Art** *(11 W 53rd St, 212-708-9400)*. Students: $12, free on Fri 4-8pm.
- **Metropolitan Museum of Art** *(1000 5th Ave, 212-535-7710)*. Students: $10.
- **The Whitney** *(945 Madison Ave, 212-570-3600)*. Students: $12, PWYW on Fri 6-9pm.
- **Guggenheim** *(1071 5th Ave, 212-423-3500)*. Students: $15, PWYW on Sat 5:45-

7:45pm.

- **Jewish Museum** *(1109 5th Ave, 212-423-3200)*. Students: $7.50, free on Sat.
- FIT Museum *(7th Ave at 27th St, 212-217-4558)*. Free.
- **Museum of Sex** *(233 5th Ave at 27th St, 212-689-6337)*. Students: $15.25.
- **National Museum of the American Indian** *(1 Bowling Green, 212- 514-3700)*. Free.
- **American Museum of Natural History** *(Central Park W & 79th St, 212-769-5100)*. Students: Suggested $12 donation.
- **Museum of Arts and Design** *(2 Columbus Circle, 212-299-7777)*. Students: $12, PWYW on Thurs 6-9pm.
- **International Center of Photography** *(1133 6th at 43rd St, 212-857-0000)*. Students: $8, suggested donation on Fri 5-8pm.

Free Galleries

- **Gagosian Galleries** *(980 Madison Ave, 212-744-2313 and 555 W 24th St, 212-741-1111; gagosian.com)*
- **Matthew Marks Gallery** *(523 W 24th St, 212-243-0200)*
- **Davidson Gallery** *(724 5th Ave, 212-759-*

7555)

- **DD172** *(172 Duane St, dd172newyork.com for more info)*

MUSIC

For some of the best jazz riffs in the city, try **Jazz at the Lincoln Center** *(Broadway & 60th St, 212-258-9877)*—student rush tickets are $10, and student after hour tickets are $5. **Iridium Jazz Club** *(1650 Broadway at 51st St, 212-582-2121)* offers half-price discounts on second sets Wednesday, Thursday, and Sunday and all sets on Tuesday. Discounted prices range from $7.50-20. For more information on free, cheap, and discounted jazz venues, visit **gothamjazz.com/venues**.

Lincoln Center also offers a variety of discounts for other musical genres. For opera, try the **New York City Opera** *(Columbus Ave at 63rd St, 212-870-5630)*, which offers students tickets at $12 if ordered one week prior to the performance. The Chamber Music Society *(70 Lincoln Center Plaza, 10th Fl and Broadway at 65th St, 212-875-5788)* offers chamber music performances for $10 rush tickets and discounts of 50% off advance tickets. **The New York Philharmonic**

(Broadway at 65th St, 212-875-5656) sells student rush tickets for $12.50.

Free Festivals

- **Celebrate Brooklyn** *(647 Fulton St, Prospect Park, 718-855-7882)* – June through August
- **Metropolitan Opera Summer Recital Series** *(various parks & locations, metoperafamily.org)* – every July
- **Central Park's Summer Stage** *(830 5th Ave, 212-360-2756)*
- **Seaside Summer Concert Series** *(W 5th St btwn Sea Breeze & Surf Ave in Brooklyn, brooklynconcerts.com)* – July and Aug at Asser Levy/Seaside Park
- **Charlie Parker Jazz Festival** *(Marcus Garvey Park in Harlem & Tompkins Square Park in LES)* – every August
- **Good Morning America Summer Concert Series** *(Rumsey Playfield, enter Central Park at 5th Ave & 69th St, abcnews.go.com)*
- **Today Show Concert Series** *(45 Rockefeller Plaza, 212-332-6522)* – May through August
- **Siren Music Festival** *(Coney Island, siren.villagevoice.com/siren)* – July

ACTIVITIES & EVENTS

While there are many untapped sites peculiar to specific enclaves of New York City, some landmarks, beaches, and parks are just too popular to sit humbly in their respective neighborhoods, while annual events draw crowds from every corner of all five boroughs.

In these pages, you'll find two striking profiles of the city. **Iconic New York** beckons backpackers from around the world, who come to pay homage to the Empire State Building and its celebrated ilk. The other is the city's less discovered, alfresco persona, **Outdoor New York**, featuring some of the best seasonal activities you can find in and around the metropolitan area.

There's never a shortage of fun and sun to be had in the tree-swept playground that is **Central Park**. You'll find historic sights, recreational activities, and scenic spots to muse away the time. From the lower loop to the upper reaches, this picturesque park is arguably as iconic as any of its concrete peers.

While many of your explorations will center around the enduring establishments and little-known nooks that have come to define New York City, you won't want to miss the exciting annual festivities listed by month on the **Events Calendar**.

An urban wonder of 843 acres, Central Park is America's first landscaped public park and arguably Manhattan's most prized single work of art, designed by architects Frederick Law Olmstead and Calvin Vaux. Irregular terrain, swamps, and rocky outcroppings made the area unsuitable for private development, which proved a blessing in disguise. Ever since its opening in 1859, the park has been the verdant playground of choice for families, joggers, sun-worshippers, bridezillas, and solitary wanderers seeking a picturesque sanctum.

central
PARK ENTRANCES

When the city's most celebrated park was still in its fetal stages of development, New York's affluent denizens urged for the construction of majestic gates to rival those of Europe's public parks. But architects Olmstead and Vaux chose to build sandstone gates instead, and named each after a particular batch of the city's motley residents. These portals, they decided, should reflect Central Park's function as a welcoming refuge for all, in the heart of Manhattan.

Over the years, these names have been carved into the 18 original gates, and emblematic statues have been installed at some. **The Children's Gate** *(64th St & 5th Ave)* is nearest to the **Central Park Zoo**, while the **Inventors' Gate** *(72nd St & 5th Ave)* is guarded by the statue of Samuel Morse, pioneer of the telegraph. Other entryways include **Artists' Gate** *(59th St & 6th Ave)*, **Engineers' Gate** *(90th St & 5th Ave)*, **Mariners' Gate** *(85th St & Central Park W)*, **Scholars' Gate** *(60th St & 5th Ave)*, and **Strangers' Gate** *(106th St & Central Park W)*.

LOWER LOOP
59th-86th St

EXPLORE

Stunning vistas aside, the park offers another kind of scenery: people. Leading to Bethesda Terrace, **The Mall** *(mid-park btwn 66th & 72nd St)* is a tree-lined grand walkway populated with mingling New Yorkers and the sculptures of Beethoven, Shakespeare, and a company of luminaries on the southern end, known as Literary Walk.

At the focal point of the lower loop, **Bethesda Terrace** *(mid-park at 72nd St)* overlooks the Lake and the Angel of Water sculpture sprouting from the Bethesda Fountain. If you see a flash of light, don't be surprised to find a fashion shoot underway on the balustraded staircase—photographers, brides, and film crews flock to this unrivaled spot every week for picturesque portraiture and scenery. Be sure to exit through the arcade beneath the terrace to see the encaustic tiles of its dazzling underbelly.

Memorializing the legendary Beatle, **Strawberry Fields** *(east side at 72nd St)* is a pilgrimage site for John Lennon fans and peace activists who come to contemplate by the Imagine mosaic, which lies opposite the Dakota building where he was tragically shot.

Recognizable from its appearances in Woody Allen scenes, the cast-iron **Bow Bridge** *(mid-*

CENTRAL PARK

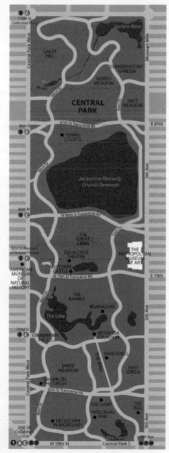

park at 74th St) is a celebrity for its aesthetically fluid arch, like the curve of a shooter's bow stretching from Cherry Hill to the Rambles. A top spot for romantics, the bridge and its views of the Lake have inspired generations of photographers and artists.

Get lost in the **Ramble** *(mid-park btwn 73rd & 79th St)*, a densely-foliaged trail through a patch of woodland that was deliberately planned to look as if nobody planned it. Birders rejoice—over 270 species of feathered friends have been spotted in this pristine hideaway.

Italian for "beautiful view," the stone observatory that is **Belvedere Castle** *(mid-park at 79th St)* is a sight unto itself. Climbing up to the balconies of this fairytale palace is to expend just an ounce of sweat for sweeping panoramas of the park and the greater cityscape.

Hold ye, and smell the primroses. In **Shakespeare Garden** *(west side btwn 79th & 80th St)*, you will only find flora mentioned in the bard's poetry and plays. Interspersed among the clusters of wormwood, quince, and cowslip are bucolic wooden benches with bronze plaques highlighting quotes from some of his masterworks.

RELAX

Ideal for the traditional Japanese pasttime of watching cherry blossoms in spring, **Cherry Hill** *(mid-park at 72nd St)* encompasses a grassy slope overlooking the Ramble and Lake as well as a fountain that formerly served as a water trough for the carriage-pulling horses.

For a stress reliever, forgo the malleable ball, and take a stroll around the serene reflecting pond that is **Con-**

servatory **Water** *(east side from 72nd to 75th St)*. From April through October, grown men and their children come to steer their own wind and radio-powered model sailboats across the pond's still waters while bird-watchers show up wearing binoculars in pursuit of Fifth Ave's famed red-tailed hawk. In winter, the pond is sometimes open for free ice-skating.

On a sun-dappled day, the **Great Lawn** *(mid-park btwn 79th & 85th St)* becomes a green seashore of sunbathers. Featuring eight baseball diamonds and hosting annual concerts by the New York Philharmonic and the Metropolitan Opera, these 55 acres of pastureland at the heart of the park gather every variety of day-tripping New Yorkers.

PLAY

You'd think that the **Carousel** *(mid-park at 65th St)* would appeal only to children and their picture-happy parents, but the twinkling calliope and pretty ponies have an almost hypnotic effect on people of all ages. $2 to rediscover your inner child.

The **Central Park Zoo** *(east side at 65th St)* is one of the wilder features of the park. Its three zones—tropical, temperate, and arctic—are homes to beloved fauna including the former gay penguin couple, Roy and Silo. Go early or on a weekday to avoid the crowds.

Rent a rowboat or a Venetian gondola at the **Loeb Boathouse** *(east side at 74th St)* and row your way around a charming country lake while the skyscrapers of the Upper East Side loom surreally nearby.

During the summer season, the line for free tickets to **Shakespeare in the Park** at the **Delacorte Theater** (west side at 80th St) starts forming in the wee hours of the morning (5am) and only grows as the day progresses. But there's a certain camaraderie in the picnic-style wait, and those who queue up before 7am are practically guaranteed tickets. Plus, the show is always worth it.

TOP 5
sculptures to take a picture with

Give sled dog hero **Balto** a pat on the head (east side at 67th St).

Let **Hans Christian Anderson** tell you a story (east side at 74th St, west of Conservatory Water).

Stop and have tea with **Alice in Wonderland** (east side at 75th St, north of Conservatory Water).

Frighten unsuspecting friends with the **Still Hunt** panther (east side at 77th St).

Marvel at the oldest manmade object in the park, the **Obelisk** (aka **Cleopatra's Needle**), erected in Greece in 1500 BCE (east side at 81st St, behind the Met).

UPPER LOOP
86th-110th st

EXPLORE

Joggers extol the scenic 1.58 mile track that runs around the expansive **Jacqueline Kennedy Onassis Reservoir** *(86th to 96th St)*, a 106-acre body of water that sits meditatively in the midst of Manhattan's colossal office buildings. But whether promenading or jog-trotting, just remember to go counterclockwise, lest you incur the scorn of hardliners.

To enter the **Conservatory Garden** *(east side at 104th St)* visitors must walk through the gates that once enclosed the demolished Vanderbilt mansion at 5th Ave and 105th St. Graced with a myriad of seasonal plants including magnolias, barberry, and Korean chrysanthemums, each of the trio of gardens is modeled after an established horticultural style: French, Italian, and English.

RELAX

Swedish for "lake," the **Loch**'s waters *(mid-park btwn 102nd & 106th St)* have thinned over the years into a gracefully cascading stream. Tucked into a wooded grove, the Loch lies at the bottom of the Ravine and flows into the **Pool**, *(west side btwn 100th & 103rd St)* whose shores shaded by weeping willows are the secluded haunts of lovers.

A favorite, but perhaps dizzying, spot for jogging is the track around the **Great Hill** *(west side btwn 104th & 106th St)*, an oval hilltop meadow that once boasted unhindered 360 degree views. Since then, surrounding American elm trees have sprung up, providing the perfect shade for families who come to picnic and those who drop by for the free film screenings, music concerts, and multicultural performances hosted on this idyllic summit.

PLAY

The thirty courts at the **Tennis Center** *(west side at 94th St)* are available only upon reservation and require a single-play pass ($7 per hour) or season pass ($100). A nearby snack bar allows visitors to kick back with a sandwich and watch the tennis enthusiasts sweat over a match point.

Swimming in the **Lasker Pool** *(mid-park at 107th St)* is free during the summer season, while winter ice-skating admission stands at $6.25 plus $5.50 for rentals. Rates are lower and the rink is usually less crowded than its popular southern cousin, **Wollman Rink** *(east side at 62nd St)*.

The **Harlem Meer** *(east side btwn 106th & 110th St)* is the only body of water in the park where catch-and-release fishing is allowed. Surrounding this lake are several "heritage trees," which had grown before the park was built around them.

For over 45 million annual visitors, schlepping to the Big Apple means checking off several items from their to-do list of lifetime activities. From towering heights to bustling plazas, each of the following five iconic landmarks, steeped in its own distinct history, offers an engrossing vantage point. Play the gawking tourist for a day, and observe the eclectic crowds from Broadway Boulevard or revel in sweeping panoramas of the city far superior than a pigeon's eye view.

THE EMPIRE STATE BUILDING

Yup, it's the Big Apple's postcard-child. Built in 1930 in the Art Deco style, this 102-story skyscraper was for 42 years the tallest building in the world, until it was surpassed by the North Tower of the World Trade Center. Once again the highest structure in New York City, the Empire State Building flaunts the most dazzling floodlights in town, with its top 30 floors alight in commemorative colors to celebrate holidays and special events such as the Yankees or Mets winning the World Series.

Since the crowds can get nauseating, it's best to avoid visiting during a holiday or in the middle of the day. Bring a date on a cloudless night, as the observation decks on the 86th and 102nd floors are open late and impress with some of the most picturesque panoramas of the city.

Location: 34th St & 5th Ave
Get There: ❸ ❿ ❺ ❹ ❹ ❹ to 34th St-Herald Sq, ❶ ❷ ❸ to 34th St-Penn Station, ❻ to 33rd St.
Admission & Hours: Observatory is open daily 8am-2am (last elevator at 1:15am). Adults $18.45 +$15 for 102nd floor observation deck.
Nearby attractions: Shopping central **Herald Square**, the **Macy's flagship store** *(34th St & Broadway)*, and **Greeley Square**

Park are just a few blocks west. Though you won't escape the swarms of tourists at this pseudo park, it's a prime spot for people-watching.

TIMES SQUARE

The LED-illuminated "Crossroad of the Worlds" was once one of New York's sketchiest areas, littered with drug dealers, prostitutes, and porn shops. Named after the old *New York Times* building, it's now the most ad-happy, congested strip of Manhattan after decades of crime-busting. Forget the New Year's Eve ball drop if you don't want to wear a diaper, but check out some less-broadcast events such as "Broadway on Broadway," a free concert showcasing musical acts by current performers from the world-famous Theater District and "Taste of Times Square," a food fest with samples from upscale restaurants in the area.

Closed off to traffic and complete with tables, chairs, and potted plants, **Broadway Boulevard** *(42nd St & Broadway)* has been described as a "pedestrian living room" by the Bloomberg administration—a testament to the sanctity of people-watching at this touristy spot.

Location: From 6th to 8th Ave, 40th to 53rd St
Get There: ❶ ❷ ❸ ❹ ❹ ❹ ❸ ❼ to 42nd St-Times Square.
Admission & Hours: Free and always open.

ICONIC NEW YORK

Nearby Attractions: For free movie screenings in the summer and ice-skating in the winter, saunter east to **Bryant Park**, which is just behind the magnificent main branch of the **New York Public Library** *(40th St & 5th Ave)*. When dinner calls, walk up 8th Ave to **Hell's Kitchen** or head south to **Koreatown** for a spice fest and karaoke *(32nd St, btwn 5th Ave & Broadway)*.

BROOKLYN BRIDGE

In the words of essayist John Perry Barlow, the Brooklyn Bridge embodied a "literal and genuinely religious leap of faith" in modern technology, a symbol of optimism at the time of its completion in 1883, when it was crowned the longest suspension bridge in the world. Designed by John Roebling and his son Washington, this elegant feat of engineering—anchored by Gothic towers and an intricate latticework stretching across the East River—has inspired generations of creative thinkers, including Frank Lloyd Wright, Walt Whitman, and Georgia O'Keefe.

Although frequently crowded with tourists, many Brooklynites commute via this overpass every day. Just over a mile long, the trek or bike ride along the raised path in the middle of six traffic lanes offers stunning views of lower Manhattan.

ROCKEFELLER CENTER

Conceived by none other than John D. Rockefeller Jr in 1929, this 22-acre complex comprising 19 buildings was the largest private project of its kind ever undertaken. Whether you're coming to salute Atlas or simply to stand in speechless wonder at the foot of the GE Building, Rockefeller Center is a mesmerizing blend of art deco and modern sculpture. Enjoy the bas-relief by Noguchi and the glinting golden Prometheus for free as you stroll through on a pleasant day.

If you're planning to attend the annual tree-lighting ceremony in December, arrive an hour early, and be prepared to get jostled in the perpetually crowded rink. The less enthused can grab a table at the Saks 5th Ave cafés and enjoy an elevated vista of the rink while sipping tea.

Location: Near Centre St, southernmost bridge between Brooklyn and Manhattan.

Get There: ❹ ❺ ❻ to Brooklyn Bridge-City Hall or **❷ ❸** to Park Pl.

Admission & Hours: Free and always open.

Nearby Attractions: In Manhattan, pause at **South Street Seaport** for a clear view of the bridge from a distance. Then head north to the many delicious cheap eats and antique shops in **Chinatown**. If you debark in Brooklyn, browse the bistros on **Mantague St** or nosh on the famous pizza at **Grimaldi's** *(19 Old Fulton St)* to taste for yourself what the fuss is about.

NBC's *30 Rock*, *The Today Show*, *Nightly News with Brian Williams*, and *Saturday Night Live* are all broadcast from Rockefeller Center. Curious TV addicts can tour the studios.

Location: 48th to 51st St, btwn 5th & 6th Ave
Get There:  B D F to 47th-50th St-Rockefeller Center, E to 5th Ave-53rd St, N,R to 49th St
Admission & Hours: The plaza is free and always open. Tickets for NBC Studios, Rockefeller Center, and Art & Observation tours can be purchased for $19.25, $30, and $21 respectively.
Nearby Attractions: Don't risk splurging on the pricey duds in this area. Instead, prowl through the polished lobby of the **GE building** *(30 Rockefeller Plz)* for a look—or a stare—at its wondrous mural. An eastward stroll brings you before the colossal **St. Patrick's Cathedral** *(460 Madison Ave)*, open daily for mass.

STATUE OF LIBERTY

While she may have been the last woman Woody Allen was inside of, the Statue of Liberty has served a less carnal purpose for millions of immigrants. An iconic beacon of hope since 1886, the statue stands 300 feet above New York Harbor, off the southern coast of Manhattan, and the only way to get there is still by boat. Conveniently, the ferry stops at both Liberty Island, home of the statue, and Ellis Island, the former point of entry and the current location of the Immigration Museum.

With a 4 1/2-foot nose and a 35-foot waist, the figure herself is imposing enough, but those who are hard to impress and willing to pay a little extra can climb the 354 steps for spectacular views from the crown to rival those of the Empire State Building and the Brooklyn Bridge.

The Immigration Museum takes visitors through the same great Hall that some of their ancestors likely passed through. Roughly 40% of the U.S. population has a forebar who entered here. Once you walk through the Baggage Hall and up the stairs to the Registration Room, you'll find sepia photos of some of the immigrants, whose poignant and arduous journeys are documented through audio recordings.

Location: Both islands are in New York Harbor and are part of New York, though the parks and all of the surrounding waters are technically part of Jersey City, NJ.
Get There: 1 to South Ferry, 4 5 to Bowling Green, N R to Whitehall.
Admission & Hours: Ferry ride costs $12, and tickets can be purchased at Castle Clinton in Battery Park or online *(statuecruises.com)*. Elevator to the pedestal is free, but access to the crown is $3. Those who depart after 2pm are restricted by the ferry schedule to visit only one of the two islands, so get out early.
Nearby attractions: Sit in **Battery Park** at Manhattan's southern tip to behold Lady Liberty in all her majesty from a reverent distance.

This cab-infested metropolis is known for wearing down its residents, but thankfully plenty of seasonal facilities do more than just provide a breath of fresh air. Nearby ski slopes and skating rinks keep New Yorkers sweating in winter, while glistening white shores and boating excursions provide breezy warm-weather escapes. No matter what season it is, you don't need fitness clubs to keep in shape—hop on a bike and roll across the Brooklyn Bridge or pack frisbee and mitts for an invigorating day trip upstate.

WINTER

New York's icy-cold winters can dampen the sunniest of spirits. But don't coop yourself up at home with the heater on full blast—'tis the season to get your blood pumping by hitting the slopes or a nearby rink.

SKIING

Just 35 miles from the George Washington Bridge, **Tuxedo Ridge**'s accessibility makes it a popular choice among those looking to escape New York's slushy streets. The small facility has nine trails open for skiers and snowboarders, as well as a lift-serviced snow tube run.
581 Rt 17a W, Tuxedo NY, 10987. 845-351-1122.

The two-hour bus trip to **Bellayre Mountain** is worth it for those looking for a more authentic skiing experience. This Catskill peak, which boasts 47 runs, a terrain park, and miles of cross-country trails, is under New York State protection, meaning less commercial development and far fewer crowds than some of its neighboring resorts.
Belleayre Mountain Highmount, NY 12441. 845-254-5600.

OUTDOOR NEW YORK

Venture an hour northeast of New York for **Mountain Creek** in the New Jersey Appalachia range. With a diverse trail selection and the amenities of a full-size resort, the mountain offers plenty to do on and off the slopes. It's best to go during weekdays or at twilight (when the resort offers nighttime skiing), as crowds can get notoriously large during weekends.
200 State Rt 94, Vernon, NJ. 973-827-2000.

ICE SKATING

The Pond at Bryant Park, which offers free general admission, is one of the largest and most popular in the city. Small temporary shops set up around the pond during the holidays make for a festive experience.
99 W 40th St. 866-221-5157.

Let out your inner tourist by visiting the famous **Rockefeller Center** rink during the holiday season, where you can squint up at the famous Christmas tree and the bustling crowds of shoppers. Check out their discounted price times for a more affordable adventure.
601 5th Ave. 212-332-7654.

As an outer borough venue, **Prospect Park Wollman Rink** is cheaper, larger, and less crowded than its Manhattan counterparts. With happily skating families and quintessential rink grub, its vibe is more small-town charm than big-city glamour.
Brooklyn Ave & Lincoln Rd, Brooklyn. 718-287-6431.

SUMMER

When the subway stations start to reek with the collective sweat of humanity, you know it's time to grab some friends and some fresh air outdoors. Turn off the AC and seek out that precious summer breeze by the shore, on your bike, or down the Hudson River.

BEACHES

A former military outpost, **Fort Tilden** on Rockaway Peninsula offers some of the most secluded and pristine beaches in the metropolitan area. It takes considerable effort to access this hideaway via public transportation, so you're guaranteed a truly relaxing, crowd-free day when you arrive.
Breezy Point, Queens. 718-318-4300. Ⓐ *to Rockaway Beach.*

Encompassing a 10-mile strip of the Nassau County coast, **Jones Beach** directly faces the Atlantic Ocean and is one of the most popular destinations for NYC beach bums. For nighttime activity, check out the Nikon at Jones Beach Theater, which hosts big-name acts throughout the summer.
Ocean Parkway, Wantaugh. 516-785-1600. LIRR to Wantaugh, $3 Shuttle, Daily dawn-dusk.

Home to Coney Island Beach, Brighton Beach, and Manhattan Beach, the peninsula of **Coney**

activities & events.outdoor new york

Nothing tops camping for an authentic outdoor experience, but choosing from New York's 178 state parks may seem overwhelming. Luckily, a few parks relatively close to Manhattan offer scenic sights and seasonal sports for every agenda.

With hiking, swimming, and boating, **Bear Mountain** *(845-786-2701)* offers classic camping easily accessible by public transportation. While getting in touch with Mother Nature, be sure to revisit your inner child, too, by riding the hand-painted carousel.

Located at the convergence of the Atlantic Ocean and the Block Island Sounds, **Montauk Point** *(50 S Fairview Ave, Montauk, NY, 631-668-3781)* is one of the best places in the world for surf fishing. For those who prefer ogling to angling, check out the historic Montauk Point Lighthouse, which was authorized under George Washington in 1792.

Minnewaska State Park Preserve *(5281 Rt 44-55, Kerhonkson, NY, 845-255-0752)* is home to a host of seasonal activities, from swimming to snowshoeing. Its best attraction, however, is available year round—incredible vistas of the Catskills and surrounding lakes form one of its many skyscraping cliffs.

Island is rife with options outside the typical corn dog and skeeball fare—experience the neighborhood's cultural influence by sampling Russian boardwalk cuisine at Brighton Beach. *Surf Ave at Atlantic Shore, Brooklyn. 718-946-1350.* **B D F N** *to Stillwell Ave-Coney Island,* **D F** *to W 8th St.*

Orchard Beach, a crescent-shaped sliver of Pelham Bay Park in the Bronx, provides over a mile of sandy coastline. Its unusual shape is outlined by a sprawling pavilion, which offers shops, guilt-laden food, and excellent people watching spots. *Pelham Bay Park, Bronx. 212-885-3466.* **6** *to Pelham Bay Park.*

While the hour-long trip on the LIRR and the beach fee ($12 daily pass) may deter some from venturing out to **Long Beach**, visiting this area feels like a true escape from the city. Consider spending time in the town itself, which holds craft fairs, art festivals, and free concerts throughout the summer. *LIRR to Long Beach.*

KAYAKING

The 72nd Street Boathouse in Riverside Park offers the best deal for boating in Manhattan. Drop by between 10am and 4:30pm on weekends and holidays to take out a kayak on the Hudson for free. **1 2 3** *to 72nd St.*

Need a speedy arm workout? **Red Hook Boaters** is a Brooklyn outpost that offers free kayaking and canoeing for 20 minutes per group. Those who consistently complete volunteer beach cleanup in exchange for this kayak rental can eventually earn a spot on longer, guided group tours. **F G** *to Smith, 9th St.*

SAILING

Departing from Chelsea Piers, **Classic Harbor Line** gives tours on Schooner Adirondacks, modern remakes of 19th-century sailing ships. Simply choose your time—options range from the Day Sail to the City Lights Sail—and enjoy the city from a fresh nautical perspective. *Pier 62, W 22nd St & 12th Ave.* ⊙⊕ *to 23rd St.*

The Shearwater schooner, owned by the company **Manhattan by Sail**, was built in 1929 and gives 21st-century passengers a taste of Gatsby glamour. Departing daily from the North Cove Marina, it offer tours of the New York Harbor and its environs. *385 S End Ave, 212-619-0885.* ⊛ ⊕ *to Cortlandt St.*

BIKE ROUTES

Hudson River Greenway
Begin at 181st St to enter this path exclusively reserved for pedestrians and bikers. After you wave to the **Little Red Lighthouse** and pass over the **GW Bridge**, you'll be greeted by a line of pink blossoms (if it's spring) as you head down **Cherry Walk**. Keep your carbon emissions low by taking a breather at the eco-friendly, vegan **Peacefood Café** *(82nd & Amsterdam, exit at 79th St)*. As you continue down the Greenway, you'll pass the various athletic offerings of **Chelsea Piers**, as well as the impressive **USS Intrepid**. End at the southern tip of Manhattan with a visit to **Battery Park**, and enjoy the spectacular views overlooking **New York Harbor**.

Brooklyn Bridge/LES
Roll with the cool kids by crossing the Brooklyn Bridge and touring the Lower East Side. Start at E 25th St, and enter onto the **East River Bikeway**. Cruise by the water down to Dover St, unbothered by cars or pedestrians. Then head west until you reach **Bridge Café** *(279*

Water St), the oldest surviving tavern in NYC. Once satiated with pub victuals, enter the Brooklyn Bridge via the **BK Bridge Path**, and indulge in the stunning views while breezing across this iconic landmark. Exit the bridge, going south on the Brooklyn Bridge Trail. Go down Clark St until you reach the BK Heights promenade. Then cool off and watch the sun set over the East River.

Central Park Loop
Start at the **Loeb Boathouse** *(E 72nd St & Park Dr N)*, where you can rent bikes by the hour or for the whole day. Head north, following the extensive, bike-friendly East Drive. You'll pass some of Central Park's most iconic features, including the **Great Lawn** and the picturesque **Jacqueline Kennedy Onassis Reservoir**. As you hit the northern regions, the path will swing westward and turn into West Drive along 110th St. Following this loop south, you'll pass **Strawberry Fields**, the memorial ground dedicated to John Lennon. Continue along this path as it turns back into East Drive and drop your bike off at the boathouse.

JANUARY

Arts & Leisure Weekend
January 6-9, 2011 (10th Anniversary)
The *New York Times* presents a series of interviews and performances featuring today's most renowned artists, musicians, entertainers, and writers—from Ina Garten to Rufus Wainwright.
TimesCenter (242 W 41st St, btwn 7th and 8th Ave). 888-698-1970. nytimes.com. Roughly $30 per event.

New York Boat Show
January 19-23, 2011
Fishing and motoring aficionados gather to buy—or simply admire—hundreds of state-of-the-art nautical beauties.
Jacob K. Javits Convention Center (655 W 34th St, btwn 11th and 12th Ave). 212-216-2000. nyboatshow.com. $12.

Winter Antiques Show
January 21-30, 2011
From Ancient Roman jewelry to 1960s furniture, this exhibition showcases intricate period pieces from the Americas, Europe, and Asia to collectors, dealers, and first-timers.
Park Avenue Armory (btwn 66th & 67th St). 718-292-7392. winterantiquesshow.com. $20 at the door, cash and check only.

Winter Restaurant Week
Late January or Early February
Some of the city's big-ticket dining establishments provide three-course prix fixe meals for two weeks at jaw-droppingly low prices.
Nycgo.com/restaurantweek. $24 lunch, $35 dinner (not including beverages, tax, and tip).

Chinese New Year Parade
January/February, depending on the lunar calendar
Feast your eyes and ears on a parade of ornate floats, popping firecrackers, acrobatics, and dragon dances as the fanfare snakes its way through Chinatown.
Mott & Hester St. chinatown-online.com. Free.

FEBRUARY

Empire State Building Run-Up
Early February
New York Road Runners hosts this mad sprint up 1,576 steps to the 86th floor observation deck, where the view is well worth the 1/5 mile exertion.
350 5th Ave (btwn 33rd and 34th St). 212-736-3100. nyrr.org. Apply for a chance to participate.

Winter Jam
Early February
Bundle up for this winter wonderland, featuring a snowboarding contest, ice sculpting, and trampoline acrobatics. Bop to live music, sip cider, and munch on free market snacks to keep warm.
Central Park, the Bandshell area (at 72nd St). nycgovparks.org. Free.

Coffee & Tea Festival
February 19-20, 2011
Providing the ultimate caffeine jolt, this festival offers classes, demos, and free samples of some of the best coffee and tea brands in the country, complemented with chocolates and sweets.
7 W 34th St. 631-940-7290. coffeeandteafestival.com. $20 all day pass.

Frigid Festival New York
Late February-Early March
A festival of more than 150 independent theater shows and events, at bargain prices. Audi-

EVENTS CALENDAR

ence selection is first-come-first-serve for the first 15 slots, followed by a lottery.
Location varies. frigidnewyork.info. Most performances $10-20.

Mardi Gras 2nd Ave Stroll

Late February or Early March

Local bars along 2nd Ave provide revelers with discount beer, live performances, and garish beads in a festive imitation of New Orleans's Bourbon St.

Near 2nd Ave and 53rd St. 800-422-7295. lindy-promo.com. $10 with two cans of food, $15 without.

MARCH

St. Patrick's Day Parade

March 17th at 11am

This classic spectacle transforms 5th Ave into a roiling sea of shamrocks to celebrate Ireland's patron saint.

5th Ave, from 44th St to the Metropolitan Museum of Art. 212-484-1222. Free.

International Art Expo

March 25-27, 2011

Touted as the largest fine arts trade show, this fair welcomes dealers and the general public to browse thousands of innovative masterpieces in painting, sculpture, photography, ceramics, print, lithography, and more.

Pier 94 on the Hudson (711 12th Ave). 212-757-9592. artexponewyork.com.

Annual Urban Pillow Fight

Late March/Early April

Scaring pigeons away, this skirmish sends feathers flying as New Yorkers vent every possible frustration in a hilarious, primordial showdown.

Union Square (14th St at Broadway). newmind-space. com. Free.

Barnum & Bailey Animal Walk

Late March or Early April

Jog to keep up with Barnum and Bailey's traveling team of circus elephants, horses, and ponies as they make the epic trek from Queens to Madison Square Garden.

Starts at Midtown Tunnel (2nd Ave, btwn 34th and 36th St). ringling.com. Free.

APRIL

Major League Baseball

Season starts in early April

It's that time of year again. Whether your tickets are in the nosebleeds or the grandstand, don your team cap and head to the ballpark.
MLB.com.

Antiquarian Booksellers Fair

April 7-10, 2011

Bibliophiles scavenge the aisles for rare editions, gorgeous volumes, maps, and manuscripts from hundreds of exhibitors.

Park Avenue Armory (643 Park Ave, at 67th St). 212-944-8291. abaa.org.

National Tartan Week's Pipefest

Mid-April

This kilted cavalcade of bagpipers and drummers serenades the city, while onlookers toast the Highlands with single malt whiskey.

6th Ave, from 45th to 58th St. 212-980-0844. tartanweek.com. Free.

Tribeca Film Festival

Late April-Early May

This popular downtown extravaganza brings

movie lovers together to enjoy a lineup of documentaries, indie flicks, shorts, and screenings. *Various theaters. 212-941-2400. tribecafilmfestival. org. Ticket prices vary.*

MAY

TD Bank Five Boro Bike Tour
May 1, 2011
Forget the bus and the Circle Line cruise—join more than 30,000 cyclists on a rigorous 42-mile ride to stretch those calf muscles and explore the outer boroughs.
Starts in lower Manhattan. 212-932-2453. bikenewyork.org. Register on Feb 1st.

Sakura Matsuri Cherry Blossom Festival
Early May
Beneath the scented canopy of cherry trees, participants watch and engage in performances ranging from bonsai trimming to a traditional tea ceremony.
Brooklyn Botanical Gardens (900 Washington Ave). 718-623-7200. Students $10 (with ID), adults $15.

9th Ave International Food Festival
Mid-May
Sample a smorgasbord of local dishes hailing from countries around the world, with everything from dumplings to jambalaya.
9th Ave (42nd to 57th St). 212-581-7217. ninthavenuefoodfestival.com. Free.

Fleet Week
Late May
Celebrate Memorial Day weekend by waving to a battalion of sleek, powerful ships or participating in eating contests and other fun events aboard the Intrepid Museum.
Pier 86 (12th Ave and 46th St). 877-957-SHIP. intrepidmuseum.org. Free.

Rooftop Films Summer Festival
Mid-May to Mid-August

Watch independent shorts on balmy summer nights at a number of atmospheric outdoor venues across the city. Screenings include Q&As with filmmakers.
Various locations. 718-417-7362. rooftopfilms.com. $8 -$10.

JUNE

Museum Mile
Second Tuesday in June
Spanning 23 vehicle-free blocks, live bands and street art celebrate this one epic evening each year when all nine museums on 5th Ave—including the Met, the Guggenheim, and El Museo del Barrio—open their doors for free to the public. Arrive early to avoid waiting in line.
5th Ave, from 82nd to 105th St. 212-606-2296. museummilefestival.org. Free.

BAMCinemaFest
Mid-June
This sassy, self-proclaimed "Brooklyn Style" festival features only the brightest new talents in the independent film industry.
Various venues. Brooklyn Academy of Music. 718-636-4100. bam.org. General screenings $9 students.

Big Apple BBQ Block Party
Weekend in mid-June
Follow your nose to the smoky aroma of grillers as the nation's top pitmasters cook and serve their award-winning grub for over 100,000 salivating enthusiasts.
Madison Square Park (Madison Ave btwn 23rd & 26th St). 646-747-0584. bigapplebbq.org. Free admission, $8 per plate of barbecue, $4 desserts, $2-6 beverages.

SummerStage
June-August
A vibrant lineup of performances from hip hop to reggae to belly-dancing take center stage at this first-come-first-serve concert series in Central Park.

Ramsey Playfield (enter at W 72nd St or E 69th St).
212-360-2756. summerstage.org. Free.

River to River Festival
June-Mid-September
A post-9/11 effort to revivify lower Manhattan with live music, this performing arts fest is the city's largest, with eclectic showcases from operatic songsters and mellow jazz musicians alike. Venues throughout Lower Manhattan. *rivertorivernyc.com. Free.*

Shakespeare in the Park
June-September
Superbly staged performances of Shakespearean classics, often starring acclaimed actors, grace the verdurous environs of Central Park. Bring snacks and blankets to wait in the wee hours of the morning for tickets.
Delacorte Theater (west side at 80th St). 212-539-8750. publictheater.org. Free.

JULY

Nathan's Hotdog Eating Competition
July 4th
Coney Island's annual gut-churning contest has been a favorite spectacle among locals for over 90 years.
Nathan's Hot Dogs (King's Plaza at Avenue U, Coney Island Boardwalk). 212-352-8651. nathansfamous.com. Free.

Macy's Fireworks Show
July 4th
This Independence Day pyrotechnic spectacular lights up the sky in dazzling swirls of red, white, and blue with over 40,000 fast-exploding shells. Traditionally held over the East River, the show—lasting some 25 minutes—has been fired off on the Hudson River in the last two years. Prime viewing spots are along the waterfront between 23rd & 59th St.
Hudson River. macys.com. Free.

NY Philharmonic in the Parks
Mid-July
A soothing program of classical music at parks in all five boroughs and Long Island provides low-key entertainment for picnicking aficionados sitting by the bandshell and less serious, chattering chums in the back. A sensational fireworks display concludes the euphonious evening.
Various locations. 212-875-5656. nyphil.org. Free.

Summer Restaurant Week
Mid-July/August
The city's classiest restaurants offer yet another chance to dine in luxury with affordable three-course prix fixe meals.
Nycgo.com. $24 lunch, $35 dinner (not including beverages, tax and tip).

AUGUST

Fringe Festival NYC
Mid-August
For two weeks, the Present Company introduces more than 1,200 up-and-coming acts by companies around the country to diehard theater geeks.
Various venues. 212-279-4488. fringenyc.org. $15 advance tickets, $18 at the door.

Harlem Week
All Month
A series of panels, street fairs, walk-a-thons, and musical performances celebrates Harlem's rich culture and history.
Venues vary throughout Harlem. 212-862-7200. harlemweek.com. Events are free or by invitation only.

US Open Tennis
Late August-Early September
Some of the sports world's most dogged competitors volley it out in Queens for the fourth and final Grand Slam.
US Open Tennis Center (Flushing Meadow Park). 914-696-7000. usopen.org. Ticket prices vary.

SEPTEMBER

West Indian Carnival Festival
Labor Day Weekend
A euphoric parade celebrating the cultures of the West Indies with delicious food, calypso music, and colorful masquerades.
Eastern Parkway, Brooklyn. 718-467-1797. wiadca. com. Prices vary.

Howl! Festival
Early September
Kicking off with a reading of Ginsberg's famous poem, this festival memorializes the counter-culture unique to the Village by incorporating painting slams, readings, hip hop performances, and even yoga sessions.
Various venues in the East Village. howlfestival.com. Free.

Broadway on Broadway
Mid-September
Some of the most acclaimed current Broadway stars perform for tens of thousands at an outdoor stage in Times Square.
42nd St and Broadway. broadwayonbroadway.com. Free.

San Gennaro
Mid-September
Vendors selling sausages, cannolis, and zeppoles line the festooned streets of this 11-day feast in honor of the patron saint of Naples.
Mulberry St and the surrounding area. 212-768-9320. littleitalynyc.com. Free.

Fall for Dance
Late September
Ten nights of exhilarating dance performances from solo artists and the best companies in the world in genres ranging from ballet to hip hop, tango to tap.
New York City Center (130 W 56th St, between 5th and 6th Ave). 212-581-1212. nycitycenter.org. $10 per event.

OCTOBER

Animal Blessing at St. John the Divine
Early October
A parade precedes this religious ceremony in honor of St. Francis of Assissi, the patron saint of animals. Attend either the procession or the service to catch a glimpse of llamas, camels, monkeys, reindeer, and more.
1047 Amsterdam Ave (at 112th St). 212-316-7490. stjohnthedivine.org. Free.

Medieval Festival at the Cloisters
Early October
Lords and ladies visit the market town that is Fort Tyron Park adorned with processional banners and flags. There are jugglers, magicians, jesters, and even rounds of jousting between dashing knights on horseback.
Fort Tryon Park (1838 Riverside Dr). 212-795-1600. whidc.org/home.html. Free.

NYC Oktoberfest
Early October
Traffic stops on Lexington Ave as milling crowds of pedestrians chomp on bratwurst sausages, guzzle German lagers, and clap their hands to exuberant singing and dancing gigs.
Lexington Ave (btwn 42nd & 57th St). 212-809-4900. Free.

Harlem Open Artist Studio Tour
First weekend in October
Emerging and internationally renowned artists based in Harlem open their studio lofts and converted bedrooms to the public for one weekend of art-feasting galore.
Various locations in Harlem, download map online. hoast.org. Free.

New Yorker Festival
Mid-October
A weekend-long series of fascinating panels and speakers, from the editors of the New Yorker and the likes of Stephen Colbert.

Various venues. newyorker.com/festival. Ticket prices vary, sales begin in September.

Greenwich Village Halloween Parade
Oct 31st
Put on your creepiest paraphernalia and join the largest Halloween procession in the country.
6th Ave, from Spring to 23rd St. halloween-nyc.com. Free.

Procession of the Ghouls
October 31st
A spine-tingling horror film sets the mood for the interactive procession of ghouls down the center aisle, accompanied by the organ's eerie groans.
St. John the Divine (1047 Amsterdam Ave at 112th St). 212-316-7540. stjohnthedivine.org. $20.

Chocolate Show
Late October-Early November
The world's best chocalatiers gather to exhibit their rich confections and demonstrate their craft. Free samples abound.
Metropolitan Pavilion (18th St at 6th Ave). chocolate-show.com. Approximately $30 per day.

NOVEMBER

New York City Marathon
Early November
The world-famous 26.2-mile course through all five boroughs is open to all, from professional trainers to Forrest Gumps.
Fort Wortsworth, Staten Island to Central Park. 212-423-2249. nycmarathon.org. $11 application fee, $171 non-member entry fee.

New York Comedy Festival
Early November
Five days of knee-slapping hilarity, as renowned stand-up comics take the theaters of New York by storm.
Various venues. nycomedyfestival.com. Ticket prices vary.

Macy's Thanksgiving Day Parade
Thanksgiving
This jolly pageant of jumbo floats and mammoth-size Disney characters soars over the streets of Manhattan.
From Central Park West and W 79th St to Broadway and 34th St. macys.com. Free.

Radio City Christmas Spectacular
Mid-November-December
Spirited families and the young at heart delight in this kickass dancing and singing show featuring high-swinging Rockettes.
Radio City Music Hall (6th Ave at 50th St). 212-307-7171. radiocity.com. Tickets $40-150.

DECEMBER

Tree Lighting at Rockefeller
Early December
This popular gala marks the official start of the holiday season as stars take the stage and merry couples and families loop around the crowded rink.
Rockefeller Center (5th Ave at 50th St). 212-632-3975. Free.

Menorah Lighting Ceremony
Hanukkah
A cherry picker lights the 32-foot-tall candelabra on these eight holy nights. Enjoy folk dancing performances while munching on sufganiyot.
Grand Army Plaza (5th Ave at 59th St). Free.

New Year's Eve
December 31st
Brace yourself for nippy frostbite when waiting for the glimmering silver ball to drop before a crazed crowd of one million.
Times Square (42nd St at Broadway). 212-768-1560. timessquarenyc.org. Free.

WALKING TOURS

Slip on a sturdy pair of shoes, grab your camera and MTA day pass, and embark on one of these custom-designed walking tours. Each will take about a half day's time as you move from one neighborhood to the next, from the west side to the east side. You'll be surprised by the timeless narratives this city has to tell.

If aesthetic design and public art catch your eye, start with **Art & Architecture**, which features mansions, Gothic churches, off-the-beaten-path sculptures, and cutting-edge edifices.

Bookworms, English majors, and aspiring novelists will have a riot wandering through the stomping grounds of O. Henry, Edith Wharton, Henry James, Dorothea Parker, and Jack Kerouac on the **Literary Landmarks** tour.

Lights, camera, action—**TV & Movie Sites** will take movie buffs from the Upper West Side to the Lower East Side, with about a dozen déjà vu storefronts, plazas, and terraces in between.

Hip Hop traces the movements of the marketable genre as it's showcased and lionized in theaters, hotels, lounges, and the playgrounds of Harlem.

Rife with a history of intrigue, **Political Landmarks** will steer you through the money vaults of Wall Street, the luxuriant foliage of City Hall park, Gracie Mansion's elegant halls, and the riverside tomb of a decorated American general.

Generations have admired New York's postcard-perfect panorama, but this city of skyscrapers is home to individual steel and concrete specimens that deserve a zoom-in. Both the grand and the elfin, the functional and the charmingly impractical constitute the striking topography of its streets. Mountainous buildings with elaborate period details humble even the bigwigs who work within, while sculptural installations have interacted with passerby and the passing seasons in unexpected ways. Scrutinize at your leisure—and, best of all, enjoy every site for free.

Start your day by taking the downtown ⑥ to 51st St. A left onto Madison Ave brings you before the courtyard of the **Villard Houses** *(455 Madison Ave)*. Originally designed by the McKim, Mead, and White firm in the late 19th century, these restored brownstones recall a time when stately mansions lined this affluent pocket of the city. Today, they serve as the antiquated entrance to the New York Palace, the nondescript high-end hotel looming in the background.

Directly across the street from the houses is **St. Patrick's Cathedral** *(460 Madison Ave)*, a Neo-Gothic brick and marble edifice that seems to have been plucked from Rome and plopped among Manhattan's glass office buildings with wry humor. Enter at 51st St and 5th Ave to check out its stained glass windows and 12 interior chapels.

Continue your journey on foot, heading south on Madison Ave and making a left onto 42nd St. As you walk toward Park Ave, you will probably spot a line of yellow cabs in the distance. 750,000 New Yorkers are conveyed to and from the city daily by the sprawling transportation hub to your left that is **Grand Central Terminal** *(87 E 42nd St & Park Ave)*. Hightailing through its cavernous halls, few commuters have seen the terminal's front façade, which features Neoclassical sculptures of Hercules, Mercury, and Minerva perched above a Tiffany glass clock. Now enter the terminal through the 42nd St doors: as you walk into the vaulted main concourse, you won't be able to help gawking at the gilded constellations painted against a teal blue skyscape in adoration of the heavens. Revoltingly, however, this ceiling mural was obscured by decades of nicotine and tar buildup until its restoration in 1998.

In Grand Central, walk—or hightail it—downstairs and catch the downtown ⑥ to 28th St. Head south one block on Park Ave S and make a right onto 27th St. Point your eyes 600 feet skyward to behold the gold pyramid of the **New York Life Building** *(51 Madison Ave)*. Cass Gilbert, architect of the Woolworth Building, designed his last magnus opus in Manhattan with Gothic details and 25,000 gold leaf tiles.

ART & ARCHITECTURE

Just a step southwest of the New York Life Building, **Madison Square Park** *(Broadway to Madison Ave, E 23rd to E 26th St)* is the perfect spot to take a breather from the pyramid's eye-popping opulence. If it's spring or summer, you will likely find a free "gallery without walls" hosted by the Madison Square Park Conservancy.

Once you've had your fill of art and greenery, cross over to the western edge of the park and stroll southward to the point where Broadway crosses 5th Ave—this is the Flatiron District, named after the wedge-shaped **Flatiron Building** *(175 5th Ave)*. This oddly-shaped skyscraper was designed in the Beaux-Arts style by Daniel Burnham. Striking though its exterior may be, the rooms at the sharp northern tip of the building require awkward and impractical configurations of furniture. Yet, somehow, they sell as some of the hottest office spaces in the city.

While musing on the Flatiron Building's quizzical appeal, walk east along E 23rd St, then turn right onto Park Ave S. At the center of **Union Square** *(Broadway to 4th Ave, E 14th to E 17th St)* you'll find the oldest park sculpture in Manhattan—Henry Kirke Brown's George Washington atop a galloping horse. But wander away from the multitudes seated by this lofty effigy and seek, instead, the statue of another revolutionary figure, the solitary Mohandas Gandhi in the southwest corner. Sculpted in his characteristic humble bearing, the inspirational champion of nonviolent civil disobedience ambles along a winding stone path in this park that has seen countless political demonstrations. At least once every spring, someone will stop by and place a flower in the Indian leader's hand.

Continue west along 14th St and make a left onto 5th Ave. Walk down 5th Ave until you spot an Arc de Triomphe lookalike. Built by McKim, Mead, and White to celebrate the centennial of the Founding Father's presidency, **Washington Square Arch** *(north side of Washington Sq Park)* serves as the impressive European-style northern entrance to the storied park by the same name. Scores of West Village boho intellectuals have touted slogans at the foot of this marble structure. In 1917 a group of artists, including Dadaist Marcel DuChamp, climbed on top of the Arch and proclaimed the Village an independent nation.

Now walk through the arch and across the park, turning left onto Bleecker St. Near the point where Elizabeth St hits Bleecker stands the landmark **Bayard-Condict Building** *(69 Bleecker St)*, the only New York skyscraper designed by Chicago architect Louis Sullivan. Impossible to pigeonhole under a particular period style, this terracotta structure features Sullivan's own natural aesthetic. Accentuating the building's height are reedy mullions that run like water pipes down the arched frames. Intricate, hand-carved floral forms in the front entrance's mantlepiece—some microscopic, others detectable only by the squinting eye—lend new meaning to the city's reputation as a concrete jungle.

walking tours.hip hop

If Jay-Z has put you in an "Empire State of Mind," look no further than the historic streets of Harlem for hip-hop's scintillating chronicle. Ever since DJ Kool Herc of the Bronx spun life into the catchy rhythmic beats, the genre has absorbed jazz influences and given birth to rap, mushrooming into a multifaceted lifestyle. Today, hip-hop music continues to evolve as sensational new artists skyrocket to the top of Z100's charts, following in the pioneering footsteps of Ella Fitzgerald and Duke Ellington.

Take the **Ⓐ Ⓑ Ⓒ** to 135th St. Amble through St. Nicholas Park along 135th St until you hit Convent Ave. Located in the heart of this neighborhood's flourishing performance arts scene, the gatehouse of **Harlem Stage** (*150 Convent Ave, at 135th St*) resembles a citadel with a striking octagonal tower and glass front doors. Promoting innovation while reflecting the artistic voices of the community, Harlem Stage showcases collaborations among musicians of different genres. Ella Fitzgerald, Celia Cruz, and Max Roach number among celebrated past performers.

Follow Convent Ave S until it becomes Morningside Ave at 125th St and turn left,

continuing on 125th St to the corner of 8th Ave, where you'll find the former site of Harlem's most cherished record shop: **Bobby's Happy House** (*2335 Frederick Douglass Boulevard, at W 125th St*). The store opened in 1946, and owner Bobby Robinson immediately became a local icon as the first black man to own a store on 125th Street. Bobby closed his shop in 2008—at the golden age of 91.

You might not spot Bobby with his streaming white locks, but it's difficult to miss the legendary **Apollo Theater** (*253 W 125th St, btwn 7th and 8th Ave*) located just a few steps east on 125th St. One of the premier music halls in the country, the Apollo is famous for its weekly "Amateur

Night," which has launched the careers of prominent figures including the Jackson 5 and James Brown. In 1934, a lanky aspiring dancer took the stage, and on the spur of the moment, decided to sing instead. Belting out a few notes to the catcalls of an unforgiving crowd, she took a deep breath and tried again—subsequently bringing down the house. Jazz singer Ella Fitzgerald made her vocal début that night, attesting to the theater's tag line, "Where Stars are Born and Legends are Made."

Before you get misty-eyed, walk one block south to the Magic Johnson Theater. The **Hip Hop Culture Center** (*2309 Frederick Douglas Boulevard, at W 124th St*), known locally as H2C2, occupies the second floor. The facility sponsors youth programs, rap and "sneaker" battles, as well as art exhibitions—appropriately, all hip hop-oriented.

Just off the eastern end of the block stands the former **Hotel Theresa** (*2090 Adam Clayton Powell Jr. Boulevard, btwn W 124th and W 125th St*). Designated Harlem's Waldorf=Astoria, the hotel was the first in Manhattan to admit black clientele, accommodating Louis Armstrong, Duke Ellington, Ray Charles, and Jimi Hendrix—four notable influences on modern hip hop. Although the building has since been converted into office space and renamed Theresa Towers, it still proudly displays its original name at the main entrance.

To get your groove on, head one block east along W 125th St to the celebrated **Lenox**

Lounge (*288 Malcolm X Blvd btwn W 124th and W 125th St*). The jazz club's performances were held in the Zebra room, where Miles Davis and John Coltrane played in front of its distinctive black-and-white wallpaper. Writers James Baldwin and Langston Hughes often accompanied the music—a prelude to hip hop's synthesis of rhythm and lyrics.

Go south on Malcolm X Blvd and turn west on 116th St to 7th Ave. The residential **Graham Court** (*1923-1937 Adam Clayton Powell Jr Bld*) spans the entire face of the block between 116th and 117th St. In 1991, the building gained a cult following in the community when it served as the fictional Carter apartment complex, housing a crack cocaine factory in George Jackson's drug-thriller *New Jack City*, starring hip hop great Ice-T.

Follow 116th St east towards Park Ave and turn south, continuing to the intersection of 106th St until you reach Manhattan's most colorful playground, the **Graffiti Hall of Fame** (*Park Ave & E 106th St, at the Jackie Robinson Educational Complex*). While hip hop is often regarded as simply a musical movement, it actually consists of four distinct pillars: emceeing, deejaying, b-boying (aka breakdancing), and graffiti tagging. In 1980, Ray Rodriguez unveiled the display, in hopes of legitimizing his beloved street art. Though the walls were originally blank canvases reserved solely for graffiti artists, today anyone accomplished in one of the four pillars can add his signature.

walking tours.literary landmarks

Groucho Marx once noted, "Practically everybody in New York has half a mind to write a book, and does." Indeed, much ink has been lovingly spilled by the likes of O. Henry, Edith Wharton, Henry James, and Jack Kerouac, who captured the city's throbbing vitality and immortalized its parks, bars, and hotels. Today, legions of young wordsmiths continue to find inspiration in roving the familiar stomping grounds of their predecessors and the eccentric characters they penned to life.

Take the , , or to 5th Ave and head south, making a right onto W 59th St. To your left stands **The Plaza Hotel** (*Central Park S, btwn 5th and 6th Ave*). Its Eloise shop playfully salutes the high-spirited six-year-old of Kay Thompson's childhood classic. Young adult lit reminiscers might also recall that a lavish suite in The Plaza was the setting for the confrontational get-together of F. Scott Fitzgerald's decadent characters in *The Great Gatsby*.

Gatsby might not have materialized on high school syllabi if Charles Scribner and Max Perkins hadn't taken the risk to publish the young inconnu's début novel, *This Side of Paradise*. A short 10-block walk south on 5th Ave from The Plaza, the publishing house of **Charles Scribner's Sons** (*597 5th Ave*) receives a regular influx of Sephora shoppers but was once a behemoth in the publishing industry, printing the timeless words of Ernest Hemingway, Edith Wharton, Kurt Vonnegut, and Stephen King, among others.

Another exclusive circle of pens gathered just four blocks south on 5th Ave. At E 44th St, turn right and walk down to the **Algonquin Hotel** (*59 W 44th St, btwn 5th & 6th Ave*), where Dorothy Parker's esteemed "Round Table" of writers, critics, and actors once luxuriated in the hotel's plush amenities. "This novel is not to be

LITERARY LANDMARKS

tossed lightly aside, but to be hurled with great force," Parker wrote, and indeed, her posse was somewhat of an intellectual menace, chucking criticism and snarkily delightful witticisms left and right.

Continue along E 44th St toward 6th Ave, then take a left and walk 10 blocks to W 34th St. Another quick left brings you before the most exalted skyscraper in town. In *The Shape of Things to Come*, H.G. Wells prophesied its demolition in C.E. 2106. Apocalypse or not, the Michael Chabon fans among us will remember the towering **Empire State Building** (*350 5th Ave*) for Sammy and Bacon's unexpected, clandestine kiss in his Pulitzer prize-winning novel, *The Amazing Adventures of Kavalier and Clay*.

Continue your jaunt down 5th Ave until you reach W 21st St, then turn left towards Park Ave S. The private **Gramercy Park** (*Gramercy Park E btwn E 20th St & E 21st St*) taunts with a tantalizing verdure that reflects the envious looks of those who can only peer in behind its locked gates. In an eponymous poem written about the park, E.B. White imagines himself and a friend stealthily climbing over the gates. His beloved character Stuart Little was lucky enough to have the distinguished address "22 Gramercy Park."

By now, you could probably use some replenishment. On the southern side of the park, walk two blocks down Lexington Ave to E 18th St. Do your legs a favor and swing by **Pete's Tavern** (*129 E 18th St*) on the left

corner for some hearty, old-fashioned brew and a plate of grilled calamari. It was here in 1902 that O. Henry sat in his favorite booth and drafted *Gift* of the Magi.

Once you've had your fill of pub fare, continue down Park Ave and head west on E 14th St before taking a left onto 5th Ave. Walk south and take a right onto W 10th St, where the homes of **Mark Twain** (*16 W 10th St*) and **Emma Lazarus** (*18 W 10th St*) sit two buildings apart. Plaques label the landmarks, although Twain's doesn't warn of the fabled 22 ghosts—including that of Twain himself—who have often been sighted floating through the hallways at night.

Before you get goosebumps, trek south on 5th Ave and enter **Washington Square Park** (*W 4th St to Waverly Pl, MacDougal St to University Pl*), where you might espy a few aspiring novelists searching for inspiration—inspiration that Edith Wharton and Henry James found while composing *New York Stories* and *Washington Square*, respectively.

For the final leg of your trip, make a left down 6th Ave to Christopher St. Tucked beneath an apartment building on the west side of the street is **Kettle of Fish** (*59 Christopher St*), a favorite evening haunt of the dearly departed Beat poets. Mingle at the bar where Kerouac and his pals got into their usual skirmishes, leaving behind a trail of football fans and bookish bohemians to savor the drops of Coney Island lager.

walking tours.tv & movie sites

Hollywood may be America's entertainment capital, but when it comes to location, location, location, New York City takes the limelight. Familiar narratives have glamorized middle-of-the-road delicatessens and corner cafés, drawing ardent film buffs snapping Canons like a flock of paparazzi. These recognizable spots recall a treasury of delightful on-screen moments, from jaw-dropping proposals to side-splitting spoofs.

Start your day by taking the ❶ to 116th St- **Columbia University** (*116th & Broadway*) and enter through the main gates. Sit on the steps of Low Library, the Romanesque rotunda on your left, where the Ghostbusters schemed their business plan. While basking in the sun, imagine such talents as *True Blood*'s Anna Paquin and *Lost*'s Matthew Fox scrambling late to class as undergrads.

Now walk south on Broadway until you see a neon sign on the corner of 112th St that should look familiar to any Seinfeld fan. Although scenes from Jerry and company's diner of choice were filmed in California, **Tom's Restaurant**

(*2880 Broadway*) was used for the exterior shots of Monk's Café. Grab a spot of breakfast before the trek ahead of you, but don't expect to find a "Big Salad" on the menu.

Hop onto the downtown 1 on 110th St and Broadway, and get off at 79th St. Another recognizable storefront in Seinfeld, **H&H Bagels** (*2239 Broadway, btwn 79th & 80th St*) also appears in *Entourage*, *The Office*, and *How I Met Your Mother*.

Continue hiking south on Broadway before heading east on 72nd St until you reach Central Park. Trek due south through the park to

TV & MOVIE SITES

Bethesda Terrace (*mid-park at 72nd St*). You might recall that Santa's sleigh clipped the wings of the Angel of the Waters sculpture in *Elf*. Take a moment to sit here and reflect as Serena does in *Gossip Girl*.

Now climb the terrace steps and make your way towards the southeast corner of the park. You'll know you've reached the periphery of the park when you spot readers sunning on the **Great Lawn** (*mid-park btwn 79th & 85th St*) in front of the Pond. You may recognize this snapshot as the backdrop for Sarah Michelle Gellar and Selma Blair's teasing kiss in *Cruel Intentions*.

Time to hit the pavement again. Walk all the way south, either through the park or along 5th Ave until you arrive at the **Plaza Hotel** (*Central Park S, btwn 5th and 6th Ave*), the only landmark that Kevin of *Home Alone II* recognizes when he's lost.

Down 5th Ave, on the corner of E 57th St is **Tiffany and Co.**—Holly's spot of relief in *Breakfast at Tiffany's* and the memorable setting of Andrew's extravagant proposal to Melanie (Reese Witherspoon) in *Sweet Home Alabama*. Head west on 57th St, and you might recognize the **Solow Building** (*9 W 57th St*) as Mugatu's headquarters in *Zoolander* (imagine an intimidating "M" on the roof).

If you hear a round of applause from the southwest, that's showbiz calling—three blocks down 6th Ave and a right turn onto 54th St brings you to the **Ed Sullivan Theater**

(*1697 Broadway, btwn W 53rd & 54th St*), home of *The Late Show* with David Letterman. Now keep to Broadway and take a left on W 49th St. At Rockefeller Center, you'll find the NBC Experience Store (*Rockefeller Plz & W 49th St*), where NBC conducts studio tours of popular shows including *The Today Show* and *Saturday Night Live* ($19.25 adult).

A 15-minute promenade seven blocks down 6th Ave followed by a left onto W 42nd St brings you to the midtown branch of **The New York Public Library** (*455 5th Ave at W 40th St*). In the summer, the library's AC will have many reaching for warmer gear, but the survivors of *The Day After Tomorrow* once took refuge here from the apocalyptic subzero temperatures outside. While most may not find dusty tomes romantic, Carrie first chose the library as the grand venue for her marriage to Big in *Sex and the City*.

By now your stomach should be craving some afternoon nourishment. Head six blocks down 6th Ave to 34th St-Herald Sq. The colossal Macy's looming on the right was the real Santa's workshop in *Miracle on 34th Street*. Duck underground from the masses of shoppers by taking the **F** to the Lower East Side station. Exit at E Houston St, and make a beeline to **Katz's Delicatessen** (*205 E Houston St*) to grab a humongous pastrami sandwich. This is where Meg Ryan demonstrated a fake orgasm in *When Harry Met Sally*. Billy Crystal's seat in the scene now bears a plaque: "Where Harry met Sally... hope you have what she had!"

walking tours.political landmarks

If money makes the world go round, then these names—Wall Street, City Hall, Waldorf=Astoria, Gracie Mansion—would make heads turn. Many of the nation's statesmen and tycoons made their fortunes (or dug their own graves) in this city of reputations. Their names have been enshrined in the enduring monuments and powerful institutions that bore silent witness to their deeds. With a camera and an unlimited Metrocard in hand, explore the landmarks, both hallowed and infamous, where political wheedlings were exchanged, slush funds pocketed, and a plummeting economy salvaged.

Start by taking the ❷ ❸ to Wall St—11 Wall St is the inconspicuous address of the **New York Stock Exchange**. Though tours are no longer offered to the public, you can stand on a street closed to traffic and gaze ceremoniously at the squat columns swaddled in an American flag. While the original Federal Hall, built in 1699, no longer stands, the **Federal Hall National Memorial** (*26 Wall St*) on the adjacent corner was erected upon the very spot where Washington was sworn in as president on April 30, 1789.

Pose with the bronze cast of the founding father, then stroll up Nassau St to visit one of

Wall Street's proudest bastions, the **Federal Reserve Bank of New York** (*33 Liberty St*). This building looks intimidating for a reason—far below the bustling streets of the financial district lies the world's largest stockpile of gold. You might expect it to be heavily fortified by goblins at the very least, but free tours of the vault are open to the public.

After you've grown weary of the city's timeless ode to wealth, tread west on Maiden Ln and make a right onto Broadway. Built in 1812, **City Hall** (*260 Broadway, City Hall Park*) is the oldest building of its kind still operating in its intended capacity. Encircled in foliage, this

POLITICAL LANDMARKS

palazzo's grandiose exterior masks a gory early history. Nicknamed "The Flats," it was once used for executions and slave burials.

Also nestled within City Hall Park is **Tweed Courthouse** (*52 Chambers St*). Now home to the Board of Education, this magnificent tribunal's most infamous defendant has become its namesake—William M. Tweed, the former head of Tammany Hall. Charged with embezzling the courthouse's construction funds, "Boss" Tweed was tried and convicted in one of its unfinished courtrooms.

If the air is beginning to smell foul, it's time to seek statelier chambers. Backtrack a few paces down Federal Plz to the Brooklyn Bridge-City Hall station. Take the uptown ❹ to 42nd St-Grand Central. Go west on E 42nd St and turn left onto Madison Ave to visit the **Morgan Library and Museum** (*225 Madison Ave at 36th St*). Built in 1906 by Charles McKim, this American Renaissance-style library holds first editions of Dickens and Hemingway as well as three Gutenberg bibles. The prominent bankers and financiers of the day, led by J.P. Morgan, convened here to put an end to the Panic of 1907.

Now journey north on Park Ave, passing Grand Central Terminal and about a dozen pygmy-length blocks. Snuggled between E 49th and 50th St is the opulent **Waldorf=Astoria Hotel** (*301 Park Ave*)—spelled with a rare double hyphen for an added distinction it probably could do without. Over the years it has accommodated American presidents, military leaders, foreign heads of state, and visiting dignitaries. Herbert Hoover and General Douglas MacArthur sojourned here, as well as the prince and princess of Monaco.

One block north, make a right on E 41st St towards the subway station on Lexington Ave. Take the uptown 6 to 86th St and set out east on E 86th St towards 3rd Ave. Turn right onto East End Ave. After another two blocks south, you'll hit **Gracie Mansion** (*88 East End Ave*). Built as a private house by Archibald Gracie, the Scotsman himself lived here until he was forced out by debt accrued during the War of 1812. It became the official residence of the mayor in the 1940s, and when Bloomberg took office, he converted the mansion into a conservancy and a venue for formal receptions. If you're not invited for a black-tie shindig, you can always call ahead to reserve a spot on a guided tour (free for students, $7 adults).

The affairs of state have now been adjourned for the day. Steer your feet crosstown by hopping onto the uptown ❶ four blocks west along 50th St. Get off at 116th St and walk a few blocks northwest to Riverside Park to discover the second largest mausoleum in the Western Hemisphere. Here lies **Ulysses S. Grant** (*Riverside Dr at W 122nd St*) and his wife Julia. The National Park Service manages the site and offers daily tours. After your visit, the question, "Who's buried in Grant's Tomb?" should no longer be perplexing.

OUTSIDE
NEW YORK

There's never a shortage of things to do in New York City, but its 24/7 hoopla can get tiring. For a break from the city's honking soundtrack, take a weekend trip to one of these conveniently close destinations, all of which offer both exhilarating and relaxing diversions.

Cultivating an innovative artistic culture, the former military outpost of **Governors Island** hosts some of the summer's hottest free concerts and art shows in its lush outdoor spaces and deserted mansions.

Don't be fooled by **Hoboken**'s one square mile landmass—its delicious breakfast spots, waterfront parks, historic niches, and euphoric nightlife will have you prolonging your stay from morning 'til way past dusk.

Get your feet wet on the untrammeled beaches of **The Jersey Shore**. Belmar's fine sands and clean waters are revitalizing, and so are its dance clubs. For a taste of the skimpy and intoxicating, dive into the boardwalk fanfare and nighttime roistering at Seaside Heights, home of the shameless Jersey Shore gang.

Mere minutes from Manhattan, the 92-acre Governors Island is one of the city's fastest-spreading secrets for a zero-cost weekend diversion. Formerly an outpost of the U.S. Coast Guard, the Island's stately military history serves as the backdrop to its active transformation into a recreational park. Art installations and music festivals have revitalized the open roads and empty mansions of this ghost town Pleasantville. No longer residential, the Island has become a weekend hangout spot for young artists and families seeking repose from the hubbub of the city.

GET THERE

From June to October, enjoy free three to five-minute Island-bound **ferry rides** direct from Manhattan's Battery Maritime Building *(10 South St)* on Fridays and weekends and from Brooklyn Bridge Park's Pier 6 *(Atlantic Ave & Furman St)* on weekends only. Check govisland. com for the season's full rundown of the ferry schedule. Keep in mind that the last boat departs from the Island at 5pm on Fridays and 7pm on weekends.

EAT

Take a tip from young families who go picnic-style, toting their own bagged sandwiches, blankets, and drinks. Grassy grounds abound, serving the sedentary needs of those who come to wax philosophical or otherwise schmooze and lounge with friends. While seasoned visitors know better than to rely solely on the Island's meals-on-wheels for sustenance, some food carts and Island mainstays are simply too irresistible.

An escape from the clamor of the city does not include leaving behind the ubiquitous Mister Softee jingle. But don't waste time wondering how the soft serve truck managed to find its way here. Instead, follow your nose to the more exotic fare of Jamaican-style curry shrimp at **Veronica's West Indian Cuisine.** This food cart will have you ditching that homemade corned beef sandwich in no time.
Off Andes Rd (near Berry Rd).

For a refreshing breather after biking around the Island, take refuge from the sun in **Pyramid Café**—the hand-scooped gelato and freshly brewed iced teas will have you thirsting for a second serving.
Clayton Rd (at King Ave).

GOVERNORS ISLAND

EXPLORE

A leisurely promenade around the Island is do-able within an hour's time, but no tour is complete without the breezy fun of biking. **Bike and Roll** has $15 rentals for two hours, $20 for the whole day, and free one-hour rental sessions on Fridays. As with all freebies, visitors come in droves on Friday mornings, so be prepared to wait for your turn or time your stop at the rental shop an hour after it opens.
515 Hay Rd (at Andes Rd). 212 260-0400. Fri 10am-5pm, Sat-Sun 10am-6pm.

One of the best gratuitous deals are the **kayak rentals at Pier 101**. Grab a life vest, a row-ing buddy, a camera, and enjoy paddling on the Hudson River.
Entrance on Carder Rd (near Andes Rd).

Each of the rooms in the crumbling brick homes of **Colonel's Row** features a minia-ture exhibit, so strolling from one to the next is a constant surprise. Some of the buildings still have their original fireplaces and chandeliers, but they've fallen into a state of spooky disre-pair, which can be great for taking pictures or envisioning yourself as the star of a low-budget horror film.
Btwn Comfort Rd and Hay Rd.

Built in 1794 and now open to the public for educational purposes, **Fort Jay**'s star-shaped edifice still has cannon balls piled up in the courtyard.

On the Parade Ground btwn Andes and Comfort Rd.

During the Island's Coast Guard days, the porticoed **Admiral's House** with its slender Doric columns hosted parties thrown by the commanding officer. Its current state of disuse is manifest in the displays of children's artwork, which now feebly adorn the expansive interiors of this manor.
In Nolan Park.

RELAX

Yesteryear's golf course, The **Parade Ground** is now the go-to playground for kite-flyers and frisbee-throwers. Humbler in size and popula-tion than Central Park, this capacious lawn is often used for concerts and exhibits, including annual interactive arts projects by FIGMENT (figmentproject.org).
Btwn Comfort and Andes Rd.

A no-charge hit or miss, the **hammocks** on the southern tip of the Island seem perpetually occupied by dubiously healthy men who never want to leave their well-nestled pouches. Des-peradoes make a beeline for them as soon as the first boat docks, and may even tip someone over to claim their spot in the shade.

An underwhelming strip of sand dressed up with plastic palm trees, **The Water Taxi Beach** compensates for its initial disappoint-ment by serving the only bar on the island.
On Carder Rd (near Hay Rd).

89

With locals scowling at the fist-pumping stereotype, take a day trip to the shore to clear up what's fact and what's MTV fiction. New Jersey's Atlantic coast is strewn with over 40 beach towns, each with its own iconic attractions and distinctive reputation. Point Pleasant is a family-friendly destination, while Sandy Hook, Spring Lake, and Barnegat Light are among the quieter getaways. Meanwhile, sun-and-surf crowds are hooked on the hopping nightlife in Belmar and notorious Seaside Heights.

BELMAR

Surf champs, skaters, and college chums retreat to Belmar's white sands and clean waters to soak up the sun and booze. Fishing is somewhat of a local pastime, but the cheap boardwalk eats and dance clubs keep young sojourners coming in droves every summer.
Beach badge: $7 daily fee.

GET THERE

Take an **NJ Transit bus** from Port Authority or the **NJ Transit North Jersey Coast Line** from Penn Station to Long Branch, then transfer to the local train to Belmar. The trip is about 2 hours.

EAT

Break from the hoagie vendors to chomp on fiery burritos at **10th Avenue Burrito Co**. Slip in on a Saturday for live band music, or on a

Tuesday for the unbeatable homemade empanadas.
817 Belmar Plz. 732-280-1515. Sun 11am-8pm, Mon-Sat 11am-9pm.

Located near the train station, the **Express Station** gives vacationers and residents good reason to crawl out of bed early for humongous omelets and personable service.
835 Belmar Plz. 732-280-0333.

EXPLORE

Rent a boat at the **Belmar Municipal Marina** to go deep-sea fishing.
905 Route 35 (near 10th Ave). 732-681-2266.

Just down the road from the Marina, **Maclearie Park** boasts its own boardwalk, soccer fields, and tennis courts—and is also a scenic spot for grilling burgers and kayaking.
Off River Rd & L St.

PLAY

Despite its capacity to hold thousands, every inch of **Bar Anticipation** is crawling with boozers and dancers. Multiple bars keep the liquor flowing, and "Beat the Clock" Tuesdays offers draft beer starting from 50 cents and increasing by a quarter every hour.
703 16th Ave, Lake Como. 732-681-7422. Daily 10-2am.

For those who like to jive post sunset, **D'Jais** spins upbeat dance tunes, rock 'n' roll, and reggae every night.
1801 Ocean Ave (at 18th Ave). 732-681-5055. Sun 11-12am, Mon-Sat 11-2am

JERSEY SHORE

For a classic night of bar fare, head to the **Boathouse Bar & Grill** for finger-licking wings, 14 beers on tap, billiards, and 30 televisions.
1301 Main St (near 15th Ave). 732-681-5221. Mon-Sat 11-2am, 12pm-2am.

SEASIDE HEIGHTS

Native beach bums scorn visiting "shoobies" and "bennys," who hit the beachside roller coasters and boardwalk snack huts. A seedy nightlife begins after dinner, when scantily clad clubbers grind to pulsating beats and reckless revelers get plastered off drink specials.
Beach badge: $5 daily fee.

GET THERE

Take the **NJ Transit bus (seasonal)** from Port Authority to Seaside Heights, or the **NJ Transit North Jersey Coast Line** to Bay Head, and then hop on a taxi to Seaside Heights. Trip time is about two and a half hours.

EAT

If you smell cheese steaks and sausage sandwiches while doing backstrokes in the water, it must be lunch hour at **Midway Steak House**, which boasts mouthwatering boardwalk grub and refreshingly cool lemonades.
Boardwalk at Webster Ave. 732-793-6617.

Skip the greasy beachside pizza to dine at **Luna Rosa Trattoria**, where the bill is well worth a plate of calamari and puttanesca.

401 Boulevard (at Hamilton Ave). 732-793-0021. Daily 5-11pm.

EXPLORE

Kids and children-at-heart crave the splashy fun of **Casino Pier**, which offers over 40 thrilling rides, a carousel, an arcade, a jumbo water park, and rooftop mini golf.
800 Ocean Terrace. 732-793-6495.

Rent jet skis from **Seaside Waverunners** to pump up your adrenaline at 45 miles per hour.
Cranberry Inlet Marina, Route 35. 732-830-4900. Daily 9am-6pm (weather permitting).

PLAY

Otherwise known as the spot where Snooki got pummeled in the face, **Beachcomber Bar & Grill** draws throngs of guidos and girlfriends as well as day-trippers who secretly can't get enough of MTV's *Jersey Shore*. Perks include a chill vibe, live band music, and no cover charge.
100 Ocean Terrace (at Dupont Ave). 732-793-0526. Sun, Mon-Thurs 11-2am, Fri-Sat 11-2:30am.

Don't let the uninspired name deter you from stopping by **The Beach Bar**. Better-than-typical bar pie cures late-night munchie cravings, while Corona and Coors Light bottles go for $2-3.
28 Boardwalk. 732-830-7700. Open daily.

Friends hang out at **Captain Hooks Bar** to play after hour ping-pong, billiards, video games, foosball, air hockey, darts, tabletop shuffleboard, pinball, and one-on-one hoops.
1320 Boulevard. 732-830-0006.

The "Mile Square City" offers more Sinatra-nostalgic pizza parlors, historic sights, and sports bars than even the most energetic can visit in one day. Once a center of transportation firsts, Hoboken's Erie-Lackawanna Railroad Terminal now receives droves of young professionals commuting daily from Manhattan and boatloads of New Yorkers and tourists alike. Known as the place to have a burger and beer while enjoying dazzling waterfront views, this former port city itself lights up after work hours with music and spirited cheers, proving that despite size, it's no mere whistle-stop.

GET THERE

It's a quick 15 to 20-minute ride to Hoboken via **PATH train** from 34th St-Herald Sq and a 10-minute ride on weekdays from the WTC station. But if you have time and cash to spare, take a ferry from one of the **NY Waterway** terminals to enjoy a picturesque trip across the Hudson.

EAT

A number of chain eateries have sprung up in recent years, replacing homegrown oldies. Fortunately, some delicious one-of-a-kind options have stood the test of time.

A grab-and-go breakfast spot, the **Bagel Smashery** uses a panini press to flatten bagel sandwiches for a creative smush on the age-old staple.
153 1st St (near Bloomfield St). 201-604-0120. Daily 11:30am-11:30pm. No credit cards.

La Isla's homey space can barely contain the abundance of Havana flavors packed into its lunch and dinner menus, yet savvy locals know that nothing beats breakfasts (Mon-Sat) or Sunday brunch. Early birds and late risers alike rejoice in the restaurant's tasty selection of omelettes à la Cubano and will avow that the huevos rancheros is this culinary island's hidden treasure.
104 Washington St (near 1st St). 201-659-8197. Sun 10am-3pm & 5pm-9pm, Mon-Sat 7am-10pm.

Tourists from all over the country queue up in front of **Carlo's Bakery** to pay homage to TLC's Cake Boss. For maximum expediency at this populous dessert shop, order on the line to the right and avoid the hordes that gather on weekday evenings (5-7pm). If the cakes are beyond your budget, try the cannolis or lobster tails, instead, for the sweetest fix per buck.
95 Washington St (btwn 1st St and Newark St). 201-659-3671. Sun 7am-5:30pm, Mon-Sat 7am-7:30pm.

EXPLORE

The **Birth of Baseball Monument** consists of a base on each street corner at the intersection of Washington and 11th St. One block east, on Hudson St, **Elysian Park** is said to mark the site of the first organized ball game, which has given H-town a unique berth in baseball history.

A stroll along the waterfront unveils panoramic views of the Manhattan skyline that can leave even a daily jogger breathless. Start from the peninsula of **Pier A Park**, which features an expansive grass field worshipped by devoted sunbathers. A northward stroll along the river leads to the recently completed **Pier C Park**, a recreational island with a playground and fishing pier. Walk further along the river, cross the street, and climb the wooden steps to **Castle Point**, home of the Stevens Institute of Technology. As you pass the Castle Gatehouse, trek

uphill through the shaded campus until you reach the **Castle Point Lookout**. The highest point in town, this tranquil spot overlooks the river and features a canon gun sculpture at its center.

From 101 Sinatra Dr (at 1st St) to Castle Point on Hudson.

PLAY

Historically strewn with Irish pubs, Hoboken is hands down the hottest PATH train stop during its festive St. Patrick's Day parade. But no matter what day of the year, there's no escaping the bar hopping carousal in this town known for having the greatest number of bars per square mile in the country.

Residents and the well-informed rave about the music scene at **Maxwell's Bar & Restaurant**. A functional space brings indie, grunge, and alternative rock bands up close in an unpretentious setting. Go for the music, but don't deprive your palate of an offbeat treat up front: chicken pot pie and 13 beers on tap provide the energy for a night of fist-pumping and mingling.

1039 Washington St (at 11th St). 201-653-1703. Sun 11am-2am, Mon-Thurs 5pm-2am, Fri-Sat 5pm-3am.

At **Green Rock Tap & Grill**, weekday Happy Hour (5-8pm) works its stress-beating mojo with $1 mug specials. Stop in on a Monday or weekend night for mouthwatering 25-cent wings and catch the football game with a clamorous crowd of locals.

70 Hudson St (btwn Hudson Pl and Newark St). 201-386-5600. Sun, Mon-Thurs 11:30am-2am, Fri-Sat 11:30am-3am.

Scotland Yard's live jazz and blues performances six nights a week and antiquated exterior are hard to miss. A onetime Prohibition-era speakeasy, this dive bar receives a mellower crowd than Black Bear Bar & Grill's boisterous frat guys.

72 Hudson St (btwn Hudson Pl and Newark St). 201-222-9273. Sun 12pm-2am, Mon-Thurs 4pm-2am, Fri 4pm-3am, Sat 2pm-3am.

WAS

&IN

In front of a Dominican bodega, a climactic game of dominoes ensues over an up-tempo merengue beat blaring in the background, while just several blocks away a family is going on a bicycle ride across the George Washington Bridge. Welcome to Washington Heights and Inwood: nestled at the northernmost tip of Manhattan, this expansive neighborhood blends residential living with urban areas, creating a geographic and cultural dichotomy. As diverse as its history, it has been reflecting a strong Latin Caribbean presence for the last 30 years.

Just blocks away from the upper end of the neighborhood—in Bennett Park, located in the Hudson Heights section—lies Manhattan's highest natural point, at 265 feet above sea level. This geographically strategic location became the grounds for Fort Washington, an essential fortification during the Revolutionary War. Well into the late 18th century, Washington Heights was a grouping of ridges filled with villas. In the 19th century the arrival of Irish settlers, along with European Jews, established the area as a haven for many generations of immigrants. By mid-century there was an emerging Greek population, but it wasn't until later decades that Cubans and Dominicans moved into the area, giving it a distinct Caribbean charm which has been greatly popularized by mainstream media—namely in the Broadway musical sensation "In the Heights" and the film Washington Heights.

INGTON
IEIGHTS
VOOD

Once notorious for its alarmingly high crime rate, the neighborhood has in recent years undergone extensive urban renewal, and although gentrification-induced demographic shifts signify a relocation of the dominant nationality, Dominicans still makeup three-fourths of the population. With Manhattan's ever-increasing real estate costs, many city dwellers have headed uptown for affordable and spacious living in this relatively safe neighborhood. Along the western end of Broadway towards the Hudson River, you can find historic homes surrounded by gardens leading up to Fort Tyron Park. Just several blocks east, the urban hustle and bustle that one would expect in the city exists in the form of countless street vendors—selling everything from fruit and ice cream to Nike sneakers and multi-colored rosaries—shopping boutiques and mega fashion stores and vibrant crowds that add to the lively dynamics of the corner. Succumb to the seductive smell of the tantalizing Dominican food, whose authenticity is enough to make anyone feel like they are Santo Domingo-bound, or stop at the local Irish pub by the George Washington Bridge for some rounds of thirst-quenching lager. Tropical uptown culture meets comfortable residential living here—providing a range of low- to high-end establishments that offer the best in dining, nightlife, and shopping.

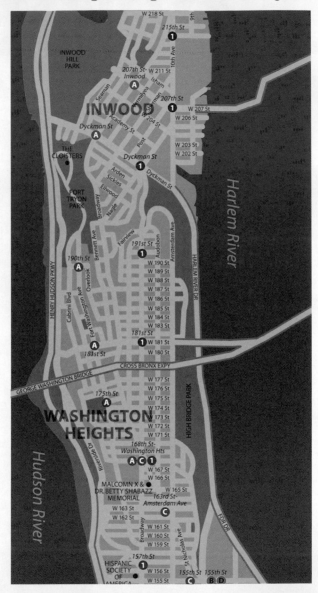

EXPLORE

Fort Tryon Park

This 67-acre ridge in upper Manhattan is the home of the Cloisters, the

Broadway and Dyckman St (bounded by Broadway, Riverside, and the Hudson)
Ⓐ to Dyckman St

Heather Garden, and extensive walking trails and meadows. The elongated strip of land was an ancillary site of the Battle of Fort Washington and named after Sir William Tryon, the last British Governor of New York. As the city rapidly developed, the expansive area was donated by John D. Rockefeller Jr. with express instructions to be turned into parkland. Undertaken during the Great Depression, the project provided jobs and heavily reshaped the upper region of the borough. On any given day, you'll see joggers navigating the paths, bicyclists zipping through the designated bikeways, children exploring the playground, and affectionate couples strolling through the blossoming garden.

George Washington Bridge

Connecting Washington Heights to Fort Lee, New Jersey, the GWB is considered

Btwn W 178th & 179th St
❶ to 181st St

one of the most beautiful bridges in the world for its eyeball-caressing views of the Hudson, the Palisades, and Manhattan. Its cables and steel beams have grown to iconic proportions, becoming a trademark of New York City. During the day, the aluminum-colored bridge provides a marvelous contrast between the water and sky. At night, the gargantuan structure radiates a mesmerizing glow from the lights that ascend its bent cords. On both sides of the bridge's upper roadway, bicycle and pedestrian walkways allow for a pleasant (but lengthy) track. With a 14-lane span and an estimated traffic flow of nearly 300,000 vehicles per day, this is the busiest bridge in the world.

The highest natural point in Manhattan is in Hudson Height's Bennett Park (265 feet).

LITTLE DOMINICAN REPUBLIC

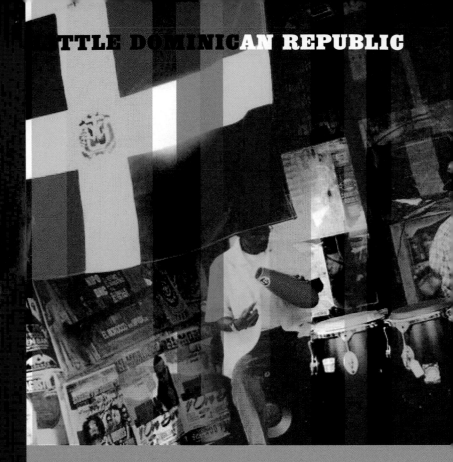

The uppermost tip of Manhattan has been home to many generations of immigrants over the 20th century, but for the last three decades no group has had as much influence in shaping Washington Heights as its Dominican population. Stroll down Fort Washington Ave at 181st (where the train station with a shout-out from "In the Heights" is) to see why it's called the heart of the Dominican Heights—a merengue rhythm wafts across street corners and an undeniable Caribbean flavor pervades the air. Although greatly affected by gentrification, the Quisqueyan (the native name for the Hispaniolan Island) spirit remains dominant from 165th to Dykman St, where vibrant family-owned shops, street vendors, and clothiers like **Broadway Fashion Boutique** (*4029 Broadway*) stand. Drop by any barbershop or beauty salon for an impeccable haircut—not to worry, Dominican stylists and barbers are experts at managing just about any hair texture—and then get a taste of Santo Domingo at the 24-hour **La Casa del Mofongo** (*1447 St Nicholas Ave*), a neighborhood staple by day and a booming dance floor at night. Try a classic Mama Juana or the national beer Presidente for a tropical buzz that'll have you dancing bachata like you were in Punta Cana.

The Hispanic Society of America

Founded in 1904 in a Beaux-Arts building on Audubon Terrace, this museum holds an impressively comprehensive collection of rare artifacts

613 W 155th St
(near Broadway)
212-926-2234
Tues-Sat 10am-4:30pm
❶ to 157th St
Suggested Donation

and literature from Spain, Portugal, and Latin America. The display begins outside with a series of sculptures by multiple artists from the Spanish-speaking world. Inside the grandiose building—graced with towering pillars and an almighty pediment—noted works by Joaquin Sorolla y Bastida hang in the newly renovated Sorolla Room. But the undisputed main attraction is the Goya collection, which encompasses the majority of the master's prints, including his revered Sleep of Reason. In the library, gawkers gather around a first edition print of Don Quijote. Visit soon, lest you miss other treasures more fleeting: recently the Society auctioned off the oldest known entire copy of the Qur'an.

Morris-Jumel Mansion

At 246 years, the Morris-Jumel Mansion is the oldest house in Manhattan and one of the precious few landmarks left from the Battle of Harlem Heights. During the Revolution, Roger Morris's grand residence was a headquarters for both British and American forces, the most notable occupant being George Washington after the Battle of Long Island was lost. Renovated and restored with elaborate furnishings from the colonial period,

65 Jumel Terrace
(near 160th St)
212-923-8008
Wed-Sun 10am-4pm,
Mon-Tues
by appointment only
❻ to 163rd St
Adults $5, Students $4

the mansion is now remarkably similar to its original state. After a brief inside tour, take advantage of the mansion's strategic location atop "Mount Morris"—it affords an unobstructed view of the Harlem River, the Bronx, Long Island Sound, downtown New York, the Hudson, and the Palisades. Visit for a first-hand experience of American history or simply to admire to the mansion's Palladian-style monumentalism.

National Track and Field Hall of Fame

Founded in Charleston, West Virginia and passing through a host of cities before establishing its permanent location in the Heights, the National Track and Field Hall of Fame is the only sports museum in New York City. Dedicated to the spirit of achievement and to the American heroes of

The Armory, 216 Fort
Washington Ave
(at 168th St)
212-923-1803
Mid Nov-Mid Apr
Tues-Sun 10am-5pm
Mid Apr-mid Nov
Tues-Fri 10am-5pm
❶ ❹ ❻ to 168th St
Admission $5

On February 21, 1965, Malcolm X was assassinated in the Audubon Ballroom.

CHEAP EATS
best dominican food

El Presidente- All the Dominican favorites—rotisserie chicken, beef tripe soup, codfish fritters—are made well at this Caribbean diner. Extra strong coffee and fresh juices served through the night. *3938 Broadway, 212-927-7011, Daily 24 hours, 1 to 168th St $*

Tipico Dominicano Restaurant- An elegant dining room and friendly service set Tipico apart from the dozens of other Dominican restaurants in the neighborhood. Housemade desserts like arroz con leche provide an excellent end to an authentic meal. *4172 Broadway, 212-781-3900, Daily 24 hours, 1 to 181st St, A to 175th St $*

La Reina del Chicarron- It's all about the fried pork belly at this Dominican hotspot, great for take-out. Aromatic rice and fried sweet plantains accompany the house special well. *4840 Broadway, 212-304-1070, Sun 12pm-8pm, Mon-Thurs 9am-9pm, Fri-Sat 9am-10pm, A to Dyckman St, 1 to 207th St $*

La Casa del Mofongo- This airy restaurant specializes in the much-loved Dominican classic, mofongo, made from mashed fried green plantains stuffed with beef, pork, or chicken (and sometimes shrimp), covered with a thin chicken broth. *1447 St Nicholas Ave, 212-740-1200, Daily 24 hours, 1 to 181st St $*

Margot Restaurant- Most of Margot's specialties are stewed and served with yellow rice and red beans, like the goat, beef tripe, and pig's ear. Fresh tropical juices are good complements to some of the heavily spiced dishes. *3822 Broadway, 212-781-8494, Mon-Thurs, Sat-Sun 10am-11pm, 1 to 157th St $*

sports, the Hall has been inducting members since 1974 and currently has 239 people enshrined. The museum's interactive exhibits are spread out over three levels: on the first, there's a theater and a history gallery, on the second, an atrium and a champion gallery, and on the third, a 40-foot-long etched glass wall with the engraved names of all the inductees. The Hall also contains a 65,000-square foot arena, a breeding ground for future record-breakers.

The Cloisters

As you walk across the lengthy Fort Tryon Park, take a detour through the Dark Ages at this amalgam of five French cloisters.

99 Margaret Corbin Dr
212-923-3700
Tues-Sun 9:30am-5pm
Ⓐ to 190th St
M4 to the Cloisters

Overlooking the Hudson River at Manhattan's north end, this branch of the Metropolitan Museum of Art specializes in art from the European Middle Ages. With over 5,000 altarpieces, manuscripts, reliquaries, and illuminated books from the 12th through 15th centuries, the Cloisters embodies its era of choice with both its collection and its hybrid building of tan stone walls, granite columns, terracotta roof tiles, and soaring towers. Come—preferably in autumn for the blazing trees atop the Palisades—for the free gallery tours and the gardens planted exclusively with the herbs and blooms that medieval monks tended.

SHOP

Nostylgia

Since the beginning of the hip hop era, sneakers have been a part of uptown culture— Uptown Jordans and crisp white Air Forces remain synonymous

251 Dyckman St (btwn Payson and Seaman Ave)
212-304-0337
Mon-Thurs 12pm-9pm,
Fri-Sun 12pm-10pm
Ⓐ to Dyckman St

with summertime among those in the know. At exclusive sneaker boutique Nostylgia, timeless style is blended with colorful everyday life, a philosophy the staff refers to as Lifestylgia. Originally just a retail website, this now larger-than-life shop has its own customized shoes and clothes, displayed on miniature fire escapes. Along with a loyal customer base, the store has also developed an online following with its daily blog, which chronicles new merchandise, store sales, tips on sneaker style, and even local sneaker-related news (yes, it exists). Get your start on the Lifestylgia path, or just get some kickass kicks.

Quisqueya Record Shop

"Quisqueya" is a colloquial term for the Dominican Republic, and although the small record shop takes much pride in its Hispaniola roots, its more than 25,000 CDs reflect Latin American diversity. The most popular genres are bachata, merengue, salsa, reggaetón, bolero, mexicana, cumbia, and tipico—a veritable rainbow of styles. A bold circular logo juts outward above the store's entrance, distinguishing it from the surrounding discount stores and diminutive bodegas. Though calm on the outside, the interior is a room-sized boombox constantly playing a shuffle of genres. Squeezed amongst the racks you'll find the latest CD by bachata sensation Aventura, a greatest hits collection from salsa goddess Celia Cruz, and the DVD of reggaetón superstar Daddy Yankee's last tour.

52 Sherman Ave
(near Arden St)
212-942-1020
Mon-Sat 10:30am-7pm
Sun 12pm-7pm
❶ Ⓐ to Dyckman St

EL MALECON
best dominican immersion

Named after the Santo Domingo boardwalk, El Malecon prides itself on its ability to immerse guests in a complete Dominican experience. It's difficult not to get lost in the chorus of Spanish conversation on the way to your table. Scenes of merengue hanging from orange walls are a reminder that even though Washington Heights experiences four seasons, the restaurant is as warm as its namesake. Begin with a longaniza sausage, or if it's on the early side, a plantain omelette. The local favorite is undoubtedly the rotisserie chicken "Malecon style"—served in garlic sauce with yellow rice and maduros, it's available both half and whole. Accompany your meal with beer by the bucket or a choice of 12 tropical juices or shakes. El Malecon has expanded to two additional New York City locations, but those who know the boardwalk know the original is always worth a visit.

4141 Broadway
(btwn 175th & 176th St)
212-927-3812
Sun-Thurs 7am-1:30am,
Fri-Sat 7am-2am
A to 175th St
$$

Washington Heights is famous for its "nutcrackers," street cocktails made of fruit punch and alcohol.

EAT

Indian Road Café

New American

Indian Road Café's coffeehouse-chic interior feels more SoHo than Inwood, minus the hordes of tourists toting shopping bags. But this cozy, honey-colored Italian fusion restaurant carries a celebrity cache to match any downtown Manhattan eatery: it's co-owned by Jason Minter, former producer of HBO's The Sopranos, and you might recognize the dark wood tables and blue-cushioned chairs from the show's restaurant set, Nuovo Vesuvio. A camel wingback chair is a perfect spot to sip on Indian Road's organic French-pressed coffee or enjoy a prosciutto panino, its saltiness offset by a subtle calimyrna fig jam. Dinner offerings include classic roast duck, served with locally-grown vegetables, a wasabi-glazed tofu steak, or, for the supremely indulgent, lobster macaroni and cheese featuring everything yummy and rich: asiago, pecorino romano, fontina, truffle oil, and fresh, flavorful lobster. Prices are also more SoHo than Inwood, but the lunch, dessert, and drink menus are quite reasonable.

600 W 218th St
(at Indian Rd)
212-942-7451
Sun 8am-9pm,
Mon-Thurs 7am-10pm,
Fri-Sat 7am-11pm
❶ to 215th St
$$

Mamajuana Café

Latino

Like so many things Latin, Mamajuana Café is breezy and romantic. The sidewalk tables cater to families and friends, chatting over pancakes and bottomless mimosas. But the couples are found indoors, among the dark wood tables and Goddesses, expertly carved out of algae-green stone. Here, a pizza kitchen churns out "Cocas" and lovers gape at a colossal wall of orange blossoms, dunked

247 Dyckman St
(near Seamen Ave)
212-304-0140
Daily 5pm-12am,
Brunch Sun 11am-3pm
Ⓐ to Dyckman St
$$

upside down in jars of cloudy water. On the dinner menu, the Octopus Ceviche is the latest addition: a series of white rings and tomatoes soaked together in a beautifully purple sauce. The Cornish Hem is also a popular dish, with flecks of lobster chorizo and a thick sherry glaze. Around midnight, customers head over to the lounge and moonlit bar. Now Mamajuana turns into a nightclub, where bangles gleam and salsa reigns for the following three and a half hours.

PLAY

Keenan's Piano Bar   *Pub, Open Mic*
Keenan's Piano Bar resembles a Midwest small-town bar from 1975—old-time slot machines crowd the corners, wooden panels cover the walls, and a square-shaped wood bar dominates the main room. Despite the name, there's no piano. Locals sprawl on nondescript bar stools or watch TV in the back of this brown-toned lounge. Cheap beer and Monday open mics draw everyone from bearded men in cowboy hats to skinny Spanish-speaking goth boys. The bar is well-stocked and straightforward: knock back a $2 Bud at happy hour, stick around for live entertainment on Tuesday "Jam Night," or shoot some pool. Food isn't served, but you're welcome to bring snacks from the deli across the street.

♫
4878 Broadway
(near 204th St)
212-567-9016
Daily 11am-3:30pm
Ⓐ ❶ to 207th St
$

LITTLE RED LIGHTHOUSE
sweetest reason to do a double take

Popularized by Hildegard Swift's 1942 children's book *The Little Red Lighthouse and the Great Gray Bridge*, this bite-sized lighthouse on the Hudson (officially called Jeffrey's Hook Lighthouse) was built in 1880, in New Jersey. In 1921, the beacon relocated across the river to aid in navigation before the George Washington Bridge was built. After more than half a century of operation, it was marked for dismantling, but young Swift readers didn't like that. The public outcry culminated in the preservation of the lighthouse and, later, its establishment as a city landmark—it has even been relit as of 2002. Today, tours run daily and every autumn a Little Red Lighthouse Festival offers free food, photo displays, and a public reading of the famous story.

Fort Washington Park
West 178th St at the
Hudson River
212-304-2365
1 to 181st St

First dubbed Nieuw Haarlem by plucky Dutch sailors, today's West Harlem lived most of its first century of settlement as inauspicious farmland. In the late 18th century, the area emerged as an elegant getaway for wealthy urbanites, spurring the construction of the same grandiose stone manors that dot Riverside Drive a few miles southward. But the difficulty of traveling downtown and the infertile soil diminished property value, and much of the land was auctioned off cheaply and written off as useless to both farmers and real estate agents. The extension of elevated railroads into Harlem in 1880 brought accessibility and successive waves of immigrants—Jews, Irish, Italians, and, beginning in the early 1900s, blacks. The last group migrated en masse from the southern states and immediately began a concerted, ultimately long-lived effort to build a true community out of fragments, reveling in the solidarity and sense of activism that the neighborhood enabled. By 1910, the Harlem region was known as the "black capital of America."

History and legends of Harlem abound, but its most famous period was in the 1920s, at the height of the Jazz Age. Then it was the center of the Harlem Renaissance, a prolific outpouring of black poetry, fiction, music, and art, driven by iconic artists like Langston Hughes, Countee Cullen, Dorothy West, and Zora Neale Hurston. But as Harlemites' cultural contributions

soared to new heights, the neighborhood itself began to deteriorate as an increasingly poor population became riddled with crime and drug addiction. The overall decline of New York in the latter half of the 20th century is well-documented, and Harlem was doubly damaged by its northern location. The cultural membrane between upper Manhattan and the south Bronx has always been porous, dating back to the first Dutch settlements of the 1600s. As the Bronx descended into arson-fueled violence, Harlem absorbed most of the heat from the blaze.

Not until the 1990s were drastic steps were taken to remedy Harlem's problems. The Upper Manhattan Empowerment Zone began to funnel money into new developments, and former Mayor Giuliani vigorously cleaned up the many housing projects. Property values soared by 300% that decade and, as the story goes, rapid gentrification followed, ushering in a lowered crime rate, Starbucks, the offices of Bill Clinton, and a small but persistent band of young, creatively-minded ex-suburbanites. Yet despite hints of a Corporate America-approved new edge, the area has maintained its original lively aura, representing modern neighborhood life and the plethora of Harlemites' countries of origin in equal measure. West Harlem still boasts some of the best jazz and soul food in the city, and on Wednesday nights, when it's showtime at the Apollo Theater, you can pop in to see the next big star.

EXPLORE

The Apollo Theater

Founded in 1914, the Apollo has for years been the gold standard in entertainment for black performers: to make it to this stage (and not get booed off) is a holy achievement.

253 West 125th St (btwn 7th & 8th Ave)
212-531-5305
Shows start at 7:30pm or 8pm
Ⓐ Ⓒ Ⓑ Ⓓ ② ③ to 125th St
Tours $16-$18

Ella Fitzgerald, Billie Holiday, Aretha Franklin, and The Jackson 5 were all discovered during the the the theater's legendary Amateur Night, a Wednesday night tradition running since the early 1930s. The Apollo's stature as a cultural gathering place far exceeds mere music hall status; after his death in 2006, James Brown's body lay in state on the Apollo stage, with Rev. Al Sharpton officiating all of the public memorial's services. The theater also provides historic tours and community outreach programs.

Maysles Institute

The only theater in Manhattan dedicated solely to documentaries is named for the Maysles brothers, the masterminds behind Gimme Shelter and Grey Gardens.

343 Malcolm X Blvd
(btwn 127th & 128th St)
212-582-6050
❷ ❸ to 125th St
Suggested Donation $10

Founded by Albert Maysles in 2005 as a nonprofit theater, the Institute expressly aims to provide training, schooling, and internships to underprivileged individuals with movie-making aspirations. Screenings take place in a chic room accented with a Persian rug and 60 plush batik cushion-lined seats, somewhat of a shift from the Loews multiplex. On occasion, Maysles will invite the filmmakers and crew members to participate on a related panel after the screening—a different kind of movie-viewing experience, to say the least.

Schomburg Center for Black Culture

The Schomburg Center for Black Culture was founded in 1926 when the NYPL purchased the collection of Arthur Schomburg, a historian who had spent his lifetime collecting papers and artifacts chronicling

515 Malcolm X Boulevard
(at W 142nd St)
212-491-2200
Mon-Wed 12pm-8pm,
Thurs-Fri 11am-6pm,
Sat 10am-5pm
❷ ❸ to 135th St

the many paths of the African-American experience. Today it contains over ten million items, and is widely regarded as one of the finest research libraries devoted to the study of black culture. The collection includes materials belonging to Malcolm X and Richard Wright, and interred within the building are the ashes of Langston Hughes, one of the Harlem Renaissance's most important champions. For years known mostly to scholars and researchers, the center has recently become nationally popular as a museum, and as an occasional host of live readings and theater shows.

LITTLE SENEGAL

Le Petit Senegal is geographically a little fish in the big ocean of West Harlem, but its cultural identity is so assertive that it often overshadows the surrounding neighborhood, rather than the other way around. An unusual immigration boom at the beginning of the millennium caused the number of Senegalese in Harlem to skyrocket, although the country has had a powerful presence above Central Park for decades. Three short blocks of hand-beaded jewelry, okra chicken curry, and men in robes that trail along the sidewalk, this enclave on 116th St between Frederick Douglass Blvd and 5th Ave rings with choppy French and a dozen African dialects. Follow the daily routine of a typical Senegal-born local by pairing a visit to the stunning **Malcolm Shabazz Mosque** *(102 W 116th St)* with a lamb lunch at **Le Baobab** *(120 W 116th St)*. The year-round outdoor **Malcolm Shabazz Market** *(52 W 115th St)* is the go-to destination for immigrants throughout Harlem who want the authentic thing from back home, be it all-natural soap or a figurine carved by hand.

Studio Museum in Harlem

A promoter of local and African-American art for over 40 years, the Studio Museum boasts a small but terrific collection encompassing James Van Der Zee and Jacob Lawrence. This modernized, deceptively simple two-floor space commands visitors' attention for much longer than other museums of its tiny size—the woefully underexposed artwork is simply that intriguing. The small sculpture garden contains some of the museum's nicest pieces, while indoors the art trends toward contemporary, with photography playing a dominant role. The Artist-in-Residence program has supported such luminaries as David Hammons, Chakaia Booker, and Julie Mehretu. Most of the floor is devoted to rotating exhibits, so don't take it for granted that a single visit will cover everything.

144 W 125th St
(btwn Malcolm X Blvd & 7th Ave)
212-864-4500
Sun 12pm-6pm, Thurs-Fri 12pm-9pm,
Sat 10am-6pm
Suggested Donation
Adults $7, Students $3, Free on Sundays

SHOP

Hats by Bunn

Bunn, the owner of this artisan Harlem millinery, has been crafting hats for more than 30 years for customers like Alicia Keys and LL Cool J, in addition to the countless neighborhood denizens who make this boutique a daily pit stop. Around the shop hang pictures of happy customers donning their hats, and reggae music blasts from the stereo. Though prices can be steep for the type of workmanship Bunn provides—the handmade headwear ranges from $75 to $200—for the true hat lover, it's worth it. Accordingly, though visitors can feast their eyes on displays of already-constructed, prêt-à-porter specimens, most of Bunn's work is made one-of-a-kind, for and with the customer.

2283 Adam Clayton Powell Junior Blvd
(btwn 134th & 135th St)
212-694-3590
Mon-Sat 11am-7pm
② ③ ⑧ ⓒ to 135th St

EAT

5 and Diamond

New American

5 and Diamond might be the kind of place where the waiters change utensils after every course, but it has a casual swagger too—its Harlem location tempers the upscale vibe, and the interior is desaturated and catalog-worthy. The $5 menu, available Tuesdays through Fridays, makes the restaurant more approachable and offers drinks and a rotating selection that can include anything from lamb belly sliders to

2072 Frederick Douglass Blvd (near 112th St)
646-684-4662
Sun 11am-3pm,
5:30 pm- 10 pm,
Tues-Fri 5:30pm- 11pm,
Sat 11am-3pm,
5:30pm- 11pm
⑧ ⓒ to 110th St-Cathedral Parkway
$$$$

North of Hamilton Heights sits Sugar Hill, which is most notable for nursing the Harlem Renaissance and dubbed for the "sweet life" its wealthy residents lead—Duke Ellington, W.E.B. Du Bois, and Thurgood Marshall once counted among them.

WEST HARLEM
best soul food

Strictly Roots- Possibly the only place for vegetarian soul food in New York, this Rasta-themed restaurant doesn't serve greasy fried chicken and ribs, but just-as-tasty, healthy alternatives like spicy black beans and red pepper, or sweet and sour tofu. *2058 7th Ave, 212-864-8699, Sun 12pm-8pm, Mon-Fri 8am-10pm, Sat 11am-10pm, 2,3, A/B/C/D to 125th St $*

Charles' Southern Style Kitchen- World-famous chef Charles Gabriel feeds patrons the best of soul food in this small uptown eatery. Highlights of the buffet include sweet roasted yams, smoky collard greens, and the much-celebrated crispy fried chicken. *2841 Frederick Douglass Blvd, 212-281-1800, Sun 12pm-7pm, Mon-Thurs 12pm-10pm, Sat 12pm-11pm, B/D/C to 155th St $$*

Africa Kine- All the African influences of soul food are apparent at this airy Senegalese restaurant: dishes with yams, okra, and fried fish resemble the cuisine of the South. Try the Thiebu Djeun: tomato sauce-covered brown rice with garlic-smothered fish. *256 W 116th St, 212-666-9400, Daily 12:30pm-2am, A/B/C 116th St $*

Fishers of Men- An odd pairing of hot dogs and soul food makes this fried fish restaurant a Harlem favorite. Finish the meal with a slice of the coconut cake. *121 W 125th St, 212-678-4268, Mon-Thurs 10am-9pm, Fri-Sat 10am-10pm, 2,3, A/C/B/D to 125th St $*

Kaloum- West African specialties of the highest authenticity are what set this restaurant apart. Fresh juices like baobab fruit with milk or yam with honey are a refreshing compliment to the heavily spiced stewed meats and fish. *120 W 116th St, 212-222-3651, Mon-Fri 8am-2am, 2/3 to 116th St $*

tempura maitake mushrooms. The burger is all that remains of Ryan Skeen, 5 and Diamond's former celebrity-chef-in-residence, and the resulting menu reveals the measured, unpretentious hand of David Santos. Seafood is the way to go when ordering: the sockeye salmon is a clean refresher, and the seared scallops swim in an apricot broth. But the doughnuts are a contender for the city's best—made with brioche dough and sprinkled with cinnamon sugar, they are exceptionally light and just sweet enough.

Dinosaur BBQ   *BBQ*

Under a clanging metal overpass in the heart of riverside Harlem, a staggering line of Harleys and cruisers mark a distinct cultural shift. The raucous, rollicking crowd at this old-fashioned roadhouse is kept at bay by the

646 W 131st St
(at Riverside Dr)
212-694-1777
Sun 12pm-10pm, Mon-Thurs 11:30am-11pm, Fri-Sat 11:30am-12pm
❶ to 125th St
$$

tried and true barbecue they came for. The bar and terrace are filled with eager diners awaiting tables, getting more fidgety with each steaming plate of wings, ribs, and fried green tomatoes going by. No one is disappointed once seated: the wings are mammoth bites of crispy, dry rubbed goodness with a complimentary kick in the mouth. The tomatoes, a lesser-known appetizer, surprise with a delightfully tarty crunch, quickly abated by a sharp pecorino cheese. But Dinosaur BBQ is a rib joint at heart, and these ribs remain king: slow-cooked marvels of fatty meat that would fall apart from the slightest poke with a fork—that is, if you weren't already eating them with your hands.

Melba's   *Southern, Soul*

This soul food joint's friendly servers encourage diners to enjoy the delicious fried fare in a formal yet relaxed setting. Dressed up diners enter the beautiful black-and-white interior in separate groups, but everyone seems to know each other. A charismatic singer and live band add chill Motown tunes to the already incandescent atmosphere. Try the special, fried chicken and eggnog batter waffles, or the mac and cheese, blended from three sorts of cheese, for a gustatory trip to the American South. If you're lucky, you'll get to meet the charming Melba herself, the Harlem native who gave her name to this swanky comfort food restaurant.

300 W 114th St (at Frederick Douglass Blvd)
212-864-7777
Sat-Sun 10am-3pm, 5pm-11pm, Tues-Fri, 5pm-11pm
B C to 116th St
$$

Patisserie Des Ambassades   *Senegalese, French, Bakery, Café*

This little Senegalese bakery collects its influences from all over the former French colonial empire. A warm café atmosphere lures diners into the nook, but the diverse brunch and dinner menu is what turns first-timers into regulars. The eclectic options range from crisp Vietnamese spring rolls to the Moroccan-tinged Charwarma. Traditional European dishes like mussels or lamb shanks equal their downtown brethren in taste but certainly not price. The sandwiches encapsulate the global theme, combining all influences—you'll lose your head over the Robespierre,

2200 Frederick Douglass Blvd (at 119th St)
212-666-0078
Mon-Thurs 7am-2am, Sat-Sun 8am-3am
B C to 116th St
$

LENOX LOUNGE
truest time warp

Perhaps the most tried and true vestige of old Harlem jazz culture, Lenox Lounge has heard the voice of Billie Holiday and the sax of John Coltrane. The zebra-striped space still stands as one of the best jazz clubs in New York, attracting music enthusiasts from well-informed college kids to elderly black men that have been regulars for decades. Along with reliably amazing live shows, the venue serves up cocktails and soul food for affordable prices. Its art-deco aesthetic makes you feel like you're in a 1930s time warp sitting at a table near James Baldwin or Claude McKay. For this reason, Lenox Lounge has been used as a set in movies such as Shaft and American Gangster, further increasing its well-deserved fame.

Music Venue, Lounge

288 Lenox Ave
(btwn 124th & 125th St)
212-427-0253
Daily 12pm-4am
2/3 to 125th St
*Live Music

a baguette filled with grilled lamb or chicken, sautéed onions, tomatoes, mayo, and French fries. For those not craving a full meal, delightful pastries, including a solid croissant, are available for under $5. This is definitely one of the finer results of the international evolution that is taking place in Harlem.

Tonalli Café and Wine Bar *Italian, Latino*

This self-proclaimed continental Italian restaurant is both a sensory and visual experiment in eclecticism. The menu offers a unique assortment of Italian-based dishes that are heavily influenced by Thai, Spanish, and Mediterranean flavors. The name itself, Tonalli, which derives from an Aztecan Nahuatl word, is a prime example of the diversity cultivated within the restaurant. Rustic Italian dishware and decorative wheels pleasantly accent the dining room, and a quaint little wine bar forms the center of the cozy space. Although quiet and intimate, Tonalli attracts both couples and families alike, from as far away as Westchester County. Highlights are the crab and avocado dumplings, the pan-seared salmon, and the lemonade, which is squeezed when you order it.

3628 Broadway
(btwn 149th & 150th St)
212-926-0399
Mon-Fri 11am-11pm,
Sat-Sun 11am-12am
❶ to 145th St,
☉ to 155th St
$$

west harlem
UNDER $20

Start at the **Abyssinian Baptist Church** *(132 Odell Clark Place)*, a stunning castle-like landmark that jolts many an early-morning worshiper awake.

Then pay your respects to twin stars of uptown history, first at famed Harlem writer **Ralph Ellison's memorial** *(150th and Riverside)*, and then at revolutionary hero **Alexander Hamilton's home** *(287 Convent Ave)*.

Take in a prix fixe brunch at **Les Ambassades Boulangerie-Patisserie-Cafe** *(2200 Frederick Douglass Blvd)* for the kind of omelette that eggs dream about becoming.

Tour the **Studio Museum in Harlem** *(144 W 125th St)* for an exemplary contemporary art experience, then cool off your senses in the sculpture garden.

Treat yourself to a traditional Senegalese dinner at **Keur Sokhna** *(2249 Adam Clayton Powell Jr Blvd)*, where the lamb is tender and the peanuts are hot.

If it's Wednesday, hurry to the **Apollo** *(253 W 125th St)*—tickets to Amateur Night sell for a meager $12.

Wind down at the **Nectar Wine Bar** *(2235 Frederick Douglas Blvd)*, with chianti and bar snacks for $4 and up.

PLAY

The Shrine World Music Venue
Music Venue

Music is religion for the mature, easygoing crowd that frequents this dimly lit Harlem hotspot. The managers work magic to reel in performers from around the world, ensuring a diverse serving of genres and styles. Musicians come from as far afield as Timbuktu, so you can expect to hear instruments, vocal techniques, and rhythms that are new to even the most well-traveled ears. If you're a musician yourself, you don't have to stick to the audience: on Sunday afternoons, Shrine hosts a jazz jam session where everyone's invited to play. Generous seating and table service allow patrons to enjoy the vegetarian-friendly food menu made up of native African and Mediterranean dishes. At midnight, DJs, disco balls, and flashing lights encourage dancing, so don't be shy. If you need liquid courage, try the Afro-trip, a ginger beer-infused cocktail.

2271 Adam Clayton Powell Jr Blvd
(btwn 133rd & 134th St)
212-690-7807
Daily 4pm-4am
②③ to 135th St
$$

SPA

HAR

Murals of traditional Puerto Rican families and great historical figures, such as Julia de Burgos, cover the walls of Spanish Harlem and capture the neighborhood's ambiance. During the day, elderly immigrant couples walk over to the closest food mart. After school, older siblings assist their younger family members back home while dodging the fluid motion of workers. At night, young couples wine and dine at Ricardo's Steakhouse, and on weekends parents take their kids to Marcus Garvey Park. Much like the murals, the people of Spanish Harlem illustrate the values of community every day.

Before East Harlem became known as Spanish Harlem, the Italians had dominated the area in the 1900s and nicknamed it "Italian Harlem." At the end of World War I, Puerto Ricans and other Latinos settled in small communities and linked together at the northern tip of the area, which they nicknamed "El Barrio," or "the Ghetto." As the Latino population expanded after WWII, the Italians migrated to areas in the Bronx, Brooklyn, and downtown Manhattan. El Barrio had become more than just a section in East Harlem—it *was* East Harlem.

Spanish Harlem is now considered the area bounded by the Harlem River to the north, 5th Ave to the west, E 96th St to the south, and the East River. During the 1960s and 1970s, the neighborhood experienced a large increase in drug abuse, unemployment, deficit, poverty,

and crime. Young locals joined together in activist and gang-related movements, like the Young Lords and Black Panthers, that took it upon themselves to pick up where the weak local government had failed them. In the late 1960s, the Young Lords picked up la basura—garbage left in the streets—and bagged it in an effort called the Garbage Offensive. They went on to seize an X-ray unit in 1970 and overran Lincoln Hospital, in order to improve health care for residents. These groups left an indelible imprint on the people of Spanish Harlem, who still currently face hardship yet depend on the unity of their community for strength.

Past artists, performers and political activists alike have left their mark on El Barrio, leaving behind their passions, philosophies, and sense of collective identity. El Museo Del Barrio, New York's largest museum geared towards uplifting Puerto Rican, Latino, Caribbean and Latin American culture, embodies the preservation of traditions and memories of the Latino Diaspora, especially in regards to the United States. The Harbor Conservatory for the Performing Arts also teaches children throughout New York the traditional foundations of dance, music and theatre, and through these courses show students not only how to read music, but also how to be a better person within their community. Watching them perform on stage is like watching the continuation of the neighborhood's history.

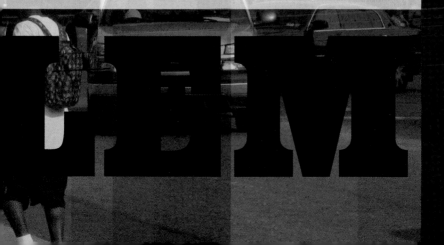

EXPLORE

Conservatory Garden

Three sections split the 71-year-old Conservatory Garden, each mimicking a different European planting tradition. The Italian-style manicured lawn, geyser fountain, and canopy of wisteria vines present a whiff of Tuscany. Turn left and walk beneath the towering cloud of purple for a trip to a prim English landscape, where the serene Burnett Fountain pools water at the feet of a bronze statue. Opposite, the Northern Garden pays homage to the more sprawling but no less delicate French tradition. As Central Park's only formal garden and a relatively unknown patch of uptown parkland, the Conservatory Garden is the photo backdrop of choice for city brides and a weekend destination for upstate yuppies. It's worth the trip just for the chance to see a butterfly in Manhattan.

105th St & 5th Ave
212-860-1382
Mon-Fri 9am-5pm
6 to 103rd St,
2 3 to 110th St
Free

neighborhhood
NECESSITIES

SUBWAYS 4, 5, 6

BUSES M1, M15, M35, M60, M98, M100, M101, M102, M103, M106, M116, Bx15, Bx33

MARKETS Mount Morris Farmer's Market *(Marcus Garvey Park, 212-369-4241)*

LIBRARIES Aguilar Library *(174 E 110th St, 212-534-2930)*, 125th Street Library *(224 E 125th St, 212-534-5050)*

MEDIA east-harlem.com

FITNESS New York Sports Club *(1400 5th Ave, 212-722-1185)*

BIKES Heavy Metal Bike Shop *(2016 3rd Ave, 212-410-1144)*

Songs that reference Spanish Harlem include: Ben E. King's "Spanish Harlem," Louie Ramirez's "Lucy's Spanish Harlem," Bob Dylan's "Spanish Harlem Incident," The Mamas and the Papas' "Spanish Harlem," and Carlos Santana's "Maria Maria."

MURAL ROW

The two-, three-, and four-story images of Mural Row hover over the residents of Spanish Harlem as they go about their day, a reminder of the neighborhood's past stars and present traditions. As graffiti artists' territory shrinks in a gentrified downtown, Harlem continues to celebrate its pockets of public art like the invaluable expressions of creativity that they are. Dancing across the murals of E 104th St and the surrounding blocks are paintings of close-knit families engaging in customary pastimes that emphasize the need for unity and community, and allusions to Caribbean and Latin American heritage. **"The Spirit of East Harlem,"** encompassing one whole peaked brick façade, is the closest a piece of art will ever get to capturing the brilliantly clashing character of the neighborhood. Its dreamily overlapping figures are epic in size and preternaturally bright in color, but these are not comic book heroes—rather, they're normal Spanish Harlem natives from every walk of life, no more and no less extraordinary than the residents who make the area come alive. From seascapes to Che Guevara, Mural Row is a monument to historical and cultural pride.

El Museo Del Barrio

Since the Civil Rights movement, El Museo Del Barrio has been the city's cornerstone for Caribbean and Latin American art and culture.

1230 5th Ave (at 104th St)
212-831-7272
Wed-Sun 11am-6pm
6 to 103rd St
Suggested Donation

With a special emphasis on Puerto Rican works, the museum collection spans dramatically across time and space, displaying both pre-Colombian and traditional artifacts and contemporary graphic design and video art. Originally developed out of the Nuyorican intellectual movement of the late 20th century, it addresses the concerns of poets, novelists, and musicians as well as visual artists by organizing local book clubs and hosting regular cultural festivals. El Museo is committed to inviting those outside of Spanish Harlem to celebrate Puerto Rican tradition—recent exhibitions have collaborated with the New York Historical Society and the Museo Amparo in Mexico.

Harbor Conservatory for the Performing Arts

For 40 years, the Harbor Conservatory for the Performing Arts has been dedicated to instilling a broad arts education in New York children between the ages of four and 19.

1 E 104th St (at 5th Ave)
212-427-2244 ext. 573
Hours vary
6 to 103rd St

SPANISH HARLEM
one-name italian restaurants

Cuchifritos Frituras- Croquettas, empanadas, chicharron—these are just some of the many fried Latino delights that are sold at this fritura. With each crunchy snack at $1, a full meal, with a freshly squeezed orange juice, does no damage to one's wallet. *168 E 116th St, 212-876-4846, Mon-Thurs, Sat 8am-2am, Fri-Sat 8am-5am, 6 to 116th St §*

La Lomita del Barrio- In the front of this overcrowded Mexican grocery store, fresh tacos and tortas are whipped up within minutes, and when paired with a fresh fruit juice from the back, make a satisfying and authentic meal. *209 E 116th St, 212-289-8138, Daily 7am-1am, 6 to 116th St §*

El Coqui Restaurant- Authentic roasted pork, baked chicken, and fried sweet and green plantains make this Puerto Rican restaurant a popular hangout for neighborhood residents. *2002 3rd Ave, 212-427-3952, Daily 10am-2am, 6 to 110th St §*

El Paso Taqueria- This taqueria is a refined upscale alternative to the Mexican cantinas along 116th St, but the overstuffed tortas and crunchy tostadas are just as authentic. *1643 Lexington Ave, 212-831-9831, Daily 9am-11pm, 6 to 103rd St §§*

"El Barrio" derives from the Puerto Rican term meaning "the ghetto." El Barrio thus symbolizes the early struggle of Puerto Rican immigrants and acculturation into New York.

The center teaches music, dance and theatre courses and explores the disciplines' folkloric, classical, and contemporary styles. Pledging to go beyond the traditional after-school program, the Conservatory is dedicated to fostering the social skills and competitive drive necessary for success in both academics and the professional world of the arts, where the rules are often bendier than anywhere else. Professional choreographers, musicians, and directors teach workshops and construct student pieces, giving these aspiring artists their first taste of a personal creative vision becoming reality. An adult music program keeps the parents busy.

Islamic Cultural Center of New York

1711 3rd Ave
(btwn 96th and 97th St)
212-722-5234
Daily 9pm-5:30pm,
prayer until 10pm
6 to 96th St
Free

New York's first mosque and a community touchstone, the Islamic Cultural Center has been dedicated to preserving Muslim traditions and providing religious guidance for two decades. Local and international believers gather here to worship, but the Center's library, school, museum, lecture hall, and even prayer hall are open to the public—a policy founded in the good faith that awareness breeds amicability. The

GRAFFITI HALL OF FAME
best felonious museum

Once a year, graffiti artists from all over the world travel to the sunken playground outside Jackie Robinson School to add a fresh coat to the legacy of the Graffiti Hall of Fame. According to young but greatly respected tradition, the graffitied playground walls are whitewashed on the last Friday of each July. On the following day, DJs, B-boys, MCs, and scores of spectators gather at a block-wide barbecue and watch famous taggers reinvent the street scenery once again. On the Sunday after the paint has dried, the artists touch up their work. If you're lucky, you'll catch JDL Wilson from the legendary hip hop group Cold Crush Groove leading a tour and explaining the history of this great street art stronghold.

106th St & Park Ave
212-714-3527
Sat-Sun 24 hours,
Daily 24 hours (summer)
6 to 103rd or 110th St

community-building effort here is firmly cross-cultural. A resplendent architectural departure from Harlem's grid complete with minarets, the trapezoidal main building's top third is radiant stained glass. A crescent moon sits atop the mosque's dome, calling all eyes to the meticulous geometric decoration that ornaments without imitating the organic forms of God's creation, in accordance with Islamic tradition.

Marcus Garvey Park

At 170 years, Marcus Garvey Park is one of Manhattan's oldest public parks and, unsurprisingly, replete with local history: the Dutch called it Snake Hill in the 1600s, a wary tribute to the area's most prolific demographic, and the 1969 "Black Woodstock" concerts were held here, during which Gladys Knight and Stevie Wonder graced the lawns. Today the park is known to locals as Mount Morris Park, where visitors come to enjoy not just the outdoors, but also the additional recreational areas, including a baseball field, basketball court, amphitheatre, and outdoor pool. There's also a rec center, where

18 Mount Morris Park
(Madison Ave btwn
120th & 124th St)
212-860-1394
Daily 24 hours
❷ ❸ ❹ ❺ ❻ to 125th St

123

young students can take courses in computer skills, karate, and a range of other fairly surprising subjects.

EAT

Ricardo Steak House

Latino, Steakhouse

Six years ago, Ricardo Steak House started as a hole-in-the-wall dream for owner Edward Mateus. However, with the combination of gourmet recipes and word of mouth, it's since transformed into today's classy two-building restaurant and bar. The dim candles and inviting red brick interior with wooden trimmings set a relaxed, embracing vibe, but the grub itself is the winner. Appropriate for Spanish Harlem, it's best described as an American steakhouse menu with a Latin twist—think surf and turf. If you're up for the challenge, try the 22oz T-Bone steak, which cuts like butter and is so rich in flavor that the A1 sauce isn't even necessary. Whether inside, on the patio, or on the roof, you're bound to hear Mateus and the staff ritually singing "Happy Birthday" to a surprised guest with 50 Cent's "In Da Club" providing backup.

2145 2nd Ave (btwn 110th & 111th St)
212-289-5895
Mon-Wed 4pm-11pm,
Thurs-Sun 4pm-12am
❻ to 110th St
$$$

GRAN PIATTO D'ORO
best use of checked tablecloth

Before the 1950s and the rise of Puerto Rican immigrants, Italians once dominated East Harlem. Since then, Spanish Harlem, as the area is now called, has been known for its chiefly Latin American influence. But in 2008, Rolando Calle brought the taste of Italy back to the neighborhood with Gran Piatto d'Oro. This unpretentious white tablecloth restaurant attracts both older upper-class socialites and young couples, and creates a serene eating environment to shake out your folded napkin. The kitchen turns out classically massive portions of pastas and chicken breasts, but the atypical risottos are of the highest caliber. If you're still having difficulty deciding, start off with the stuffed mushrooms and Pinot Grigio. For dinner, try the seasoned lamb chops, which comes with mashed potatoes and ground spices.

Italian

1429 5th Ave
(btwn 116th & 117th St)
212-722-2161
Mon-Fri 11am-10pm,
Sat-Sun 11am-11pm
2/3 to 116th St-Lenox Ave, 6 to 116th St-Lexington Ave
$$$
*Delivery, Take Out

Your inside guide to
DINING
NIGHTLIFE
& EVENTS

insideNEWYORK.com

With the increase in gentrification, advertisers and new residents have begun calling Spanish Harlem "SpaHa." Locals detest the phrase.

125

MORNI

As recently as one hundred years ago, Morningside Heights was a wooded and mostly undeveloped area. Before Columbia University purchased the grounds of the Bloomingdale Insane Asylum in 1896 for its new campus, the neighborhood was perhaps most notable for being the site of a battle in the Revolutionary War. In a wheatfield that once stood at the present site of Barnard College, a group of American soldiers halted a retreat and gave the British heavy casualties, boosting the rebels' weakening morale.

Aside from a small plaque commemorating the event, no sign of any conflict remains. Home to Columbia, Barnard, Teachers' College, the Union and Jewish Theological Seminaries, Manhattan School of Music, Bank Street College of Education, and a variety of parochial and private secondary schools, Morningside Heights has been thoroughly stamped by the imprint of higher education. Those institutions own a large percentage of the real estate, and it is common to see professors and students run into one another on the sidewalks.

Of course, education isn't the only attraction in Morningside Heights. Ulysses Grant's tomb and the Cathedral of St. John the Divine are popular among tourists, and upper Manhattan dwellers craving fresh air flock to the paths and fields of Riverside Park. On a sunny day, the neighborhood provides a plethora of entertainment—snag a bite at Tom's Restau-

HEIC

rant (the exterior of Seinfeld's Monk's Café), browse in one of the neighborhood's book shops, and hit the (Hudson) Beach in Riverside Park's lower level. Though the nightlife doesn't compare to the downtown scene, fun can be had in the bars of lower Morningside and the dives of next-door Manhattan Valley.

Unfortunately, not everything is coming up roses in Morningside Heights. In June 2010, the state upheld a decision allowing the Empire State Development Corporation to take over land in northern neighbor Manhattanville. Columbia plans to develop the property into a 17-acre expansion. Though construction has yet to begin, the plan has raised ire among some students and neighborhood residents who cry foul over its use of eminent domain.

Whatever the end result, one thing is sure to remain unchanged. As long as education remains the lifeblood of Morningside Heights, future notables in business, politics and the arts will continue to live in the neighborhood. From Barack Obama (Columbia '83) to Jhumpa Lahiri (Barnard '89), Morningside intitutions have turned out some of the best and brightest. If you bump into a student, be sure to get his name. In ten years, he might be in your bookstore or on your ballot.

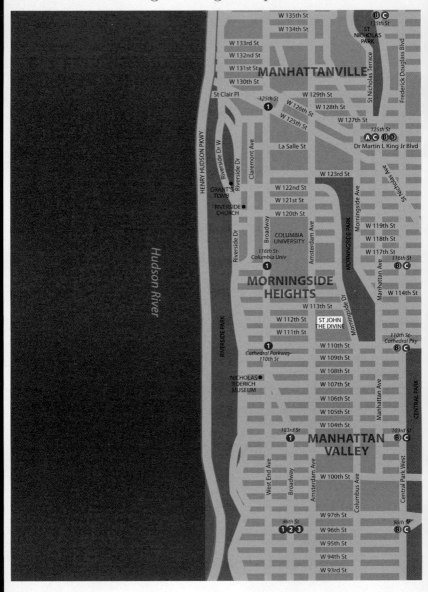

EXPLORE

Columbia University

A compact campus boasting magnificent Neoclassical architecture and lush lawns sits in the tranquil terrain of Morningside

**114th-120th St
(btwn Broadway &
Amsterdam)
❶ to 116th St**

Heights. New York's photogenic Ivy League institution was founded in 1754 through a charter of King George II. Since then, some of its buildings have been written into the perennial chapters of history: Pupin Hall, on the northwest corner, was the site of atomic research that launched the Manhattan Project. All who stand on College Walk, the pedestrian-only path across campus, can't help but ogle at Low Library—its sweeping steps and plaza accommodate student performances, hookah sessions, and protests. Seething with coffee-binging workaholics, Butler Library radiates formidable erudition with the engraved names of dearly departed luminaries. Before leaving, try to find Alma Mater's shy owl hiding somewhere about her majestic person, but a tip to the wise: don't look too hard.

Grant's Tomb

Since 1897 the man who led the Union Army to victory in the Civil War has rested on one of the highest points of Manhattan, an exceptional Hudson panorama on one side and the tranquil

**Riverside at 122nd St
212-666-1640
❶ to 125th St
Daily 9am-5pm
Free**

Riverside Park on the other. The tomb, which contains both Grant and his wife, has a respectable display detailing the life and times of the 18th president and some rare Civil War flag reproductions, but most people come here for the spectacular neoclassical architecture: at 150 feet, the columned cupola crowns the second-largest mausoleum in the Western hemisphere.

neighborhhood
NECESSITIES

SUBWAYS 1, 2, 3, B, C

BUSES M4, M5, M7, M11, M60, M116

MARKETS Columbia Greenmarket *(Broadway btwn W114 and 115th St, 212-788-7476)*, Westside Market *(2840 Broadway, 212-222-3367)*

LIBRARY NYPL of Morningside Heights *(2900 Broadway, 212-864-2530)*

MEDIA *Columbia Daily Spectator,* bwog.com

FITNESS Pilates Shop Yoga Garage *(2805 Broadway, 212-316-9164)*, Capoeira School *(610 W 112 St, 917-653-9339)*

BIKES MODSquad Cycles *(2119 Frederick Douglass Blvd, 212-865-5050)*, Innovation Bike Shop *(105 W 106th St, 212-678-7130)*

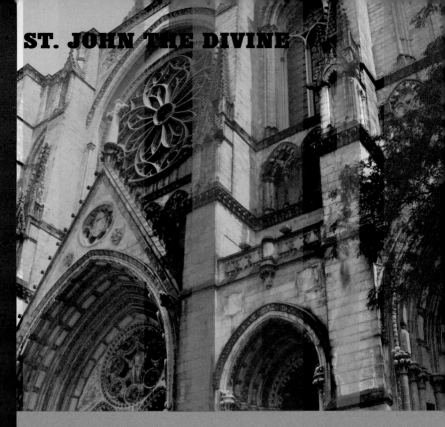

ST. JOHN THE DIVINE

Known by some parishoners as "St. John the Unfinished," this massive Neo-Gothic cathedral towers above Morningside Park. Spanning three blocks and 11 acres, the Cathedral and its grounds are something of a neighborhood landmark. Set across from the Hungarian Pastry Shop's cramped quarters, its lawn and gardens provide a rare bit of open space in which to read and admire the resident peacocks.

Although a fire destroyed the north transept and burned much of the exterior in 2001 (appropriately darkening scenes from Revelations carved above the front entrance), a full restoration effort was completed last year. Now clean of soot and dust, the stunning stained glass windows and 8,500-pipe organ attract tourists from all over the world.

While its chief function may be spiritual, St. John provides a world-class selection of music. From the New York Philharmonic (which plays a concert in the Cathedral every summer) to jazz saxophonist Paul Winter, the Cathedral's programming caters to diverse tastes.

In addition to its concerts (almost all of them free), St. John hosts one of Morningside's most spectacular events, the **Feast of St. Francis**, each October. Pet-owners from all over New York bring their animals—from birds to camels—to receive a blessing. From the top of St. Paul's tower (accessible by tour), the ark-like potpourri is a sight to behold.

Though the memorial's urban hinterland took its toll in the '70s and '80s, when vandals attacked unchecked, today locals picnic on The Rolling Bench, a 1972 art installation of 17 mosaic-covered benches around the white stone plaza.

Historic Mansions on Riverside Drive

Today the residential stretch of Riverside Drive, winding parallel to Riverside Park, is home to luxury apartment buildings and a few of the luckier Co-

	Riverside Dr
	btwn 72nd & 125th St
	❶❷❸ to stops btwn
	72nd & 125th St

lumbia fraternities. But in the 1950s and '60s, the street's cream-colored brick facades housed members of New York's Jewish intellectual circle, including philosopher Hannah Arendt, novelist Saul Bellow, and Manhattan Project director J. Robert Oppenheimer. A few of those elegant townhouses still stand, including the curving Colosseum and Paterno, twin apartment buildings at 116th St boasting over-the-top marble lobbies. The so-called Cliff Dwellers' Apartment at 96th St is particularly striking for its asymmetrical wedge shape and limestone friezes depicting the Arizona cliff dwellers, the ancient predecessors of the Manhattan "cliff dwellers." At dusk, enjoy the view of twinkling

New Jersey beyond the river, and imagine yourself as one of the Riverside nouveau riche of decades past.

The New York Buddhist Church

	331-332 Riverside Drive
	(btwn 105th & 106th St)
	212-678-0305
	❶ to 103rd St

Housed in the former abode of 1930s film star Marion Davies, which nestles in a row of Beaux-Arts brownstones on Riverside Drive, the New York Buddhist Church is one of Morningside Heights' best-kept secrets. In front stands one of the Hiroshima bombing's few survivors: a towering statue of 12th-century Japanese monk Shinran Shonin. In addition to offering services patterned on Shinran's teachings, the church hosts weekly classes in calligraphy, martial arts, taiko drumming, and tachibana dance in the annex, as well as traditional ceremonies like the annual Obon festival. Though some classes cost money, the daily meditation sessions aren't to be missed—the chants and dharma talks will wash away the stress of city life, at least for a little bit

Nicholas Roerich Museum

The paradigmatic Renaissance man, St. Petersburg-born Nicholas Roerich tried his hand at art, fiction, philosophy, and natural science,

President Obama, a transfer to Columbia, claims to have spent his first night in the neighborhood sleeping in an alley at 109th and Amsterdam, after arriving too late to get into his apartment.

earning worldwide recognition and several Nobel Prize nominations in the process. Founded two years after Roerich's death in 1947, this small museum, housed in a lovely bay-windowed brownstone just a block from Riverside Park, holds the world's most extensive collection of his paintings, drawings, and sketches. In addition to peaceful, pastel-hued temperas depicting Christian, Hindu, and Buddhist subjects (Roerich was committed to the goal of infusing art with a solid ethics), terra cotta heads, stone Buddhas, and other findings from his travels throughout the East are on display. Today the museum maintains the values of the Roerich Pact, the artist's treaty urging the protection of artistic and scientific centers in the Americas, by hosting poetry readings, chamber music, and lectures.

319 W 107th St
(near West End)
212-864-7752
Tues-Sun 2pm-5pm
❶ to 103rd St

Union Theological Seminary
Founded in 1836 by clergy leaders with the unique vision to create a theological seminary that is wholly influenced by its urban surroundings, the Union Theological Seminary in the City of New York focuses its ministerial training with an ultimate objective to, in turn, benefit the city. The school itself is an architectural masterpiece—beautiful English Gothic towers surrounding a spacious, tree-filled quad. Stop by simply to admire the building or to attend one of the innovative daily chapel services among the diverse neighborhood community.

3041 Broadway
(at 121st St)
Daily 24 hours
212-662-7100
❶ to 116th St

SHOP

Book Culture
Used by most students as an alternative to the Columbia Barnes & Noble, Book Culture at first has all the markings of a mediocre independent bookshop. There are socialist magazines on the rack at the door, philosophy and "Area Studies" titles are interspersed between the usual tables of new releases and fiction, and

536 W 112th St (btwn Broadway & Amsterdam)
212-865-1588
Sun 11am-7pm,
Mon-Fri 9am-10pm,
Sat 10am-8pm
❶ to 110th St

all the commune-dwelling cashiers are bearded and friendly. Books are inconveniently stacked on the stairwell, making it impossible for more than one person to pass at a time. Yet the upstairs belies Book Culture's role as a bustling university bookstore: dozens of shelves bear the labels of academic disciplines, box sets designated for classes, textbooks, and thousands of cheap, used books. For more traditional fiction genres and children's books, check out their other location, at the corner of 114th & Broadway.

EAT

Community Food and Juice

American, Brunch

2893 Broadway
(btwn 112th & 113th St)
212-665-2800
Mon-Fri 8am-9:30pm,
Sat-Sun 9am-9:30pm
❶ to 110th St or 116th St
$$

Constantly packed with splurging students and farmer's market devotees, Community is an entirely green restaurant that distinguishes itself through noble ideals and a health-inspired, locally sourced menu. The sleek space is well divided by the bar and backroom, offering both quiet and communal options, while the dark wood tables set a pleasant, low-key tone. The menu reflects the restaurant's ideology, offering a lush variety of health foods, including a vivid Bowl O' Beets and a well-seasoned, veggie-heavy rice bowl. One of the neighborhood's better burgers is ground from all-natural grass-fed beef, depositing its wealth of flavor into the sturdy buns. Community truly shines at breakfast and brunch, offering a keen variety of egg dishes, and a sinfully good brioche French toast. Prices may be a little high, but the dedication to green living guarantees a superior freshness.

Hamilton Deli

Sandwiches

It's hard to say exactly what makes one everyday sandwich shop better than another, but Hamilton Deli (aka HamDel) offers a few solid

theses. Perhaps it's the welcoming staff, recognizing the large base of regulars, happily churning out burgers and sandwiches as fast as the orders come in—which is fast. Or maybe it's the daily

1129 Amsterdam Ave
(btwn 115th & 116th St)
212-749-8924
Sun until 9pm, Mon-Sat
24 hours
❶ to 116th St
$

delivered fresh rolls, subs and H&H bagels that make a superior sandwich suitable for any meal. But money's on the massive green board listing the 30+ named sandwiches and burgers, changing daily with laminated printouts offering newfangled inventions. The smattering of superior classics are interspersed with subtle genius, such as the NYPD: roast beef, bacon, onions, and hot

MORNINGSIDE HEIGHTS
best places you're never been

Voza- A 20-seat mom and pop joint that serves a diverse range of French and Italian options. Make sure to try the Snapper—like almost everything, it's served with a surprising little kick. *949 Columbus Ave, 212-666-8602, Sun 11pm-2am, Mon-Fri 6pm-2am, Sat 11am-2am, 1 to 110th St, B,C to 110th St $$*

Malaysian Grill- A serious contender for best Malaysian food in the city—and certainly the best above 59th St. Authentic and refreshing, especially in an area so dominated by Thai food. *224 W 104th St, 212-579-1333, 1 to 103rd St, Daily 11am-12am $$*

A Café- Chef, owner, and waiter Al will make you feel right at home in this miniature eatery. The menu, however, is a gourmet masterpiece, with a $20 prix fixe option. Remember to BYOB. *973 Columbus Ave, 212-222-2033, Tues-Sat 6pm-11pm, 1 to 103rd St, B,C to 110th St-Cathedral Parkway $$*

peppers covered in melted American and BBQ sauce. Come late at night to ask for secret off-menu gems like the Gipper, a melted mess of roast beef, provalone, gravy, and fried onions on an oiled roll.

Kitchenette
American, Brunch

You'll find delicious spins on comfort classics at this charmingly decorated Morningside favorite. Mismatched chairs surround glass tables, while spinning bar stools with floral cushions provide the best view of the extensive selection of housemade sweets, including a dangerously creamy version of a Nutter Butter cookie. The food is decadent despite its humble origins: try the mac & cheese with smoked mozzarella, easily swapped with any side dish for an additional dollar. But where Kitchennette truly shines is weekend brunch, when people flock for cherry vanilla French toast and apple-brie omelettes. Expect to wait anywhere from 20 minutes to an hour for a table on Sundays. Not in the mood to linger in line? Visit during the week and choose from the "breakfast for dinner" selection. Don't forget to try the homemade biscuits with housemade strawberry butter and jams.

1272 Amsterdam Ave (at 123rd St)
212-531-7600
Mon-Fri 8am-11pm,
Sat-Sun 9am-11pm
❶ to 125th St
$$

SAJI'S
best reason to learn how to use chopsticks

A five-seat hole in the wall that you could walk by every day and still miss, Saji's offers the standard quick and cheap meal. The entire menu consists of seriously authentic Japanese home cooking, some of which may not have a broad appeal. However, there are some gems that make Saji's an indispensable resource for lovers of Japanese food. The chicken kara-age—Japanese fried chicken—offers mouthwatering bites of lightly sauced white meat, so moist it would stick to the rice on its own. The true highlights are the donburi: bowls of sushi rice cooked in sake, soy sauce, and brown sugar, layered with green onion, steamed egg, and your choice of chicken, pork, or beef. The resulting mash of heartwarming flavors is about as homey a meal as you can get from a take-out joint.

Japanese
256 109th St (near Broadway)
212-749-1834
Mon-Fri 11am-11:30pm,
Sat-Sun 12pm-10:30pm
1 to 116th St
$
*Delivery/Takeout, Cash Only

Koronet Pizza · *Pizza*

2848 Broadway
(btwn 110th & 111th St)
212-222-1566
Sun-Wed 10am-2am,
Thurs-Sat 10am-4am
❶ to 110th St
$

While Koronet's doesn't offer much in the way of charm, seating, or variety, what they do have is a cheese slice the size of a boogie board. Koronet's signature jumbo slice is the stuff of local legend: immense, incredibly satisfying, and dripping with grease. Every weekend until 4am, local collegians stagger over from nearby bars and line up out the door for a $3.50 continent of cheese, sauce, and crust. The staff is no-nonsense and the pizza is hot, fresh, and damn good—and if you're lucky enough to grab a seat on a Saturday night, you're sure to see just about everyone you know in the neighborhood drop by.

Max Soha · *Italian*

Serving up student-priced, high-caliber Italian food in a collegiate area, Max Soha is always appropriately mobbed at dinnertime. While crowds alone are not indicative of a worthwhile trip, most Soha (South Harlem) residents are more than willing to drop a few words confirming Max's excellence. Certainly light on the luxury, the simple wooden tables and floor-length windows radiate a modest charm appropriate for the blooming area. An inspiringly fresh buffalo mozzarella makes for an excellent appetizer, especially when paired with paper-thin prosciutto. Richly sauced, the pastas come as hearty tributes to the virtue of al dente—special mention goes to the excellent carbonara and stout lamb ragu. The easygoing waiters, in addition to listing the above-average specials or recommending a decent wine, provide quick and friendly service, inspiring many relaxed sighs from burdened students.

💲 🥡 🕶
1262 Amsterdam Ave
(at 123rd St)
212-531-2221
Daily 12pm-12am
❶ Ⓐ Ⓒ Ⓑ Ⓓ to 125th St
$$

Milano Market · *Grocery Store*

2892 Broadway
(near 113th St)
212-665-9500
Daily 6am-12am
❶ to 116th St

In a city with endless supermarkets, bodegas, and niche markets, your everyday mini-market has a difficult time standing out. Yet Milano Market achieves distinction by dedicating over half of its shelf space to pre-packaged foods and drinks, including a grand

135

selection of both beer and coffee, and a mouth-watering parade of freshly made meals. The hot food bar, which changes daily, is a standby dinner stop for many busy Morningside Heights residents craving pesto tortellini and chicken parmesan. The top-notch sandwich menu lures many a Columbia student with a dizzying selection of breads, meats and creative combos. The real star is the salad bar, which continues to outshine the others in the neighborhood by a simple dedication to freshness and an unlimited toppings option.

Pisticci

Italian

Tucked away on the outer edges of Morningside Heights, this absolute gem of transplanted Italian hospitality serves humble, filling dishes at very reasonable prices. The black and white family photos on the wall, as well as a yellowing birth certificate and a bookshelf trompe l'oeil, make the restaurant feel like a Tuscan trattoria. The warmly lit dining room is an amalgam of

125 LaSalle St
(btwn Broadway &
Claremont Ave)
212-932-3500
Sun 11am-1am,
Mon-Thurs 11am-11pm,
Fri-Sat 11am-1am
❶ to 125th St
$$

nooks and crannies, accommodating both the hand-holding couple and the large, gregarious group on their fifth bottle of wine. A bowl of La Spaghettata with meatballs is Pisticci's quintessential dish: hearty and simple, it looks as if it came straight from the hands of your steady-handed, loving grandmother. To complete your homage to the time-honored tradition of Italian comfort food, get the homemade tiramisu for dessert, an ethereal blend of chocolate, coffee, and mascarpone.

Rack and Soul

Soul Food, BBQ

With a diner vibe and Harlem legend Charles Garbiel's back, Rack and Soul woos Morningsiders with an all out revival of the art of fried

258 109th St
(near Broadway)
212-222-4800
Mon-Fri 11am-11pm,
Sat-Sun 10am-11pm
❶ to 110th St
$$

chicken. A fuzzy feeling pervades the restaurant, coming from a mixture of the warm lights, lacquered wood, and red booths. The friendly service and the crumbling savory cornbread help to complete the sensation. The chicken lives up to the hype—accompanied by the traditional waffle that perfectly compliments the crispy golden crust and ethereally moist meat.

But the soul doesn't stop at chicken; the menu is full of excellent barbecue standards such as succulent pulled pork, beef short ribs, and gut-stuffing sides of mac and cheese. The comfort food and equally comfortable atmosphere make Rack and Soul a choice destination for both down-home dinners and hangover cures.

Sookk   *Thai*

Never mind the lanterns that look more like birdcages—this sleek Thai den surpasses nearby competitors when it comes to the sheer variety of tasty Yaowarat street food that it dispatches from an efficient kitchen. Part of Sookk's endearing charm comes from its kitschy polychromatic cushions and the gimmicky yin yang symbolism of mismatched chopsticks. Have a tissue handy when braving the spicy basil noodles, and be warned that the sidewalk noodles with tender chunks of roasted beef drenched in a fragrant Thai cinnamon soup could have you relinquishing Vietnamese pho forever. Don't overlook the ear-tingling beef tartare served on a paunchy bed of chili-drizzled sticky rice, although nothing tops the cinnamon duck for a steaming meal with the exotic accents of goji berries, ginkgos, and red dates. Wash it all down with lychee sangria, and you won't even realize you've forgotten to order Pad Thai.

2686 Broadway
(btwn 102nd & 103rd St)
212-870-0253
Sun-Thurs 11:30am-11pm,
Fri-Sat 11:30am-11:30pm
❶ to 103rd St
$$

DING DONG LOUNGE
best ex-heroin addict hangout

Dive

929 Columbus Ave
(btwn 105th & 106th St)
212-663-2600
1,B,C to 103rd St
Daily 4pm-4am
$

This spacious, barely lit dive was built in the remains of a vacated crack den and has defiantly retained much of its seedy LES vibe in the face of neighborhood evolution. The draught levers are guitar handles, and the mahogany bar was—according to lore—bankrolled by the sale of pornography left behind by the former owners. Grungy bartenders serve a mixed crowd of neighborhood regulars and Columbia students seeking asylum from the overplayed campus dives. Concert posters, graffitied bathrooms, and live DJs every night give Ding Dong a punk rock feel. Ultimately more of a place to hang out than to head bang, the perennially available plush chairs and candlelit tables offer a welcome retreat. Feel free to test your skills at the pool table or vintage Ms. PacMan/Galaga set.

Part of a Cuban restaurant and bar chain since 2006, Havana Central once entertained the likes of Allen Ginsberg and Jack Kerouac when it went by "The West End."

Taqueria y Fonda la Mexicana *Mexican*

968 Amsterdam Ave
(near 108th St)
212-531-0383
Daily 11am-12am
❶ ❸ ❼ to 110th St
$

Morningside Heights residents know where to find the quality Mexican cuisine that Southwest transplants to New York City pine for: Taqueria y Fonda la Mexicana serves up plate-covering mounds of freshly made traditional Mexican fare that fit a student's budget. The main event is the expertly rolled Big Burrito—at $10, it might be able to feed a family of two. Those not interested in a burrito with its own zip code can opt for the Baby Burrito, a smaller, more reasonable version of its larger cousin. But the real draw for the hungry college students seems to be the endless homemade tortilla chips served at every meal with not one, but three kinds of salsa.

The Hungarian Pastry Shop and P&W Sandwich Shop *Hungarian, Café, Sandwiches*

1030 Amsterdam Ave
(btwn 110th & 111th St)
212-866-4230
Sun 8:30am-10:30pm,
Mon-Fri 7:30am-11:30pm,
Sat 8:30am-11:30pm
❶ to 110th
$

The Hungarian Pastry Shop, known affectionately as simply "the Hungarian," is a Morningside Heights legend. It's not just a café but a modern-day salon, a tribute to the old Viennese standard of comfortably lingering on a refilling cup of coffee. Despite the dim lighting and grime, Columbia students and local writers still throng the small shop's two-person tables. But you don't need to be a Kafka-quoting poet to enjoy the Hungarian's croissants—some of Manhattan's best—or a rich cappuccino. Eat indoors to soak in the languid atmosphere (a wandering cat and the famous bathroom graffiti), or choose a table outside for a view of St. John the Divine. Craving something more savory than a Sachertorte or apple strudel? Visit P&W next door and pick up a gourmet sandwich, grape leaves, and a piece of fruit for under $10—all packed in a brown bag for nostalgia's sake.

PLAY

1020 *Dive*

1020 Amsterdam Ave
(at 110th St)
212-531-3468
Daily 4pm-4am
❶ ❽ ❾ to 110th St
$

It's almost impossible to figure out what makes 1020 so damn appealing. Sure, it's cheap, but not astoundingly so. You can play darts with a friend, but there's usually a line. It's easy to meet new people, but that's just because it's so crowded. 1020 is undoubtedly a dive, and it feels that way, right down to the permanent coat of dried beer on the bar. Despite these apparent setbacks, there's something about this dimly lit haven that just works. On busy weekend nights, when Columbia students flood in for $3 pints, you'd be hard-pressed to find someone having a lousy time. At the coveted back mezzanine, new couples guzzle Gin and Tonics and canoodle on busted leather couches. Two TV screens and a projector show a motley collection of cable flicks, but most visitors prefer to solicit hookups and knock over each other's Brooklyn Lagers.

Suite *LGBT, Karaoke*

992 Amsterdam Ave
(at 109th St)
212-222-4600
Daily 5pm-4am
❶ ❽ ❾ to 110th St
$$

Karaoke in Morningside? Yes, please! Join an eclectic crew of Columbia students, middle-aged men, and curious adventurers in belting out your favorite 90's classics at this low-key and chic LGBT lounge. Most come to enjoy the beautiful singer-dancer hostess, Sahara, who performs nightly and orchestrates each of the venue's signature events, including traditional karaoke, "ghetto" karaoke, drag night, and game night. If your drunken hunger pains start kicking in, don't hesitate to order a few Bombay frankies to the bar from the fast food Indian restaurant, Roti Roll, conveniently located next door.

Tap A Keg
Dive

📶

2731 Broadway
(btwn 104th & 105th St)
212-749-1734
Daily 12pm-4am
❶ to 103rd St

Although Da Vinci pre-dates Tap a Keg by nearly 500 years, his insight that "simplicity is the ultimate sophistication" can easily be applied to this charming Morningside Heights watering hole. An unassuming and appropriately gritty entrance leads to an equally casual interior: a bar lines one side of the room opposite tables and booths; a pool table and jukebox sit in the back. If you're feeling hungry, feel free to order in from a local eatery (ask the bartender for their collection of menus). Stay awhile, and take advantage of the free Wi-Fi while you chat up some of the many regulars devoted to this cozy little hangout. After a few rounds, you'll be itching to join their ranks.

The Abbey
Pub

237 105th St
(near Broadway)
212-222-8713
Sun 12pm-4am,
Mon-Sat 4pm-4am
❶ to 103rd St
$

Stained glass windows and pew-like booths only hint at the sanctity of this holy place: an age-old neighborhood pub that houses great beer, close friends, and a seriously sinful brownie. Antique lamps cast dim light on the worn brick space, where couples and solo riders of varying generations sit at the bar as bigger groups compete for wooden tables and booths. The crowd is a mix of professionals after work, Columbia students, and locals with decades of patronage under their belts. Burgers, soups, and nachos emerge hot and fresh from the kitchen, which stays open past 1am on weekends. Come in for a cold draught beer from the always changing selection, but don't be surprised if you stay for the three flavors of chicken wings and some sports talk with a stranger.

The Underground Lounge
Comedy, Games

🎵

955 West End Ave
(at 107th St)
212-531-4759
Daily 4pm-4am
❶ to 103rd or 110th St
$$

Depending on the night of the week, the Underground is either a comedy club, a fratty party spot, or a laid-back blues lounge. This chameleonic venue seems to have as many personalities as it does rooms—grab a table in the front if you want a view of the daily sports game, or head to the adjoining pool area for a round and new company. On show nights, the back lounge fills up with happy onlookers there to support the local musicians and comedians on stage. Like most bars in the neighborhood, it houses its fair share of Columbia students, especially on Thursdays, but the Underground generally welcomes a slightly older crowd than other nearby bars. Whatever your age, beware: with such cheap drink specials, the small flight of stairs can be a doozy on the way out.

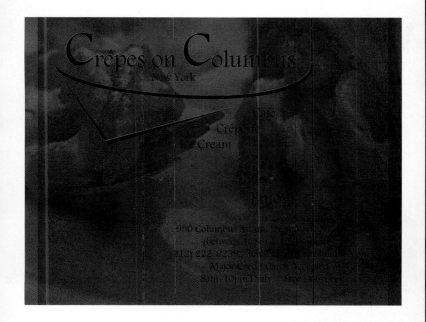

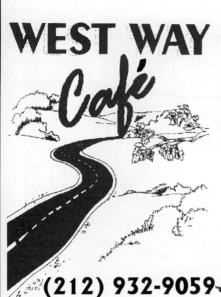

144

145

COLUMBIA UNIVERSITY CENTER FOR
Career Education

Inside New York is part of Columbia University's Student Enterprise (CSE) program hosted by the Columbia University Center for Career Education.

The mission of the CSE program is to provide students with a unique opportunity to cultivate and develop transferable entrepreneurship and enterprise management skills through leading and running student-operated businesses.

The program dates back to 1965, when students created their own businesses to offset the cost of tuition. Today, these businesses provide experiential learning and employment opportunities to over 200 students annually.

Participants of this program emerge as experienced business managers, with a strong foundation in leadership, business ethics, and professional responsibility through direct, hands-on experience.

UP. W. SI

In the battle of the Upper Sides, the thin swath of buildings bordering Central Park's western edge loses in a lot of categories: affluence, prestige, and cleanliness (Alec Baldwin once called the UWS "one of the dirtiest neighborhoods in town"). But the residents who have been pouring into these high-rises for centuries come for the uniquely diverse, refreshingly laid-back aura that distinguishes this enclave of culture and commerce.

From the its early days, the neighborhood has fulfilled myriad functions. It originated as a cluster of august "country" homes and farms for the monied class, but slowly became a shipping, transportation, and manufacturing corridor, as prime riverfront property was in equally high demand for those outside the housing market. In the following years, it served as a sort of haven for otherwise displaced individuals, from recent immigrants to squatters. The growing commercial sector eventually forced out those on the fringes of society in favor of the elite, who appreciated that the area was rapidly assuming a place in the thick of things. This gentrifying movement reached a crescendo during the 1950s and 1960s with the inception of the Lincoln Square Renewal Project, which centered much of the City's artistic and cultural endeavors into one concentrated location. As the Upper West Side amassed more and more land, its historical population shifted higher and higher up on the island.

PER
ST
DE

Today, the UWS is notorious for its high property values, and for the fact that they weren't always that way. The neighborhood affords easy access to the many walking and biking paths of Central Park—in fact, between those lush landscapes and the lawns of the somewhat less infamous Riverside Park, one of the UWS's major draws for families is how many swingsets are within easy reach. And though the beauty of the waterfront is tempered by the West Side Highway, the Hudson River vistas are another huge part of this area's character. Lincoln Center attracts herds of theater-goers and opera aficionados, while down the block, movie theaters alternate between screening indie flicks and box-office behemoths. Stores are an inescapable presence along the north-south avenues, catering to the needs of every imaginable shopper: athlete and adventurers flood Sports Authority and the North Face, while fashionistas on all budgets attack the racks at discount designer stores, including Loehmann's, Filene's Basement, and the Barneys Co-Op. National chains more or less define the consumer scene, as Zara, Urban Outfitters, the Gap, Best Buy, Bed Bath & Beyond, and Banana Republic all have multi-level complexes along Broadway. But the smaller-circulation boutiques, like Tani and Wink, are just as busy as the giants, keeping the local pulse more neighborly than anything else.

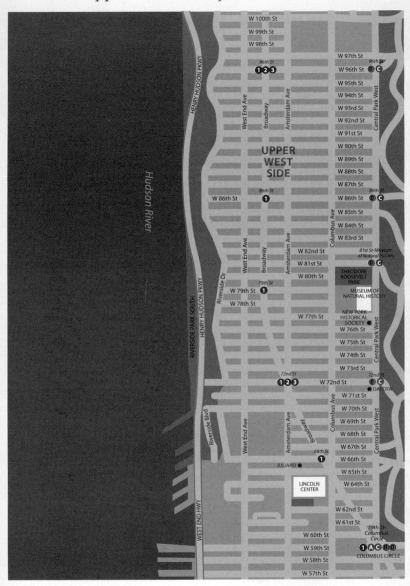

EXPLORE

Lincoln Center

Conceptualized in the late 1950s, Lincoln Center was the first successful attempt by any metropolitan area to centralize its cultural offerings. Today, Josie Robertson Plaza forms the core of the artistically diverse locale and is surrounded by Avery Fisher Hall, the Metropolitan Opera House, and the David H. Koch Theater. Home to the city's top performing arts companies, including the Opera, the New York City Ballet, and the New York Philharmonic Orchestra, Lincoln Center also welcome dance, music, and theater acts from as close as Boston and as far as Thailand. During the warmer months, there are free dance performances on the plaza steps and the "Mostly Mozart" classical music festival. Jazz at Lincoln Center, a year-round program, is as celebrated a New York institution as Shakespeare in the Park. Don't worry if you're strapped for cash: the Center offers starving students discounts and a rush option on the day of the show.

> 10 Lincoln Center Plaza (btwn Amsterdam and Columbus Ave)
> 212-875-5456
> ❶ to 66th St

New York Historical Society

The city's oldest museum is housed in this distinguished research institution, which features an exhaustive, four-centuries-spanning collection of artifacts, artwork, and documents indispensable for any scholar of American culture. Galleries on the second floor showcase a rotating selection of paintings, while on the fourth floor the Henry Luce Center houses thousands of sculptures, pieces of furniture, decorative objects, glass work, Tiffany lamps, silverware, ceramics, textiles, accessories, toys, coins, buttons,

> 170 Central Park West (btwn 76th & 77th St)
> 212-873-3400
> Sun 11am-5:45pm, Tues-Thurs, Sat 10am-6pm, Fri 10am-8pm
> ❶ ❸ to 81st St
> Adults $10, Students $6

badges, and other ephemera. When your head has finished reeling, stagger back downstairs to the library and reading room. Here, in the shadow of Ionic columns, researchers and the general public alike can burrow through over four million books, maps, newspapers, broadsides, photographs, and architectural drawings, all relating to American history.

Riverside Park

While picnicking or roller blading in this family-friendly strip of natural woodland, one barely notices the traffic buzz or police sirens from nearby Broadway. Tucked within the park are several notable statues and memorials, all easily acces-

Btwn 72nd & 158th St
(along the Hudson River)
❶ ❷ ❸ to stops btwn
72nd & 125th St

sible from the jogging and biking paths. Among the most notable are the Eleanor Roosevelt statue, which can be reached through the 72nd Street entrance, and the Joan of Arc Memorial, which guards the park at Riverside Drive and 93rd Street. Grant's Tomb, Ulysses S. Grant's granite-and-marble resting place and the largest mausoleum in North America, looms on 122nd Street. Other notable landmarks include the Amiable Child Memorial, the only private single-person grave on public land in the City, and the Warsaw Ghetto Memorial at 83rd Street.

Symphony Space

Reflective of the UWS's well-deserved reputation for being progressive and culturally aware, Symphony Space is a venue devoted to promot-

upper west side
UNDER $20

Buy some organic strawberries at **Zabar's** *(2245 Broadway)* and have a pensive country breakfast at **Strawberry Fields** *(CPW at 72nd St)*, the understated John Lennon memorial across the street from the **Dakota** *(1 W 72nd St)*, best appreciated in the early morning.

Balance the peace with a little chaos at **Uptown Birds** *(522-526 Amsterdam Ave)*, where macaws are thousands of dollars but a friendly feeding is free.

A lunch of topping-heavy brick-oven pizza at **Coppola's** *(206 W 79th St)* contains all your recommended veggie servings for the next week.

Take a walk under the whale at the **Museum of Natural History** *(CPW at 79th St)*. Pretend to be krill that got away.

Learn the salsa basics at **El Taller Latino Americano's** *(2710 Broadway)* biweekly early evening classes.

Sup on the Recession Special while it lasts at **Gray's Papaya** *(2090 Broadway)*: two hot dogs and a drink for $4.50.

ing artistic literacy in all areas. It screens old flicks for absurdly cheap prices ($5), and hosts orchestral performances, plays, dance performances,

2537 Broadway
(at 95th St)
212-864-5400
Check website for listings
❶ ❷ ❸ to 96th St
Prices vary

and book readings throughout the year. Kids can enroll in literature and arts camps, for a few days or a few weeks. For the super-ambitious, Symphony Space's theaters and studios are available for individual use seven days a week. There's a small used bookstore in the lobby and the Thalia Café a step away, which is usually filled with post-storm-of-creativity patrons. Prices and times follow no rhyme or reason—inspiration can strike at any moment.

The Dakota

Best known, rather gruesomely, as the site of John Lennon's murder, the Dakota has in fact been one

1 72nd St
(at Central Park West)
212-362-1448
❶ ❷ ❸ Ⓑ Ⓒ to 72nd St

of the city's premier apartment buildings for decades. And it still is: most visitors can only

admire the palatial edifice from the outside and hope for a peek at the courtyard through the 72nd St gate. A subway entrance cleverly blends into the façade at the corner of 72nd, and an iron railing styled with mini-busts of Poseidon flanked by dragons wraps around the building, adding to its castle-like aura. Leonard Bernstein and Rudolf Nureyev once resided here, and Yoko Ono maintains her quarters to this day, across the street from Strawberry Fields. Roman Polanski fans also know the Dakota as the unsettling setting for Rosemary's Baby.

SHOP

Citarella

This high-end Italian market does a few things very well. The cheese section is extensive, the fish is famously divine, and the butchery has a wide variety of prime cuts. Between barrels

2135 Broadway
(at 75th St)
212-874-0383
Sun 9am-7pm, Mon-Sat
7am-9pm
❶ ❷ ❸ to 72nd St
Additional locations: 1313
3rd Ave, 424 6th Ave,
461 W 125th St

The Upper West Side features prominently in a number of Woody Allen movies, including *Annie Hall*, *Manhattan*, and *Hannah and Her Sisters*.

of different coffees and huge beefsteak tomatoes sit boxes of obscure little British shortbread cookies and fruit that's always guaranteed fresh. The overabundance of apron-clad staff answers inquiries and fulfill your requests with speed. Crowds tend to be less severe here than at Zabar's, so things are easier to find, there's no constantly bumping into other shoppers, and legs won't ache afterwards. It's more expensive and much smaller than the nearby Fairway, but Citarella has a lockdown on customers who want the minimum hassle, especially during an emergency four- or five-item trip.

Maxilla & Mandible, Ltd.

Its storefront may be tiny, but this enclave of fossils and other osteo-related wares is hard to miss as you walk down Columbus Ave. With display windows crammed with skeletons, skulls, and teeth from myriad human and non-human specimens, Maxilla & Mandible feels slightly out of place alongside prissier UWS shoe boutiques. Yet its survival instinct is strong: offering insect jewelry, dinosaur teeth, seashells of every color, and both real and replica versions of human, ostrich and sabertooth cat skulls, the store entertains children, amateur archaeologists, and seasoned collectors alike.

451 Columbus Ave
(btwn 81st & 82nd St)
212-724-6173
Sun 1pm-5pm,
Mon-Sat 11am-7pm
Ⓑ Ⓒ to 81st St,
❶ to 79th St

After wandering the halls of the Museum of Natural History just down the block, come in for a femur, and stay for the ossified springbok horns.

Zabar's

Covering almost an entire block of prime Broadway real estate, this multi-level, family-run mega-bazaar sells seemingly anomalous wares: high-quality food, competitively priced and in supermarket-style bulk. In addition to the exhaustive grocery floor, where meat, fish, imported cheese, fruit,

2245 Broadway
(btwn 80th & 81st St)
212-787-2000
❶ to 79th St
Sun 9am-6pm,
Mon-Fri 8am-7:30pm,
Sat 8am-8pm

vegetables, and gourmet pickles coexist, an upper level offers cookware and specialty kitchen items. If you crave immediate satisfaction, be it in the form of frozen yogurt, paninis or smoothies, the store's adjoining café makes everything in-house with fresh ingredients. Budding chefs may attend a number of classes, demos and samplings in the store itself. More than a (humongous) corner grocer, Zabar's is a rather intense culinary experience, and a traditional destination for New Yorkers.

EAT

Bar Boulud   *French*

With an impressive selection of meats, cheeses,

AMERICAN MUSEUM OF NATURAL HISTORY
best place to never grow up

Holden Caulfield's favorite haunt, whose blindingly white neoclassic facade dominates the Upper West Side, has been popular with New Yorkers ever since its inception in 1877. Boasting an impressive array of life-sized dioramas and interactive displays, this Upper West Side biology majors' haven is dedicated to the most interesting aspects of nature and science, from the heavens of the gargantuan planetarium to the dirt of the Fossil Halls. Tours of P.S. 6 schoolkids love the Hall of Human Origins, the Hall of Ocean Life, and the life-size mammalian exhibits, all of which provide dramatic, up-close encounters with prehistoric and exotic life. Periodic live exhibits feature animals ranging from lizards and snakes to butterflies, and the extensive natural science library is a peerless resource.

Central Park West
(btwn 77th & 81st St)
212-769-5100
Daily 10am–5:45 pm
BC to 81st St, 1 to 79th
Suggested Admission
$16, Students $12

UPPER WEST SIDE
best gourmet markets

Mani Market Place- While it lacks the grandeur of its competitors, Mani Market may be the perfect local grocery, with friendly staff who remember your name and a daily shipment of fresh breads, fruit and vegetables. *697 Columbus Ave, 212-662-4392, Sun 7am-10pm, Mon-Sat 7am-11pm, 1,2,3, B,C to 96th St $$*

Fairway Market- This king of grocery stores pairs unbeatable prices with an impressive stock. The meat, fish, and organic sections are awe-inspiring. *2127 Broadway, 212-595-1888, Daily 6am-1am, 1,2,3 to 72nd St $*

Westside Market- With everything a gourmet grocery could possible have—basic dairy products, gourmet spreads, packaged prepared foods—this market is the king of temptation. You can get lunch at the extensive salad bar, hot food bar, or full-stocked deli. *2171 Broadway, 212-595-2536, Daily 24 hours, 1 to 79th St $$*

wines, and pâtés, Bar Boulud is the easiest way to experience classic French charcuterie without going to France. The elegant yet simple design is meant to evoke a wine cellar—meats and wines are prominently displayed amidst classic wooden furniture. Nestled conveniently across from the cultural mecca of Lincoln Center, Bar Boulud caters to the pre-theater crowd with a prix fixe menu featuring a fantastic steak roti with glazed market carrots. The waiters are expert and knowledgeable and will gladly pair wine with your dish of choice. The crowd is unpretentious and fairly casual—trendy couples of all ages mingle before a night on the town—and in the summertime, the outdoor tables are packed with people-watchers enjoying the bustle of Broadway. Noted restaurateur and chef Daniel Boulud has created an oasis of rare, but fantastic French fare.

1900 Broadway
(at 64th St)
212-595-0303
Brunch Sat-Sun 11am-4pm, Lunch Mon-Fri 12pm-2:30pm,
Dinner Sun 5pm-10pm,
Mon-Thurs 5pm-12am,
Fri-Sat 5pm-1am
❶ to 66th St
$$$

Barney Greengrass   *Deli*

Head to this Upper West Side temple of smoked fish for some of the best sturgeon, smoked salmon, and Nova in the city. For just over a century, Barney's has offered up the same dazzling spread of smoked,

541 Amsterdam Ave
(near 86th St)
212-724-4707
Tues-Fri 8:30am-4pm,
Sat-Sun 8:30am-5pm
❶ ❻ ❼ to 86th St
$$

cured, and pickled Jewish delights. The space appears epic from the outside but a peek inside will reveal a line of cramped and crowded counters. Expect the same curt, efficient service when ordering a single H&H bagel or the $280 Supreme Caviar Sampler—die-hards don't come to Barney's for the hospitality, they come for the lox. Though newcomers complain about the expense ($12.75 for a bagel with cream

cheese and Nova), out-the-door lines on the weekend show that Barney's popularity hasn't suffered for it.

Flor de Mayo
Latino, Asian

2651 Broadway
(at 101st St)
212-663-5520
Daily 12pm-12am
❶ to 103rd St
$$

A restaurant that serves both East Asian and Latin American foods is undoubtedly an anomaly. But Flor de Mayo has specialized in the combination of both tastes for the past 30 years, resulting in an exotic Chino-Latino blend. This rare cultural cuisine originates from Peru, where Asian-Peruvians account for little over four percent of the country's population. Upon entering the contemporary restaurant, customers are greeted warmly by both the waiters and the yellowish-orange ceiling light. Bring a friend and explore the selections, which range from carnes (meats) and mariscos (seafood) to lo mein (soft noodles) and wanton soup, for less than $20.

Good Enough To Eat
American, Brunch

483 Amsterdam Ave
(at 83rd St)
212-496-0163
Sun 9am-10:30pm, Mon-Thurs 8am-10:30pm, Fri 8am-11pm, Sat 9am-11pm
❶ to 86th St
$$

The first thing you'll see—and will undoubtedly be charmed by—when you enter Good Enough To Eat is the adorable white picket fence that surrounds both the indoor and outdoor dining areas. This choice of a divider is very telling about what Good Enough To Eat is

LEVAIN BAKERY
best chocolate chip cookie

There's a reason people flock to this easy-to-miss bakery on the Upper West Side. The infamous four-dollar Levain cookie has been called "the most divine chocolate chip cookie in Manhattan" by The New York Times—and they're certainly worth their hefty six ounces in quality butter, sugar, and chocolate. The selection is fairly classic: oatmeal raisin, dark chocolate chip, chocolate peanut butter chip. Levain also boasts a fine selection of artisanal breads, all made fresh daily in-house. Try the fluffy brioches for a semi-sweet portable treat. The line on weekend mornings may be eye-catching, but with Manhattan's best cookie at the other end, the wait just might be well worth it.

Bakery

167 W 74th St (near Amsterdam Ave)
212-874-6080
Sun 9am-7pm, Mon-Sat 8am-7pm
1,2,3,B,C to 72nd St
$

Ranging from 800 to 1200 feet, the avenues west of Central Park are significantly longer than their East Side counterparts.

going for with their food: warm, weighty dishes of the American "heartland"—the kind of breakfasts that would be served in the kitchen of a two-story farmhouse with, yes, a white picket fence. From the intimidatingly hefty strawberry pancakes that come with the Lumber Jill meal to little touches like the inclusion of a warm and flaky biscuit with the more savory egg dishes, Good Enough To Eat captures in its meals that fortifying tastiness of a classic Midwestern breakfast with delicious, if not completely authentic results (though it's doubtful that many Ohioans seek out Belgian chocolate and coconut pancakes).

Ouest   *New American*

Pronouncing the French name may call for a lip pucker, but there is nothing pompous about chef Tom Valenti's cavernous two-story den. Furnishing the lamp-lit saloon interior, circular cherry leather booths provide comfy alcoves for bespectacled septuagenarians and pairs of self-absorbed younger couples. Valenti's vaunted main courses impress with their fine-tuned perfection, while his appetizers bedazzle with ingenuity. A chickpea pancake heaped with fine slices of salmon gravlax is girdled by a shimmering ring of mustard oil dotted with three kinds of caviar and minutely diced scallions. Succulent chunks of short ribs, the star of the entrées, are braised for hours—then paired with a layered vol-au-vent pastry and a smattering dip of parsley, rosemary, and thyme pesto. Ouest's potent portions pack the stuffing power of a Thanksgiving feast. Mercifully, the crème fraîche panna cotta sloshed with syrupy passion fruit punch is exquisite for its austerity.

2315 Broadway
(near 84th St)
212-580-8700
Sun 11am-2pm,
5pm-9pm,
Mon-Tues 5pm-9:30pm,
Wed-Thurs 5pm-10pm,
Fri-Sat 5pm-10:30pm
❶ to 86th St
$$$$

THE DEAD POET
best place to pretend you like poetry

Poetry adorns the walls at what may just become your new favorite neighborhood bar. The well-worked pool table takes up what little space there is in its cozy interior, but it only adds to the charm of the place. Be prepared to scoot by your neighbor to reach the lively bartenders, who just may take some shots with you. The top-notch beers on tap are moderately priced, and signature drinks like The Dead Poet Cocktail, a combination of seven liquors, are strong enough to kill.

Irish Bar

450 Amsterdam Ave
(btwn 81st & 82nd St)
212-595-5670
Sun 12pm-4am, Mon-Sat
10am-4am
1 to 79th St
$$

Picholine

Picholine's menu is a showcase of the art of 21st-century cooking. The dishes alternate cleverly between inventive demonstrations of what can be achieved by a modern chef, like the light and clean mint, peach, and prosciutto palate-cleansing foam, and smart blends of the traditional and the experimental, such as a classic rack of lamb topped with sharp and crisp "Moroccan flavors and textures." Between these two extremes, you'll be shown around the worlds of both molecular gastronomy and classic cooking in one fantastic meal. The popular creamy gnocchi made of sheep's milk might very well convince you that Picholine is worthy of its reputation as one of New York's top restaurants.

35 64th St
(at Central Park West)
212-724-8585
Tues-Sat 5pm-10pm
❶ to 66th St
$$$$

PLAY

Barcibo Enoteca

Wine Bar

The tall marble-topped tables and high stools provide an elegant setting for good times over great wine, and Barcibo knows great wine. It houses an impressive selection of over 130 Italian varieties, 40 of which are available by the glass. Go for a glass of the Montepulciano or Valpolicella, and rely on the staff to make knowledgeable suggestions if you're unfamiliar with Italian varietals. Pair your wine with something from the equally extensive tapas selection, like shrimp risotto, marinated octopus, or calamari salad. Perfect for a pre-theater drink, Barcibo encourages patrons to give free reign to their inner connoisseur.

2020 Broadway
(at 70th St)
212-595-2805
Mon-Fri 4:30pm-2am,
Sat-Sun 3:30pm-2am
❶❷❸ to 72nd St

Cleopatra's Needle   *Jazz, Middle Eastern*

Serving a Mediterranean medley of couscous and kebab—plus American extras like French fries and chicken wings—this eatery and bar hosts live jazz every night of the week. The bar swallows most of the space, serving happy hour specials for about three-and-a-half "happy" hours every day. Still, the best thing about this Upper West Side spot isn't the menu or the twinkly light décor: it's the free cover charge for music. There is, however, a $10 per person minimum—so the exodus of your cash is inevitable.

2485 Broadway
(at 92nd St)
212-769-6969
Daily 11am-11:30pm
❶ to 96th St
$$

Jake's Dilemma   *Dive*

New York City is home to an incredibly diverse range of bars, with one block running the gamut from ritzy cocktail lounges to Irish pubs. Jake's Dilemma, however, mashes two of the most disparate scenes possible: the sports-loving fratty dive and the laid-back, 30-something ex-pat lounge. Dilemma? No, because this bar is master of both. Upstairs, the singles-laden bar scene resounds with loud music, gregarious crowds, and enough beer pong to bring you back to Everystate U. Downstairs, a circle of low-key intellectuals converse intimately in oversized armchairs, surrounded by the mostly-for-show bookshelves of "The Oak Room." While cross-group mingling may seem unlikely, the bar then accomplishes its job of social lubrication with a cut-rate happy hour and commodious beer selection.

430 Amsterdam Ave
(near 81st St)
212-580-0556
Mon-Fri 4pm-4am, Sat-Sun 12pm-4am
❶ to 79th St
$

2010 – 11 SEASON
NEWYORKCITYBALLET

REPERTORY
September 14 – October 10
January 18 – February 27
May 3 – June 12
STUDENT RUSH TICKETS $15

George Balanchine's
THE NUTCRACKER™
November 26 – January 2
TICKETS START AT $20

nycballet.com

CenterCharge 212-721-6500   David H. Koch Theater at Lincoln Center
Sébastien Marcovici   Photo by Henry Leutwyler © 2010

UPPER EAST SIDE

Arguably the wealthiest and most coveted (in an old-world kind of way) neighborhood in Manhattan, the Upper East Side is home to quaint parks, beautifully aged cathedrals, flower shops, and cafés that make it an essential area to visit and a picturesque place to live. The neighborhood is a former stronghold of German and Eastern European immigrants, with a highly concentrated Jewish population cropping up at the turn of the last century. Prominent souvenirs of the area's past abound, if you know where to look: restaurants and meat markets specializing in German fare, marvelously understated synagogues and Jewish community centers, and a generous smattering of mansions and art collections named after wealthy Austrian families. UES residents represent most of the oldest wealth in New York City, a leftover demographic quirk that proves that even if the original underdog spirit of those immigrant populations is long gone, the past has not been forgotten.

Pockets of commercialism certainly exist, primarily on Lexington Ave, where the neighborhood's only subway line runs. But the Upper East Side is mostly residential—the famous pre-war apartment buildings on Park Ave constitute some of the most expensive places to live on the isle of Manhattan. Equally chic are the townhouses on tree-lined side streets between the main avenues. At the same time, virtually all of New York City's luxury-brand art institu-

tions run along 5th Ave, including the much celebrated Metropolitan Museum of Art and the Solomon R. Guggenheim Museum. This, somewhat confusingly, also makes the residential neighborhood a top tourist destination—one that drains of practically all its pedestrians at night. Visitors also come for the elegant parkside architecture of Manhattan's biggest mansions, or the many upscale boutiques and art galleries along Madison Ave where the upper crust do their shopping.

But while tourists immediately flock to high-end fashion stores and Museum Mile, perhaps what makes the area most interesting are the numerous historical sites with hardly any name recognition. Visitors to the Upper East Side are greeted with these landmarks every way they turn: Manhattan's most prestigious private schools and social clubs, old-school restaurants, and pharmacies established over a century ago. Even though today the streets betray a surprisingly eclectic mix of people, the Upper East Side has a strong foundation in its past, making it an extraordinarily old-fashioned neighborhood that still manages to move, financially and socially, at the speed of light. The doormen still wear full suits, caps, and gloves, but the Upper East Side has all the essentials of every residential neighborhood in New York: local pizzerias, cheap diners, pocket parks, and quarter laundromats.

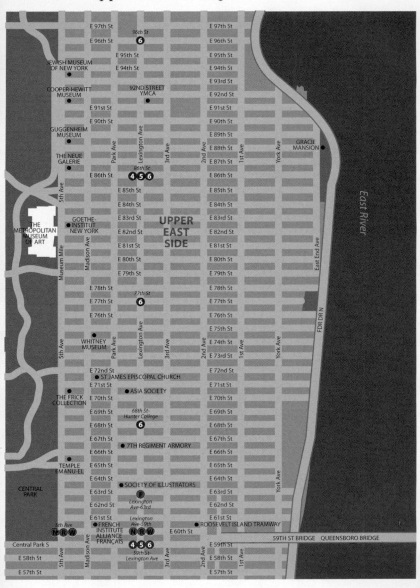

EXPLORE

92nd Street Y

The 92nd Street Y is definitely not to be confused with the YMCA of Village People fame:

1395 Lexington Ave
(at 92nd St)
212-415-5500
6 to 96th St

it's actually a Young Men's Hebrew Association, but welcomes guests all faiths. Although the security checks, which unfortunately come standard nowadays in Jewish institutions, may be off-putting to a casual member just looking for a place to work out, the 92nd Street Y's cultural offerings make it worth the inconvenience. This social center frequently hosts concerts and performances of all genres, stand-up comedy, workshops, and lectures and readings by everyone from Tony Blair to Jon Stewart. With kids taking art and music classes next to the cavernous fitness center where their parents work out, the 92nd Street Y is a genuine-article neighborhood gem.

Big Cinemas

This one-room theater comprises the lone Manhattan outpost of India's largest cinema chain. A venue for refreshing alternatives to the latest blockbust-

239 E 59th St
(btwn 2nd & 3rd Ave)
212-371-6683
●●●●●● to
59th St, **F** to 63rd St
Films $12.50, $5 on
Wednesdays

ers playing in Loews across the city, "Big Cinemas" is anything but: the American fare here is strictly indie and documentary. On the Indian side, the movie house specializes in mostly non-Bollywood movies, so don't expect much song and dance—rather, come to see the latest big budget thriller or comedy out of Bombay. Sundance is a regular player on these screens, as well as the occasional Japanese minimalist flick. Foreign movies are mostly subtitled, so don't forget your glasses. Downtown indie theaters can waver all over the map in terms of sound quality and cleanliness,

SUBWAYS 4, 5, 6, F

BUS M1, M2, M3, M4, M101, M102, M103, M15, M31, M96, M86, M79, M72, M66

MARKETS Grace's Marketplace *(1237 3rd Ave, 212-737-0600)*

LIBRARY Yorkville Library *(222 E 79th St, 212-744-5824)*

HOSTEL Residence at 92nd Street Y *(1395 Lexington Ave, 212-415-5500)*

MEDIA The New York Observer

FITNESS May Center at 92nd Street Y *(1395 Lexington Ave, 212-415-5700)*

BIKES Bicycles NYC *(1400 3rd Ave, 212-794-2929)*

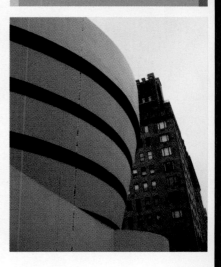

MADISON AVE SHOPPING

The specialty household boutiques hawking mink bathmats and high-end fashion showcases of Madison Ave dominate the shopping scene of the Upper East Side. While tourists flock to brand-name megastores on 5th Ave, these shops cater to a more exclusive crowd, one more in the know and more in the black. World-famous clothiers like **Dolce & Gabbana** (*825 Madison Ave*) and **Giorgio Armani** (*760 Madison Ave*) have their smaller New York locations here, and sprinkled in between are institutions that skew funkier, like **Juicy Couture** (*860 Madison Ave*) and **Lilly Pulitzer** (*1020 Madison Ave*). But it's the one-off beauty shops and miniature pharmacies (**Jo Malone**, *946 Madison Ave*), antique stores (**Florian Papp**, *962 Madison Ave*) and the most affluent of art galleries (**Beretta Gallery**, *718 Madison Ave*) that set this block apart from other consume-or-be-consumed shopping havens around SoHo, Williamsburg, and the East Village. The surrounding side streets are just as quaint, dotted with trendy eateries and a healthy lining of trees.

but Big Cinemas is a dependably enjoyable experience every time.

The Frick Collection

Housed in a Victorian mansion complete with turrets, Persian carpets, and crystal chandeliers, the Frick is cozier than its marbled Metropolitan counterpart, and its collection is no less significant. Inside, you'll recognize the old masters from your art history textbook: Henry Clay Frick's holdings include paintings and sculptures by Titian, Vermeer, El Greco, Velazquez, and Whistler. Frick's home is almost as spectacular as his art: wind through the Roman busts scattered throughout the Neoclassical courtyard or inspect the Chinese porcelain. The 16 living rooms, dining rooms, and parlors-turned-galleries are arranged according to Frick's original design. Remember to take a free audio guide at the entrance, as none of the pieces on display are accompanied by information plaques.

1 E 70th St (at 5th Ave)
212-288-0700
Sun 11am-5pm,
Tues-Sat 10am-6pm
❻ to 68th St
Adults $18, Students $5

Museum of the City of New York

A must-visit for any local history enthusiast, the Museum of the City of New York features vintage photographs, drawings, and prints of New York City from every conceivable viewpoint, as well as specialty collections of New York-manufactured toys and Broadway memorabilia. Among the museum's noteworthy artifacts are John Jay's velvet frock-coat and a chair belonging to the first child born in New York to European parents. Located at the far northern tip of Museum Mile, MCNY also offers historical education and community clean-up programs for the youth of East Harlem. If you experience déjà vu on your first visit, it's because the building's neo-Georgian façade stands in as the Constance Billard School for Girls on Gossip Girl.

1220 5th Ave (at 103rd St)
212-534-1672
Tues-Sun 10am-5pm
❷❸ to 110th St,
❻ to 103rd St
Suggested Donation
Adults $10, Students $6

Solomon R. Guggenheim Museum

Today the Guggenheim is perhaps the most prestigious home of contemporary art in the country, but such wasn't always the case: before it opened in 1959, Willem de Kooning and 20 fellow artists protested the presentation of their work on its walls. Fearing for their reputations, they argued that the Frank Lloyd Wright-designed building was itself so spectacular that the art it contained could only pale in comparison. It's true that New Yorkers walk up 5th to admire again and again the seemingly weightless white spiral (Wright even boasted that his curled concrete structure made the Met look like a Prot-

1071 5th Ave (at 89th St)
212-423-3500
Sun-Wed, Fri
10am-5:45pm,
Sat 10am-7:45pm
❹❺❻ to 86th St
Adults $18, Students $15,
Art After Dark $25

Old-style mansions like that of the Frick Collection once characterized 5th Ave. Most were demolished and later replaced by the elegant high-rises we see today.

estant barn). Inside, visitors shuffle single file up the seven-story winding ramp beneath the illumination of a mollusk-shaped skylight. The permanent collection features works by Cezanne, Picasso, and Mondrian; contemporary exhibitions have included revered performance artist Tino Sehgal's playful "constructed situations."

Sotheby's

Founded 266 years ago, this auction house how takes up a 10-floor residence in a sleek modern building on York Ave, and is widely acknowledged as a fundamental cog in the rarity market. The strength of the collections put on auction biannually is self-evident, as many sales chronicle the rise and fall of fortunes—recently the Lehman Brothers' corporate art collection was subject to the gavel here. Activity dies down during the summer and winter months, peaking in May and November. Peruse the galleries of pieces up for bidding and brush shoulders with wealthy art collectors and their minions. Then sit in on a high-pressure

1334 York Ave
(at 72nd St)
212-606-7000
Sun 1pm-5pm,
Mon-Fri 10am-5pm,
Sat 10am-5pm
6 to 68th St

auction and marvel at the prices called out by the auctioneer.

The Metropolitan Museum of Art

Rising from the trees of Central Park, this neoclassical behemoth makes no attempt to blend in. Possibly New York's single most celebrated institution, the Met shelters an exquisite permanent collection of over two million objects, from the reconstructed ca. 15 BC Temple of Dendur to 1850s microscope photographs of nematodes to a reliquary containing Mary Magdalene's tooth. And then there are all the da Vincis. In summer the Roof Garden is a must, with site-specific seasonal sculptures, a café, and views of the park that will make you understand the price of a 5th Ave apartment. It's equally pleasant to catch the sunset from the front steps as the limestone façades across the street glimmer with gold.

1000 5th Ave (at 82nd St)
212-535-7710
Sun, Tues-Thurs
9:30am-5:30pm,
Fri-Sat 9:30am-9pm
4 5 6 to 86th St
Suggested Donation
Adults $20, Students $10

Whitney Museum of American Art

As one of the largest showcases of American art of the 20th and 21st centuries, the Whitney is as crucial in giving under-the-radar young artists their big break today as it was decades ago, when it propelled Edward Hopper and Robert Rauschenberg to stardom. It comes as little surprise that the Whitney Biennial, that celebration of the undiscovered held every even-numbered year, is received as a momentous event on the arts circuit. Brag-worthy gems of the permanent collection include works by Alexander Calder, Jasper Johns, Mark Rothko, and Willem de Kooning. Visit to discover both the budding trends of today and our national artistic heritage of the past century.

945 Madison Ave
(at 75th St)
212-570-3600
Sat-Sun 11am-6pm, Wed-Thurs 11am-6pm,
Fri 1pm-9pm
6 to 77th St
Adults $18, Students $12,
Fri 6pm-9pm PWYW

SHOP

J Leon Lascoff & Son

A throwback to the days when a Duane Reade didn't take up every city corner, Lascoff is classier than the Ritz-Carlton and friendlier, too. The apothecary is over a century old, and has resided in its current building since 1931, taking

1209 Lexington Ave
(at 82nd St)
212-288-9500
Mon-Fri 9am-6pm
4 5 6 to 86th St

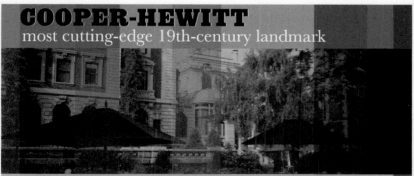

COOPER-HEWITT
most cutting-edge 19th-century landmark

Housed in one of the few remaining palatial estates that once lined 5th Ave, the Cooper-Hewitt is worth visiting as much to get a sense of how New York's old storied families once lived as it is to view its first class design collections. A celebration of the artistic creativity behind the everyday items we use, these collections encompass over 250,000 objects, ranging from Chinese hand-painted wallpapers to furniture designs by Frank Lloyd Wright. One particular highlight is the recently identified Michelangelo drawing for a candelabrum which was originally acquired for $60 in 1942. Be sure to drop by on Friday nights during the summer months, when jazz musicians and cocktails await you in the museum garden.

2 E 91st St (at 5th Ave)
212-489-8404
Sun 11am-6pm,
Mon-Fri 10am-5pm,
Sat 10am-6pm
4, 5, 6 to 86th St
Adults $15, Students $10

full advantage of the beautiful Gothic two-story windows and polished ironwork. Inside, modern pharmaceutical necessities are stocked next to archaic goods and memorabilia in original glass vials, sitting on antique wooden furniture. Salvador Dali came here to pick up bloodsucking leeches to use as models for his paintings, but you can take the less creepy route and treat yourself to one of the scented soaps or bubbly organic shampoos on sale.

Margoth Consignment Shop

For those seeking Upper East Side boutique chic but unable to throw around Rockefeller money, Margoth Consignment Shop provides a great alternative to the stores of Madison Ave.

Any normal passerby would fail to notice this thrift store—it's tucked into the ground floor of a townhouse on a tree-lined residential block. For the many locals who make up the regular customer base, Margoth Consignment is the source for lightly used formalwear at a terrific discount. The unpredictable pickings of accessories for men and women include ties, belts, shoes, and jewelry. With all the ritzy wares of Madison Ave's bold-face names, this is one of the few places in the neighborhood where you can nab the best without breaking the bank.

218 E 81st St
(btwn 2nd & 3rd Ave)
212-988-7688
Sun 12pm-5pm,
Mon-Sat 12pm-8pm
❻ to 77th St

CAFE SABARSKY
best three-hour cup of coffee

The Neue Galerie, a member of Museum Mile, accompanies its superior presentation of early 20th-century German and Austrian luminaries with a fascinating venture: the artistic milieu of the area has been replicated in the wooden walls, marble tables, and languid atmosphere of Café Sabarsky, an authentic Viennese café. The café stays true to Old World traditions by offering starters like a beet salad with goat cheese and pine nuts drizzled with vinaigrette. Viennese staples such as the Wiener Schnitzel (a thinly sliced breaded veal cutlet, pounded and pan fried) and cheddar-filled Bratwurst are sure to please. The real highlight is the Viennese coffee, served on a silver tray and best paired with a Sachertorte, Viennese dark chocolate cake. The combination provides a sensual experience that rivals any of the works in the Galerie itself.

Austrian
1048 5th Ave (at 86th St)
212-288-0665
Mon, Wed 9am-6pm,
Thurs-Sun 9am-9pm
4, 5, 6 to 86th St
$$

EAT

Café D'Alsace — *French*

1695 2nd Ave (at 88th St)
212-722-5133
Sun 9am-4pm,
5:30pm-10:30pm,
Mon-Fri 10:30am-4pm,
5pm-11pm,
Sat 9am-4pm, 5pm-12am
❹ ❺ ❻ to 86th St
$$$

Café D'Alsace promises "Alsatian cuisine with a contemporary New York flair," and it delivers, with a selection of well-executed traditional French dishes, including duck sausage, mussels in wine, and a number of organic offerings with seasonal ingredients. The bustling café has been packed since its opening day a few years ago, and diners will swoon when they learn that its price point is surprisingly welcoming. For starters, order a serving of gougeres (gruyere cheese puffs) and be prepared to order more. Among the entrées, the organic chicken breast with Yukon mashed potatoes and snap peas is a must-have and the seafood choucroute is a classic French favorite. Do not miss the caramelized apple tart for dessert. Service is usually fast and friendly, but expect to wait on weekends unless you've made a reservation.

Maz Mezcal — *Mexican*

316 E 86th St (at 2nd Ave)
212-472-1599
Sun 12pm-11pm,
Mon-Thurs 5pm-11pm,
Fri 5pm-12am,
Sat 12pm-12am
❹ ❺ ❻ to 86th St
$$$

A staple of Upper East Side Mexican cuisine, Maz Mezcal is always crowded, especially in the summer months when the outdoor seating is the perfect spot from which to witness the bustle of 86th St from a safe distance. Luckily, the eclectically-decorated restaurant is big enough that you can expect to be seated inside fairly quickly. The extensive menu includes all of your Mexican favorites as well as a solid selection of flavored margaritas. For a break from classic fajitas, try the flautas combinados, crispy deep fried tor-

UPPER EAST SIDE
best quick lunch joints

Papaya King- One of the most famous spots to get the classic New York City hot dog, the King's odd but magical pairing of snappy skin dogs with tropical fresh fruit juices keeps customers coming in 365 days a year. *179 E 86th St, 212-369-0648, Sun-Thurs 8am-12am, Fri-Sat 8am-2am, 4,5,6 to 86th St $*

Nick's Pizza- Reputedly the neighborhood's most authentic pizzeria, Nick's serves pies the way they're made in the old country. Extra thin and perfectly crispy, the most popular pizzas—ricotta and sausage—come with fresh mozzarella and basil leaves. *1814 2nd Ave, 212-987-5700, Daily 11:30am-11pm, 6 to 96th St $$*

Yorkville Creperie- This popular lunch spot serves both delectable dessert crepes—banana nutella, banana peanut butter, fresh berries with whipped cream—and savory classics like the croque monsieur. *1584 York Ave, 212-570-5445, Sun 9am-9pm, Mon-Thurs 10am-10pm, Fri-Sat 9am-10pm, 4,5,6 to 86th St $*

Hungarian Meat Market- A wide array of German and Eastern European products are sold at this delicatessen, where you can get an unctuous liverwurst and salami sandwich or a bag full of paprika-coated pork cracklings. *1560 2nd Ave, 212-628-5147, Daily 8am-6pm, 4,5,6 to 86th St $*

Park East Kosher- With a large selection of kosher meats and prepared foods, this neighborhood favorite makes meat-packed Jewish deli classics like pastrami and chopped liver. *1623 2nd Ave, 212-737-9800, Sun 9am-6pm, Mon-Wed 7am-7:30pm, Thurs 7am-9:30pm, 4,5,6 to 86th St $$*

tillas rolled around beef, chorizo, and chicken. And don't miss out on the quesadilla, which is plump with Mexican Oaxaca cheese and cooked to perfection. Be aware that there is a $15 minimum per person, but you will most likely meet it without even trying.

Pascalou

French

Upper East Side locals depend on this bistro's reliable selection of French and New World dishes. Though the restaurant itself is small (avoid the upstairs unless you don't

1308 Madison Ave
(at 93rd St)
212-534-7522
Daily 11:30am-3:45pm,
5pm-10pm
6 to 96th St
$$$

mind low ceilings) Pascalou offers a surprisingly diversified menu featuring classic French appetizers such as escargots and cheese soufflé, as well as Thai-inspired warm crab dumplings with peanut sauce. The three-course "twilight dinner" prix fixe ($19.95-24.95) is an unbeatable deal offered daily from 5pm to 6:30pm. Try starting with the classic goat cheese salad with garlic toasts, followed by duck confit with seasonal vegetables. When ordering à la carte, the molten dark chocolate soufflé is heavenly, and the classic profiteroles stuffed with ice cream and crème anglaise are equally delicious. If you want to sit in the restaurant's airy first floor, don't forget to make a reservation on weekend nights.

STIR
best blueberry mojito

Stir is a little black dress amid a sea of polos, valiantly breathing life into the frat boy abyss that is the Upper East Side bar scene. While it may occasionally come off as trying too hard—with an affected downtown vibe and a fussy drinks list—Stir definitely has its perks: the crowd is diverse and the music's a danceable melange of hip hop and funk. Sleek, dark, and minimalist decor dresses the bar area. In the back, charming candlelit banquettes offer perfect first date seating. Enjoy signature

Lounge

1363 1st Ave
(btwn 72nd & 73rd St)
212-744-7190
Mon-Wed 5pm-1am,
Thurs 5pm-2am, Fri 5pm-
4am, Sat 8pm-4am
6 to 68th or 77th St
$$

martinis like the Temptation, a mojito Stoli muddled with fresh blueberries, lime, and mint, or sip the Passion, a genteel Southern peach tea cocktail. Just be prepared to share the space with raucous birthday and bachelorette parties on weekends.

Sfoglia — *Italian*

1402 Lexington Ave
(at E 92nd St)
212-831-1402
Mon-Sat 11:30am-
2:30pm, 5:30pm-11pm
6 to 96th St
$$$

Wooden tables and dishtowel tablecloths create a farmer's market aura, which is mirrored in the rustic dishes on the seasonal menu of this neighborhood favorite. While most plates at Sfoglia mimic rural Italian classics, some are more innovative in their not-so-traditional pairing of ingredients, like the watercress salad with walnut pesto and apricots, or the mozzarella crustini smothered with pickled cherries. The regular items on the menu, although more simplistic, are also done with a creative spin: pan-seared chicken is served with a squeeze of lemon and a sprinkling of hot pepper seeds, and the pappardelle bolognese is made with a combination of veal, pork, lamb, and chicken liver to thicken the sauce. The fruit pie, which must be ordered with your main courses, combines season's freshest fruits in a buttery pie crust—a truly delicate end to an already refined meal.

PLAY

Aces and Eights Saloon — *Bar*

While the nonstop beer pong tournaments might seem more frat row than LES, Aces and Eights offers a grown-up version of the college

An elevated railway once ran up 3rd Ave. Its demolition has left the 6 train overcrowded ever since.

drinking experience. There's bottle service and a DJ on the second floor, and the dark wood bar and leather booths on the first floor are more conducive to deep conversa-

1683 1st Ave (at 87th St)
212-860-4020
Sun 5pm-12am, Mon 12am-4am, 5pm-4am, Tues-Sat 5pm-4am
❹ ❺ ❻ to 86th St
$

tion than getting schwasted. Patrons in their late twenties and early thirties flood the bar around midnight, making it a lively end-of-the-night spot. The bartenders are friendly, many more than willing to have a drink or three and dance on the bar with customers. A jukebox of rock, pop, and hip hop classics encourages drunken singalongs, and video games like Buck Hunter offer diversions from the booze. Aces and Eights has what your college frat never had—six beer pong tables and twelve-dollar Michelob pitchers.

The Big Easy

Dive

1768 2nd Ave (at 92nd St)
212-348-0879
Sun 1pm-2am, Mon-Fri 5pm-4am, Sat 12pm-4am
❻ to 96th St
$

You'll run into the crowd (and the smell) of this rowdy joint before you've cleared the sidewalk. A frat boy's dream awaits within—bras decorate one full wall, simple concrete outfits the floors, and a hot all-female waitstaff wearing skimpy uniforms give The Big Easy an anything goes spirit. Be careful not to spill your slightly warm, slightly stale beer or unidentifiable mixed drink as you navigate through hordes of happy bros. Take your glass to the cavernous backspace and play a game of pong. Fridays boast the $20 open bar special, aptly named "Road to Rehab." So brush up on your Journey sing-along skills, warm up your throwing arm, and kick back with nearly half of Jersey's male population.

upper east side
UNDER $20

Start with a stroll down **5th Ave**'s stretch of historical park-side mansions *(96th to 84th St)* to take in some of the oldest and most beautiful buildings in Manhattan.

Grab the true New Yorker's breakfast of a coffee and a bagel and schmear at **Tal Bagels** *(333 E 86th St)* for $2.80, and dine al fresco on the **Great Lawn** of Central Park.

Spend some time with Vermeer and Cézanne at Manhattan's largest museum, the **Metropolitan Museum of Art** *(1000 5th Ave)*.

For lunch, **Papaya King** *(179 E 86th St)* serves up two signature wieners with sauerkraut and fresh fruit juice (papaya, obviously, being the drink of choice) for $4.95.

Walk south along the **East River** among joggers and fishers. At 60th St, turn west to pick up a chocolate morsel at **Dylan's Candy Bar** *(1011 3rd Ave)*.

Cross the street and window-shop at the immortal **Bloomingdale's** *(1000 3rd Ave)*.

On a Friday, catch the happy hour special at **Third and Long** *(532 3rd Ave)*, the first among equals of the neighborhood bar scene.

Cavatappo Wine Bar

Wine Bar

1728 2nd Ave (near 90th St)
212-426-0919
Sun 4pm-11pm, Mon-Thurs 5pm-12am, Fri-Sat 5pm-1am
❹ ❺ ❻ to 86th St
$$

A tiny red and blue awning, a small patio, and a narrow room make one of the most romantic places to drink on the Upper East Side. The gregarious sommelier will chat you up as he fills your glass, recommending his favorite cheese to accompany your selection. The list of bottles (mostly under $40) are categorized by their sensuous characteristics, like "soft and supple" and "full-bodied, robust." Pair a glass with some Foxy cheese fondue or hand-pressed finger sandwiches—food specials change almost daily and are always worth sharing. Visit on Sundays, when the weekend's opened reds are sold-half off until they're gone, to build your knowledge of global wines.

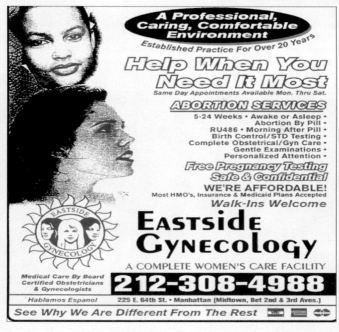

175

MIDT

Park Ave is famous as home base for Manhattan's affluent, and Wall Street gets all the attention for its trading floors, where bundles of theoretical money fly through the air. But Midtown West is where all the business is—neither polished nor romantic, it's just the densest commercial quarter on the island, catering to the flat broke college dropout in need of a one-dollar taco and the richest power broker looking for a nightclub that offers champagne footbaths.

While the island's southern tip established itself as a political stronghold throughout the 17th and 18th centuries, the area above 14th St was left to soak up the more pedestrian real estate, both residential and mercantile. But Midtown West wasn't destined to develop undisturbed like the comparatively sleepy Upper West Side, simply by virtue of its position as the rest of the country's gateway to Manhattan. Ferries were bringing hundreds of commuters and tourists across the Hudson by the 1850s, when downtown's storied playhouses gradually began to chase cheaper rents uptown. The century turned, the golden age of the musical began in earnest, and the construction of Penn Station and the Lincoln Tunnel upped the day-tripper ante considerably. A skyscraper craze also descended on midtown in the 1920s, resulting in the landmarks our postcards bear today and providing office space to business giants. Restaurants, small museums, and retail chains flooded in, looking to siphon tourists and the after-work

WE

crowd. Inexorably, the area accrued a reputation for being family-friendly, even as crime rates soared and architects insisted on walk-up after hideous post-war walk-up. The neighborhood was a perfect storm of commerce.

Because it's been so crucial in keeping the business of the city going, Midtown West's narrative since the early 20th century has largely been Manhattan's narrative as well. The rise in population slowed, but never slackened entirely; productivity increased even as living conditions worsened; and finally, the great 1990s revitalization of New York was epitomized in Mayor Giuliani's campaign to sanitize Times Square. Today there is no Manhattan neighborhood more devoted to families and tourists than Midtown West. Times Square has traded peep shows and choking traffic for lawn chairs and the M&M's store. The blighted rail yards edging the neighborhood to the west are slated to be rebuilt as a residential area, complete with its own riverfront park. Even the pedi-cabs and horse-drawn carriages that congregate along 59th St seem classier, sitting as they do in the shadow of the sparkling Time Warner Center, a high-priced urban shopping mall not yet ten years old. You'd have to be insane or deaf to want to live here, the one place in the city where you're guaranteed to never have a moment's peace. But peace isn't the point—Midtown West is important because it is, simply, the heart of it all.

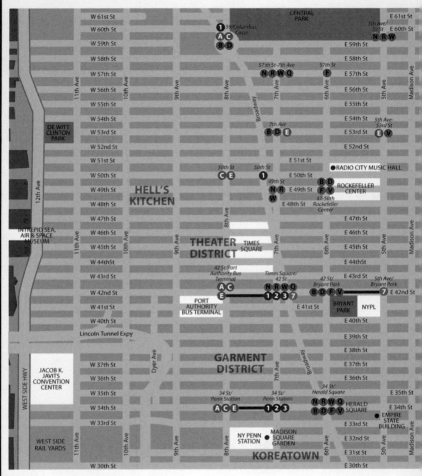

EXPLORE

Carnegie Hall

Music lovers, be grateful for the guilty conscience. Steel tycoon Andrew Carnegie built this fantastically prestigious concert hall as part of his late-in-life shift to philanthropy after 30 years as one of America's most powerful robber barons. Since 1891, Carnegie Hall's three stages have showcased the finest in international symphonies, classical soloists,

881 7th Ave
(btwn 56th and 57th St)
212-247-7800 (tickets),
212-903-9765 (tours)
Hours vary
🄵 🄽 🅀 🅁 to 57th St
Students $7

jazz ensembles, and progressive rock and pop. The sleekly imperial white and gold interior makes for an atmosphere of luxury, but the hall is surprisingly accessible. The Weill Institute for Music offers several free concerts a season as well as moderately priced music lessons for all ages, and the Rose Museum, wedged into one of the building's innumerable side nooks, invites visitors to survey mementos from legendary performances at no charge.

Herald Square

Welcome to the commuter hub of New York City: with close proximity to over 10 subway lines and Penn Station, Herald Square teems with tourists and bridge-and-tunnelers year-round. Named in honor of the New York Herald newspaper, the triangular park in the middle of the intersection is surrounded by iconic attractions like the Empire State Building and Madison Square Gardens. Sit and enjoy the crowds with a cup of coffee from the nearby 'wichcraft or explore one of the most concentrated shopping centers in the world—the titanic Macy's store, self-proclaimed as "the biggest store in the world," sits comfortably on an entire city block just minutes away from Manhattan Mall. Don't miss its annual Flower Show and Thanksgiving Day Parade, a balloon-bearing national institution that ends in Herald Square before a crowd that regularly exceeds 3 million.

34th and Broadway
B D F N Q R to 34th St-Herald Sq

International Center of Photography

ICP, midtown's original, pre-Steve Jobs glass box, is the museum most relevant to today's Facebook Age. Founded in 1974 by Cornell Capa in order to preserve documentary work, the Center is devoted exclusively to the display and study

1133 6th Ave (at 43rd St)
212-857-0000
Tues-Thurs 10am-6pm, Fri 10am-8pm, Sat-Sun 10am-6pm
B D F M 7 to 42nd St-Bryant Park, 1 2 3 N Q R S to Times Square, Adults $12, Students $8, free Fridays 5-8pm

neighborhhood
NECESSITIES

SUBWAYS 1, 2, 3, 7, A, B, C, D, E, N, Q, R, S

BUSES M4 M5 M7 M10 M16 M20 M34 M104 Q32

MARKETS Amish Market (731 9th Ave), D'agostino Supermarkets (815 10th Ave), 57th St Greenmarket (9th Ave btwn 57th and 56th St)

LIBRARY Columbus Library (742 10th Ave)

MEDIA Tmidtownlunch.com/blogroll

FITNESS Manhattan Plaza Health Club (482 W 43rd St), Exhale (150 CPS)

BIKES Midtown Bicycles (360 W 47th St), SBR Multisports (203 W 58th St)

COLUMBUS CIRCLE

On nice days, the New Yorkers too lazy to venture into the touristy lower wilds of Central Park instead lounge around the tower in the center of Columbus Circle. They munch on bean sprout pitas (or something) from **Whole Foods**, which occupies the entire basement of the **Time Warner Building**, now the intersection's most prominent and brilliantly spiffy feature. At the confluence of 8th Ave, Broadway, and 59th St, Columbus Circle is the southwestern entrance of Central Park and the gateway to the Upper West Side. Here, pedicabs and horse-drawn carriages circle the roundabout, looking for out-of-towner prey. To the east, an imitation of the World's Fair globe fools no one. The statue of Columbus atop the tower is the point from which all distances from New York City are officially measured, an ironic designation when one considers Columbus' navigational history. Admire the architecture or find your way to the park's greener pastures; just don't step in the horse crap.

of the art of photography in all its permutations. Feats of artistry, technology, and journalism are equally revered: couture shots, Iraq war documentation, and vintage prints share wall space. Students of the School at ICP can take a five-week digital video course or graduate from the MFA program fully versed in black-and-white darkroom technique. The current headquarters opened in 2000 and has extensive underground galleries specifically designed for mounting photography shows.

Madison Square Garden

Squatting atop North America's busiest train station and casting its shadow over the tight-laced Garment District, Madison Square Garden might be Manhattan's most improbably placed landmark. The World's Most Famous Arena seats over 20,000 and is home to the Knicks, the Liberty, the Rangers, Cirque du Soleil, the Westminster Kennel Club Dog Show, and the blockbuster boxing matches of the year. It's also where Springsteen and Gaga play when they come to town. A seat in the nosebleeds will only cost you something in the double digits, but you'll almost certainly want to make use of the binoculars available for rent. Still, visitors appreciate the echoing complex—this is large-scale entertainment in a city where space comes at a premium.

> 4 Pennsylvania Plaza (7th Ave, btwn 31st & 33rd St)
> 212-465-6741
> Tours daily 11-3, adults $18.50
> ❶❷❸Ⓐ Ⓒ Ⓔ to 34th St-Penn Station

NASDAQ MarketSite

The lure of Madame Tussaud's and the Naked Cowboy notwithstanding, tourists go to Times Square simply for a sight of its cacophonous lights. Embedded in the neon jungle is one display that actually has something to say: at seven stories of curved LED screen, the façade of the NASDAQ stock market's headquarters is the ticker that never sleeps. Twenty-four hours a day, the MarketSite gives up-to-the-minute market quotes and news from the financial sector, while inside a host of international news networks use the ground floor TV studios to film economic reports. The building

> 4 Times Square (at 43rd and Broadway)
> 646-441-5200
> ❶❷❸❼ⓃⓆⓇ Ⓢ to Times Sq

is well known among suits for being a splashy place to launch a new product, but visitors are better off attending Opening and Closing Bell Ceremonies, which are presided over by anyone from the pianist Lang Lang to Ringling Brothers acrobats.

Radio City Music Hall

Behind a blazing neon façade that still retains every bit of its 1932 Art Deco glamour, the world's largest indoor theater hosts concerts, stage shows, film premieres, and the annual Rockette-heavy extravaganza that is the Christmas Spectacular. Developer John D. Rockefeller, Jr.'s last-ditch effort to save midtown Manhattan from itself during the Great Depression is today known as the Showplace of the Nation. Daily tours of the building bring visitors through the splendid Grand Foyer, an exercise in red velvet restraint, and onto the Great Stage, whose stately, stupefying proportions mask one of the most advanced technical systems in theater. Any auditorium that hosts Willie Nelson, MGMT, and the Tony Awards

> 1260 6th Ave (btwn 50th and 51st St)
> 212-247-4777
> Box office: Mon-Sat 11:30am-6pm
> Ⓑ Ⓓ Ⓕ to Rockefeller Center-50th St

has got to sound great under all circumstances.

SHOP

Diamond District

Not many student budgets allow for precious gemstones, but this short, absurdly busy strip of street

47th St
(btwn 5th & 6th Ave)
Ⓑ Ⓓ Ⓕ to Rockefeller Center-50th St, Ⓖ to 51st St

offers the closest thing to a discount diamond there is. Amidst sidewalk hawkers and tacky diamond-shaped streetlights, wholesale vendors and technically brilliant jewelers work almost on top of one another to keep this hub of the international diamond trade going at breakneck speed. The larger shops can guarantee certified stones and won't try to persuade you to forget about your receipt, but the sketchier single-window stalls are where the real deals are. If you're coming to buy, be prepared to haggle and don't let on that you can't tell a culet from a shank. If you're coming to window shop, you've found one of the city's best browsing blocks.

Garment District

As good a place to spot Diane Von Furstenburg as to stumble across a whispered sample sale, the Garment District has de-

5th Ave to 9th Ave,
34th St to 42nd St
Ⓐ Ⓒ Ⓔ to 34th St-Penn Station, Ⓑ Ⓒ Ⓔ Ⓔ Ⓢ to Times Square

signed and produced American fashion for over a century. The high concentration of major label showrooms, ateliers, and specialty suppliers makes the neighborhood a meeting point for the industry's most creative minds and a working environment that allows start-ups to rise through the ranks—Jason Wu, the Obama-consecrated wunderkind, began here as an unknown. Stop in at B&J Fabrics (525 7th Ave), Toho Shoji (990 6th Ave), or Project Runway landmark Mood (225 W 37th St) for utterly unique raw materials, and remember to look up for a glimpse through Vera Wang's or Calvin Klein's office window.

EAT

Burger Joint   *Burgers*

A rowdy, crowded burger shack might be low on the list of things you'd expect to find at the end of a dark and hidden hallway in the lobby of one of New York's

119 West 56th St
(btwn 6th & 7th Ave)
212-708-7414
Ⓑ Ⓒ Ⓕ to 57th St
Sun-Thurs 11am-11:30pm,
Fri-Sat 11am-12am
$$

fanciest hotels. Nevertheless, in a back room of the Parker Meridien lies the trendy and often mobbed Burger Joint, serving up some of their specialty NYC-famous burgers. Sure, the shakes and fries are above average, but there's no doubt that the namesake sandwich is where this

HELL'S KITCHEN

What kind of neighborhood emerges from a muddle of antebellum tenements, kept short and squalid by the twin demons of low-rise zoning laws and overcrowding, boxed in on all sides by humongous transportation portals? Never glitzy, Hell's Kitchen, which extends from 34th to 57th Streets west of 8th Ave, is the Manhattan underbelly of generations past. During the 19th century's immigration flood, dirt-poor Irish and German laborers packed the reputed "most dangerous area on the American Continent," the Prohibition turned the mafia-ruled neighborhood into the nucleus of speakeasy life, and West Side Story was Amsterdam Avenue's answer to Beaver Cleaver. Today Hell's Kitchen is workaday but not dangerous and is better known for its high concentration of compact ethnic restaurants and all the struggling actors who were kicked out of Brooklyn. An afternoon at the weekend **Hell's Kitchen Flea Market** *(39th St at 9th Ave)* is perfectly capped with a jazz performance at the hallowed **Birdland** *(315 44th St)* and a late-night sushi roll at **Kyotofu** *(705 9th Ave)*. Otherwise, continue the great bathtub gin tradition at **The Snug** *(751 9th Ave)*.

THEATRE ROW

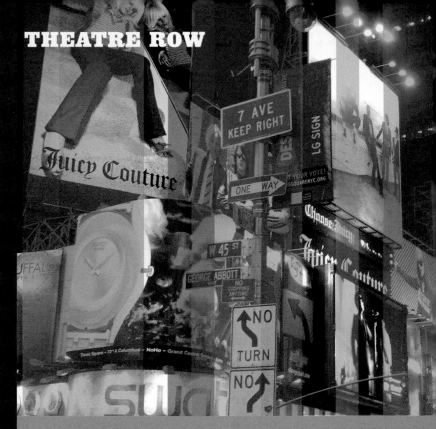

Way back in 1933 when director Lloyd Bacon released 42nd Street (which would become the template for every let's-put-on-a-musical musical thereafter) the titular thoroughfare was in its first incarnation as a highly regarded performing arts district. The theaters of western 42nd Street between 9th and 11th Avenues survived the Great Depression but had taken a financial beating by the time stagflation rolled around. Times Square remained notoriously seamy throughout the 1970s, but the marquees of Broadway could take it, having good name recognition and even better funding. However, along the side streets, stages were transformed into brothels, burlesque shows, and porn theaters, and the clientele switched from families and Times critics to the kind of businessman Leonard Cohen sings about.

But the street's priceless location was undeniable, and in 1975 the troupe Playwrights Horizons embarked on a mission to restore traditional drama to the run-down theaters. The company launched a two-pronged attack of urban renewal and play production, enlisting aid from Broadway's biggest names, other theater groups, and the many resident prostitutes with acting aspirations. Today Theatre Row is a string of pearls in midtown: six gorgeously renovated historical theaters and a gaggle of brand new stages, each presenting an acclaimed, unprecedented Off- or Off-Off-Broadway work. It's Peggy Sawyer's kind of place again.

shack excels. Their secret here is that the meat is flame-grilled, making the resulting burger far leaner and cleaner than the usual, greasy deli burgers New Yorkers are used to. Add to that a toasted bun, a melted mix of cheddar and swiss, and your choice of condiments, and you're left with one of the best-tasting burgers in the city.

Casellula Cheese & Wine Café *Wine Bar*

This small Hell's Kitchen restaurant serves up a diverse array of—you guessed it—cheeses and wines, alongside a brief, well-selected, mostly pork-

401 West 52nd St
(near 9th Ave)
212-247-8137
Daily 5pm to 2am
❶ ❻ ❸ to 50th St
$$

centric menu. While the wait can be long and the seating a bit crowded, the space is anything but uninviting: give your server some idea of your preferences, and he or she will help you navigate the potentially intimidating selection of cheeses. The stuffed peppadew peppers, oozing with fresh mozzarella and wrapped in deliciously salty speck, are not to be missed. Nor is the Pig's Ass Sandwich, which New York Magazine appropriately dubbed the "Jennifer Lopez of Cuban sandwiches." You can leave the choice of cheese up to your well-informed server, but don't play it safe—Casellula is the

place to try products you won't be able to find elsewhere. The wine and beer menus, both of which also feature rare and unfamiliar offerings, are also not to be overlooked.

DB Bistro Moderne *French*

Wedged between Manhattan's theater and fashion districts, DB Bistro Moderne caters to Conde Nast business lunches and pre-theater tourists alike. The menu's "house specialties" effectively showcase both the restaurant's philosophy as well as its culinary strengths.

55 W 44th St
(near 5th Ave)
212-391-2400
Breakfast Mon-Fri
7am-10am, Sat-Sun 8am-
2:30am, Lunch Mon-Fri
12pm-2:30pm, Dinner
Sun-Mon 5pm-10pm,
Tue-Thurs 5pm-11pm,
Fri-Sat 5pm-11:30pm
❶ ❷ ❸ ❼ ❶ ❶ ❶ ❸
to Times Square
$$$

The Alsatian tart, which traditionally contains caramelized onions, fromage blanc, and bacon, is impossibly thin for the depth of flavor it contains. And then, of course, there's the infamous DB Burger, which goes above and beyond paying tribute to the quintessential American fast food. Packed with red wine-braised short ribs and black truffle and served on a Parmesan bun, it's the most decadent burger you will never be able to eat with your hands. For dessert, forgo

MIDTOWN WEST
best street food

53rd and 6th Halal Stand- Only after 7:30pm does the most famous food cart in the city churn out hundreds of platters of chopped chicken and lamb gyro over rice with its much celebrated white sauce and incredibly spicy hot sauce. Beware of the lines! *53rd St & 6th Ave. Daily 7:30pm-4am, B/D/E to 7th Ave-53rd St $*

Hallo Berlin German Food Cart- Stop by this food cart at lunchtime for liberal servings of grilled sausages—pork, veal, and beef—braised red cabbage, and onions, accompanied with a crusty roll and a super-sized pickle. *54th St and 5th Ave, 212-333-2372, Mon-Fri 11:30am-3:30pm, E to 5th Ave-53rd St, N/R to 5th Ave-60th St $*

Carnegie John's- A cross between a halal stand and a burger joint, Carnegie John's delivers one of the best burgers in the area for one of the best values: get it with peppers and onions for under $5. *56th St & 7th Ave, Mon-Fri 11:30am-6pm, N/Q/R to 57th St-7th Ave, B/D/E to 7th Ave-53rd St $*

Kim's Aunt- This cart offers a wide array of cuisines for cheap, but stick with the chicken. It's fresh, well-spiced, and made to order, a rarity for halal carts. *46th St btwn 5th & 6th Ave, 917-805-3519, Mon-Fri 11am-4pm, B/D to 47th-50 Sts-Rockefeller Center, N/R to 47th St-7th Ave $*

The Jamaican Dutchy- There's always a line at this food cart with the finest Caribbean fare. Apart from the heavily spiced jerk chicken, the sides—plantains, boiled dumplings, yellow yams—are the highlights of a hearty meal here. *51st St near 7th Ave, 646-287-5004, Mon-Thurs 6am-8pm, Fri 6am-12am, 1 to 50th St, N/R to 49th St, B/D/E to 7th Ave $*

the temptation of trying the popcorn ice cream in favor of the homemade mini madeleines, served warm and dashed with powdered sugar.

Il Punto   *Italian*

507 9th Ave (at 38th St)
212-244-0088
Sun-Thurs 11:30am-11pm,
Fri- Sat 11:30am-12am
❶❷❸Ⓐ©Ⓔ to
34th St-Penn Station
$$$

Good Italian restaurants are about as common as yellow cabs in New York City, so it's an inspired menu that makes us remember one plate of penne over another. At elegant but unpretentious Il Punto, chef Tony Pecora offers his own contemporary interpretation of traditional Bari cuisine in an unlikely location between Port Authority and the Lincoln Tunnel. Pass over the standard meat and fish dishes (beef rollatini, roast monkfish) for the updated pastas, each of which forgoes hearty tomato or pesto for light and tangy flavors. On the menu, the pasta della selva reads like a summer salad—linguine with raspberry-infused vodka sauce, blueberries, cherries, and cranberries—but Pecora balances the sweetness so skillfully that the odd combination seems perfectly obvious. Il Punto's yellow walls and white tablecloths may be simple, but the wait staff doesn't hesitate to show personality, detailing recommendations for every course.

Kyotofu   *Japanese, Dessert*

🍦
705 9th Ave (btwn 48th
& 49th St)
212-974-6012
Sun, Tues-Wed
12pm-12:30am,
Thurs-Sat 12pm-1:30am
©Ⓔ to 50th St
$$

A dessert bar may be the last thing you expect to find in a Hell's Kitchen Japanese restaurant, but find it you will. While a late-night tofu joint may scream dainty pastries, those who venture to Kyotofu will be rewarded with desserts worthy of a four-star restaurant. The Far East-centric menu offers a flight of light and refreshing dishes and cocktails, all nutritionist approved and appropriately sized for either full meals or quick snacks. Flashes of brilliance shine in the meltingly warm miso chocolate cakes and the insanely rich scoop of maple-spiked soy mascarpone atop the toasted walnut vanilla parfait. The restaurant is divided by the open chef's quarters into a bar area and a back dining room. Adorned in pink and white with modern furnishings, Kyotofu is meant to feel like a traditional Japanese home—minus the need to take off your shoes.

Landmarc *Breakfast, Brunch, American*

With a music selection highlighted by Kid Cudi and a floor-space large enough to accommodate the rhythm, stepping through Landmarc's doorway is evocative of entering a nightclub. Add to this a coveted third floor view from the Time Warner Building

10 Columbus Circle
(Time Warner Building,
3rd Floor)
212-219-2126
Daily 7am-2am
Ⓐ Ⓒ Ⓑ Ⓓ ❶ to 59th
St-Columbus Circle
$$$

and an international wine list including full and half bottles, and the resemblance is welcome. Wine, in fact, symbolizes Landmarc's fusion concept, as represented by the Babel-inspired wine rack standing in the center of the dining room. Begin with the prosciutto and fontina flatbread or the evening's pasta special. Next, choose your cut of steak and one of six signature sauces—all prepared on the open grill, a popular view from the bar. Between the white brick wall above the grill and the islands of barstool tables, you are sure to have a landmark experience.

Má Peche *New American, Asian*

The hymns of praise sung for the newest property in the David Chang empire have only been slightly dimmed by the fact that, at this point, no one is surprised. That

15 W 56th St
(btwn 5th & 6th Ave)
212-757-5878
Daily 7am-2:30pm,
5pm-11pm
Ⓕ to 57th St, Ⓝ Ⓡ to
5th Ave-59th St
$$$

the Vietnamese-inspired fare is both marvelously inventive and totally satisfying is par for the course. That the young staff is as casual as it is expert is de rigeur. That the wait for a (non-reservable) spot at the communal plywood tables can be long is expected. The restaurant's massive size and Midtown location, however, have garnered some attention. Though a sizable raw bar (try the hamchi) and killer cocktails hint at Chang's new postal code, Má Peche is Momofuku through and through, from the familiarly excellent crispy pig's head torchon, to the new and predictably glee-inducing lemongrass-caramel glazed ribs. This outpost of downtown cool may be the best thing to happen to Midtown in years.

Margon

Cuban, Sandwiches

136 W 46th St
(btwn 6th and 7th Ave)
212-354-5013
Mon-Fri 6am-5:30pm,
Sat 6:30am-3pm
B D F to 47th-50th
St-Rockefeller Center,
1 2 3 7 N Q R S
to Times Square
$

Just off of Times Square, Margon caters to guests busy with a Manhattan schedule. In fact, at first glance, the restaurant can easily be mistaken for a traditional American diner. Yet past the stainless steel takeout counter and white tile walls, small pictures of Havana accent the room and an animated staff waits to explain the authentic Cuban dishes on display under the countertop. Steady favorites include pork chops

and the Cuban sandwich with large sides of rice and plantains, although specials rotate daily, including Wednesday's well-known roast pork. After your meal, calm your palate with one of nine tropical shakes. True to its original 1970s decor, Margon has successfully brought the tastes of Cuba to the look of a New York diner.

Norma's   *Brunch, American*

Tucked in an airy, modern dining room off the lobby of the Parker Meredien, Norma's has long catered to those who view breakfast as not only the most important meal of the day, but also the only one worth having. Of course, it doesn't hurt that after eating at Norma's—an experience which necessarily includes a free shot of

the day's smoothie and glass or three of the signature orange juice—diners won't be very much inclined for dinner that night, or the next day. But given the size of the offerings and the staff's eagerness to package items to go, leftovers won't be in short supply, should there be a late night craving for, say, Upstream Eggs Benedict or the classic Waz-Za, a fluffy waffle layered deep with mangos and berries and crowned with a crackly brûlée top. Take note, breakfast believers: this is a pilgrimage not to be missed.

118 W 57th St
(btwn 6th & 7th Ave)
212-708-7460
Mon-Fri 7am-3pm,
Sat-Sun 7:30am-3pm
●●● to 57th St-
7th Ave
$$$

THE PARIS THEATRE
best non-brie taste of france

Alongside the Plaza and the tired carriage horses just across the street, the Paris Theatre completes Central Park South's trifecta of old-world romanticism. At 62, it's the nation's oldest continually operating arthouse theater. Its commitment to international films was initially considered scandalous: in 1950, Catholic activists succeeded in banning the Paris from screening Roberto Rossellini's Miracle. Still, the Paris has remained remarkably constant in appearance and practice over the years. Its single screen shows only one film a week, each of which begins with the parting of the stage curtains, and the theater holds fast to its no-preview policy. Most offerings are French, but other European and American indies are screened sporadically, and the Paris's worn-in charm lures Continent-flavored Hollywood premieres like Moulin Rouge.

4 W 58th St (at 5th Ave)
212-688-3800
N,Q,R to Fifth Ave-
59th St

189

The gold stage curtain that falls in front of the Great Stage at Radio City Music Hall is the largest stage curtain in the world.

Pam Real Thai Food   *Thai*

Pam Real Thai's name makes a bold promise of superlative authenticity. While it's hard for a New Yorker to judge whether Pam's offerings are real or not, it's clear that they come at a real value. Popular standby Thai dishes like massaman curry, pad thai, and pad se ew all cost less than $8, but taste better than what one might find for double that price at the plethora of other locally touted Thai joints. If you're willing to venture beyond the lowest price bracket, Pam also has some more exotic options, such as a calamari pad thai or the curiously named "jungle curry." If Pam has a downside, it's that they're cash only, but at least you won't have to bring much to get an ample meal here.

404 W 49th St
(near 9th Ave)
212-333-7500
Sun-Thurs 11:30am-11pm,
Fri-Sat 11:30am-11:30pm
Ⓒ Ⓔ to 50th St
$

Sullivan Street Bakery   *Bakery*

Just avenues away from the bustle of Times Square, this gem of a bakery tucked inside Hell's Kitchen manages to stay on the radar. Sullivan Street famously provides delicious, hearty breads for fine restaurants across the city, including the much-

533 W 47th St
(btwn 10th & 11th Ave)
212-265-5580
Sun 8am-4pm,
Mon-Sat 8am-7pm
Ⓒ Ⓔ to 50th St
$

celebrated Gramercy Tavern and Babbo. But the small bakery also offers a delicious selection of paninis ($6), pizzas ($2-3.50/slice), and dessert breads ($2-3.50) to be enjoyed at the very limited window seating, or taken to go. Expect to find unusual and exciting panini pairings—pork and peach, beets and goat cheese—alongside classic caprese and prosciutto-mozzarella, all served on fresh bread. Don't forget to leave without a pane di comune to share with friends.

Woorijip
Korean

12 W 32nd St
(btwn 5th & Broadway)
212-244-1115
Sun-Thurs 24 hours,
Fri-Sat 6am-2am
B D F N Q R to 34th St-Herald Sq,
A C E 1 2 3 to 34th St-Penn Station
$

At the door, Woorijip's guests are welcomed by a wooden arrow signpost pointing toward the dining options. Woorijp means "our home," and the menu adds that home should be "a place where delicious food is always waiting for you." This philosophy, along with low prices and a nearly 24-hour schedule, has attracted a busy crowd that often fills the room, but lines move quickly due to the efficient system. Beneath the paper lanterns suspended from the ceiling, stool tables run down the center of the room while guests serve themselves along the perimeter. Start with a traditional Korean ricecake, with seasonings ranging from brown sugar to pumpkin and sweet potato, followed by an à la carte sautéed beef or pan fried squid. Complete your meal with a side of kimchi, available in 17 salad varieties. But whatever you order, our home will not disappoint.

PLAY

123 Burger Shot Beer
Gastropub, Sports Bar

738 10th Ave (btwn 50th & 51st St)
212-315-0123
Daily 11am-4am
C E to 50th St
$

True to its name, a good time at this Midtown sports bar is as easy as 1, 2, 3. Come through at game time and you'll likely find yourself wedged among raucous fans, teetering beer towers, and piles of dirt-cheap sliders (tasty morsels that come with a carousel of sauces). On off nights and afternoons, "123" can be the perfect spot to unwind with friends. Check out the backyard seating while you chow down on the generous portions of classic bar and BBQ comfort food. The peanut buffalo wings deserve special mention, as do the beer tubes for larger parties. With a steady stream of $1 angus sliders and beers on tap, this is one sports bar that deserves the game-winning shot.

Bar-Tini Ultra Lounge
LGBT

642 10th Ave
(btwn 45th & 46th St)
917-388-2897
Daily 4pm-4am
A C E to 42nd St
C E to 50th St
$$

Hidden behind a quaint white wood and blue awning, Bar-Tini is discreet and unassuming, but it's slowly attracting the attention of more and more locals. The swanky space was recently transformed into a modern cocktail hangout with plush velvet couches, colorful lights, and room for 75-person private parties. Friendly bartenders who are conscious of the morning after headache recommend the specialty "White Lotus" vodka-based cocktail, infused with vitamins and minerals to avert hungover regret. If you're a day drinker, be sure to hit the half-price happy hour, but don't get sloppy. Bar-Tini is a grown up type of place, less for the prepubescent-looking and more for the man girls will flirt with until they realize he don't swing that way.

Mé Bar
Cocktails, Bar

On the 14th floor of La Quinta Inn, Mé Bar puts the Empire State Building at the drinker's fingertips. After-work happy hour happens on this spacious rooftop, modestly decorated with a quaint white picket fence, Christmas lights, and pillowed benches to accommodate a crowd looking to relax. Young professionals swap industry gossip and try their best pickup lines while sipping on pomegranate martinis, and middle-aged hotel guests wander shyly around. Whether or not you meet some potential business contacts here, an evening of laid-back conversation is a guarantee. Insider's tip: make use of the affordable Korean food across the street, as this budget-friendly bar is BYOS (Bring Your Own Snacks).

17 W 32nd St
(btwn 5th & 6th Ave)
212-290-2460
Sun-Thurs 5:30pm-12am,
Fri 5:30pm-1am,
Sat 5:30pm-3am
❶❷❸Ⓑⓓ🅕Ⓝ🅠🅡
to 34th St
$$

Terminal 5

Music Venue

ALL
AGES

610 W 56th St
(btwn 11th & 12th Ave)
212-582-6600
Hours and ticket prices
vary by performance
❶Ⓐ🅒Ⓑⓓ to 59th St

This tri-level, all-ages venue is one of the largest and most popular new places to see indie acts play live. Despite the 3,000+ capacity, Terminal 5's superior sound system makes the space feel aurally intimate. The main floor is the easiest place to snag a spot, but avoid it on sold-out nights when mobility is nearly impossible. Instead, aim for a railing spot on one of the three balconies and take advantage of the excellent views of both stage and crowd that it provides. If you're hungry, grab an empanada from the cart on the third level. In addition to the four bars dotting the enormous space, the new, fully stocked rooftop lounge, resembling an airplane hanger (an homage to the venue's namesake), is now open for business.

Vintage

Cocktail Lounge

753 9th Ave (at 51st St)
212-581-4655
Daily 5pm-4am
🅒Ⓔ to 50th St
$$

With 80 beers and a bible of cocktails, this lounge is a little bit of heaven in Hell's Kitchen...if heaven served up 201 specialty martinis. Choosing a drink can be a challenge, so jump mouth-first into a candy-flavored martini like the Caramel Apple or Tootsie Roll. A solid stream of 80s tunes caters to the after work crowd, though weekends tend to draw in younger droves. Due to its location, Vintage is also popular with the after-theater scene, and Broadway stars have been known to hide out at its dimly lit bar and dark wood tables. Bring friends, sample several cocktails, and share the nachos—a salty mess of chips and melted cheese that pairs perfectly with your sweet sip.

194

195

MIDT

When the daily army of commuters and tourists rides off into the sunset on the last few rush hour buses, they leave behind a much quieter Midtown East, peopled by only a quarter of its daytime population. During the day the streets of this overwhelmingly corporate zone go worsted wool-gray as Lexington and Park fill with ambassadors from the business world. Those remaining after dark are residents of conservative Murray Hill and the Brooklynesque Sutton Place, mostly professionals and the invariably affluent. Midtown East is a notoriously expensive locale for both companies and families to set up camp, due to its curious geographic status as a neighborhood both completely secluded and in the middle of it all.

Since the earliest Manhattan settlements, the Hudson-side swath of today's Midtown has been an important transportation channel, while the eastern half languished in the shadow of Roosevelt (née Welfare) Island. Then the commercial centers of Midtown West—Times Square, Herald Square, virtually everywhere along the Avenue of the Americas—grew exponentially during the 19th and 20th centuries, and inevitably leaked across the island. The district was bitten by the skyscraper bug, giving us the Chrysler Building and the Empire State Building, and daring developers dreamed of bigger and bigger offices. Headquarters and flagships went up around the clock. Up to about Third Ave, Midtown East was where Things were Happening in a capital-letter sort of way.

But the neighborhood's extreme east quarter went neglected, there being no subway and

OWN

no significant demand for a bridge to Queens. Without fire-breathing CEOs snatching up the land, developers instead poured money into grand brownstones and luxurious high-rise apartments, in complexes expressly landscaped to leave room to breathe. More varied and floral for developing without outside pressure, it became a favorite for the old money crowd (a reputation that lingered until the yuppie invasion at the turn of this century). Quirks of the area's quasi-isolation include the now-lost golf course of Tudor City and Turtle Bay, the mile or so of peaceful, leafy riverfront property that once had a different industrial plant on each corner.

Above 42nd St are the remnants of Edith Wharton's "Gilded New York": the Plaza hotel, the Waldorf=Astoria, and the Villard Houses. A night amble by St. Patrick's Cathedral reminds tourists and natives alike that city history still animates the area. Unlike its crosstown neighbor, Midtown East isn't known for its vibrant nightlife; locals spend their evenings at classy restaurants with spectacular East River views. Tourists come for the architectural land-marks—Rockefeller Center, Grand Central Station, the Morgan Library—and for the iconic 5th Ave shopping and store window displays. Classic flagships like FAO Shwartz, Bergdorf Goodman, and Bloomingdale's, as well as the more recent NBA Store and an enormous Abercrombie and Fitch draw hoards. A day-tripper's haven by day and a playground for the wealthy by night, Midtown East has something for everyone—unless you're cheap.

ST

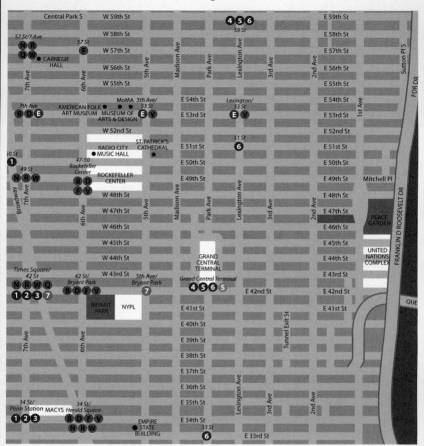

EXPLORE

Bryant Park

"Manhattan's Town Square" doesn't provide much relief from the city crowd—because of its proximity to Times Square,

42nd St (at 6th Ave)
Hours vary seasonally
B D F to
42nd St-Bryant Park,
7 to 5th Ave

20,000 people flood in every day when the weather's pleasant. Yet the park still manages to enclose a splendor of outdoor charms, including tree-lined gravel paths, an army of dark green tables and movable chairs, a picturesque fountain, a carousel, six flowerbeds, and an aptly-named Great Lawn. Free wireless attracts businesspeople on their lunch breaks, and those unarmed with laptops should still drop by to grab a snack from one of the four 'wichcraft kiosks (when the weather gets cold, be sure to sample their three flavors of hot chocolate). Come during Fashion Week to catch a glimpse of mingling models and designers, or take advantage of free movie screenings during the HBO Summer Film Festival.

The Chapel of the Good Shepherd

Once known as "Welfare Island," Roosevelt Island was an Australia-like destination for New York's destitute, criminal, and mentally ill for over a century. In 1889, the Episcopal Church opened this chapel with the goal of spiritually enlightening "the most neglected class of humanity." Since the 1970s refurbishment of the island, the Chapel of the Good Shepherd continues to carry on this tradition. The church shares its grounds with the Catholic Parish of St. Frances Cabrini and other groups so as to function as a community center. Its imposing Gothic-style brick façade and brownstone interior are reminiscent of old English parish churches. With views of midtown Manhattan from its wings, the Chapel affords a contemplative space mostly unavailable on the mainland.

543 Main St
917-843-3338
Sunday services 10am
🄵 to Roosevelt Island,
tram at 59th St & 2nd Ave

Chrysler Building

This monolith of steel is marked by a fluctuating flow of suits and ties: as the business of the day dies down into the early evening, the men and women of the workplace dissipate, leaving ogling tourists in their wake. Built between 1928 and 1930, the building was the world's tallest skyscraper for a brief 11 months before the Empire State Building came along. Its purpose has seemingly taken a backseat to its art deco design, celebrated for an emphasis on geometric precision and detail.

405 Lexington Ave
(btwn 42nd & 43rd St)
Mon-Fri 8am-6pm
(Lobby only)
④⑤⑥⑦Ⓢ to
42nd St-Grand Central

KOREATOWN

Just east of Broadway, 32nd and 35th Streets demarcate midtown Manhattan's Koreatown—its massage parlors, noodle joints, barbecues, and karaoke bars are squeezed into a cluttered three blocks. The area showcases some of New York's finest examples of Korean art and tradition: **Lee Young Hee Museum** *(2 W 32nd St)* and the **Hun Gallery** *(12 W 32nd St)*, both on the same block, display Korean painting, photography, traditional costumes, and furnishings. At night, the neighborhood transforms into a popular destination for college students who end their barbecue dinners with rounds of drinks and karaoke. Try the gogi gui at **Kunjip Korean Restaurant** *(9 W 32nd St)*, though you may find yourself waiting in a line out the door for the extensive meat and vegetarian options and generous free samples. If you'd prefer something more traditional, cut into the pork belly at **Wonjo** *(23 W 32nd St)* or the **New York Kom Tang House** *(32 W 32nd St)*, the last two BBQ joints that still use charcoal for grilling.

The Chrysler's lobby, adorned in onyx and amber, is flanked with Egyptian motifs and images of the manufacturing assembly line. Foreboding yet grand, the spires of the crown are often hidden behind the clouds, which gave rise to the name "Cloud Club," a legendary private dining area on the upper floors (sadly, it no longer exists).

Museum of Modern Art

MoMA is not only an internationally known art site but also one of the most remarkable architectural structures in the city. Designed by Yoshio Taniguchi in 2004, the building is a masterpiece in itself, with clean lines, open, airy

11 W 53rd St (near 6th Ave)
212-708-9400
Sun-Mon, Wed-Thurs, Sat 10:30am-5:30pm, Fri 10:30am-8pm
E to 5th Ave-53rd St, **B** **D** **F** to Rockefeller Center
Adults $20, Students $12

spaces, and floor-to-ceiling windows providing views of nearby brownstones and skyscrapers. Besides its permanent collection from modern masters like Dali, Picasso, Van Gogh, Mondrian, and Warhol, the museum also features a large-scale (and often overwhelming) sculptural exhibit in its atrium, as well as rotating cutting-edge exhibits by renowned artists. For cinema lovers, there are contemporary and international film screenings. During warmer months, drop by the hushed sculpture garden on the ground level for a pleasant respite from exhibit-browsing.

New York Public Library

Polymaths and plebeians alike make the pilgrimage to this "Splendid Temple of the Mind." As the NYPL's central research center, it comprises a vast

476 5th Ave (at E 42nd St) Sun 1pm-5pm, Mon, Thurs-Sat 11am-6pm, Tues-Wed 11am-7:30pm
7 to 5th Ave, **B** **D** **F** to 42nd St-Bryant Park

network of divisions that contain over 15 million items in 1,200 languages, ranging from historical documents and rare books to maps and photographs. The autographed manuscript of Washington's Farewell Address and a copy of the Gutenberg Bible are some of its most distinguished treasures. Architecturally speaking, this building is not only a feast for the mind, but also one for the eyes—it's a Beaux-Arts masterpiece, inside and out. Its marble-floored hallways are graced with rococo ceilings, from which dangle elaborate glass-orbed chandeliers that emit a soft radiance. On the third floor, don't miss the murals in the McGraw Rotunda or on the ceiling of the Rose Reading Room.

The Pierpont Morgan Library

The only survivor of three brownstones that once stood on midtown's section of Madison Ave is now the home of the Pierpont Morgan Library and Museum. A tribute to the extensive literary and artistic collection of legendary financier J.P. Morgan, the museum features numerous galleries showcasing the work of Da Vinci, Michelangelo, Raphael, Rembrandt, and

A toilet sits inside the highest point of the Chrysler Building's spire.

Picasso, among other masters. Outfitted with marble staircases and intricately carved ceilings, the Charles McKim-designed building also includes the renowned McKim Library, which is home to three Gutenberg Bibles, and a restaurant, located in the Morgan family's orginal dining room. Thankfully outside the trampling ground of Museum Mile, the Morgan's collection stands up to any of the must-sees on the Upper East Side.

225 Madison Ave
(at 36th St)
212-685-0008
Sun 11am-6pm,
Tues-Thurs 10:30am-5pm,
Fri 10:30am-9pm,
Sat 10am-6pm
4 5 6 7 S to
42nd St-Grand Central

The Plaza Hotel

Since 1907, this 19-story Renaissance "château" has opened its doors to visiting kings, dignitaries, presidents, and all those rich and fabulous, including Katherine Hepburn, Truman Capote, and the Beatles. Located at the corner of 5th Ave and Central Park West, it maintains what many would consider the best real estate in the city, ornamenting its prime lot with a full array of marble lobbies, mahogany doors, and over 1,000 crystal chandeliers. The hotel, which recently celebrated

5th Ave at Central Park S
(near 59th St)
212-759-3000
N R to 5th Ave-59th St,
1 A C B D to
Columbus Circle

DAWAT
Best Argument for High-Class Indian

Opened in 1902, Luna Park was a wildly popular entertainment spot featuring thousands of electric lamps, performing monkeys, and rides on domesticated elephants. Fire damage forced its closure in 1944, but after massive renovation, the grounds were reopened in May 2010 with a fresh array of rides, games, and spectacles. Lunatics can swing up to 50 feet on the Eclipse Pendulum, brave switchback curves on the Tickler, or attempt to keep down their cotton candy on the Electro Spin half pipe. Sandwiched between the notorious Cyclone roller coaster and Deno's Wonder Wheel Amusement Park, the revamped park has muscled its way back into Islanders' hearts. When you're sick of feeling your stomach drop, head next door to get your fortune told or take a picture with a live snake.

Indian
210 E 58th St
(btwn 2nd & 3rd Ave)
212-355-7555
Sun 5:30pm-10pm, Mon-
Thurs 11:30am-2:30pm,
5:30pm-10:30pm,
Fri-Sat 11:30am-2:30pm,
5:30pm-11:15pm
N,Q,R,4,5,6 to 59th St
$$$
*Delivery/Takeout

its 100th birthday, plays central roles in North by Northwest, Sleepless in Seattle, The Great Gatsby and, of course, the ever-beloved children's book Eloise at the Plaza. However, most citygoers will only admire the Beaux Arts décor from afar: rooms, all of which include 24-hour butler services, start at around $700 a night.

Saint Patrick's Cathedral

The largest Gothic-style Catholic cathedral in the United States, the imposing St. Patrick's takes up an entire city block.

460 Madison Ave
(btwn 50th & 51st St)
212-753-2261
Daily 6:30am-8:45pm
E to 5th Ave–53rd St,
6 to 51st St

Constructed in 1858, today the cathedral towers clash strikingly with the skyscrapers of midtown, while the inside is a spacious sanctuary of marble and stained glass. Layered arches open onto the central altar, from which sermons and the three church organs resound during service hours. Besides serving as the seat of New York's Roman Catholic Archdiocese, St. Patrick's is a major destination for both midtown worshipers and out-of-town visitors. Lying in the shadow of the great nave, the outside steps are dotted with pedestrians on their lunch breaks and awed tourists craning their necks for better views of the full 330-foot spire.

United Nations

Along a stretch of riverside international territory lies New York's very own province of peace. The U.N. houses its 192 member-nations in four central buildings, including the Sec-

United Nations Plaza,
1st Ave
(btwn 42nd and 48th St)
212-963-8687
Tours Mon-Fri
9:45am-4:45pm
4 5 6 7 S to
42nd St-Grand Central
Adults $16, Students $11

retariat skyscraper, an exemplar of modernist architecture. Both guided and audio tours take visitors past floors of gifts from neighbor countries, a roomful of translators simultaneously spouting different languages, and the General Assembly, where representatives convene to discuss the most crucial issues in the world. Within the imposing complex is a comprehensive sculpture park, with work originating from all over the globe. Pause a moment here, or get a coffee and a personalized stamp on the Public Concourse, where the territory's own post office squats between gift shops.

The Waldorf-Astoria

Conrad N. Hilton proclaimed in 1932 that the Waldorf-Astoria is the "greatest of them all," and many

301 Park Ave (at 50th St)
6 to 51st St

maintain that this still holds true. The present 1400-room art deco building began as two separate hotels that were connected by a corridor in 1897, and was relocated to Park Ave after 34 years. Franklin Delano Roosevelt was a frequent guest—during his presidency a special track at Grand Central Terminal took him directly here. If you've ever enjoyed a Waldorf salad, you too have taken part in a bit of the hotel's history, as its chefs were the original creators. As famous for its central position in the highbrow social scene as for its transformative influence on the hotel industry, the Waldorf=Astoria has always been, in the words of a 1900 Harper's Bazaar article, "the chosen gathering place of New York society, which comes here to see and to be observed."

EAT

2nd Avenue Deli

Jewish Delicatessen

162 E 33rd St (btwn Lexington & 3rd Ave)
212-689-9000
Sun-Thurs 7am-12am,
Fri-Sat 7am-4am
6 to 33rd St
$$

Pictures of famous performers from Yiddish theater hang from the walls of this kosher deli, a constant reminder of its rich cultural history. Although the restaurant recently relocated, it still serves all the classics of Jewish cuisine, like the much-celebrated sandwiches stuffed with layer upon layer of cold cuts including hot pastrami, roasted turkey, tongue, and salami. An extensive salad bar, with a variety of coleslaws and

TINSEL TRADING COMPANY
Classiest Tassels

If beauty is in the details, Tinsel Trading Company keeps the prettiest inventory in Manhattan. Devoted to the small touches that really make an outfit—trims, buttons, buckles, feathers, ribbons, and fringe—the family-owned business specializes in vintage finds. Sort through the collection of '50s-era raffle and straw ornaments from Italy, hand-twisted gold cords and tassels, and antique chenille flower appliqués dating as far back as the 1880s. Founded in 1933, the Company manufactured metal threads for soldiers' uniforms during World War II. Today, the Bergoffen family store is endorsed by none other than Martha Stewart, a long-time patron.

1 W 37th St (btwn 5th & 6th Ave)
212-730-1030
Mon-Fri 9:45am-6pm,
Sat 11am-5pm
N,Q,R to 34th St-Herald Sq

pickled vegetables, provides the quintessential kosher accompaniments to any meal, like the beet and sweet onion salad or the homemade sour and half-sour pickles. While the takeout bar is always well-staffed, some traditional dishes, like gefilte fish or chopped chicken liver with onions, are best enjoyed in the dining room with a homemade matzoh ball soup to open the appetite.

Gilt Restaurant
New American

Housed in the Villard Mansion of the New York Palace Hotel, Gilt is unabashedly opulent: you'll have to pass through wrought-iron gates and ascend a sweeping staircase to reach the main dining

455 Madison Ave
(btwn 50th and 51st St)
212-891-8100
Tues-Thurs
5:30pm-9:30pm,
Fri-Sat 5:30pm-10pm
E to 5th Ave-53rd St,
6 to 51st St
$$$$

room, which is graced with rich oak panels, mosaic tile floors, a marble fireplace, and intricate ceiling moldings. The seasonal menu—available in three, five, and seven courses—is just as sumptuous. An extremely attentive staff will help you navigate Justin Bogle's reinterpretations of traditional dishes, which innovatively mingle abstruse ingredients: heirloom tomatoes are accented with a strip of wild boar and an olive oil sponge, chicken is paired with truffles and a foie gras-infused piece of sausage, dry-aged strip loin is served with potato terrine, bone marrow custard, and morel mushrooms. The flavors are rich but not overwhelming, especially when complemented with wines from the 2,100+ selection and the mouthwatering assortment of breads, all of which are baked daily in the kitchen at 3pm. This is fine dining at its utmost finest, but with none of the pretension.

Oms/b
Japanese

Make sure to come here with clean hands, because fingers are not just accepted—they're encouraged. Similar to sushi, Omusubi is cooked rice packed together with a variety of fillings and toppings to give flavor. The difference be-

tween the two is that Omusubi is an easy-to-carry food, perfect as a quick bite to eat—which probably accounts for why oms/b is particularly packed during lunchtime

156 E 45th St (btwn 3rd & Lexington Ave)
212-922-9788
4 5 6 7 S to 42nd St-Grand Central
$

hours. Or maybe the crowds come for the Special Set (three rice balls, appetizer, and soup), which is only $7.25 from 11:30am to 2pm. Get the spicy tuna, chili shrimp, kinpira (cooked burdock, carrot, ad renkon) rice balls, the rice noodle salad appetizer, and udon noodle soup for a winning combination. Or swing by after work to pick up a Japanese tea and a traditional sesame panna cotta snack.

MIDTOWN EAST
best chinese places

Grand Sichuan Eastern- Grand Sichuan's outrageously spicy dishes are a favorite among Chinese locals looking for something authentic. *1049 2nd Ave, 212-355-5855, Sun 12pm-10pm, Mon-Fri 11am-10pm, Sat 12pm-11pm, 6 to 51st St, E, V to Lexington Ave $$*

Peking Duck House- The chefs here have mastered the art of the Peking duck, roasting the succulent bird to moist but crispy perfection, and bringing it whole to the table. *236 E 53rd St, 212-759-8260, Sun-Thurs 11:45am-10:30pm, Fri-Sat 11:30am-11:30pm, E, V to Lexington Ave $$$*

Chin Chin- This trendy restaurant offers Chinese cuisine with an innovative twist. It's no place for takeout—enjoy a tea-smoked duck or sake shiitake chicken in the chic dining room. *216 E 49th St, 212-888-4555, Sun 12pm-11pm, Mon-Sat 12pm-12am, 4,5,6 to 51st St $$$*

Gossip Girl Blair Waldorf takes her name from renowned luxury hotel the Waldorf=Astoria.

PLAY

Rink Bar

Cocktails, Bar

601 5th Ave
(btwn 49th & 50th St)
212-332-7620
Sun 10am-9pm,
Mon-Fri 11:30am-10pm,
Sat 11am-11pm
❶ to 50th St
$$

Situated on the grounds of Rockefeller Center's winter ice rink, this chic outdoor restaurant-cum-bar attracts an unpredictable crowd that ranges from tourists to cubicle types. A canopy covers the bar, and after a few piña coladas, you'll get that familiar rush—it's summertime, and the living is easy. Should you get hungry, the bar serves food from the Rock Center Café. The drinks, though a tad expensive, are no more overpriced than they would be anywhere else in the area.

The Ginger Man

Beer Bar

The impressive selection of nearly 70 draughts and bottles gives true brew fanatics a chance to branch out, pick the brains of the well-trained, knowledgeable staff, and find themselves a new favorite. Ginger Man's extensive options are organized

11 E 36th St
(near Park Ave)
212-532-3740
Sun 3pm-12am,
Mon-Thurs 11:30am-2am,
Fri 11:30am-4am,
Sat 12:30am-4am
❷ ❹ ❺ to 34th St,
❻ to 33rd St
$$

by country and type: beer connoisseurs can tour the menu without sipping the same style twice. Luckily, the bar is large enough to accommodate the weekend pilgrims that flock from all over to this Midtown beer mecca. Past the long, dark wood bar and row of booths is the back lounge, which resembles a gentleman's scotch room, outfitted with relics of taverns past. Have a seat here and sip a Southampton Abbey Dubbel or pair a flight of four draught samples with the special house hot dog wrapped in bacon and topped with melted cheddar.

CHE

What started out as a family farm in 1750 transformed into a bustling shipping hub by 1900, and is now a Manhattan enclave of high art. Yet Chelsea hasn't eluded its industrial past, much as it would perhaps like to. Instead, its rugged history has been translated into an aesthetic of recycled sophistication and juxtaposed extremes. Nowhere else can you find a few blocks separating Roy Lichtenstein from low-income housing, or decades-old bodegas from high-fashion brasseries.

In the early 20th century, the neighborhood's piers made it an industrial center that housed a mostly Irish population of longshoremen. Warehouses, freight lines, and even uranium storage facilities abounded. When flying eventually replaced shipping, the formerly essential docks stood abandoned and decaying. But while industry declined, the cultural scene boomed. The still-standing Chelsea Hotel was the long-term home of counter-culture legends in the '50s, '60s, and '70s. Behind its doors, Bob Dylan wrote Sad Eyed Lady of the Lowlands, Jack Kerouac penned On the Road, and Sid Vicious maybe/probably stabbed his girlfriend Nancy Spungen. Allen Ginsberg, Jimi Hendrix, Patti Smith, and Robert Mapplethorpe also checked in at the Chelsea during downtown's bohemian heyday.

The stretch of 8th Ave running through Chelsea became a thriving center of gay culture in the late '70s and '80s, earning the neighborhood a reputation for quartering the bronzed and muscled "Chelsea boys," many of whom stuck around to form the area's current large

SEA

gay population. Finally, in the 1990s, New York's established visual art community made the move from SoHo to West Chelsea. Since then, over 350 galleries and countless artist studios have moved into the area bounded by 10th and 11th Avenues and 18th and 28th Streets. Walking these streets during Thursday night gallery openings means a wade through a sea of critics, gallerists, and fashionistas clutching glasses of chardonnay and hefty checkbooks, or otherwise equipped with compensating egos. Older, suit-wearing collectors admire the latest exhibit alongside self-important art school dropouts in bright yellow overalls and models running on liquid lunches.

Today the neighborhood is postindustrial, but many traces of the past have been revamped rather than removed. The Chelsea Piers no longer receive freighters and luxury liners, but were transformed into a colossal entertainment and sports complex in 1994. Similarly, what were once elevated train tracks is now the High Line Park: in 2006, the rusted, 30-foot-high rail lines were replaced by native flower plantings, benches, and a walking path.

More than ever, Chelsea is growing into a center of dining, nightlife, fashion, and art. Recent years have seen a construction boom, with destinations like the Chelsea Market bringing more tourists to the neighborhood. Projects going up by Frank Gehry and Jean Nouvel might ultimately turn the neighborhood a little more new than old, but for now Chelsea's charm is still the unpolished history that lies behind its recently refined exterior.

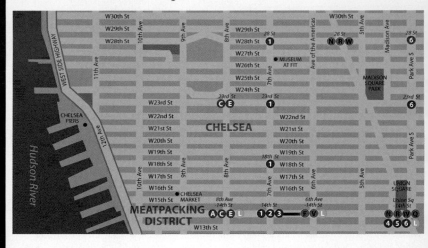

EXPLORE

Chelsea Art Museum

At first glance, this arts space looks like another too-big-for-your-budget stop on one of Chelsea's crowded art walks. But a second glance reveals that the museum distinguishes

556 W 22nd St
(at 11th Ave)
212-255-0719
Tues-Sat 11am-6pm,
Thurs 11am-8pm
C E to 23rd St
Adults $8, Students $4

itself from the neighborhood scene. With three floors of exhibition space, CAM aims to bring little-known international artists to New York's attention, and takes a special interest in timely political themes. Its permanent collection, set off by the natural light that pours through warehouse windows, includes work by Jean Miotte, Joan Mitchell, and the abstract European school L'Informel. Programs include rooftop yoga and, in the summers, a rooftop film series. Yet what really sets the Chelsea Art Museum apart is its "ambassadors"—in lieu of information plaques, friendly volunteers offer information and lead discussions. This helpful approach makes the CAM a nice starting point for those who appreciate art but are not necessarily well-versed in art history.

Chelsea Piers

Originally a passenger ship terminal (and the never-reached destination of the Titanic), Chelsea's four piers were transformed in 1994 into what is today a monstrous $120 million sports, dining,

Piers 59-62:
W 17th-W 23rd St &
the Hudson River
212-336-6666
Hours and prices vary
A C E L to
8th Ave-14th St

and entertainment complex. Try your hand at rock climbing, sailing, and ice skating, all under the same roof, or train on a soccer, football, or golf team. The Sports Center offers a more traditional workout with fitness classes, a swimming pool, cardio and strength training equipment, and an indoor track, while pleasure-seekers can drop the kids off at youth hockey or summer camp and head to the full-service spa. Those who prefer gin to Gatorade can sip cocktails at the 32-lane bowling alley, which features an electric blue bar. With an ice theater, four restaurants, and a brewery, this adult playground is an all-encompassing destination for your morning workout or your TGIF celebration.

Rubin Museum of Art

The only museum in the city dedicated exclusively to Himalayan culture, the Rubin makes a good crash course for novices of Eastern art and religion. Its collection, the largest holding of Himalayan religious

150 W 17th St
(btwn 6th & 7th Ave)
212-620-5000
Mon, Thurs 11am-5pm,
Wed 11am-7pm,
Fri 11am-10pm,
Sat-Sun 11am-6pm
❷❸ ❻❶ to 14th St
Adults $10, Students $2

art in the Western hemisphere, features works dating as far back as the 12th century from Nepal, Tibet, Bhutan, India, Mongolia, and China. The 25,000-square foot space is organized thematically, not chronologically, around a six-story spiral staircase, originally designed for Barneys by Andrée Putman. History buffs can kill a few hours in the museum's many alcoves, each containing books and computer resources to better explain the political context of the artwork. Admission is free on Fridays from 6-10 pm—come for a festive tapas menu, a wine and martini bar, live music, and special gallery tours and programs.

Trapeze School of New York

For the best view of the Statue of Liberty, you need nerves of steel: New York's daredevils can step off a 23-foot high platform atop Pier 40 and catch a glance of the East River as

Pier 40
(at West & Houston St)
212-242-8769
❶ to Houston St
Classes $35-70
Additional locations:
518 W 30th St and
Governors Island

they soar headfirst through the air. From May to October, skilled instructors give flying trapeze classes open to beginners and experienced athletes alike—in the past, TSNY has trained students from the ages of six to 82. The School

THE MEATPACKING DISTRICT

Hundreds of slaughterhouses and packing plants called the Meatpacking District home in 1900, but today you're more likely to find a pack of glamazons smoking outside of the latest trendier-than-thou nightclub than a meat market of the Upton Sinclair variety. In the 1980s the area was an infamous hangout for drug dealers, prostitutes, and a gay BDSM community, but throughout the next decade they were supplanted by high-end designer boutiques and glitzy restaurants, attracted by the still-quaint cobblestone streets and low rents. Today, naught but an occasional meat hook is visible among riverfront high rises. Some of the city' hardest-to-get-into nightlife spots reside here, including **APT** *(419 W 13th St)*, which hides behind an unmarked entrance and surly bouncers. Gastronomes in stilettos frequent the legendary **Pastis** *(9 9th Ave)*, which nearly perfectly replicates a 1930s Parisian brasserie and serves up classics like steak frites and oysters. Parked beneath the High Line is **The Standard Grill** *(848 Washington St)*, a good place to get bistro cuisine and a look at fashion industry honchos and A-list actors.

also offers classes in silks and rope (the most popular, but also requiring the most upper body strength), static trapeze, trampoline, and aerial conditioning. For New Yorkers willing to take the plunge, there isn't a better place to find an adrenaline rush combined with a workout.

SHOP

Angel Street Thrift Shop

Angel Street Thrift looks more like a showroom at Bloomie's than a second-hand store, but don't let sleek glass display tables and the typically anti-thrift cleanliness fool you: high-end designer brands are sold

118 W 17th St
(btwn 6th & 7th Ave)
212-229-0546
Sun 12pm-5pm,
Mon-Fri 11am-7pm,
Sat 10am-6pm
❶❷❸❻❺❻ t to 14th St,
❶ to 18th St

here for surprisingly reasonable prices. YSL and Marc Jacobs pieces run at $50-$80 each—truly a steal—while brands like Zara, H&M, and Banana Republic sell at under $15. Find coffee table paraphanelia, wall art, and kitchen knick knacks neatly stacked against shelf after shelf of Burberry checks. Proceeds from the store benefit those with substance abuse, mental illness, and HIV/AIDS, so feel doubly pleased about dropping $40 for gently used Prada pumps.

Chelsea Market

This shopping complex gives the traditional mall a sophisticated Chelsea makeover. In typical Chelsea style, it presents high fashion and

75 9th Ave
(btwn 15th & 16th St)
Sun 8am-6pm,
Mon-Fri 7am-9pm,
Sat 7am-7pm
Ⓐ Ⓒ Ⓔ Ⓛ to 14th St

dining in an industrial setting. A long alley of brick columns and overhead pipes that once belonged to a National Biscuit Factory contrast the 35 vendors selling their high-end wares. While the Market is more food court than retail space, there's a great deal to keep any shopper occupied: multiple high-end bakeries, restaurants, takeout lunch places, and grocery stores, as well as a wine, a book, a basket, a chocolate, a lobster, and a flower store. The venue even functions as an art exhibition space and music performance venue at times. Join tourists and local businessmen alike in browsing, shopping, tasting, and eating at the trendy and always bustling Chelsea Market.

Mantiques Modern

With everything from Hermes cigar boxes to World War II-era binoculars packed into a single small aisle, Mantiques Modern resembles a storage space for the entire 20th century. Apothecary bottles are stacked on antique barber chairs, while what seems to be a giant

The Chelsea Hotel was the long-term residence of numerous artists and musicians in the '60s and '70s, including Bob Dylan, Janis Joplin, Patti Smith, Leonard Cohen, Dylan Thomas, and Robert Mapplethorpe.

elephant skull looms between abstract photography prints. The store's usual clientele includes interior designers and architects, but anyone is welcome to browse—it's the

146 W 22nd St
(btwn 6th & 7th Aves)
212-206-1494
Mon-Fri 10:30am-
6:30pm,
Sat-Sun 11am- 7pm
Ⓒ Ⓔ Ⓕ Ⓕ to 23rd St

perfect place to pick up a one-of-a-kind statement (read: oddball) piece for the home without the designer mark-up price. Even so, prices range from under a hundred to the hundreds of thousands, and a genuine Roy Lichtenstein sculpture is mixed in among vintage teddy bears and handmade robots.

Pippin Jewelry

If you don't have a wealthy aunt from whom to inherit trunks full of costume jewelry, Pippin has everything you would desire at not much more than free. The

112 West 17th St
(btwn 6th & 7th Ave)
212-505-5159
Sun 12pm-6pm,
Mon-Sat 11am-7pm
Ⓞ Ⓐ Ⓑ Ⓕ Ⓛ to 14th St,
Ⓞ to 18th St

crowded, exposed brick shopping space displays Victorian coin bracelets, cameo brooches, clip-on baubles, and Mexican silver cuff links on wooden armoires. The collection ranges from pre-1900s to the 1980s, while prices start at $1—be sure to rummage through the "$5

drawers"—and rise to $1200 for diamonds and rubies. Owners Rachel and Stephen Cooper gather thousands of pieces from estate sales along the East Coast, and also stock lace gloves, felt top hats, and delicate clutches wreathed in seed pearls. Once you've had your fill of cigar-band rings and beaded Japanese collars, venture across the courtyard to Pippin Home, the Coopers' vintage furniture store.

EAT

Blossom Restaurant   *Global, Brunch*
Blossom's food, like that of all other vegan res-taurants in the city, is fastidiously guilt-free: it's prepared from organic, mostly fair trade, and strictly meat-free ingredients. Despite these strict requirements, one cannot taste a single compromise in the final product. The French toast pairs fresh, crisp berries in perfect proportion with the fluffiest bread this side of $20, drizzled in authentic maple syrup for a perfect breakfast or brunch. More imaginative dishes are equally well-executed, such as the avocado purée gaspatcho that will

187 9th Ave (at 21st St)
212-627-1144
Daily 5pm-10pm, Brunch
Fri-Sun 12pm-2:45pm
1 **A** **C** **E** to 23rd St
$$

HIGH LINE PARK
most rewarding walk-up

A defunct elevated freight railway hardly seems an obvious place for kids to play or lovers to snuggle, but the High Line Park, opened in 2009, is actually one of the most picture-perfect spots in the city. With the train tracks' abandoned skeleton peeking out from untamed swaths of purple coneflowers and birch groves, the High Line's 30-foot-high landscape is designed to have a look of disrepair, as though visitors have

Gansevoort St to 34th St
(btwn 10th & 11th Ave)
Daily 7am-10pm
L,A,C,E to 14th St-
8th Ave

stumbled upon a ruined paradise. An amphitheatre offers views of Chelsea high rises, the piers, and the Empire State Building in one sweeping glance. The park, the backers of which include Philip Falcone and Diane von Furstenberg, has sparked something of a development renaissance in the area: more than 30 projects, including an expansion of the Whitney designed by Renzo Piano, are in the planning stages.

CHEAP EATS
best gallery tour pitstops

Ronnybrook Milk Bar- The Columbia County dairy farm brings organic ice cream and milkshakes to Chelsea Market, but also offers light dishes for lunch which make use of the farm's fresh products, like an asparagus and farmer's cheese omelette. *75 9th Ave, 212-741-6455, Mon-Fri 8:30am-8pm, Sat-Sun 9am-7pm, A, C, E to 14th St $*

People's Pops- This quaint stand in Chelsea Market is famous for its frozen treats made from fresh, locally-grown herbs and fruit. Try the seasonal special of the week in popsicle or shaved ice form or the popular raspberry-basil. *425 W 15th St, 212-111-1111, Daily 10am-8pm, A, C, E, L to 14th St-8th Ave $*

Le Zie- This neighborhood favorite prepares refined Italian classics like osso buco with sage-infused marrow and oven-roasted tomato sauce with spaghetti and meatballs, all of which can be delivered right to your door. *172 7th Ave, 212-206-8686, Mon-Fri 12pm-11pm, Sat-Sun 11am-11pm, 1 to 18th St $$*

Lezzette Mediterranean Cucina- This lunch stop has the standard pizza and salads of any upscale New York deli, but the hot food counter in the back is the way to go. It offers generous portions of grilled kebabs, rice, and roasted veggies for a reasonable price. *369 W 34th St, 212-244-8301, Daily 6:30am-9pm, 1,2,3,A,C,E to 34th St $$*

Tebaya- Extra crispy fried chicken wings and potato mochi collectively make the quintessential Japanese fast food meal at this small, quirky snack bar. *144 W 19th St, 212-924-3335, Mon-Fri 11:30am-9:45pm, Sat 12pm-9:45pm, 1 to 18th St $*

make lovers of the creamy fruit swoon. Blossom proves that a dedication to great taste can make both veteran vegetarians and carnivores fans of the vegan kitchen.

El Quinto Pino
Basque, Tapas

401 W 24th St
(btwn 9th & 10th Ave)
212-206-6900
Breakfast
Mon-Fri 8am-2pm,
Dinner Sun 5pm-11pm,
Mon-Thurs 5pm-12am,
Fri-Sat 5pm-1am
C E to 23rd St
$$

Another venture from the Chelsea tapas kings Belz, Dawes, and Raij, El Quinto Pino is instantly recognizable via its signature marbled horseshoe-shaped bar. The small rustic storefront conceals no cavernous, subterranean rooms; rather, a tiny but well-used space awaits the gathering crowd of local foodies open to the bar side of tapas. Here, the traditional Spanish and Basque menu gets a modest global makeover—overplayed classics are traded for sophisticated concoctions like the uni panini, a lovingly buttered baguette topped with a touch of wasabi and chunks of vibrant orange sea urchin. Cocktails are equally as inventive, with choices like the Pomada, a frozen blend of lemonade, gin and basil. El Quinto remains loyal to its roots with a rotating "Turistico" menu, which features dishes from a new region of Spain every month.

Matsuri
Japanese

369 W 16th St
(near 9th Ave)
212-243-6400
Sun-Wed 6pm-12am,
Thurs-Sat 6pm-1am
A C E L to 8th Ave-
14th St
$$$

This hangar-sized restaurant holds fast to a grandeur that has all but disappeared in leaner times. Its Japanese-inspired décor is edged with modern taste: giant misshapen paper lamps highlight the rough-grained wooden tables and large format bottles of sake that line the walls. The menu shows a commensurate level of refinement that is attentive to the importance of fresh ingredients—fish is flown in daily from Japan. The standard sushi bar is made exceptional by unparalleled freshness and masterfully prepared rice that yields effortlessly to the bite, crumbling away. However, the entrees showcase the chef's vision with options such as the Sake Marinated Black Cod—a lightly charred filet, steeped in a complex sake, soy and ginger sauce, so flaky that it seems like a pastry. The dish blooms when tasted alongside one of the premium sakes from the restaurant's discursive list

Scarpetta   *Italian*

Scarpetta literally means "little shoe" in Italian, but it also refers to the piece of bread used to sponge up the last bit of sauce off a dish. This appropriately named, moderate-sized white restaurant on the edge of the Meatpacking District gracefully contrasts its posh surroundings. The opulent yet tranquil interior contains a relaxed bar in front of a spacious dining area illuminated by subtle skylights—the ideal setting for a late evening dine. Chef Scott Conant prepares a masterful lineup of classic and innovative dishes, all of which are made in-house with imported Italian ingredients. Such authenticity makes the traditional spaghetti a signature dish, prepared shy of al dente and served in hot, bubbling tomato

355 W 14th St
(at 9th Ave)
212-691-0555
Sun 5:30pm-10:30pm,
Mon-Thurs
5:30pm-11pm,
Fri-Sat 5:30pm-12am
Ⓐ Ⓒ Ⓔ Ⓛ to 8th Ave-
14th St
$$$

chelsea
UNDER $20

Start the morning with something you've never seen before at **Gallery David Zwirner** *(525 W 19th St)* and **Tanya Bonakdar Gallery** *(521 W 21st St)*, two showcases of international and progressive artists.

For a palate cleanser that smacks more of Lower East Side culture, the **Daniel Reich Gallery** *(537 W 23rd St)* is young and provocative, and displays several alums of the 2010 Whitney Biennial.

For a lunch break, **Bottino Take Out** *(246 10th Ave)* offers inexpensive Italian-inspired sandwiches, soups, and salads. Take your prosciutto to the giant lawn at **Hudson River Park's Pier 64** *(24th St & the River)* and enjoy the view outside gallery doors.

After lunch, get to Chelsea's heavy hitters: the **Gagosian Gallery** *(555 W 24th St)* curates museum-caliber shows and exhibits everything from Monet's Water Lilies to Cy Twombly, and the **Barbara Gladstone Gallery** *(515 W 24th St)* screens films by Matthew Barney, a living legend.

For dinner stop by **Co.** *(230 9th Ave)* for thin-crusted Neapolitan pizza on your way to **People's Improv Theater** *(154 W 29th St)* to unwind after a long day of white walls.

The Village People's 1978 hit "YMCA" was inspired by the McBurney YMCA that was once located on W 23rd St.

sauce with basil. For the true Scarpetta experience, ask your server for wine pairings—the rare Torre Dei Beati is sure to leave any rosé-lover impressed.

Tia Pol
Tapas, Bar

From its wooden, rustic interior to the casual yet fun atmosphere, Tia Pol perfectly executes all that is necessary in a modern wine and tapas bar. The food here is, as it should be, bite-sized and cheap, yet oh-so-filling and deli-

205 10th Ave (at 22nd St)
212-675-8805
Sun 11am-3pm, 6pm-10:30pm, Mon 5:30pm-11pm, Tues-Fri 12pm-3pm, 5:30pm-11pm, Sat 11am-3pm, 6pm-12am
❶ ❻ ❺ to 23rd St
$$

cious. The drink selection encompasses a surprisingly good and ever-rotating choice of rich and robust Spanish wines—perfect to pair with the spicy and savory lamb skewers and chorizo with chocolate that overflow from the kitchen. There are few places in Chelsea better suited to entertain a small group looking for a foreign culinary adventure.

Txikito
Tapas, Basque, Spanish

The second restaurant from power couple Alex Raij and Eder Montero (of Tia Pol), Txikito—pronounced "Chee-KEE-toe"—is a minuscule yet standout tapas joint serving authentic, refined, and small-portioned Spanish food in a comfy and casual setting. The menu is divided into four sections: bar snacks, Basque cana-

DICKSON'S FARMSTAND MEATS
best place to join the cult of meat lovers

Housed in the unique Chelsea Market, Dickson's has found an equally singular niche: an artisan quality butcher at the retail level. Local, sustainable farms provide the best of their harvest; beautifully marbled cuts line a glass case that emanates a visible excellence. The open butcher shop offers interested meat fanatics a view of the humble staff masterfully carving away. The shop also runs a whole animal program, making use

Market, Sandwiches

75 9th Ave
(btwn W 15th & 16th St)
212-242-2630
Mon-Fri 10am-8pm,
Sat-Sun 10am-7pm
A/C/E/L to 14th St-8th Ave
$$$

of every bit of meat—the lesser cuts going to gourmet sausage or sloppy joes served at lunch. The lunch is nothing short of stellar, offering a rotating buffet of options such as pulled pork and meatball subs served between noon and 2:30pm. The roast beef sandwich, a pile of vivid supple meat that manages to contrast fluffy pieces of rye, will win your heart—it's delicate without sacrificing the carnal push against the teeth.

pés, cold items, and hot items. While your server will encourage you to consider one of the many entrée-sized specials, you mustn't forget that the real pleasure here is in sharing an array of delicately plated tapas. Vegetarians beware, as the dishes are largely fish-and-fatty-meat-focused, garnished with exceptional Spanish cheeses and vibrant Greenmarket salads. The lamb meatballs in minted broth are a standout, as are the crisp fries with spicy cod roe mayo—an interesting riff on the traditional patatas bravas.

240 9th Ave
(near 25th St)
212-242-4730
Sun 5pm-11pm,
Tues-Thurs
12pm-3pm, 5pm-12am,
Fri 12pm-3pm, 5pm-1am,
Sat 5pm-1am
 C E to 23rd St
$$

PLAY

Brass Monkey

Beer Bar

55 Little W 12th St
(near 11th Ave)
212-675-6686
Daily 12pm-4am
A C E L to 14th St
$$

Packed in the early evenings with trendy business folk, young creative types, and thirsty Chelsea locals, Brass Monkey is the place to be for an after-work drink. Ascend to the rooftop bar to watch the sun set over the Hudson, or hang downstairs in one of the cozy candlelit rooms. The open brick walls and rich wooden booths are reminiscent of Ireland, as is the food, with menu picks like bangers and

manhattan.chelsea.play

mash, mussels, and shepherd's pie. The beer selection is even more impressive—there's 20 on draught and over 75 in total, and featured brews change to fit the season. But if you aren't in the mood for an ale or a lager, opt for the Brass Lemonade cocktail, a refreshing blend of sweet and sour with the kick of Absolute Citron.

Club Rush
LGBT, Nightclub

18
579 6th Ave
(btwn 16th & 17th St)
212-243-6100
F **L** to 14th St,
1 to 18th St
Cover $10-20
$$

Rampant twink fun awaits at this refuge for beautiful youths. Coined as the only 18+ club in the City, Rush is usually the first stop for new college students looking to experience the quintessential gay dance club. There are weekly themed parties like the Black Out Beach Party, when a pool is set up on the lower level, or Superhero Saturday, when entry is half price if you dress up, so it never feels like a typical club. Explore the three colorful floors or have a smoke in the gated outdoor area, but make sure you're ready to move. On any given weekend, Club Rush is a great place to shimmy off your freshman 15 among bright lights and vibrant go-go dancers.

Splash
LGBT, Nightclub

50 W 17th St
(btwn 5th & 6th Ave)
212-691-0073
L **N** **Q** **R** **4** **5** **6** to
14th St-Union Square
$$

With its flashing lights and blaring top 40 hits, this nightclub is not for the shy or those unwilling to unleash their wild side, so be forewarned: you will have your butt pinched, and someone may try to dance on you. Be prepared to pay a hefty cover, but with high-energy music and beefy go-go dancers, the price is well worth a full night of shenanigans. Yet despite all the testosterone-driven bustle, Splash provides a great fix to anyone yearning for an eventful night. And for those bound by a black X on their hands, Campus Thursday is a weekly party for Splash's not-yet-ripe crowd—admission is free with a college ID.

The Standard Hotel Biergarten
Beer Garden

Above the Highline stands one of the most happening hotels in Manhattan, and beneath it lies the hotel's Bavarian-inspired beer garden. New Yorkers in everything from board shorts to business suits line up to purchase a ticket (representative of the coins used in Southern Germany) that can be exchanged for one of three draught beers, a sausage, or an oversized pretzel

served by a waitress in Bavarian garb with a modern twist. Crowds fill the long wooden tables, lined between iron subway support beams, or mingle by one of the garden's two bars—one for beer, one for liquor. With no reservations, no dress code, and no cover, this swanky hotel has created a red brick refuge for the summertime.

848 Washington St
(at 13th St)
212-645-4646
Sun 12pm-12am, Mon-
Thurs 4pm-12am, Fri
4pm-1am, Sat 12pm-1am
Ⓐ Ⓒ Ⓔ Ⓛ to 8th Ave-
14th St

The Frying Pan   *Bar*

After spending three years at the bottom of the Chesapeake bay, this lightship was resurrected by the gods of booze and revelry as the ultimate floating dive bar. The boat is permanently docked to a railroad car barge with multiple decks that have sweeping views in all directions—at sunset, climb up the long spiral staircase to reach the 360 degree observation deck. The Palisades cliffs serve as the backdrop to the stage in the back, which hosts live jazz several nights a week. Though Frying Pan is grungy, wet, and not altogether safe for high heels, it's frequented by young professionals who dress up for a night on the town. Enjoy seafood and barbecue classics at the grill, and be sure to explore the boat's rusted bowels to find the old sailors' quarters—perfect for impromptu make-out sessions.

Pier 66, W 26th St
(West Side Highway)
212-989-6363
Daily 12pm-12am
(May-Oct)
Ⓒ Ⓔ to 23rd St
$

Upright Citizens Brigade   *Comedy Club*

Best known for its Sunday night ASSS-CAT 3000 shows (featuring special guests from SNL and Conan), this improv and sketch comedy theater showcases the freshest funny faces with affordable shows seven nights a week. Founded by Second City alums like Amy Poehler in 1996, UCB maintains a spirit of community through its many sought after classes, including Sketch Comedy Writing, Improv Basics, and long-form improv study called "Harold." Make sure to reserve space ahead of time and come early—seats are assigned on a first come, first serve basis.

18·
307 W 26th St
(near 8th Ave)
212-366-9176
❶ to 28th St,
Ⓒ Ⓔ to 23rd St
$$

GRAM

In a city that worships at the altar of progress, Gramercy is a district whose present character is still wholly defined by its past. Here, historical landmarks are almost as frequent as "I<3NY" t-shirt vendors are in Times Square, and immaculately preserved buildings are called home by the downtown patrician set. Even though a number of chain stores and office buildings have stealthily instituted themselves recently, Gramercy still clings to one persisting original characteristic—exclusiveness.

Development in the area began in 1831, when lawyer Samuel Ruggles proposed a private square to replace the untamed swampland covering the area, with Gramercy Park as the centerpiece of the new construction. Following the turn of the century, some of New York's first apartment buildings cannibalized the neighborhood's old low-rises. Then came one of the city's earliest skyscrapers (the triangular, ultra-iconic Flatiron Building) and, in 1963, the world's tallest building at the time (the octagonal MetLife Tower). Many of Gramercy's denizens had money to burn and put it towards charitable and arts organizations, making the district a hub of philanthropic societies in the late 19th and early 20th centuries. Socially conscious groups like the Federation of Protestant Welfare Agencies existed alongside the exclusive creative societies that the neighborhood is now known for. Still standing today is the Player's Club, a society founded by actor Edwin Boothe, an influential man-about-town in

ERCY

his own right despite being the brother of Abraham Lincoln's assassin. The Club continues to support theater and the arts as a secondary pursuit to its main purpose as a social meeting place, and draws a velvet rope far more exclusive than any in the Meatpacking District.

Some things have changed on the streets—buggies have become yellow taxis, commercial buildings have risen, and any bohemian mystery the area once had has been driven out with apparent finality. In the boisterous '80s, office space and chain stores began to absorb the non-historical sites and many public spaces fell into disrepair, though not nearly to the degree of neighboring locales. Since the new millennium, Gramercy has committed to the upkeep of both old and new spaces, renovating Madison Square Park and turning the historic Gramercy Park Hotel into famously luxurious accommodations. And old symbols of affluence retain their grandeur: today, only residents who pay for Gramercy Park's upkeep can step within its fenced bounds, unlocking the gate with keys that change yearly.

Because the well-heeled have an easier time keeping their footing in New York's tumultuous real estate market, the demeanor of the district has been a rare constant in a city known for its continual evolution. Gramercy seems impervious to urban decay, but it basically can't get any richer—what we can expect from this enclave in the future is probably the business of life as usual.

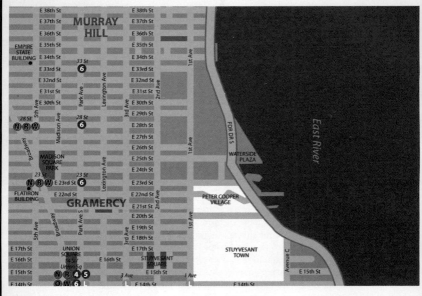

EXPLORE

Gramercy Park Hotel

Since serving as the unglamorous, un-up-tight digs of the likes of The Clash and Bob Dylan, the Gramercy

2 Lexington Ave
(at 21st St)
212-920-3300
6 to 23rd St

Park Hotel has metamorphosed into one of New York's premier luxury hotels. After a 2003 renovation, the space adds exorbitant expense to its old edge, with works by Cy Twombly and Andy Warhol complementing its lush velvets and dark wood. The Rose Bar and Jade Bar, decorated as you might think, offer late night drinks and surprise musical guests, like Rufus Wainwright and Guns N' Roses. Restaurateur Danny Meyer conceived the ground floor trattoria Maialino, which puts a spin on classic Roman cooking. The exclusivity even extends outdoors, where only residents receive keys to Gramercy Park, the fenced-off flower patch visible from every room in the hotel.

Museum of Sex

The Museum of Sex brings together New York City's two defining components: sex and tourism. While small, the exhibits bring to light the ar-tifacts and tidbits of

233 5th Ave
(btwn 27th & 28th St)
212-689-6337
Sun-Thurs 11am-6:30pm,
Sat 11am-8pm
6 6 6 to 28th St
Adults $17, Students $16

history rarely found outside of a Planned Parenthood, from the development of the condom to a sampling of '60s porn. An exhibit on animal intercourse covers dolphin threesomes, bonobo monkey heavy petting, and dragonfly courtship, or lack thereof. Wall plaques are dutifully informative, but most visitors come for the spectacle. The gift shop is easily the most entertaining in the city, with only a little more modesty than the East Village's fetish shops. Free-love adherents, get your carnal viewing on the cheap: check the museum's website for reduced fares and other specials before visiting.

Madison Square Park

busy bit of lawn straddles the epicenter of activity in the Flatiron District, offering everything from comfort food to contemporary

Madison Ave at 23rd St
212-538-5058
Daily 9am-11pm
N R 6 to 23rd St

art. After a major renovation in 2002, the park is now pristine, but only slightly more peaceful than its chaotic surroundings. The emblematic Flatiron Building presides over its southern end with another neighborhood landmark—the deliciously unhealthy Shake Shack. Patrons await on a winding, sometimes hour-long line to savor the Shack's famous hearty burgers and creamy frozen custard. Gardens, grass, and a playground make this 6.2-acre pentagon an attractive option for all New Yorkers. Come in the summer and fall for free concerts and outdoor art exhibitions, in the winter to people-watch.

National Arts Club

The austere Tilden Mansion, home to the National Arts Club and a National Historic Landmark, was founded in 1898 by

15 Gramercy Park S
(btwn 20th & 21st St)
212-674-8824
Daily 12pm-5pm
N R 6 to 23rd St

Charles de Kay, then a literary and art critic for the New York Times. De Kay conceived of the Club as an intellectual gathering spot for American artists, and set about recreating the building as a Victorian exhibit space. Only the best are selected to join the NAC's ranks, which currently count Martin Scorsese and Uma Thurman among them and once included Mark Twain and Theodore Roosevelt. Non-art luminaries can still appreciate the burgundy and stained glass interior on gallery show nights, the only time the NAC opens its doors to the public (all other events are for members only). Business casual dress code is mandatory, upper-crust attitude is optional.

The Gramercy Theater, now a music venue but once a movie house and off-Broadway theater, was the location for The Fugee's "Killing Me Softly" video.

FLATIRON DISTRICT

Named for the logic-defying **Flatiron Building**, one of New York's first skyscrapers, the Flatiron District sits within the boundaries of 23rd and 18th Streets, and 6th Avenue and Park Avenue South. Despite the domination of big businesses in big buildings, the District is undergoing a humanizing mini-renaissance, with new renovations sidling up to old architecture. **Madison Square Park** *(1 Madison Ave)* along the north border offers contemporary outdoor sculpture, and **Shake Shack** *(11 Madison Ave)* dishes out burgers and frozen custard to park picnickers. Look up for the four clock faces of the **Met Life Tower** *(200 Park Ave)*, a historic landmark and fixture of the New York skyline. Take a step off the beaten path to the **Gershwin Hotel** *(7 E 27th St)*, where pop-themed budget accommodations are offset by original Warhol and Lichtenstein pieces littering the lobby walls. But like every New York neighborhood, the residents are the most interesting part—nestled between the funky crowd of the southern neighborhoods and the well-heeled residents to the north, the Flatiron District provides ample opportunity to people watch.

SHOP

Fishs Eddy

In a neighborhood rife with high-class home goods stores, Fishs Eddy holds the spot as the everyman's cheap 'n' classy alternative. Focusing on flatware and other kitchen paraphernalia, this sunny corner store boasts prices that rival Ikea's, but a much more individualistic selection. The Alice in Wonderland and Brooklyn Bridge motifs splashed across the painted glassware trumpet the shop's whimsy, but Fishs Eddy also offers basic china and simple wooden cutlery for those who prefer more conservative trappings. Reprinted cookbooks and antique dishes scavenged from countryside nooks are scattered throughout the crowded but organized space. Don't forget to give the sale tables at the back the once-over, for top-tier pieces at rock-bottom prices. The penny-pinching postgrad yearning for water steins emblazoned with bare-assed men will be delighted.

889 Broadway
(btwn 19th & 20th St)
212-420-9020
Sun 10-9pm,
Mon 10am-9pm,
Tues-Sat 9am-9pm
🅑 🅦 🅖 to 23rd St

Idlewild Books

For every tourist ogling the grandeur of New York City, there is a harried native looking to escape—at least for a little while. Idlewild Books is the place for every would-be world traveler who wants to stay informed, as its two stories are stocked with country guides, paperbacks full of trip advice, and city handbooks. There's also opportunity for a less literal, more literary voyage: a guide to modern Moscow sits alongside Dostoevsky's Crime and Punishment, and a book on Parisian walking tours is accompanied by a tome on verlan, the French slang du jour. If you're looking to trek through a culture verbally instead of physically, Idlewild offers ten-week language courses.

2 W 19th St
(btwn 5th & 6th Ave)
212-414-8888
Sun 12pm-7pm,
Mon-Fri 11:30am-8pm,
Sat 12pm-7pm
🅕🅗 🅦 to 23rd St
🅕 🅛 🅕🅜🅔 to 14th St

EAT

Artisanal

Bistro, French

Picholine's Terrance Brennan is also the chef responsible for this Parisian-style fromagerie and bistro. Ladies who lunch and foodies come together in the beautifully tiled restaurant to share their love of all things related to cheese. The artisanally-made fromage is lovingly kept in the "cave" in the back of the eatery and is diligently paired with one of the 160 wines. Sample a tray

2 Park Ave
(at 32nd St)
212-725-8585
Sun 10:30am-10pm,
Mon-Fri
10:45am-10:45pm,
Sat 10:30am-10:45pm
🅖 to 33rd St
$$$

of cheese—the creamy Roquefort is bold and complex—and an appetizer of an impossibly thin slice of tomato saturated with fine spices and a topping of vegetables. A steak feels just right for the main course—simple, yet quite tender and perfectly peppered. Be sure to order some fromage to go, so that you can continue the cheese-loving party at home.

imported directly from Southern Italy. And there are actually entrées too: anything from the diverse pasta list is highly recommended, as is the sole picatta, which is lightly floured and flavored with lemon, butter, and capers. Be sure to finish off your meal with the housemade limoncello, made in a one-week process developed by the owner's great-grandmother.

Bar Stuzzichini   *Italian, Tapas*

"Stuzzichini" is a Southern Italian term for "little pickings," which are the specialty at this Flatiron tapas bar. Many of the recipes come from the Campania region of

928 Broadway
(btwn 21st & 22nd St)
212-780-5100
Sun 11am-10pm, Mon-Thurs 11:45am-11pm,
Fri-Sat 11am-12am
● ● ● to 23rd St
$$

Italy, and each dish is a tribute to simplicity. Try the fried Jerusalem artichokes in lemon juice, the grilled octopus, or the lightly spiced meatballs in marinara, and you'll find that the fresh ingredients speak for themselves. Even the plate of pure pecorino romano tastes as if it's been

Baoguette   *Vietnamese, Sandwiches*

Pork-lovers rejoice at Baoguette's ambitions to fuse deli-style sandwiches with Vietnamese street food in its version of the banh mi. There is a mouthwatering selection

61 Lexington Ave
(at 25th St)
212-518-4089
Mon-Sat 8am-8pm
● ● ● to 23rd St
$$

of traditional Vietnamese sandwiches, but the banh mi is the star, served on a crisp baguette with carrots, cucumbers, cilantro, chili, pate, mayonnaise, and various cuts of pork, including pork pâté and pork terrine. Devotees to the traditional preparation of the sandwich might

notice a lack of crunch due to their exclusion of pig ears, but at $5 each with an unlimited supply of Sriracha hot sauce, one would be hard-pressed to complain.

Gramercy Tavern — *New American*

42 E 20th St (btwn Broadway & Park Ave S)
212-477-0777
Sun-Thurs 12pm-11pm, Fri-Sat 12pm-12am
N 6 to 23rd St
$$$$

Though Gramercy Tavern's dining room plays host to celebrities and senators every night, the Tavern is a surprisingly relaxed environment. Yes, your napkin is folded each time you leave the table and your tap water comes pre-filtered, but the bustling bar area keeps the atmosphere lively. The menu boasts an unpretentious use of local seasonal ingredients, and although options may be limited, it's impossible to go wrong—each dish is exquisitely prepared and presented. Be forewarned: the chicken with vegetables will put every other chicken you've tasted to shame. Incomparably tender and brimming with flavor, it's carefully cooked sous-vide to maintain its natural jus. The Tavern does not accept reservations and the restaurant's merits are no secret to New York diners, so expect to wait once your name's on the list. Try coming early (5:30pm) or towards the end of service (10:30pm) to avoid a long line.

Hill Country BBQ — *BBQ*

30 W 26th St
(near Broadway)
212-255-4544
Sun-Wed 12pm-10pm, Thurs-Sat 12pm-11pm
N R W to 28th St, **6 V** to 23rd St
$$

Widely rated the best Texas barbecue joint in town, Hill Country is unabashedly kitschy: the silver star tops every menu, ram horns adorn the brick walls, and cute waitresses serve up lagers in denim shorts and cowboy hats. Yet the cavernous and always-packed space consistently draws in displaced Texans looking for quality smoked brisket and live honky tonk. Order a bucket of Lone Star and join the pay-by-the-pound buffet-style food

CHEAP EATS
best indian food in curry hill

Tiffin Wallah- A South Indian restaurant with a lunch buffet that will impress all five senses—and your wallet. All the classics are done well but the Dosas take the cake. *127 E 28th St, 212-685-7301, Mon-Fri 11:30am-3pm, 5pm-10pm, Sat-Sun 12pm-10pm. 6 to 28th St, R to 23rd St $*

Saravanaas- Wonderful for a delicious quick lunch, this high turnover venue will bring out fantastic vegetarian, Southern Indian fare before you can say Mysore Masala Dosa. *81 Lexington Ave, 212-684-7755, Mon-Fri 8:30am-10pm, Sat-Sun 8:30am-10:30pm, 6 to 28th St or R to 23rd St $$*

Dhaba- A modern and evocative dining room that turns out a variety of Indian dishes hailing from all over the vast country. The homemade lemonade is a must! *108 Lexington Ave, 212-679-1284, Sun 12pm-10:30pm, Mon-Thurs 12pm-2am, Fri-Sat 12pm-1am, 6 to 28th St, R to 23rd St $$*

Tamarind- A high-class option, but you do get what you pay for. If you've ever wondered what a great chef would do with Indian food, your answer lies inside the elegant dining room, where plates of grilled fish and lamb are accompanied by spicy basmati rice. *41-43 E 22nd St, 212-674-7400, Lunch: Daily 11:30am-3pm, Dinner: Sun-Thurs 5:30pm-11:30pm, Fri-Sat 5:30pm-12am, 6, R to 23rd St $$$*

Chennai Garden- Strictly vegetarian but don't think for a second that dulls the taste. The food is perfectly spiced and bursting with flavor—try the fried onion bhaji served with a spicy mint sauce. *129 E 27th St, 212-689-1999, Mon-Fri 11:30am-3pm and 5pm-10pm, Sat-Sun 12pm-10pm, 6 to 28th St, R to 23rd St $$*

In 1912, an upper crust residence built specifically for bachelors went up in Gramercy. These apartments did not include kitchens.

line, modeled after central Texan barbecue markets. Butchers pile on the buttery but never greasy brisket (moist or lean), pork spare ribs, and jalapeno sausage, accompanied by the classic hot and cold sides (combine the ultra-rich mac'n'cheese with the firehouse chili to feast like a true longhorn). The communal tables are too crowded to allow for conversation, so snag one near the stage and enjoy the Willie Nelson tribute band.

Lamazou
Sandwiches

Lamazou boasts all the culinary artistry typical of Gramercy eateries but with uncharacteristically affordable prices. Italian heroes are made with exceptionally fresh ingredients—the meat is sliced to order, and the ciabatta bread, crunch on the outside with a wonderfully soft center, is baked on premises. The Black Forest sandwich is a harmonious blend of a large quantity of prosciutto, melted brie, and roasted peppers, while the Manou is a genius fusion of a generously portioned chicken breast with sundried tomatoes and gouda cheese. The large stock of quality meats and artisanal cheeses for sale add just one more reason to visit this deli, as if the twenty some-odd sandwiches weren't enough.

370 3rd Ave
(btwn 26th & 27th St)
212-532-2009
Sun 11:30am-6pm,
Mon-Sat 10am-8pm
6 to 28th St
$

VERITAS
best crash course in wine

A meal at Veritas is nothing short of an education on both wine and the food paired with it. The phonebook-sized 3000+ bottle wine list would fluster the most seasoned connoisseur, yet the sommelier is eager to advise and edify any wide-eyed wayward. Don't take the recommendations lightly, as the menu is constructed from the wine up—the main dining area is even reserved for those partaking in tasting menus. Chef Grégory Pugin shows a conductor-like familiarity with the rhythm and timbre of his ingredients, crafting incredible wine-centric dishes and menus that unfold like music. Robuchon-trained, he's certainly up to date on all modern techniques, but shows a wizened maturity in their application, not letting any particular fad dominate his French-fed, New American menu. While the unforgettable meals are undeniably expensive, they come with new eyes for fine wines and food, unable to separate the two again.

Nightclub, Salon

New American, French
43 E 20th St (btwn
Broadway and Park
Ave S)
212-353-3700
Mon-Sat 5:30pm-
10:30pm
6RW to 23rd St
$$$$

Rickshaw Dumpling Bar

Asian, Dumplings

61 W 23rd St (at 6th Ave)
212-924-9220
Sun 11:30am-8:30pm,
Mon-Sat
11:30am-9:30pm
❶ ❻ ❻ to 23rd St
$

Those who believe that there's nothing special about dumplings clearly haven't been to Rickshaw Dumpling Bar. Five years ago, the first Rickshaw was founded in New York, based on one simple principle: "Do one thing and do it very well." This phrase has not only formed but also popularized the restaurant, attracting customers from all over the world to "enter the world of dumplings." With its energetic waiters excited to invite you to serve over seven different dumpling styles alongside a salad, an ice-T, and special dips, Rickshaw Dumpling Bar—and their new venue, Rickshaw Dumpling Truck—can turn anybody into a fanatic of dumplings, both for its taste and its history.

Shake Shack

Burgers

A stroll through Madison Square Park will inevitably trap one in the crowd gathering at Shake Shack—the city's proud solution to its lack of "hometown fare." The Shack elevates traditional comfort food to high cuisine, offering a blend of street vendor convenience with quality befitting The Union Street Café, one of owner Danny Meyer's other restaurants. Chomp into the famously affordable ShackBurger, which accompanies normal toppings with ShackSauce, a mayo-based sauce whose other ingredients are top-secret. Potential variations include the doubling of meat and the substitution (or addition) of a crisp, cheese-filled portabello mushroom patty. Make sure to order the eponymous shake, so thick, sweet and nostalgic that it will take you back to days of drugstore soda fountains, or a modernized "Concrete" if you're seeking a complex and refined twist.

Madison Square Park
(Madison Ave & 23rd St)
212-889-6600
Daily 11am-11pm
❻ ❻ to 23rd St
Additional Location:
366 Columbus Ave

PLAY

Beauty Bar

Nightclub, Salon

Get a manicure from a tattooed chick, sip a complimentary dirty martini, and rock out to The Smiths and Nirvana at this salon-turned-club. The $10 cocktail-and-mani special is a

The family in E.B. White's *Stuart Little* lives at 22 Gramercy Park. It's described in the book as "A pleasant place near a park in New York City."

great deal, but stick around, because the space transforms into a dance bar by midnight. At Beauty Bar, kitsch is king (or queen), with pink glitter wallpaper, old hair-dryer chairs, black-and-white female silhouette-stenciled walls, and '80s records on blast. It's the ideal place for girls to wreak havoc (with perfect French tips or blood red nails, of course). Still, the bar's status as bachelorette party central draws in dudes that equalize the testosterone-estrogen ratio at what one might expect to be an overwhelmingly feminine hangout.

212-539-1389
231 E 14th St
(near 2nd Ave)
Mon-Fri 5pm-4am,
Sat-Sun 7pm-4am
❹❺❻ⓁⓃⓆⓇ to
14th St-Union Sq,
Ⓛ to 3rd Ave
$

Crocodile Lounge

Dive, Games

🎵 🏌 🥟

325 E 14th St (near 1st Ave)
212-477-774
Daily 12pm-4am
Ⓛ to 1st Ave,
❹❺❻ⓁⓃⓆⓇ to
14th St-Union Sq
$

Crocodile Lounge will woo you with attractive mismatched seating, reel you in with a beautiful selection of eclectic draughts, and go for the kill with its cooking. That is to say, you get a free pizza with every beer—no joke—and it's made to order. Of course, by beer five, the pizza could be crap and it would still taste like Christmas. Wind your way behind the bar to find a small arcade with the classic Big Buck and the all-too-rare magic of Skee-ball. The hallway ends in a lovely open courtyard, perfect for happy hour ($3 Yeunglings) as it closes at 10pm. It's a popular spot for NYU and New School students along with younger Gramercy locals. Whatever crowd you're with, you're getting both beer and pizza, so make sure to tip like a pro.

Fillmore New York at Irving Plaza

Music Venue

ALL AGES

17 Irving Pl
(btwn 15th and 16th St)
212-777-6800
Hours vary by event
❹❺❻ⓁⓃⓆⓇ to
14th St-Union Sq
$$

In an age-old space that has housed everything from a Yiddish theater to a Polish Army veteran's club, Irving Plaza now stands as one of NYC's premier rock clubs. With a 1000-person capacity floor area and a mezzanine space overhead, the venue is deceptively big and well-suited to performers of different styles and levels of popularity. Whether it be a long-awaited rock reunion or a brand new emocore band's EP release party, Irving Plaza doesn't discriminate. For this reason, it's not like other venues you just show up to for some live music. Also unlike other rock clubs in the city, Irving Plaza is surprisingly ungrimy—the space is decorated with chandeliers, fancy mirrors, velvet couches, and neon lights. But that's not to say you won't get knocked in the moshpit, so keep your wits about you.

Your inside guide to
DINING
NIGHTLIFE
& EVENTS

insideNEWYORK.com

GREENWICH VILL

More than anywhere else in New York, Greenwich Village invites you to get lost. Its side streets are a maze of loops and switchbacks leading to main north-south thoroughfares that run like freight trains through clusters of pocket-sized cafés and boutiques. This landscape is a result of the Villagers' petition to exclude their domain from the Manhattan grid plan of 1811, thereby preserving its relatively provincial character within a rigid megalopolis. Today the neighborhood can no longer remotely be labeled "small-town," but it continues to be defined by an idiosyncratic spirit.

The area once known as Greenwyck began as a country outpost for the city's well-to-do. After almost two hundred years of life as a virtually independent suburb, a series of cholera outbreaks in the 1800s caused thousands of displaced Manhattan residents to descend on the settlement. This influx was closely followed by waves of German, Irish, and Italian immigrants who came for work at nearby factories, breweries, warehouses, and lumber yards. The Village's distinctive cultural heritage and one-time designation as "The American Bohemia" traces its roots to this period.

A reputation for social and intellectual liberality began to form even before World War I, but didn't solidify until the antics of the Beat Generation. Anti-materialist artists, actors, writers, and musicians gathered in coffee shops and bars to play needling folk music, produce avant-garde theater, author poetry about the virtues of free love, and generally drive the American

middle class insane. All manner of artistic giants are also former Greenwich residents, from Edgar Allen Poe and Mark Twain to Marcel Duchamp and Bob Dylan.

The Village is also historically a sanctuary for those segments of the population initially considered outcasts. In its infancy, the neighborhood welcomed black freemen, who were able to eke out a living in the fledgling industries along the Hudson River. In the mid-20th century it was home to a large, active community of gay, lesbian, and transgender transplants from around the nation. In June 1969, the Stonewall riots on Christopher Street kick-started the gay civil rights movement.

Some lament increasing property values and the wealthy families they bring as the downfall of the Village's irreverence, but these complaints are as old as the area's notoriety. The student scene around NYU and the New School tends to keep real estate prices out of the stratosphere, in addition to maintaining a healthy mix of head shops, tattoo parlors, sex emporiums, and fancy restaurants. Throughout its lives as an industrial center, a bohemian enclave, a haven for transvestites, drug addicts, and the Weathermen, and a real estate developer's dream, Greenwich Village has been a symbol of a utopia in which all transgressions against accepted models are forgiven. It's precisely the open-minded adaptability of Villagers that makes this radical progression possible. So if you trip over a designer stroller while taking a photo of the White Horse Tavern, stay sanguine: you just stubbed your toe on what makes the Village unique.

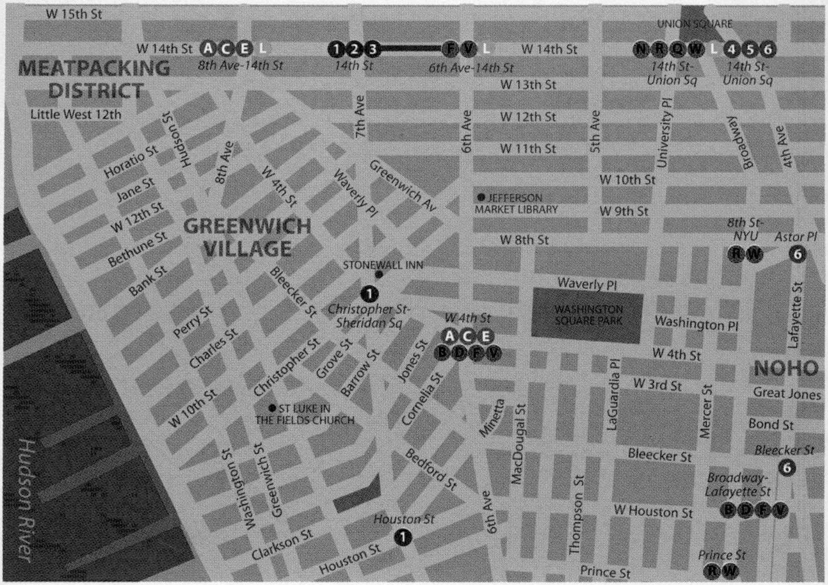

EXPLORE

Center for Architecture

536 LaGuardia Pl (btwn W 3rd & Bleecker St)
212-683-0023
Mon-Fri 9am-8pm, Sat 11am-5pm
B D F C E to W 4th St, 6 to Bleecker St
Free

A Center for Architecture may seem redundant when the city is itself a celebration of urban design, but this sleek museum, opened in 2003, promotes the sustainability of New York's steel and concrete masterpieces. Home of the nonprofit organizations American Institute of Architects-New York Chapter and the Center for Architecture Foundation, the Center was one of the first buildings in New York to use geothermal heating systems. The largely underground exhibition space enjoys natural light, which pours in through subterranean skylights. Three galleries host engaging, rotating exhibits: past shows have honored new and innovative architecture firms and explored possibilities in environmentally-friendly transportation. Try to catch one of the many free night lectures (see website for postings).

Cherry Lane Theatre

38 Commerce St (btwn Barrow & Bedford St)
212-727-3673
Box Office: Tues-Fri 3pm-8pm, Sat 1pm-8pm
1 to Christopher St

In 1928, a group of artists led by Edna St. Vincent Millay, the first woman to receive the Pulitzer Prize for Poetry, turned this former grain-storage silo into an avant-garde force. Stuffed into a back corner of shady Commerce St, the Cherry Lane Theater has remained an off-Broadway presence for over 85 years, attracting internationally prominent playwrights and distinguished actors. The playhouse has been host to major developments in American drama, including The Living Theatre and the Theatre of the Absurd. Cherry Lane continues to push

the envelope, producing plays, musicals, and re-
vivals as a nonprofit venue for experimental and
nonconformist artists, as well as programs like
master classes and stage readings.

Film Forum

Cinema buffs chased
this silver screen
around Manhattan for
40 years until it finally
settled into its per-
manent location on Houston in 1990. The Forum—one of the few nonprofit movie theaters
in the country—hosts three screens: while one
auditorium showcases the premiers of American independents and foreign art films, another
plays American and foreign classics, and the
third shows extended runs of all-time favorites.
Film Forum not only shuns the big action flicks,
but also the usual theater fare: forego the Sour
Patch Kids for a piece of fresh baked carrot
cake and a strong coffee at the concession stand.
An excellent date spot, the theater will satisfy
any cinematic craving with its charming Chap-
lins, playful Godards, and tearful Bergmans.

209 W Houston St
(near 6th Ave)
212-727-8112
❶ to Houston St

Garden at St. Luke in the Fields

Public but quasi-hid-
den, this small garden
just off Hudson St is
where locals are in on the
secret go to eat lunch
or gossip on benches
sequestered away in the lush vegetation. Some
flowerbeds are well-manicured, and some
look like the overgrown courtyard of a country church—a trick that transports the weary
back in time to the still-pastoral patch of land
on which the church was built in 1821. St.
Luke's itself is a chapel of the Episcopal Trinity
Church and includes a gym and a school, used
by members of the current outreach program.
Grab a snack from a nearby café and spend a
few minutes here recuperating before heading
back into the fray.

487 Hudson St (btwn
Barrow & Christopher St)
212-924-0562
Daily 10am-5pm
❶ to Christopher St

neighborhood
NECESSITIES

SUBWAYS 1, 2, 4, 6, B, D, F, M, N, R

BUS M1, M2, M3, M5, M8, M20

MARKETS 9th St Farmer's Market (64 W 9th St, 212-505-7194)

LIBRARIES NYPL Jefferson Market Regional (425 6th Ave, 212-243-4334)

MEDIA thevillager.com

FITNESS Wu Mei Kung Fu Association (219 Sullivan St, 917-885-8598), Bikram Yoga Greenwich Village (401 6th Ave, 212-366-5060)

BIKES West Village Waterfront Bike Shop (391 West St, 212-414-2453), Hudson Urban Bicycles (139 Charles St, 212-965-9334)

LITTLE BRITAIN

Although only half a block long, it's hard to deny the stretch of Greenwich Ave between W 12th and 13th St the nickname "Little Britain." Three stores in a row, all run by Nicky Perry, have the goods to sooth any homesick lad or bird. **A Salt & Battery** *(112 Greenwich Ave)*, reputed to be the best hangover remedy in the Village, serves the closest thing to good fish and chips on this side of the pond. Local secret: the prawns are what keep the regulars coming back for more. Just next door is **Tea & Sympathy** *(108-110 Greenwich Ave)*, both a store and a restaurant. Decorated top-to-tails in floral wallpaper and tablecloths for a cozy, eccentric-aunt ambiance, the restaurant serves its vast selection of teas in quaint Alice in Wonderland teapots. For nibbles, there's a Victorian sponge cake that has been featured on the Food Network, and a Sheppard's pie that sends a line out the door on cold winter nights. Otherwise, check out the grocer **Myers of Keswick** *(634 Hudson St)* one block over for jams, teas, and crisps imported from our Wellies-wearing cousins. Gorblimey.

The Stonewall Inn

A mafia-run gay bar in the '60s, the Stonewall Inn ballooned in popularity by painting the interior black, playing the music loud, and overcharging for watered-down drinks.

53 Christopher St (btwn Waverly Pl & 7th Ave S)
212-488-2705
Daily 2pm-4am
❶ to Christopher St
$$

Despite the mob's best efforts to exploit their clientele, patrons enjoyed a sense of solidarity while outside homophobia reigned, even in a New York overrun with flower children. Infamy came to the bar on July 28, 1969, when police raided the establishment and symbolic resistance to this harassment turned violent. The Stonewall Riots raged for three days, sparking the modern gay pride movement. Reopened in 2007 after a brief period of neglect, the bar maintains its original fly-by-night charm. Visit in the afternoon and talk to Tree, a veteran of the riots and a long-time Stonewall bartender.

Village Vanguard

The gold standard in New York jazz clubs for 75 years, the Village Vanguard is as much of a classic as A Love Supreme. Established in 1935, the cramped club began by hosting Yiddish poets and, later, folk musicians. However, it made its name for its progressive jazz acts, and the nation's top musicians continue to flood into this distinctly triangular basement to catch the edgiest sounds of the time. On any given night one could hear the rhythmic grooves of Josh White, Leadbelly, and Enid Mosier—the same holds today, as recent

178th 7th Ave S (btwn W 11th and Greenwich St)
212-255-4037
Doors open at 8pm, nightly sets begin at 9pm- 11pm.
❶❷❸ to 14th St, Ⓐ Ⓒ
Ⓔ Ⓛ to 8th Ave-14th St
$35 per show, $30 on Mon. $25 student discount Sun-Thurs.

lineups have included the Eric Reed Trio and the Lewis Nash Quintet. Jazz fanatics pack the place almost every night to see pictures of the genre's familiar faces papering the walls. The $35 cover charge may seem a bit steep, but it includes a free drink—and remember, this is the gathering place of legends.

Washington Square Park

Pass through the 77-foot marble Arch, erected to commemorate the 100-year anniversary of Washington's inauguration, to find the Village's most popular watering hole. The Arch, built in 1892 and modeled after the Arc de Triomphe, isn't the park's only mark of history—it was also the

5th Ave & Washington Sq N
Ⓐ Ⓒ Ⓔ Ⓑ Ⓓ Ⓕ to W 4th St

Edgar Allen Poe called four different places in Greenwich Village home during the late 1830s and early 1840s. He is rumored to have composed his poem "The Raven" at all four locations. Legend has it that Poe enjoyed the easy access to mind-altering substances readily available in the Village.

site of the famous 1961 "Beatnik riots," during which more than 500 folksingers performed without permits. You'll still see Izzy Young-types strumming away by the fountain, often encircled by doe-eyed teenage girls. Sandwiched between NYU buildings, the park bustles with study groups flipping through textbooks and napping couples, but the small lawns and flower gardens also lure tourists, musicians, hippies, resting shoppers, and dozens of daredevil skateboarders. If you're feeling overwhelmed by the crowds, buy an ice cream cone from one of the countless carts and head to the northwest lawn, where you'll find a shady reading spot.

SHOP

Greenwich Letterpress

For those seeking a more personal greeting card than what Duane Reade has to offer, Greenwich Letterpress is a saving grace. This stylish, welcoming store was started by a pair of third-generation printing sisters, who carry on the family tradition of printing exclusively with letterpress in an effort to keep the artisanal technique alive. All products are made on 100% tree-free post-consumer cotton or 100% recycled paper. Stroll along the side wall for birthday, thank you, and holiday cards, or pick out invitations and placecards for a fancy shindig. Filled with postcards and posters of Washington Square Park's landmark arch and antique maps of New York City, this shop is a hybrid of artist's pride and city pride.

39 Christopher St
(near Waverly Pl)
212-989-7464
Mon 1pm-6pm (closed
during the summer),
Tues-Fri 11am-7pm,
Sat-Sun 12pm-6pm
1 to Christopher St, **B** **D**
F **V** **C** **E** to W 4th St

Joanne Hendricks Cookbooks

Warm wallpaper, a petite fireplace, and a cozy location in an 1850s brick-faced townhouse make this one-of-a-kind cookbook store feel just like a visit to grandma's house. Here

Joanne Hendricks sells her personal collection of old and rare cookbooks, a mix of genuine antiques, unpublished volumes, and highly specialized pamphlets that all

488 Greenwich St (btwn Canal & Spring St)
212-226-5731
Daily 11:30am-7pm
(call ahead)
C E to Spring St, **1 A**
C E to Canal St

make you want to throw on an apron. Although Hendricks admits to having a hard time parting with certain tomes, she's eager to share her love of food and wine with visitors. You can also find archaic menus, photographs, and collectible tableware among the shelves, but be quick to beat the dealers and top NYC chefs who frequent this treasure chest.

Music Inn World Instruments

If you're looking for a keyboard or trumpet, don't bother rummaging through Music Inn's comfortably clustered shelves—this place steers away from Western instruments

169 W 4th St
(near Jones St)
212-243-5715
Daily 12:30pm-6:30pm
(call ahead)
A C E B D F to W 4th St, **1** to Christopher St

toward an assortment of African percussion sets, Indian sitars, and Russian balalaikas. Instruments are not this music hub's only gig, however. Search amongst shelves of bamboo and eucalyptus didgeridoos for jewelry, carved statues, and records from around the globe, or walk downstairs to watch the shop's handymen carve out artful basses. Music Inn is also open to making trades—it's no wonder this place has been around since Bob Dylan cruised the village streets.

EAT

'ino Café and Bar   *Italian*
Inside this cubbyhole of a restaurant awaits a delightful dining experience, complete with a lengthy wine list, generous paninis, and friendly service. No matter the time of day—'ino serves

brunch, lunch, and dinner—the eight candlelit wooden tables and general warmth of the décor strike the perfect balance between friendliness and romance. The no-

21 Bedford St
(at Downing St)
212-989-5769
Mon-Sun 9am-2am
1 to Houston St,
ACEBDF to W 4th St
$$

reservation policy means you may not be seated immediately, but ordering wine or beer at the bar passes the time pleasantly, and a surprisingly quick turnaround keeps waits manageable. The menu of classic Italian dishes—like the antipasti, rucola salad, and olive bowl—will woo any diner, and sharing an order of bruschetta before a meal is highly recommended.

August   *Mediterranean*
Accenting Old World classics with fresh, local ingredients is August's signature modus operandi. Devotees of this cobblestone hideaway with a glass conservatory roof can't get enough of the wood-fired oven's tarte flambée—a thin

359 Bleecker St (btwn Charles & W 10th St)
212-929-8727
Sun 11am-3:30pm, 5:30-10pm, Mon-Thurs 12-3:30pm, 5:30-11pm, Fri 12-3:30pm, 5:30pm-12am, Sat 11am-3:30pm, 5:30pm-12am
1 to Christopher St
$$$

dough pie heaped with tangy Alsatian onions and bacon tart. More exotic, the grilled baby octopus consists of a tender, serpentine tentacle soaking in the juices of smoked kalamata olives, pickled honeydew melon, and burst tomatoes. Garnished by picholine olives and fine herbs, the whole roasted dourade is the year-round star of the mainstays, swimming in a citronette of preserved lemon, honey, and vinaigrette. You'd expect chic couples bearing hipster babies to delight in something a tad fruitier, but chocolate reigns over the guilt-ridden dessert menu. Encircled by macadamia nuts, the popular pavé consists of a fluffy banana bavarois filling sandwiched between two chocolate patties with enough teeth-coloring cocoa goodness to sate the bottomless cravings of a child.

Barbuto

Italian

775 Washington St
(near W 12th St)
212-924-9700
Sun 12pm-10pm,
Mon-Wed 12pm-11pm,
Thurs-Sat 12pm-12am
Ⓐ Ⓒ Ⓔ Ⓛ to 8th Ave-
14th St
$$$

The buzzing hub-bub on the corner of Washington and W 12th St is sure to draw curious passersby even before they set eyes on the restaurant, reminiscent of an open garage. After a short wait at the crowded bar, the bruschetta is a light, refreshing appetizer. Then go for the soft, creamy cod topped with zucchini, squash, and tomatoes, or tender lamb arranged like a fan over warm eggplant. Barbuto's menu changes almost daily to reflect fresh, seasonal ingredients, but the roasted chicken is a house favorite and is the single item that remains year-round. To finish off the evening, order the fruity tart with raspberries and peaches and cream, topped with crispy biscuit layers, or indulge in the chocolate sundae for an ice cream experience completely worth the temporary pangs of a guilty conscience.

Bill's Bar and Burger

American, Burger

22 9th Ave (near 14th St)
212-414-3003
Sun-Wed 12pm-1am,
Thurs 12pm-2am,
Fri-Sat 12pm-4am
Ⓐ Ⓒ Ⓔ Ⓛ to 8th Ave-
14th St
$

Set in an open brick bar room, Bill's Bar and Burger is as simple as its name. The bar is the room's decorative centerpiece, and the full menu is displayed on a chalkboard. Luckily, when it comes to Bill's burgers, simplicity goes hand in hand with quality. Using a secret beef blend, all the meat is ground fresh daily and hand pressed, bringing the restaurant's old-fashioned ambiance to its recipes. You can't go wrong with the Classic, served on a toasted bun with lettuce and tomatoes. The Fat Cat, with American cheese on an English muffin, is another perennial favorite. Deliberate between sweet potato or classic French fries with gravy on the side, and for dessert, head to the bar to try an original Stout Float. Crowds gather around the bar as the night progresses, but they never seem to overlook the burger.

Commerce
New American

Tucked away at the back of one of the most picturesque side streets in Greenwich Village, Commerce attracts large crowds with its elaborate yet refined cuisine. A bread basket, with an assortment of freshly baked heavenly delights—sourdough, onion, pretzel—and homemade salted butter forebode the decadent meal ahead. While sophisticated cooking techniques are used to prepare the food (parmesan foam, for instance, covers a mushroom and Fontina cheese ravioli), most of the dishes feature rustic ingredients, like the famous "Ragu of odd things"—handmade orrechiette pasta in a hearty tomato sauce with tripe, oxtail, and pork trotter. The best entrées are the portions for two, including a porterhouse steak with cheese-filled hash browns, creamy spinach, and pearl onion glaze, or whole roasted duck with peas and ginger fried rice. No less excessive are the desserts, including an incomparable strawberry-rhubarb pie.

50 Commerce St
(near Bedford St)
212-524-2301
Sun 1pm-9:30pm, Mon-Thurs 5:30pm-11pm, Fri-Sat 5:30pm-11:30pm
Ⓐ Ⓒ Ⓔ Ⓑ Ⓓ Ⓕ Ⓥ to W 4th St
❶ to Christopher St
$$$$

Ditch Plains
Seafood

This is where the oyster shooter reclaims its dignity. Ditch Plains is the glossiest self-styled "fish shack" around, a large den swathed in metal and recessed lights that traffics in only the heartiest of lobster rolls. Here a tenderly grilled filet of salmon ringed with spring vegetables and a zingy fish taco are treated with equal respect, and the generously portioned shrimp gumbo, soaking in cayenne and garlic-tinged andouille

29 Bedford St
(at Downing St)
212-633-0202
Daily 11am-2am
❶ to Houston St, Ⓐ Ⓒ
Ⓔ Ⓑ Ⓓ Ⓕ to W 4th St
$$$

CHEAP EATS
best food to walk with

Maoz- An amazing chain of falafel stores that are cropping up all over the city. Clean and healthy baked falafel with a full salad bar to pick, choose and pack your pita as you see fit. *59 E 8th St, 212-420-5999, R to 8th St or 6 to Astor Place, Sun-Thurs 11am-11pm, Fri-Sat 11am-12am $*

NY Dosas- This humble street cart in Washington Square Park regularly churns out hundreds of dosas, thin flaky crepes from southern India made of rice and black lentils and filled with well-spiced vegetarian dishes like curried chickpeas and potato. *50 Washington Square S, 917-710-2092, A, C, E, B, D to West 4th, R to 8th St, Mon-Sat 11am-4pm $*

Sammy's Halal- Large portions of chicken or lamb with rice and salad are doused with the signature hot sauce and tangy white sauce at this halal street cart. *W 4th St (at Broadway), 917-446-9948, A, C, E, B, D to West 4th, Daily 10am-12am $*

Bleecker Street Pizza- Open late into the night, this fast-food pizzeria still uses quality ingredients to make the New York classics like cheese and pepperoni, but the authentic Italian slice is their Sicilian with fresh roasted tomatoes, chopped garlic, and basil leaves. *69 7th Ave S, 212-924-4466, A, C, E, B, D to West 4th or 1 to Christopher St, Daily 10am-4am $*

SanPanino- A killer sandwich that will win you over with the fluffy rosemary-infused foccacia bread and a delectable spread of fresh, vibrant fillers. *494 Hudson St Frnt, 212-645-7228, 1 to Christopher St, A, C, E, B, D to West 4th, Mon-Fri 7am-7:30pm, Sat-Sun 8am-6:30pm $*

sausage, could probably kill a man. Non-fish options, including piping hot mozzarella-and-ricotta fritters and a classic pairing of barbecue chicken and potato salad, represent the upscale boardwalk spirit just as well. The food is the star of the place, but the commanding attitude extends to the clientele, an even mix of guffawing young Villagers looking to get drunk somewhere respectable and businessmen hoping to impress clients from the seaside.

Doma Café & Gallery *Cafe, Sandwiches*
Have a heart-to-heart over breakfast or snag a book from the well-stocked library and munch on your favorite classic Mediterranean sandwich for lunch—you can't go wrong with any

of Doma's simple, flavorful selections. Stay late and witness the sunset transform this easygoing writer's retreat into an intimate date spot; the café has gained a second life with the addition of a pitch-perfect contemporary dinner menu, elevated by seasonal offerings. Highlights include an ethereal ricotta gnocchi, roasted chicken on a bed of tangy bread salad, and scallops with an unforgettable corn purée. Even after lunch, the West Village vibe remains strong: politics can be heard over a spread of artisanal cheeses, a single diner admires the array of original art-

17 Perry St (at 7th Ave)
212-929-4339
Daily 8am-12am
❶ to Christopher St
$

MURRAY'S CHEESE SHOP
hottest wheels

Caseophiles who dream of grainy chaource, salty broccio, or sharp gorgonzola will feel like kids in a candy factory at Murray's Cheese Shop. Around in one form or another since 1940, the current headquarters on Bleecker St is the center of operations for three locations in the city. Beyond cheese, sausages, ham, bread, chocolate, and nuts from all over the world, the shop also organizes tastings and classes, in order to spread a little bit of its expertise around. The cheerful interior is filled with enticing aromas and a staff that obviously knows its stuff. Come prepared to spend a chunk of time perusing and elbowing giddy chefs who try to cut in line.

254 Bleecker St
(at Leroy St)
212-243-3289
Sun 10am-7pm,
Mon-Sat 8am-8pm
A, B, C, D, E, F, V to
W 4th St,
1 to Christopher St-
Sheridan Sq

work, and somewhere someone can't pick just one dessert. Don't let the critics of this "new" dinner spot fool you, Doma is still about individual choice—hey, even Bohemians have to eat.

Num Pang Sandwich

Cambodian

21 E 12th St (btwn.
University Pl & 5th Ave)
212-255-3271
Sun 12pm-9pm,
Mon-Sat 11am-10pm
❶❷❸❹❺❻ to
14th St-Union Sq
$

This modest, unassuming shack, distinguished by its street-crowding lunch line, is the perfect place to fall in love with banh mi. Num Pang serves the Cambodian equivalent of New York's favorite sandwich—and you'll thank the sandwich gods it did. The pork belly melts in your mouth, and the catfish is closer to the texture of butter. Balanced by a tangy and refreshing combination of pickled carrots, cucumber, cilantro, and a creamy chili mayo, the fatty meats are served on a crusty Parisi Bakery baguette and flanked with a homemade pickle. While the sandwich travels well, you'll be tempted to stay in the small, comfortable room hiding up the spiral staircase. Replenish with a homemade watermelon juice, blood orange lemonade, or a classic Cambodian dessert. There's a gentle request for no substitutions, but you'll see why when you get here.

The expression "I heard it through the grapevine" originated at a historic roadhouse located at 6th Ave and W 11th St called The Old Grapevine. In the mid to late 1800s, it was the place where actors and artists flocked to hear the latest news.

Mamoun's Falafel

Falafel, Mediterranean

119 MacDougal St
(near W 3rd St)
212-674-8685
Daily 10am-5am
Ⓐ Ⓒ Ⓔ Ⓑ Ⓓ Ⓕ to
W 4th St
$
Additional location:
22 St. Marks Place
(btwn 2nd & 3rd Ave)

A New York favorite since 1971, Mamoun's is known for one thing: falafel. Cheap, delicious falafel. The tiny, dimly-lit restaurant is about the size of a walk-in closet and is frequented by a mix of NYU students, foodies, and neighborhood folk. The chefs put together the food so quickly and dexterously that it's hard to tell if they've been trained in cooking or karate. Try the falafel sandwich (obviously), and for dessert, savor a thick gooey baklava. Because Mamoun's has few tables and many customers, take your food to go. If it's a nice day, eat your meal at Washington Square Park, only a few blocks away. Peel away the tinfoil, and sigh at the perfectly mixed combination of lettuce, tomato, soft, moist falafel, warm, fluffy pita bread, and cool, creamy tahini.

Peanut Butter & Co.

Sandwiches

240 Sullivan St
(at W 3rd St)
212-677-3995
Sun-Thurs 11am-9pm,
Fri-Sat 11am-10pm
Ⓐ Ⓒ Ⓔ Ⓑ Ⓓ Ⓕ to
W 4th St,
❶ to Christopher St
$

It will be hard to go back to mom's old-fashioned PB&J once you've had one of Peanut Butter & Co.'s signature peanut butter, banana, and honey grilled concoctions. With over 20 varieties of peanut butter, this creative sandwich shop transforms your classic childhood favorites into gourmet delights—and they all feature some incarnation of the tasty nutty paste. The nostalgia-ridden cafe takes you back to elementary school with an old-fashioned ice cream parlor vibe and vintage decor. Some of the modern updates include "The Elvis," a bacon-and-honey-addled sandwich, and the "Lunchbox Special," served with freshly ground peanut butter

and strawberry, raspberry, or apricot preserves. Prefer your sandwich with the crusts cut off? Just ask, and they'll do it with pleasure.

Perilla

New American

9 Jones St (near W 4th St)
212-929-6868
Sun 11am-2:30pm,
5pm-10pm, Mon-Thurs
5:30pm-11pm,
Fri 5:30pm-11:30pm,
Sat 11am-2:30pm,
5:30pm-11:30pm
❶ to Christopher St,
Ⓐ Ⓒ Ⓔ Ⓑ Ⓓ Ⓕ to W
4th St
$$$

After working together at the upscale Tribeca restaurant the Harrison, Harold Dieterle (the winner of Bravo's debut season of Top Chef) and Alicia Nosenzo teamed up to open this wonderfully charming seasonal American neighborhood restaurant. The food is prepared and presented in a beautifully rustic manner, incorporating many earthy vegetables and ingredients made in-house. The spicy duck meatballs, ground duck mixed with some mint cavatelli and topped with a quail egg, are a definite must-have for their full flavor—just make sure to mix in the egg to thicken the sauce. Perilla also offers a fun and more affordable bar menu, featuring interesting bites like duckfat popcorn to satisfy your late night food cravings. The casual vibe is certainly not what you'd expect from a TV chef's inaugural debut, but no one is heard complaining over the satisfied diners.

Taim

Isreali, Falafel

222 Waverly Pl
(near W 11th St)
212-691-1287
Daily 11am-10pm
❶ ❷ ❸ to 14th St, Ⓐ Ⓒ
Ⓔ Ⓛ to 8th Ave-14th St
$

While the NYC falafel war rages between disciples of Mamoun's and the initiates of its various competitors, this small Israeli joint has quietly changed the game with a superior quality of toppings, lush velvety hummus, and three flavors of falafel. In typical Israeli fashion, the options for customization are endless, with a large bank of gourmet Mediterranean salads, including less healthy (but certainly authentic) options such as fries in aioli. The falafels are true marvels—fried to order, with both the exterior crunch and the downy mass of chickpeas spiced with red peppers, harissa, or cilantro and mint. The result is a solid brick of falafel and fillings: sublimely spiced, perfectly arranged, impossibly delicate, yet surrounded by a whole wheat pita that defies the presumed incompatibility of fluffiness and sturdiness. While the debate may never settle, Taim's Israeli- inspired perfection has added an essential stop to the pilgrimage.

The New French   *New American*
The name of this charming West Village bistro is deceiving: it's new all right, but it certainly isn't French. Wood floors, black wooden banquettes, yellow walls covered in child-like sketches, and a chalkboard back wall listing the day's specials set the quirky-romantic tone for the chattering crowd. Welcoming service and reasonable prices make the eclectic, seasonal menu all the more enticing. The chicken liver and date crostini serve as a wonderful sweet-savory start to the meal. Main dishes like tender roasted chicken with mushrooms are classic bistro fare, while vegetable curry veers toward Thai-

522 Hudson St
(near W 10th St)
212-807-7357
Sun 10am-4pm, 5pm-10pm, Mon-Fri 11:30am-4pm, 5pm-11pm, Sat 10am-4pm, 5pm-11pm
❶ to Christopher St
$$

greenwich village
UNDER $20

Pop in the organic bakery chain **Le Pain Quotidien** *(1 W 8th St)* for a blueberry muffin breakfast and a cup of brew, all for $4.35.

A stroll down through Washington Square Park brings you to the **Center for Architecture** *(536 LaGuardia Pl)*, where the cutting-edge exhibits are free.

Queue for a $6 vegan South Indian crepe from the **Dosa Cart** *(50 Washington Sq S)* and take a seat on the park fountain to watch street performers.

Re-energized, head west to **Music Inn** *(169 W 4th St)* to dig through the collection of rare instruments, then swing by **Bleecker Street Records** *(239 Bleecker St)* to marvel at the $900 Bob Dylan tracks. Don't worry, everything in the back—from CCR to Chopin—goes for only 99¢.

Pick up a gelato on a stick at **Popbar** *(5 Carmine St)* for $3.75 and enjoy it in the sun at Father Demo Square Park.

A 99¢ slice of pizza at 6th and 8th, followed by a $6 happy hour cocktail at **Dove Parlour** *(228 Thompson St)*, is the classic Village dinner.

land, and a beer-braised pulled pork sandwich takes a happy jaunt into Germany. After a bottle from the eclectic (and equally reasonable) wine list you won't be any surer of The New French's geographic pedigree, but with food this tasty at prices this reasonable, it's better not to ask too many questions.

Wallsé *Austrian*

Located in the heavily residential West Village, Kurt Gutenbrunner's 10-year old Austrian mainstay remains refreshingly aloof from the trends of downtown dining with a sanctification of the maxim that food should, above all, be tasty. The modestly adorned dining area embraces a loosened crowd of regulars with the humble comforts of neutral tones and minimalist art. Chef Guttenbrunner's flagship is no slouch in technique and flare, advancing lovingly crafted plates that revel in delicacy instead of comfort food excess or overly inventive spins. A slow-cooked salmon comes to life amid the contrasting crunch and cream of spaghetti cut cucumber in a dill and sour cream sauce. A duck breast comes crisped in caramelized onion-apricot chutney without losing any of its moisture or jus. With such culi-

344 W 11th St
(at Washington St)
212-352-2300
Mon-Sun 5:30pm-11pm,
Brunch Sat-Sun 11am-
2:15pm
❶ to Christopher St
$$$

CORNER BISTRO
best bohemian burger and beer

This relic of West Village bohemia has been serving some of the best burgers in Manhattan since the Beat movement. Though it's best known for its famous Bistro Burger, Corner Bistro doubles as an old school pub, where bartenders know the regulars by name and drink just as much as the patrons. Locals, students, and artists alike fill the wooden booths and benches late into the night, drinking $2.50 McSorley's Ale on draught and munching on stringy french fries. No matter the hour, you'll never find Corner Bistro empty (though you may find yourself in line—to avoid the wait, come by on weeknights and weekday afternoons). So if you're looking for a reliable escape from the upscale snobbery that plagues the surrounding neighborhood, CB is your spot.

331 W 4th St (at Jane St)
212-242-9502
Sun 12pm-4am, Mon-Sat
11:30am-4am
A,C,E,L to 8th Ave-14th
St, 1,2,3 to 14 St

nary accomplishments, Wallsé may well remind you of the true meaning of elegance: a pleasurable, graceful, and restrained sense of style.

PLAY

124 Rabbit

Beer Bar

$

124 Macdougal St
(at Minetta Ln)
212-254-0575
Sun-Thurs 6pm-2am,
Fri-Sat 6pm-4am
Ⓐ Ⓒ Ⓔ Ⓑ Ⓓ Ⓕ to
W 4th St
$$

An anonymous black door sits along Macdougal St, lost among the hubbub of its less subtle neighbors. Upon closer inspection, one might notice the tiny label that reads "124 Rabbit—Beer Bar." Ring the doorbell and enter the contradiction that is Rabbit—a secret bar that greets guests with a smile, turns away rowdy groups while blasting crunk rap, and serves specialized European beer to a young crowd that looks more PBR than Wittekerke. Even the decor is at odds with itself, with candlelit brick and pressed tin giving a classy cover to spray-painted designs and chalk-drawn messages. Yet these apparent discrepancies come together in perfect harmony at this subterranean beer bar.

55 Bar

Live Music, Bar

♫

55 Christopher St
(near 7th Ave)
212-929-9883
Daily 3pm-2am
❶ to Christopher St, Ⓐ
Ⓒ Ⓔ Ⓑ Ⓓ Ⓕ to W 4th St
$$

Be prepared to scoot your chair and make room for the musicians at this cozily cramped underground jazz venue. 55 Bar's lack of a formal stage puts audiences and performers on the same level, allowing everyone in the room to connect over intimate, blues-tinged jazz. The diverse crowd of listeners perch on their bar stools, tapping their feet hard enough to shake the dust off the ancient record sleeves hanging on the walls. Friendly waitresses weave through rickety round tables, delivering beer and cocktails to delighted customers while moving to the music themselves. It's an unpretentious yet in-the-know sort of scene, with jazz cats young and old chatting up anybody savvy enough to walk through the door. Whether it's a sing-a-long to "Sweet Georgia Brown" or a guitar showcase from Mike Stern, every night is right for good tunes and good vibes at this West Village favorite.

Bowlmor Lanes

Games, Lounge

18⁺

110 University Place
(btwn 12th & 13th St)
212-255-8188
Sun 11am-12am,
Mon, Thurs 4pm-2am,
Tues-Wed 4pm-1am,
Fri 4pm-3:30am,
Sat 11am-3:30am
Sun-Thurs 18+ after 7pm,
Fri-Sat 21+ after 7pm
❶ Ⓐ Ⓒ ❻ ❻ Ⓑ ❶ Ⓛ to
14th St-Union Sq

Bowlmor Lanes brings NYC chic to the old school bowling alley. With a total of 40 lanes, there's plenty space for the mix of multi-generational regulars and fresh competitors to play back-to-back rounds. Tired bowlers and their tag-a-long friends unwind with drinks in the adjacent bar area, full of sleek leather couches and cozy private booths. On screens above the lanes, computer-animated pins keep track of scores and bounce rhythmically to recent radio hits. The complex's multiple floors provide additional lounging space up the stairs at Pressure Nightclub & Billiards. Though the prices can put a hole in your wallet ($11/game per person+$6.50 shoe rental), $4 games on Formerly Employed Wednesdays and drink deals on Monday Night Strike—when DJs spin all night—bring trendy bowling to the masses.

Dove Parlour — *Cocktails, Bar*

228 Thompson St (btwn W 3rd and Bleecker St)
212-254-1435
Daily 4pm-4am
Ⓐ Ⓒ Ⓔ Ⓑ Ⓓ Ⓕ to W 4th St
$

Descend the white wooden steps of the Dove to find a veritable Victorian salon, complete with red velvet brocade wallpaper, satin pillows, upholstered couches, and a candle-studded fireplace. Don't be intimidated—the dimly lit space is as mellow as it is elegant, and the bartenders are as friendly as they are attractive. The bar prides itself on its impeccable selection of imported French boutique wines and its devastating cocktail menu—try the Spiced Peach Cobbler, a saccharine fusion of peach vodka, honey, cinnamon, and organic vanilla soy milk, or the French Lavender, lavender-infused gin and orange liqueur with a splash of grapefruit. Prices are unpretentious, especially if you come during happy hour, when all martinis, wines, cosmos, and margaritas are only $6. And come hungry, because the Dove offers a kitchen menu of modernized "tea party fare" with sandwiches, toasts, and an elaborate cheese tier.

Fat Cat — *Live Music, Games*

75 Christopher St (at 7th Ave)
212-675-6056
Mon-Thurs 2pm-5am,
Fri-Sun 12pm-5am
❶ to Christopher St
$

Seven nights a week, this iconic college lounge hosts three live jazz acts plus a jam session that lasts until 4am. For a cheap $3 cover, take in the tunes and choose from an endless selection of games to play: though Fat Cat is best known as a pool hall, it also provides ping-pong, foosball, shuffleboard, chess, checkers, Scrabble, and Othello. Dull your sensory overload with a hard cider, beer on draught, or one of the three custom cocktails—the Hairy Monk is a particularly innovative blend of tequila and fresh organic juices. If you're in it solely for the jazz, pop a squat on one of the vintage couches that line the stage before they fill up. The friendly dog that lives here might sit next to you and keep you company during the show.

HERE Arts Center — *Theater*

ALL AGES
145 6th Ave (at Dominick St)
212-647-0202
Shows start between 7pm-11pm
Ⓒ Ⓔ to Spring St,
❶ to Houston St,
❻ ❻ to Prince St
Tickets $15-30

Twenty to thirty visitors keen on the cutting edge congregate in two small theaters to experience a punk rock Kabuki, a puppet Kafka, the sweet musical venom of Taylor Mack, or other hybrid stage-breeds of multidisciplinary performer. Hosting artists-in-residence, visiting artists from across the globe, and even puppeteers and playwrights, this alternative center supports and curates some of this city's strangest and most entertaining works sure to wow theater nerds and newbies alike. Stop by the cozy side lounge before shows for beer, wine, and bistro fare. Just be sure to come early for a good seat—you don't want to miss seeing a captain engulfed by a slide projection of Antarctica, or something equally ludicrous.

Le Poisson Rouge — *Music Venue, Lounge*

For a music space that looks intimidatingly hip at first glance (sinister, coffin-like fish tanks dangle ominously over the dark entrance hall), the mood at LPR is refreshingly lively and unpretentious. Take in the contemporary visual art and sip on pre-show drinks in the warmly-lit Gallery Bar before moving upstairs for the main event. The circular stage morphs with chameleonic ease to accommodate everything from experimental indie bands to classical quartets, making the versatile venue a new favorite among all kinds of music fans. Food offerings are as diverse as the music and include sushi, chicken satay, and a $5 comfort food menu to sate late night PB&J cravings.

🎵

158 Bleecker St
(near Thompson St)
212-505-3474
Daily 1pm-4am
Ⓐ Ⓒ Ⓔ Ⓑ Ⓓ Ⓕ Ⓥ to W
4th St, ❶ to Houston St
Tickets $10-15

Love

Dance Club

The ghost of '90s rave culture still haunts this West Village nightclub, and everybody's digging it. With a cave-like DJ booth made out of fake reflective rock, walls covered in blacklight art, and hypnotic neon visuals projected on gigantic screens, Love feels like a hedonistic underworld. The club's high-end sound system is loud and crystal clear, pumping house, trance, dubstep, and the like to a crowd that's dying to dance. If your legs get tired or you find someone to smooch, there's a fluffy white lounge space behind the waterfall

🔫

179 MacDougal St
(at W 8th St)
212-477-5683
Daily 10pm-4am
Ⓐ Ⓒ Ⓔ Ⓑ Ⓓ Ⓕ Ⓥ to
W 4th
❶ to Christopher St
$$

(yes, there's a waterfall) and tables along the walls. Lines can get long, and there's usually a cover, but it's more laid-back and less out-of-towny than the Meatpacking District. Check the schedule and go on a night that suits your style.

Vol de Nuit

Beer Bar

The tiny chalked sign above Vol de Nuit's door seems intended to let wandering eyes glide over the bar's small, dark entryway. But venture through and down the dark corridor to reach a little bit of Belgium in

👓

148 W 4th St
(near 6th Ave)
212-982-3388
Sun-Thurs 4pm-1am,
Fri-Sat 4pm-3am
Ⓐ Ⓒ Ⓔ Ⓑ Ⓓ Ⓕ to
W 4th St
$$

the West Village. With its hidden wine bar and more public and popular beer and frites garden, Vol de Nuit offers visitors some of the best imported Belgian brands like Chimay and Delirium Tremens, accompanied with mussels and authentic Belgian-style french fries (mayo and all). For those looking for a lighter brew, there's the tasty Lindeman's Framboise raspberry beer on tap. If you're lucky, you can snag one of the comfy couches and lounge in the glow of the interior's warm red lights. It's the closest you can get to a Brussels beer garden this side of the Atlantic.

EAST

Partying students and local artists keep the bars of the East Village pulsating all night. A niche for nightlife and creativity, the Village has a rich history of immigration and rebellious counterculture sentiment that fueled many artistic movements. Despite its notoriety as a bohemian hotbed of rebellion, the neighborhood has in recent years contended with gentrification and the ever-expanding NYU, whose buildings and dorms speckle the area.

Long before collegiate hipsters moved in, Peter Stuyvesant began the development of this piece of southeastern Manhattan when he bought the property in 1651 from a fellow Dutch colonialist. It stayed in his family until the 19th century, when the land was partitioned and sold off and large numbers of German immigrants started to move in. He and his descendants can still be found in the neighborhood, buried at St. Mark's Church in-the-Bowery.

From the 1890s to the middle of the 20th century, Ukrainians came to the area and made it predominantly theirs. Waves of immigration from the Eastern European country lasted from the 1890s to the middle of the 20th century. Today the Village remains the Ukrainian capital of Manhattan, with the descendants of settlers running restaurants and shops and even staging an annual festival in front of the massive St. George Church.

The moniker East Village was coined in the '60s, when the area became a neighborhood distinct from the Lower East Side, set apart by its position at the forefront of contemporary art,

VILL

music, and literary scenes. Cheap real estate prices attracted beatnik writers and artists and encouraged the proliferation of post-modern art galleries and music venues, which have since moved across the bridge to Brooklyn. The punk movement originated here, with venues like the infamous CBGB hosting acts such as The Ramones, The Misfits, and Blondie until its closure in 2006. Tompkins Square Park, arguably the center of the East Village, played host to a riot of over 7,000 unemployed workers in 1874 demanding help from the government and again in 1988 fighting against the city's 1am curfew. Low prices also attracted Puerto Rican immigrants, which gave way to the Nuyorican movement, a Puerto Rican-New Yorker renaissance of art and literature.

In the last decade the East Village has changed drastically, due in large part to the expansion of NYU. Relations with the university are complex—many are opposed to the spread of the school and the subsequent crowding out of characteristically East Village establishments.

Today the East Village offers the most nightlife venues in the city as well as excellent shopping and dining—a recent wave of Asian immigration to the area has escalated the number of Japanese and Korean eateries and bars. Although most of the undercurrent restlessness has dimmed, hints of all the counterculture activity of years past still endure amidst the trendy boutiques and restaurants.

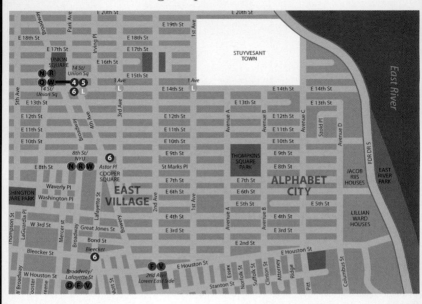

EXPLORE

Merchant's House Museum

Nineteenth-century Manhattan's equivalent of today's Upper East Side was just above Bleecker St, where narrow row houses stood side by side, a stately showing of the city's haute bourgeoisie. Now the Merchant's House Museum is all that survives, preserving in perfect condition its lavish furnishings, intricately carved ceilings, and creaky stairwells. Owned by the Tredwell family for almost 100 years, the four stories of red brick and white marble display characteristics of both Federal and Greek revivalist styles. While the kitchen and family room are dark and cavernous, the majestic parlors feature Roman columns, Staffordshire china, bronze chandeliers, crystal candle holders, and a rosewood piano. The Museum offers such a vivid portrait of centuries-old New York that one wouldn't be surprised to see the Tredwell patriarch, Seabury himself, reading in the library.

> 29 E 4th St (btwn Lafayette St & Cooper Square)
> 212-777-1089
> Thurs-Mon 12pm-5pm
> ● to 8th St, ● to Astor Pl
> Adults $10, Students $5

The Public Theater

Shakespeare's work gets an update—and often a celebrity cast—at the long-beloved Public Theater. A city institution since it began as the Shakespeare workshop in 1954, The Public has expanded its program to include works by artists as varied as Zora Neale Hurston and Paul Simon. Every summer, the iconic Shakespeare in the Park inspires Bard devotees to line up for free tickets before the sun rises. Consistent critical support aside, big

> 425 Lafayette St (btwn Astor Pl & 4th St)
> 212-539-8500
> Sun-Mon 1pm-6pm, Tues-Sat 1pm-7:30pm
> ● to 8th St, ● to Astor Pl
> Prices vary, Students $25

names are part of the draw—past casts have featured Anne Hathaway in Twelfth Night and Al Pacino as the vengeful Shylock in The Merchant of Venice. During the year, emerging playwrights stage new productions at the elegant headquarters, the former Astor Library. If you're a Public regular, make a visit next door to the theater's newest performance space, Joe's Pub. Its intimate stage hosts solo performances by former Broadway stars and local musicians and spoken word artists.

St. Mark's Church in-the-Bowery

This steepled church is the oldest place of worship in New York City, having begun as Peter Stuyvesant's family chapel in 1660. Now Stuyvesant rests here, in the same dusty graveyard as Daniel D. Tompkins, the sixth vice president and the namesake of nearby Tompkins Square Park. Although this Episcopalian church retains as much of its original appearance as possible, it stages utterly modern performances of dance and poetry, and houses a dance studio and theater in which literary greats like William Carlos Williams and Sam Shepard have had exhibitions. Artsy types habitually relax in front of the signature lions on the front steps, eating goods from the nearby organic market or looking at the plaques in the dusty graveyard.

131 E 10th St (btwn 2nd & 3rd Ave)
212-674-6377
Check website for services and performances
⬤Ⓝ⬤⬤❹❺❻ to ⑭ St-Union Sq

Tompkins Square Park

This three-block long stretch at the heart of Alphabet City was the site of the infamous Tompkins Park Riot in 1988, in which police clashed violently with protesters who opposed the park's 1am curfew. Since then, the park has maintained its rebellious atmosphere, marking the yearly anniversary of the riot with an annual rock concert, as well as holding other events such as the Charlie Parker Jazz Festival,

Entrance on E 7th St & Avenue A
Ⓛ to 1st Ave

neighborhhood
NECESSITIES

SUBWAYS N,Q,R,4,5,6,L,F

BUSES M1, M2, M3, M8, M9, M14A, M14D, M15, M21, M103

MARKET Trader Joe's *(142 E 14th St, 212-529-4612)*

LIBRARY NYPL Ottendorfer Branch *(135 2nd Ave, 212-674-0947)*

HOSTEL Village Inn Hostel *(27 E 7th St, 212-228-0828)*

MEDIA *The Village Voice,* eastvillagevisitorscenter.com

FITNESS *Yoga to the People (12 St. Mark's Pl, 917-573-9642)*

BIKES NYC Velo *(64 2nd Ave, 212-253-7771)*

UNION SQUARE

At the center of lower Manhattan lies Union Square, New York's unwritten gathering spot for political activism, artistry, and greenmarkets of monstrous proportions. It's been the site of massive protests since the political demonstrations of the Civil War, and more recently erupted in a riotous celebration on the night of the 2008 election. Farmers have set up stalls of locally-grown fresh produce, breads, cheeses, and wine five times a week since 1976, though gentrification has added a Whole Foods to the chain stores lining the square. During the winter months, the grasses host an annual Holiday Market, known to draw the odd local along with the tourists into the seasonal spirit. Beloved by street dancers, buskers, fanatical religious preachers, textbook-laden NYU students, and be-suited business folk taking a power lunch, and surrounded by restaurants, bars, coffee shops, and clothing stores, the square is a universal meeting place. This extends beyond the human sphere: the Square is the geographical union of Gramercy, Chelsea, and the two halves of the Village, distinguished by stone steps and the nationally-known George Washington statue.

the New Village Music Festival, and the more low-key French film festival in the summer. With its many monuments, dog run, and Sunday farmers' markets, Tompkins invites visitors of all kinds to enjoy its space—which still stubbornly retains its grungy glory of two decades past, but is not unwelcoming to those who prefer sunbathing to revolution.

Ukrainian Museum

In the heart of Ukrainian Manhattan, this museum is committed to edifying New Yorkers about the culture of the largest country in Eastern Europe after Russia. Inside this very modern building,

> 150-03 Jamaica Ave (at 150th St)
> 718-206-0545
> Thurs-Fri 12pm-2pm, Sat-Sun 1pm-5pm
> ❸ ❿ ❷ to Jamaica Center, ❻ to Parsons Blvd
> Suggested admission $5, Students $3

which was finished in 2005, visitors can trace the thousand-year-old Ukrainian history up to the settling of immigrants in the East Village. The spacious galleries of polished wood house stunning collections of folk art and costumes, elaborately decorated Easter eggs, richly detailed textiles and jewelry, and painting and sculptures from preeminent Ukrainian artists. The opulent display of traditional clothing for weddings and other rituals is particularly fascinating. Visit to marvel at the artistry of the culture and to learn more about Ukraine than what you may have heard concerning its clashes with its more famous easterly neighbor.

SHOP

No Relation Vintage

No Relation is the epitome of old-school thrift—grungy, trendsetting, unpredictable, and huge in the special way that makes you lose track of time as you root around for that perfect faded tee

> 204 1st Ave (btwn 12th and 13th St)
> 212-228-5201
> Sun 12pm-8pm, Mon-Thurs 1pm-8pm, Fri 1pm-9pm, Sat 12pm-9pm
> ❶ to 1st Ave, ❹❻❽❹
> ❺ ❻ to 14th St-Union Sq

or pair of biker boots. Prices are outer borough cheap for flowery bohemian skirts, bulky military jackets, and flamboyant sequined dresses alike. The only downside is that the pieces seriously have "no relation" to each other: you'll need to dig through a plethora of racks unorganized by either style or quality. Still, this is one of the few secondhand shops left in Manhattan that actually wants to make your student budget work for you. Come for the extensive collection of '70s apparel, and stay for the $10 shoe section.

St. Mark's Bookshop

Although you may come across a copy of Dan Brown's latest at this independent bookstore, most shoppers come for its spe-

> 31 3rd Ave (btwn 9th and 10th St)
> 212-260-7853
> Mon-Sat 10am-12am
> ❻ to Astor PIF to 169th St

cialties: tomes expounding on cultural theory and criticism, poetry, and film studies, as well as colorful pages of art, photography, and a solid collection of indie zines (including some very radical publications). The regulars—mostly NYU students and artists—spend hours perusing the carefully-selected merchandise and finding bargains in the sale section at the back of the store. More specialized and smaller than the Strand and with more of an intellectual focus than larger chain bookstores, St. Mark's carries obscure and unconventional volumes to provoke the thoughts of its customers.

Sunrise Mart

A discreet, almost indiscernible, elevator takes shoppers up to the second floor of a Cooper Union dorm to this Japanese super-

29 3rd Ave (at 10th St)
212-598-3040
Sun-Sat 10am-11pm
6 to Astor Place

market. But the cornucopia of Asian products within is worth the shady entrance. Customers fill their carts with seafood ranging from fish to octopus and choose from a vast selection of imported green teas, dining sets, incense sticks, and chopsticks in the back of the store. Although the Japanese beers are numerous and

well-priced, the best selection may be the candy and snacks. There are two aisles dedicated to chips, nuts, and crackers in unconventional flavors like shrimp and wasabi, as well as a profusion of Pocky sticks, rice cakes, mochi balls and various gummy animals. You may find it hard to leave without a newly-bought pack of chocolate-covered panda bears in your pocket.

Strand Bookstore

Don't be put off by the daily crowds browsing the disheveled $1 racks on the sidewalk. Enter this three-level store to see a bibliophile's wet dream: 18 miles of towering shelves, book spines of every height

828 Broadway (at 12th St)
212-473-1452
Sun 11am-10:30pm,
Mon-Sat 9:30am-10:30pm
L N 0 0 4 5 6 to
14th St-Union Sq

and thickness, and signs denoting the complete rainbow of literary genres. The Strand makes it easy for the overwhelmed by placing new, classic, and "perfect gift" ideas on front display tables. Past the hot commodities, spend an hour weaving through neatly-labeled books representing every era and country. The prices are just as admirable: The Strand sells used titles at an extremely respectable discount. The stock

MARK
best burgers for small hands

Passersby on St. Mark's Place might be quick to overlook Mark, thinking it to be just another mediocre burger stand. Those passersby are wrong: despite its kitschy appearance, Mark offers one of the most freshly ground, freshly grilled, lean, and delicious sliders in New York. And that's not even the best part: each burger is only $2! In fact, one bite of a Mark burger will make you reconsider spending $12 on burgers at many of the city's other restaurants. With its late-night hours and hip location, Mark is an irresistible stop for East Village partygoers on a night out—a burger paired with an equally cheap beer or shake, like the intriguingly named "Guinness Shake," makes for the perfect midnight snack.

33 St. Mark's Place (near 2nd Ave)
212-677-3132
Daily 12pm-3am
6 to Astor Pl, R to 8th St
$
*Outdoor Seating

---

is continually changing, and you'll never find a row of books in the same order twice—one of the reasons why locals make a daily pilgrimage.

EAT

Apiary · *New American*

A lesson in streamlined refinement, this chic dining room sets a high bar, with sharp, geometric dark wood tables, lit by side lamps painting the shadows of chandeliers on cream walls. The food does not disappoint. Chef Scott Bryan quietly returns from his self-imposed exile, serving up a stellar wine list alongside his signature style of modest yet surprising dishes that are, simply put, delicious. An eclectic appetizer menu includes colorful options such as crisp sweetbreads served in romesco, uplifted by a refreshing frisée. The entrées will floor the unprepared: a wonderfully firm monkfish in a summer corn soup, or a Peking duck breast with peppercorns and Tokyo turnips, served over an impossibly airy parsnip purée. All the dishes unfold a unique and complete flavor, a marriage of disparate ingredients that is, like Apiary itself, more than the sum of its magnificent parts.

60 3rd Ave (near 10th St)
212-254-0888
Sun-Mon 5:30pm-10pm, Tues-Thurs 5:30-10:30pm, Fri-Sat 5:30pm-11:30pm
6 to Astor Pl, N to 8th St, L to 3rd Ave
$$

259

ST. MARK'S PLACE

Walk 10 minutes south from Union Square and a three-block section of 8th St transforms into the infamously grungy cultural phenomenon that is St. Mark's Place. From 3rd Ave to Avenue A, tattooed men and pierced, mohawked punks try to run sequin-wearing clubbers off the sidewalk. The aromas streaming from the doors of cheap falafel joints, pizzerias, and numerous Japanese stir-fry places blend together to inundate the senses. Trendsetting youngsters flock to the iconic vintage punk purveyor **Trash and Vaudeville** *(4 St Mark's Pl)* for its plethora of knockoff sunglasses, hats, scarves, and jewelry. Beyond the overzealous salesmen at every other stand are a few singular stores worth a stop, including **St. Mark's Comics** *(11 St. Mark's Pl)* and **Mandala Tibetan Store** *(17 St Mark's Pl)*. The beloved strip has seen its share of counterculture heroes take a stand, from Basquiat to Jimi Hendrix. Party-goers, snarling rockers, and genuinely indescribable eccentric passerby make it the oddest, most dynamic three blocks in the East Village. A hard-won title.

BONDST
Japanese

6 Bond St (near Lafayette St)
212-777-2500
Sun-Wed 6pm-12am,
Thurs-Sat 6pm-1:30am
⊕ to Bleecker St, B, D,
⊕ to Broadway-Lafayette Ave
$$$

This ain't your everyday sushi bar—BONDST has the feel of a chic celebrity hangout and a menu that's as bold as it is exquisite. Chef Marc Spitzer describes a meal at his restaurant as an "experimental eating experience" rather than just a fancy way to fill your belly. With dishes like braised pork belly over an NYC-style pretzel cake, soba risotto with baby octopus and smoked trout butter, and raw red snapper tacos, BONDST goes for a shock and awe attack on your taste buds. Those looking for the full effect should order the Omakase tasting menu—designed nightly by Chef Spitzer, it brings to the table everything from oysters wrapped in edible gold to a tuna tart topped with shaved black truffles and ponzu sauce. Pair whatever you order with one of the equally innovative cocktails: the Maker's Mark with Asian pear nectar is a house favorite.

DBGB Kitchen and Bar
Gastropub

299 Bowery St (btwn Houston and 1st St)
212-933-5300
Daily 12pm-12am
⊕ to 2nd Ave, **⊕** to Bleecker St
$$

An uptown-directed attempt at a downtown pub, DBGB is Daniel Boulud's (of the upscale standard Daniel) precision applied to the rough-hewn world of Gastropubs. While the multifaceted menu can seem slightly overwhelming because of the sheer number of options, don't be afraid to share lots of plates. Highlights include a wide selection of decadent homemade sausages, the raw bar, and the sensational haute-burgers, such as the "piggie" burger, topped with pulled pork and house barbecue sauce. Getting acquainted with the extensive global collection of brews is reason in itself to visit—DBGB proudly aims to "give beer its proper place at the table." Coasters promoting said place are pre-set on

EAST VILLAGE
best artisanl pizza

Pizza Gruppo- Classic Italian pies are made thin and crispy here, with the freshest of ingredients. Try the Margherita with chopped tomatoes and basil leaves on top for garnish. *186 Avenue B, 212-995-2100, Sun 12pm-11pm, Mon-Thurs 11:30am-11pm, Fri 11:30am-12am, Sat 12pm-12am, L to 1st Ave $$*

Luzzo- All pizzas are stretched thin and smothered in a tangy sweet tomato sauce before entering the coal-burning oven—an anomaly for pizzerias in New York—at this quaint restaurant with a quirky interior design. *211 1st Ave, 212-473-7447, Sun, Tues-Thurs 12pm-11pm, Fri-Sat 12pm-12am, L to 1st Ave $$*

Artichoke Basille's Pizza- Swarms of pizza lovers and party-goers alike crowd into this small eatery to grab a slice of the famous pies—the cheesy spinach and artichoke or the classic Margherita with fresh parmesan and basil. Some domestic beers on tap. *328 E 14th St, 212-228-2004, Daily 11am-6am, L to 1st Ave $*

Totale Pizza- A newcomer to a crowded pizza scene, Totale has distinguished itself by offering cheaper personal pizzas without fudging the quality. *36 St. Mark's Place, 212-254-0180, Daily 12pm-11pm, 6 to Astor Pl $*

he musical phenomenon *Rent* chronicles the East Village art scene of the 1990s.

dark wood tables, surrounded by floor-to-ceiling shelves filled with bottles of wine, various dry goods, and an impressive collection of cooking containers donated by various celebrity chefs—all of which lend the space a stylish elegance.

Euzkadi

Tapas, Basque

108 E 4th St (btwn 1st & 2nd Ave)
212-982-9788
Sun 5pm-10:30pm, Mon-Thurs 5:30pm-11pm, Fri-Sat 5:30pm-12pm, bar open until 2am
F to 2nd Ave
$$

Euzkadi sports the clichéd exposed brick and chalkboard, but the cave paintings and imported odds and ends—"Piment d'Espelette" reads the sign on the bathroom door—give the restaurant its warmth. While one could simply order main dishes, opt for a dinner of tapas instead. The salty Datiles Euzkadi, dates filled with cabrales and wrapped in a jerky-like serrano ham, packs a surprising amount of flavor into its snack-sized portions. Pulpo a la Brasa is another must: the dish's lightly charred octopus, nested in a bevy of crisp vegetables, impressively avoids resembling rubber. Other items somewhat successfully prod diners' expectations, like the duck meatballs and the Bomba de Queso de Chivo, which soaks fried goat cheese in honey and echoes the Indian dessert gulab jamun. The beauty of Euzkadi is that you can try them all.

The Hummus Place

Mediterranean

109 St. Mark's Pl (btwn 1st Ave & Ave A)
212-529-9198
Sun-Fri 10:30am-12am, Sat 10:30am-2am
L to 1st Ave, **6** to Astor Pl
$
Additional Locations: 71 7th Ave S, 99 Macdougal St, 2608 Broadway, 305 Amsterdam Ave

Distressed brick walls, visible ceiling pipes, and wooden tables create a low-key setting for hummus fanatics to indulge in the creamy Middle Eastern spread, oil-drenched and dusted in spices. Purists take one glance at the streamlined menu and pick out the blandest offerings, the hummus tahini and the hummus masabacha, the latter topped with a happy overkill of chickpeas. Generous portions have diners hankering for another platter of pita bread ($1 per loaf). But while most come to sample the eatery's namesake specialty, it's impossible to ignore the ravishing $9.95 three-appetizer combination of falafels, lemony roasted eggplant, and vinegary rice-stuffed grape leaves served with mint yogurt sauce. Enjoy both an appetizer and entrée during lunch hours for an even guiltier steal of $7.95.

Ippudo

Japanese

65 4th Ave (btwn 9th and 10th St)
212-388-0088
Sun 11am-10:30pm, Mon-Thurs 11am-3:30pm, 5pm-11:30pm, Fri-Sat 11am-3:30pm, 5pm-12:30am
6 to Astor Pl
$$

This popular Japanese chain brings the traditional noodle house to the East Village. Once visitors get past the long lines stretching out the door and the hoard of people clustering around the front bar, the staff shouts a Japanese welcome, followed by more shouts when food is ready. Lauded by many as having the best noodles in New York, Ippudo's appetizers are just as noteworthy—the most popular is a bun stuffed with tender pork and crunchy lettuce in mayonnaise, a delightfully spicy combination of flavors and textures. Also worth trying are the fried pork belly and the cold Miyazaki soy milk and sesame soup. Visitors can reward their patience by ordering the famed ramen, a generous bowl of thin, homemade noodles in a pork broth with additions like miso paste. Keeping with tradition, diners must tell their waiter "kae dama" for a noodle refill.

Momofuku Ssam Bar *Korean, Southern*
The second establishment in David Chang's highly regarded Korean American empire, Momofuku Ssam Bar is a carnivore's dream. The menu, which changes daily and features produce from local farms, treats vegetarianism as a sin. The superstar chef is known for doing things his own way, especially the house special: the extravagant bo ssam. Designed for your entire party, this feast is the only dish that grants a reservation—the lettuce wrap contains a whole slow-cooked pork shoulder, a dozen oysters, rice, bibb lettuce, and a couple of sweet and savory Korean sauces. A late night menu is included as well, appropriately composed of stoner food and caviar. Ssam Bar's dark brown wooden in-

207 2nd Ave (at 13th St)
212-254-3500
Daily 11:30am-3:30pm,
Sun-Thurs 5pm-12am,
Fri-Sat 5pm-2am
N Q R 4 5 6 to 14th
St-Union Sq, **L** to 3rd
Ave
$$

BOWERY POETRY CLUB
best place to drop your ironic façade

The grungy alternative to schmancy Poet's House, Bowery Poetry Club attracts just as prestigious a crop of talent. Founded in 2002 by Bob Holman, the club became a landmark almost as soon as it opened, hosting critically acclaimed poets Tuli Kupferberg, Anne Waldman, and Sapphire. The dark and claustrophobic space is punctuated by an altar to the greats of English language verse: portraits of Alan Ginsberg, Langston Hughes, and Walt Whitman peek between Lagers at the ever-crowded bar. Welcoming visitors of any style or income bracket, the BPC snatches poetry from the hands of the elite: past events have showcased the work of Guatemalan migrant workers, beatboxers, and the deaf. Poetry gigs begin in the early evening, so come early to snag a seat and order a coffee from the wireless-accessible café. No beret or wasted heart needed.

308 Bowery (btwn
Houston and Bleecker St)
212-614-0505
Mon-Fri 4pm-4am, Sat-
Sun 12pm-4am
F to 2nd Ave, 6 to
Bleecker St
Free to $10 per show
*Live music, Wi-Fi

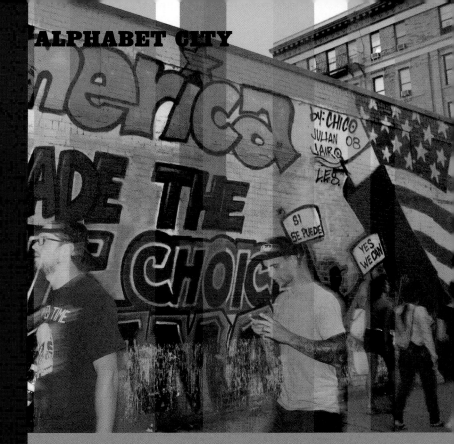

ALPHABET CITY

Alphabet City, the one-time home of an 1840s Little Germany and Rent's bohemian tragedians, covers the extreme southeastern corner of the Village, where the avenues shift from numbered to lettered names. In the last century, the neighborhood has largely consisted of Puerto Rican immigrants. The '80s riots, along with prevalent drug use and crime in Tompkins Square Park, made the area one of Manhattan's most dangerous. In the '90s came gentrification (admittedly the process has been slower here than in the rest of downtown), with shiny new storefronts trailblazing a change in local character. The Nuyorican Movement actively introduced Puerto Rican art forms, musical styles, and poetry to the neighborhood's cultural mainstream. **Nuyorican Poets Café** *(236 E 3rd St)*, where artists hold poetry slams, Latin Jazz Jams, and hip hop events, remains the heart of the movement. Alphabet City's turbulent '90s are of course best captured in Rent, which highlights AIDS, poverty, and the grassroots creativity that thrived at the time. Today the neighborhood accommodates students seeking rock-bottom downtown rents and families needing more permanent low-income housing. Crime rates decrease and sidewalks are polished every year, but Alphabet City still sustains its alt-culture vibe.

terior is stacked with tiny black benches that are rarely vacant, making the wait a chore—but as patrons attest, the pork buns are well worth it.

Otafuku   *Japanese*

Who said the Japanese only eat sushi? Japanese street food is tough to find in NYC, but Otafuku delivers Tokyo's secret to the East Village— drenched with various

236 E 9th St (off 2nd Ave)
212-353-8503
Mon-Fri 1pm-10pm, Sat-Sun 11am-10pm
6 to Astor Pl
$

sauces, mayo, and bonito flakes. Adventurous taste buds may be necessary, but this rare international bite is worth the risk. Rising sun flags sway all over the tiny building's ceiling while the duo behind the counter whips up incredibly true Japanese dishes. Try the okonomi (Japanese for "what you want"), a pancake filled with a mix of pork, beef, shrimp, or squid or the takoyaki, a batter dumpling filled with boiled octopus. Combine either dish with a solid yakisoba, pan fried noodles with squid and shrimp, and battle it out for the only bench outside.

Porchetta   *Italian, Sandwiches*

Since its opening, Porchetta has done one thing, and has done it magnificently. At the outset of New York's pork obsession (which shows no

sign of abating), this bright, clean storefront started peddling a classic Italian preparation of the meat. A gutted and deboned pig's body is layered with fat and various herbs, usually heavy on garlic and rosemary, then carefully

110 E 7th St (btwn Ave A & 1st Ave)
212-777-2151
Sun-Thurs 11:30am-10pm, Fri-Sat 11:30am-11pm
L to 1st Ave, **6** to Astor Pl
$

rolled and roasted. The rolled meat is then cut down and served either as a sandwich on floury, chewy ciabatta, or on a platter with a helping of vegetables. Either way, it's the meat—earthy and herbal and tasting like the very essence of pig—that steals the show. Vegetarians don't know what they're missing.

Tsampa   *Tibetan*

Even before the waitress begins to recite the native significance of the day's specials, Tsampa's décor betrays its Tibetan heritage. Perhaps it's the Shakyamuni prayer flags draped from the ceiling or the white shawl hanging over the Dalai Lama's smiling

Tibetan
212 E 9th St (btwn 2nd and 3rd Ave)
212-614-3226
Daily 5pm-11:30pm
N to 8th St, **6** to Astor Pl
$$

portrait, but the food is served with befitting tranquility. Tibet's most popular dish—Momo dumplings in a spicy red or green sauce—is an essential starter, welcomely followed by vegetarian, fish, or chicken entrées accented with thick seasoning or curry. Tsampa itself, the namesake of the restaurant, is roasted barley flour—a signature dessert when prepared with cranberries and honey. While the wall on the left side of the restaurant is ornamented with tapestries, the urban brick wall on the right reminds its visitors they are still in the heart of the East Village: the intersection of Astor and St. Mark's Place.

Veselka *Polish, Ukraine*
A relaxed atmosphere and 24 hour service

certainly make this 55-year-old restaurant an excellent choice for standard diner fare, but the vast offering of Ukranian comfort food makes it a New York original. The friendly staff retains a large memory of regulars' favorites, yet is certainly eager to guide newcomers through traditional dishes like bigos (sauerkraut and sausage stew), kielbasa (classic pork sausage), stuffed cabbage, potato pancakes, and blintzes (Ukrainian style crepes). There's an extensive selection of pierogi, with fillings ranging from traditional potato variet-

144 2nd Ave (at 9th St)
212-228-9682
Daily 24 hours
6 to Astor Pl
$$

BANJO JIM'S
best no cover music venue

Banjo Jim's may not take up a lot of space, but it can sure make a lot of noise. Mind you—this isn't the type of noise you're used to hearing in Alphabet City. Rather, it's the kind of noise you might hear up in Appalachia or down in Dixieland: the sound of joyous jazz, bluegrass, and folk with a lively crowd singing, dancing, and drinking along. All types of cats make up the crowd, from truly too-cool college students to mountain men just passing through. Those that are skilled enough get up to swing and square dance in the space between the stage and the wooden stools that seat the rest of the audience. All the rest fit snugly in the back or at the bar, sipping on wine or a bottle of Smuttynose. There's no cover here, so remember to tip the musicians.

Music Venue
700 E 9th St (at Avenue C)
212-777-0869
Sun-Thurs 6pm-2am, Fri 5pm-4am, Sat 2:30pm-4am
L to 1st Ave
$
*Dancing

ies to the uncommonly good goat cheese and arugula. With a neighborhood feel and hearty meals, Veselka is an essential stop for homesick Ukranians or a unique choice in the district of the late-night snack.

PLAY

Anthology Film Archives   *Cinema*

An old brick-slab warehouse may seem like an unlikely setting for a movie theater, with a leaky ceiling, gray walls, and uncomfortable seating.

32 2nd Ave (at 2nd St)
212-505-5181
Open Daily
F to 2nd Ave
Admission $9, Students
$7

However, this roughened gem is one of the city's leading underground cinemas and has promoted innovative filmmaking for over 40 years. Trendy artists and movie geeks alike flock to Anthology to find the best and most obscure in avant-garde and independent film. Anthology also functions as a museum of cinematic history, featuring a reference library, a world-famous film preservation department, and a gallery that boasts obscure classics and fresh treasures alike.

Blind Barber   *Lounge*

This brand new barbershop-meets-bar has fast become a weekend hotspot for artsy socialites in the East Village. Brought to you by the minds behind Ella and Gallery Bar, it's a place for the hip and youthful

339 E 10th St (near
Avenue B)
212-228-2123
Sun 12pm-8pm, Mon-Fri
6pm-4am, Sat 12pm-
4am
L to 1st Ave
$$

to drink in a classy, old-school environment—with a twist, of course. That twist is the barbershop in front, which stays open until 9pm and offers free specialty cocktails with $30 shaves and $40 haircuts. It's the perfect pregame, for when the clock strikes 9, you can strut into the

back lounge looking fly and feeling fine. Stay late enough and notable DJs will hit the decks, prompting an impromptu dance party. Don't want to mess up your hair? Grab a Lemongrass Gimlet and have a seat in the round leather booths under the vintage photos on the wall.

Cooper 35   *Gastropub*

A cheapo staple of the East Village, Cooper 35 (also known as Asian Pub) boasts strong $4 mixed drinks that become $5 at midnight and Asian-fusion entrées for under $10. Sure,

35 Cooper Square (at E
6th St)
212-375-9195
Sun-Thurs 5pm-12am,
Fri-Sat 5pm-2am
6 to Astor Pl
$

the California rolls are heavy on the rice, and the pad Thai is a tad overcooked, but your wallet won't notice and neither will you once you take a lycheetini to the face. Plus, Cooper is a pub first and a restaurant second, so don't complain—nobody forced you to order the warm beef salad. If weather permits, grab a table in the outdoor area, which is draped in vines and looks out onto the Bowery. Weekends get crowded with Cooper Union and NYU students, so arrive early to beat the rush

Eastern Bloc   *LGBT*

This Soviet-themed dive bar meets raunchy dance club is owned by Anderson Cooper's boyfriend, Benjamin Maisani, and has become a favorite for gay, adventurous twenty-

505 E 6th St, #A (btwn
Avenue A & Avenue B)
212-777-2555
Daily 7pm-4am
F to 2nd Ave, **L** to
1st Ave
$$

somethings. A self-described "true man meat bar," the Eastern Bloc gives visitors a taste of the East Village LGBT scene's uncensored flavor with a stripper pole, topless bartenders, and porn vids playing on TV screens. Weekends attract a younger crowd less interested in the bar's commie propaganda decorations and more interested in cruising for dudes. Sex comes first and shyness comes last here (with drinking and dancing somewhere in between), so throw caution (but not protection) to the wind! Become a regular, and you might be lucky enough to run into pop goddess/sex symbol Madonna, who is said to come by the bar with Cooper himself.

dience for local writers who share their work at events like the monthly "Drunken! Careening! Writers!" reading series. It feels like a friendly, secret club—perfect to hone your craft, feed your head, and nurse an extremely strong drink under a judgmental bust of Lenin.

KGB Bar

Bar, Lounge, Lit Club

85 E 4th St (at 2nd Ave), 2nd Fl
212-505-3360
Daily 7pm-4am
F to 2nd Ave
$

Up a steep flight of stairs gather expatriates, eccentrics, and the occasional real ex-KGB to drink Baltika beers at this former local headquarters of the Ukrainian socialist party. The red walls are plastered with Socialist Realist art, authentic propaganda posters, and Soviet souvenirs. Misha the bear, a 1980 Olympics Soviet mascot, watches from the corner while a quiet bartender spins the Pixies and pours 20 different kinds of vodka. This is the only bar in New York that publishes its own literary journal, and several times a week barflies metamorphose into an au-

Lit Lounge

Dive

93 2nd Ave (btwn 5th and 6th St)
212-777-7987
Daily 5pm-4am
6 to Astor Pl, **F** to 2nd Ave
$

Looking for a place in the East Village to drink for cheap, dance like a freak, catch a live band, and see pretty people all in one night? For nearly nine years, Lit Lounge has been your destination. Though past its supposed "peak" of Ryan McGinley's-favorite-bar stardumb, it's one of the few East Village hangouts that hasn't been infiltrated by bridge-and-tunnel boneheads. With cave-like walls under dim red lighting, it feels like a dive with lots of space. Reliable DJs spin by the dance floor upstairs and live indie bands put on sweaty shows down below. Having hosted acts like Devendra Banhart and Chairlift, Lit has an ear for what's up-and-coming. If you're lucky, you might catch an open bar downstairs, which happens at least once a week.

McSorely's Old Ale House — *Beer Bar*

Since 1854, this classic East Village bar has served its famed house ale to everyone from Abe Lincoln to John Lennon. Although it was forced to allow women entry in 1970, McSorley's continues to cater to a crowd almost entirely composed of manly men—those who cheer loudly when their baseball team scores and burst into fist-pumping chants of "USA!" Busts of John F. Kennedy and the decorative clovers scattered amongst dusty knickknacks remind customers of the joint's beginnings as an Irish working-man's pub, as does the simple menu, which offers a cheese and onion plate or small bowl of soup for just $3.50. And with mugs of the house ale served in pairs for only $4.50, drinks seem

15 E 7th St (at 3rd Ave)
212-473-9148
Sun 1pm-1am, Mon-Sat 11am-1am
⊕ to 8th St, ⑥ to Astor Pl
$

priced for a different century too.

The Stone — *Music Venue*

ALL AGES ♫

16 Avenue C (at 6th St)
212-228-5201
Tues-Sun 8pm and 10pm
⓮ ⓳ ❷ to Essex-Delancey St
Admission $10

This platform for avant-garde and experimental music is one of the last non-profit performance spaces left to serve the underground music scene of lower Manhattan. Artistic director John Zorn allows a different musician each month to curate a project, and gives him or her the entire nightly revenue. The black box theater is a hub for creative, inspirational sounds that shock and surprise the audience: Zorn chooses artists who turn ordinary objects into instruments, or who use instruments in strange and obscure ways. Unlike other underground live performance spaces in New York City, the Stone doesn't sell overly priced drinks or promote T-shirt marketing incentives—it's all about the music, raw and innovative.

269

270

271

Once the highest point in the pint-sized 1700s Manhattan, the area today called SoHo was the site of army fortifications for George Washington before quieting down to become a post-colonial suburb. The region's next big moment came in the 1840s, when a peculiarity in the 19th-century construction boom brought upwards of 250 cast iron office buildings, rowhouses, and large freestanding homes. It was these ornate iron gables and curlicues that would earn SoHo its status as a Historic District in 1978—but first the neighborhood had to go through its rough adolescence. If you asked about the area south of Houston Street in the 1960s, you'd hear about abandoned warehouses, sweatshop factories, dangerous bars, and dens of ill repute.

Today the neighborhood has a reputation as the most chic place in Manhattan, a place so hip that designers name handbags in its honor. As is typical in New York, this transformation was catalyzed by those eternally-starving artists who swarmed the derelict area to take advantage of loft spaces and cheap rent. After the artists came the galleries, and after the galleries came the boutiques and posh retail chains that hawk babydolls and earrings to a different kind of starving client. The lofts that the artists rented decades ago remain as a defining feature of the area, only transformed into high-end housing for Soho's celebrity-studded residential population.

Tribeca may not be as famous or as hip as its border to the north, but its evolution from industrial black hole to refined residential area followed mostly the same pattern: money in, artists out. Its typically glossy scene of boutiques and dining establishments may invoke a SoHoesque feel, but Tribeca is an entirely separate creature. For one thing, it seems to have escaped the notice of the tourist population—an interesting oversight considering it's the first stop for any mainlander entering town via the Holland Tunnel. Tribeca is also less dense in its layout and, as a result, far more family-friendly. Occasional events like the Tribeca Film Festival might have a brief effect on the size and constitution of the crowds on the pavement, but for the most part it's quiet. Expensively quiet. In 2006 Forbes Magazine ranked Tribeca as the priciest zip code in the city, and not much has changed since then.

Visitors tend to group Tribeca and SoHo in the same category (Gentrified Playgrounds), but they're better defined by their contributions to urban life—New York has always been changing, and just because bohemians can't afford to live in the airy singles they once commandeered for studio space doesn't mean that the area has lost its capacity for inventiveness. Tribeca is, increasingly, the ultimate place for first-time independent filmmakers to present their work, and SoHo rivals old guard 5th Ave as the fashion capital of the city.

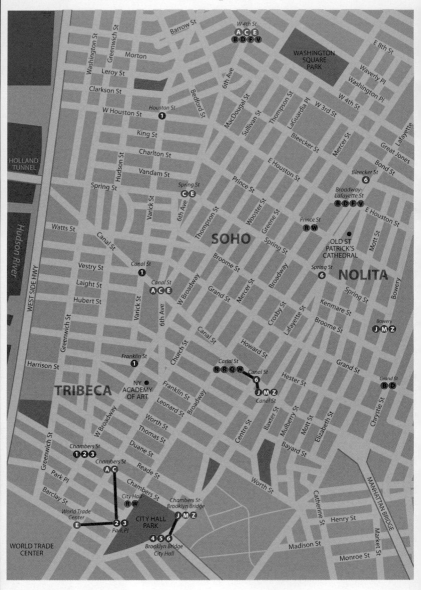

EXPLORE

Angelika Film Center

Instead of overpriced "buttered" popcorn, indulge in gourmet coffee and a pastry in the bright, spacious

18 W Houston St
(btwn Broadway & Mercer St)
212-995-2000

lounge of this six-theater independent movie house just north of the SoHo shopping district. The flagship SoHo theater opened in 1989, followed by three Texas locations in quick succession. Come early, settle on a leather couch or at a marble-topped café table, and engage your neighbor in a debate on the merits of modern cinema. The screens below ground play contemporary independent and foreign films in equal parts, to the occasional rumbling accompaniment of a subway car passing by. Angelika's movies are off the beaten path, but not inaccessible—this is simply arthouse cinema for a crowd tired of the multiplex.

The Flea Theater

"A joyful hell in a small space" is the fitting self-description of the Flea Theater, whose nightly flurry of off-Broadway artistry is barely contained by its walls. Featuring

41 White St
(Btwn Broadway & Church)
212-226-0051
❶ *to Franklin St,*
Ⓐ Ⓒ Ⓔ Ⓖ Ⓙ Ⓩ Ⓝ Ⓠ Ⓡ
to Canal St

everything from straightforward, introspective dramas to edgy performances by clown school students, the Flea earns its reputation as one of the most eclectic and unique theaters in the city. Although the acts are seasonal, events like Music with a View and Dance Conversations are quickly becoming annual staples of the experimental performance circuit. For those who would rather write than watch, The Flea also hosts workshops through its Pataphysics program—particularly talented students have had their material staged in-house.

neighborhood NECESSITIES

SUBWAYS 1, 2 ,3, 6, 9, A, C, E, N, Q, R, J, M, Z

BUSES M5, M20, M21, M22

MARKET Gourmet Garage *(453 Broome St, 212-941-5850)*

LIBRARIES Mulberry Street Library *(10 Jersey St, 212-966-3424)*

MEDIA *Soho Journal*

FITNESS New York Sports Club *(503-511 Broadway, 212-925-6600)*, Dance With Me SoHo *(466 Broome St, 212-840-3262)*

BIKES Bicycle Habitat *(244 Lafayette St, 212-431-3315)*

Nelson A Rockefeller Park

Rockefeller Park's sweet location between the Hudson and the glassed high-rises

River Terrace
❶ ❷ ❸ Ⓐ Ⓒ *to Chambers St*

of River Terrace gives it a cliff-like feel, as if it's hanging off the edge of the island. One of Manhattan's least visited parks, this serene plain is usually tourist-free, making it an exceptional place to survey the Hudson in peace. The up-close and personal views of the Statue of Liberty and New Jersey are perfect for photographers hoping to capture the uninterrupted skyline or a late sun sinking into the river. Kids will take pleasure in the pedal-powered carousel and free jump rope rentals, but the adult charm of this park is the open and outdoors-y feel that's unique in the cluttered downtown area.

New York City Fire Museum

The legendary feats of New York's fearless fire department are deeply ingrained in local history, but for 20 years, the New York City Fire Museum has been commemorating

278 Spring St (btwn Varick & Hudson St)
212-691-1303
C **E** to Spring St,
1 to Houston St
Sun 10am-4pm,
Tues-Sat 10am-5pm
Suggested Donation $7

the FDNY's contributions in a sublimely low-key remodeled firehouse. Visitors work their way around two floors of artifacts from the department's 500-year history: antique fire carriages, historic records, portraits of 19th-century ladder chiefs, and polished silver badges, all presided over by a friendly staff of retired FDNY officers and enthusiasts. The museum's singularly definitive knowledge base came in handy in the early 2000s, when its regalia was used as a reference point for Martin Scorsese's period film Gangs of New York.

The Wooster Group Experimental Theater

The Wooster Group is known as one of the premier purveyors of experimental theater in New York, a title quite fairly earned

33 Wooster St
(at Grand St)
212-966-9796
1 **A** **C** **E** **G** **J** **Z**
N **Q** **R** to Canal St

by any standard. Stationed in The Performing Garage at 33 Wooster since the 1980s, the collective puts on original productions that use a multimedia stage experience to reflect our culture's changing relationship with theater. Their innovation in incorporating dance, film, light,

SoHo & TriBeCa
UNDER $20

Have a froufrou $4.25 breakfast of chocolate bread and coffee at **Petite Abeille** *(134 W Broadway)*.

Now de-froufrou by paddling in the Hudson at **Downtown Boathouse**'s Pier 40 location *(W Houston & West St)*, where kayak rentals are free.

Dry up with a dose of culture at a 30-year-old installation called **The New York Earth Room** *(141 Wooster St)*, a loft filled with 280,000 pounds of dirt. It's art, or something like it.

Get an $8 plate of rice and beans—it's big enough for two—at **La Nueva Conquista** *(236 Lafayette St)*. If you're feeling extravagant, add some succulent pork for an astronomical extra two dollars.

Work off your lunch with a trek to **Nelson A. Rockefeller Park** *(River Terrace and Park Place W)*, where you can watch boats go by and pretend you don't want to try out the pedal-powered carousel.

Conclude your day with a $4.50 bowl of chili at the **Broome Street Bar** *(363 W Broadway)* and spend the rest of your money on a frothy stein of beer.

sound, and architecture into traditional drama has influenced the modern era of contemporary theater so deeply that their entire body of work has been toured internationally. Tickets go for prices to be expected of a non-profit theater company, but they're still cheaper than most seats off-Broadway, and it's impossible to feel cheated after considering that some of the troupe's actors are living legends.

SHOP

Housing Works Bookstore Café and Thrift Shop

This homey bookstore, café, and thrift shop is an extension of Housing Works, an organization that uses all of its profit to provide safe housing and support for people with HIV/AIDS. Even if it weren't for a good cause, you would enjoy browsing at the Housing Works because of its handsome wooden bookshelves and hundreds of attractively worn books at charitably low

126 Crosby St (btwn
W Houston & Prince St)
212-334-3324
Mon-Fri 10am-9pm,
Sat-Sun 12pm-7pm
B D F to Broadway-La-
fayette, **N R** to Prince St

prices. The little eatery at the back, staffed entirely by Housing Works volunteers, cranks out the many pots of coffee and urns of tea needed to fuel the literary crowd that comes for the cheap books and out-of-season duds dropped off by SoHo fashionistas. Pick up designer clothing and vintage shoes, or furnish your apartment with endearingly dusky pieces—buyers' remorse has no place here.

J. Crew Men's Shop at the Liquor Store

Two guys walk into a bar. (A beat.) They walk out toting bags brimming with cuff links, ties, dress shirts, and slacks. When the famous Liquor Store Bar closed its doors

235 W Broadway
(at White St)
212-226-5476
Sun 12-6pm,
Mon-Fri 11am-8pm,
Sat, 11am-7pm
1 to Franklin St,
A C E to Canal St

in 2006, it was reincarnated as a unique all-menswear extension of the J. Crew franchise. The store maintains a few relics of the old hangout—the bar is still intact—but amps up the preppy manliness with creaky leather chairs, haphazardly stacked Kerouac novels, and rugged wooden shelves. The merchandise itself is a

An abstract pattern of inlaid rods in the sidewalk at 110 Greene St actually depicts the NYC subway map. It was designed by Francoise Schein, a Belgian artist and architect, in 1986.

step above the typically pitiful selection of men's clothing stuffed in the back of J. Crew, with limited-edition shirts and vintage pieces circulating amongst the standard fare. Bite down on the end of your cigar and shop like a man.

Pearl River Mart

This one-stop shop for all things East Asian is a more than adequate alternative to the hustle and haggle of Chinatown. Pearl River

477 Broadway (btwn Broome & Grand St) 212-431-7388
6 to Spring St, **6 J Z** **N Q R** to Canal St

Mart is an indoor bazaar whose shelves carry the beautiful (samaurai swords, lanterns), the useful (patterned tea services), and all manner of cheaper oddities, like a kimono to be worn by a beer bottle. The ground floor is presided over by a winding silk dragon suspended from the ceiling that keeps a close eye on the racks of Chinese clothing, kitchenware, and home goods, while Chinese furniture crowds the top floor. If you get tired of playing with the cornucopia of knickknacks, calm down with one of Pearl River's exotic blends up in the tea balcony.

Topshop

Topshop is a beacon for fashionistas who need to be told what to wear and when to wear it. Famous long before Kate Moss introduced her in-house

478 Broadway (btwn Broome & Grand St) 212-966-9555 Mon-Fri 10am-9pm, Sat-Sun 10am-8pm
6 to Spring St, **6 J Z** **N Q R** to Canal St

fashion line, this upscale answer to H&M stocks a host of runway-ready fashion, complemented by the thumping vibes of the resident DJ and a flashy lighting design that makes all four stories feel like a club rather than a glorified department store. Heavily mascaraed women and the occasional dude grab a Topshop personal shopper and mob the racks, hoping to buy themselves into a state of fashion nirvana. Surrender, and emerge a better (or maybe just better-dressed) person in the mecca of SoHo's shopping district.

Uniqlo

Walking into Uniqlo is like taking a step into an obsessive-compulsive's idea of shopping heaven. Pure white walls and a shiny clean floor set off neatly-spaced racks of basic shirts, organized to a T, and stacks of solid-colored jeans are piled like layers of ribbon candy. Pearly staircases lead you up to a men's section where casual tees exude, improbably, immaculate class. Everything is presented with simplicity and grace, a quality that makes this store, the only Uniqlo in all of North America, a uniquely

546 Broadway
(btwn Spring & Prince St)
917-237-8800
Sun 11am-8pm,
Mon-Sat 10am-9pm
 to Prince St,
 to Spring St

calming shopping experience. The highly affordable Japanese brand is known for making high-quality, unassumingly beautiful clothing that looks good on just about everybody. To perfect the ease of your shopping experience, an on-site tailor will alter any pair of jeans you bring in.

EAT

Alidoro   *Sandwiches*

Scents of artichoke hearts and out-of-the-oven focaccia bread speak for themselves upon entry to this Italian sandwich shop. Baked loaves are kept under the glass cashier's counter and

MUSEUM OF CARTOON AND COMIC ART
best museum for museum haters

This museum actually encourages you to laugh at its offerings. While some of the rotating exhibits speak to more serious literary and artistic endeavors, much of the work is just what you would expect from a permanent collection supplied by cartoonists of the radical, notorious, and adventurous varieties. There are plenty of superheroes and a dusting of Peanuts one-liners amongst the outlandish drawings and fascinating commentary. Artists' original sketches and the rare rejected

594 Broadway (btwn
Houston & Prince St)
212-254-3511
Tues-Sun 12pm-5pm
6 to Bleecker St,
N,R to Prince St, B, D, F to
Broadway-Lafayette St

version create microcosmic narratives within exhibits: the progression of a comic from its birth as a zany idea to its published completion. In the same spirit, the layout of the gallery is designed for fluid movement throughout the space, with the single exception of the mysteriously roped-off 18+ section.

vintage Italian posters cover the walls of the tiny, takeout-only room. A few tables have recently been added, but have not kept customers from lining up on Sullivan St to order their choice of the menu's 40 sandwiches—the only thing Alidoro offers. Signature selections include the Pinocchio, a favorite among fans of prosciutto, and the Gepetto, for those who prefer sopressata and eggplant. Make sure you order your sandwich by name, as this has become part of the tradition. And though this rule won't reduce the line, it's a key to some of Manhattan's most delectable sandwiches.

105 Sullivan St
(btwn Prince & Spring St)
212-334-5179
Mon-Sat 11:30am-5pm
C E to Spring St
$$

Blaue Gans

All dark wood and high ceilings, with a long central table, Kurt Gutenbrunner's Blaue Gans might resemble Beowulf's mead hall if it weren't for the posters covering every inch of wall space and the leather booths along the sides. Fans of traditional Austrian fare should skip the wurst platter and go straight for Käsekrainer, a juicy beef sausage with cheese. The Wiener schnitzel is simple and unadorned—just breaded pork with sweet and tart lingonberry sauce. For those who find Germanic dishes too heavy, the striped bass is

Austrian

139 Duane St (btwn W Broadway & Church St)
212-571-8880
Sun-Wed 11am-12am,
Thurs-Sat 11am-1am
1 2 3 A C to
Chambers St
$$$

S.O.B.'s
coolest caipirinhas

Inside this renowned venue for world music—with a special focus on Brazilian and Caribbean styles—the young and old mingle together to show off their dance moves, imbibe caipirinhas, and revel in hypnotic beats. The minimally adorned, swanky space offers nightly performances of everything from Afro-Brazilian to salsa grooves. Catch your breath from dancing on the expansive and often packed floor to lounge at a small table along the wall or near the back bar. The food menu features generous portions of Latin and Brazilian specialties, like grilled snapper and feijoada, and the bar serves everything from domestic Bud to Cuban mojitos. Whether stopping by for a drink after work, shaking it at a late night samba session, or attending a private party, Sounds Of Brazil's promises to deliver a top notch multi-sensory experience.

Music Venue,
Gastropub

Music Venue, Gastropub
212-243-4940
204 Varick St
(at Houston St)
Sun-Thurs 7pm-2am, Fri
5pm-5am, Sat 7pm-5am
1 to Houston St
$$
*Dancing, Live Music

delicious, with a crispy skin covering soft, hot meat. Leave room for the black forest chocolate cake for dessert: its richness is nicely offset by the amaretto ice cream.

Blue Ribbon Brasserie — *New American*

97 Sullivan St
(near Spring St)
212-274-0404
Daily 4pm-4am
Ⓐ Ⓒ to Spring St
$$$

The appropriately worn "Blue Ribbon" sign on the door reflects a Brasserie that has weathered the growth of a brand without compromising quality. Open for almost 20 years, this restaurant has retained an adept hold on the subtleties of a successful Brasserie, though eight diverse restaurants have splintered off with the Blue Ribbon name. Erudite waiters nonchalantly enforce the relaxed atmosphere, providing helpful suggestions in how to pair or consume the unequivocally upscale cuisine. While many dishes come with their own utensils, the gourmet plates are unimposing, with many updated to lean towards comfort food. The beef marrow and oxtail marmalade take the potentially ominous ingredients and create a spectacularly savory jam to be spread over challah toast sprinkled with rock salt. The catfish, served with an herb-crisped skin, playfully jumps between sweet and spicy—an urbane dish that you can eat with your elbows on the table.

Café Gitane — *French, Moroccan*

242 Mott St
(near Prince St)
212-334-9552
Sun-Thurs 9am-12am,
Fri-Sat 9am-12:30am
Ⓑ Ⓓ Ⓕ to Broadway-Lafayette,
Ⓝ Ⓡ to Prince St,
$$

With a royal blue awning and a red brick exterior, Café Gitane is a Mott St standout. Yet on any given lunch hour, the restaurant attracts attention not from its colorful entrance, but from the brightly clad line of customers extending out the door. This French-Moroccan café lures Nolita's Euro-centric trendsetters looking for an equally dapper meal. Begin with the seven-grain toast topped with avocado and lemon juice—one of Gitane's signatures, it's impossible to resist. A standout entrée is the Moroccan couscous specialty with hummus and eggplant, along with your choice of organic chicken or merguez sausage. For a relaxing end to the experience, enjoy the vin chaud, mulled wine served with cinnamon and clove. And although each plate is elegantly prepared, the prices are not unbearable, making repeat visits an inevitability.

The world's first successful passenger elevator was installed in the E.V. Haughwout building on the corner of Broome and Broadway on March 23, 1857.

Calexico
Mexican, Food Stand

Wooster St
(near Prince St)
917-674-1869
Mon-Fri
11:30am-3:30pm
N **R** to Prince St,
C **E** to Spring St
$

This trendy SoHo Mexican truck is run by three brothers transplanted from California looking to take part in the newly popular New York City movement to establish Mexican cuisine in Manhattan dining establishments. Come for lunch to be shocked by the hefty mass of hungry people crowded around the metallic box parked casually on the sidewalk. Calexico serves up overstuffed tacos, burritos, and quesadillas, all worthy of their West Coast heritage. Choose between the house specialty carne asada, chicken, pork, black beans, or whatever the daily special happens to be, and watch in awe as the truck's three employees shuffle around spastically, yet gracefully to keep up with the lunch rush.

Ceci-Cela
French, Patisserie

55 Spring St (at Lafayette)
212-274-9179
Mon-Fri 9:30am-5pm
6 to Spring St
$$

The classic French patisserie is something of a rarity on the streets of New York City. Ceci-Cela is one of the few places where it's possible to settle down for a crispy croissant or a creamy éclair as if you were on the banks of the Seine, rather than the Hudson. Owned by French pastry chef Laurent Dupal, the tiny Spring St café has a wonderful storefront display case of decorative cakes, tarts, and pastries as well as a variety of sandwiches, quiches, and savory snacks that taste as good as they look. Ceci-Cela brings the best of both worlds: it also serves the kind of rich, cold iced coffee that is only available on this side of the Atlantic. For the New York stalwarts, there is even a small corner of bagels near the register, though they are wrapped in plastic and best avoided.

Hundred Acres

New American

38 MacDougal St (btwn Prince & W Houston St)
212-475-7500
Sun 11am-10pm,
Mon-Fri 12pm-11pm,
Sat 11am-11pm
❶ to Houston St,
❻ ❹ to Spring St
$$

The interior of Hundred Acres is a medley of rustic meets modern, with wood-paneled walls and a bar lined in white ceramic tiles. The menu changes seasonally, but executive chef Joel Hough is comfortable adjusting it daily according to the bounty of local suppliers from farms in New York and New Jersey. The harmony of French techniques and Southern dishes makes creative use of pickles, which the restaurant house-makes for its dishes as well as its cocktails. For starters, split the fried green tomatoes—they're matched in flavor by a crispy envelope of Panko breadcrumbs, and topped with pickles for an appealing contrast. Follow this with the Amish chicken, a generous, no-fuss dish that is perfectly seasoned. End with the decadent brioche bread pudding, a sweet and flavorful dessert topped with a well-balanced, slightly bitter caramel ice cream.

Kittichai

Thai

60 Thompson St
(near Broome St)
212-219-2000
Sun-Wed 5:30pm-11pm,
Thurs-Fri 5:30pm-12am
❻ ❹ to Spring St
$$$$

High-end Asian restaurants in the mold of Spice Market are not exactly fashionable anymore, but Kittichai has always been a little different than its brethren. The mercifully quiet dining room is comfortable and attractive, if a touch generic, with its reflecting pool, candles, and various Thai artifacts. Focusing on a Thai palate rather than misguided attempts at pan-Asian fusion, the food steers toward bold—if not strictly authentic—flavors. Kittichai's basic curries will not disappoint, though a dozen cheaper Thai spots around town do them equally well. Dishes like the banana blossom and artichoke salad and the baked sea bass demonstrate far greater creativity and skill, and at its best—namely the coconut-braised short ribs—the food can be glee-inducing. For $65, the five-course tasting is an exceptional deal and provides ample opportunity to sample the best of what this kitchen has to offer.

L'Ecole at the French Culinary Institute

French

462 Broadway (btwn Broome & Grand St)
212-219-3300
Sun 11:30am-2:30pm,
Mon-Fri 12:30pm-2pm,
5:30pm-7pm, 8pm-9pm,
Sat 11:30am-2:30pm,
5:30pm-7pm, 8pm-9pm
❻ ❹ Ⓜ ❷ ❻ ❻ ❻ ❶ to Canal St
$$$

L'Ecole at the French Culinary Institute inhabits an unusual space in the Manhattan dining scene. For starters, students comprise almost the entire staff. Arty, black-and-white pictures of instructors guiding them through the perfect steak au poivre, along with the self-assured strut of the wait staff, fosters a "Look Mom, no hands!" attitude that deflates the usual hauteur of French cuisine. But the cooking isn't remotely pre-professional. A five-course summer offering includes skate carpaccio splashed with yuzu vinaigrette, an exercise in maturity and balance. Duck breast and its corresponding confit leg are cooked perfectly—the acid from a port wine and cherry concoction cuts through the bird's richness. Perhaps most impressive is the frozen goat cheese, a palate cleanser that alludes to executive chef Nils Noren's molecular gastronomy background. But like the best restaurants, L'Ecole doesn't let itself become content—the menu is constantly changing.

La Esquina

Mexican

La Esquina means "the corner" in Spanish, and while the taqueria's location suggests that the name is meant literally, it also exists on a culinary corner. Both authentic and experimental, the menu is composed of dressed-up street food, like tongue tacos made with veal and a light-as-air avocado mousse. The pulled pork tacos, in a nod to Southern barbecue, are harmonized with fearsome habenero-pickled onions. Other offerings include Mexican staples like tortas and plates heaping with expertly spiced sauces and stick-to-your-ribs portions of rice and beans. Enjoy your food in a number of settings—the outdoor stand by the order window, the room itself (a small but functional converted diner car), and the subterranean bar. But in the summer, al fresco seating is the superior option—tacos and a glass of horchata, the famed Mexican rice-and-cinnamon elixir, are an unbeatable combination in the heat.

114 Kenmare St
(at Lafayette St)
646-613-7100
Sun 11am-12am, Mon-Thurs 12pm-12am, Fri 12pm-1am, Sat 11am-1am
6 to Spring St,
❶ Ⓜ ❷ to Broad St
$$

Salt *New American*

58 MacDougal St
(near W Houston St)
212-674-4968
Sun 11am-10pm,
Mon 6pm-10:30pm,
Tues-Thurs 12pm-3pm,
6pm-10:30pm
Sat 11am-11:30pm
❶ to Houston St,
Ⓒ Ⓔ to Spring St
$$$

Upon reading that salt is offered as a house-warming gift in Hebrew tradition, owner and chef Melissa O'Donnell fashioned her restaurant after the mineral's time-honored significance. Pushing together whitewashed benches to form communal tables, her young staff created an intimate, candle-lit space where chums and coworkers sup nightly. Honey-glazed dates bundled in bacon and mussels sluiced in an addictively flavorful stew of Thai chili, coconut, and cilantro are among the juiciest appetizers. Besides a standard list of entrées, Salt's "protein +2" option allows diners to customize their main course with a choice of a meat and two sides. While the menu is seasonal, the zesty whole-grilled dourade is a perennial favorite. Dessert holds dainty surprises: the lemon tart's shortbread is composed of subtle whiffs of lavender, while leftover slices of lemon rinds form

a pyre to prop up the accompanying dollop of Earl Grey ice cream.

Snack *Mediterranean*

105 Thompson St (btwn Prince & Spring St)
212-925-1040
Sun 12-9pm,
Mon-Wed 12pm-10pm,
Thurs-Sat 12-11pm
Ⓒ Ⓔ to Spring St
$$

With a name that rouses memories of the kitchen counter, SoHo's most acclaimed Greek restaurant welcomes guests as a mother would her kids after school. Originally a Greek grocery market, the dual kitchen and dining room is ornamented with imported honey, breads, and boxed juices—all readily on sale alongside homemade hummus and stuffed grape leaves. And if the temptation isn't enough, an open cookie jar sits atop the glowing stove. Snack directly translates to Meze, an appetizer, such as the signature Pikilia platter—the pita-dipping dish is ideal for sharing across the stainless steel tabletops. Next, add a side of lentil rice to balance a rich entrée followed by a Baklara pastry to soothe your sweet tooth. While it may be easy to lose track of time relaxing in momma's kitchen, two clocks complete the back wall, seven hours apart: New York and Athens.

Welcome to India *Indian*

369 Broome St
(near Mott St)
212-334-9145
Daily 11am-11pm
❶ Ⓜ ❷ to Bowery St,
❸ Ⓓ to Grand St,
6 to Spring St
$

Unlike its sparkly counterparts in Murray Hill and Jackson Heights, Welcome to India sticks to the basics: there no multicolored Christmas lights, no Bollywood posters, just plastic trays, disposable silverware, and fluorescent lighting. However, this tiny takeout restaurant—the smaller spinoff of Joy of India in midtown—doesn't skimp on the spice. Chef Kukun Jubir's menu is limited to classic Indian-American dishes, but that doesn't mean he tones down the heat factor for unaccustomed diners. All meat

is Halal and dishes made to order, not frozen, resulting in perfectly crispy veg samosas, tender paneer in spinach, and chicken tikka so flavorful that it will put you off the microwavable kind forever. Pair the lamb vindaloo with a sweet lassi—you'll need the yogurt drink to keep the tears from rolling down your cheeks.

PLAY

Circa Tabac

Smoking Lounge

It's not difficult to imagine Hemingway or Kerouac calling this cigar lounge their haunt of choice. Cosmopolitan types sit with furrowed brows lit by the cherried embers of their cigarettes, and the burgundy trim and velveteen curtains that adorn the walls of the dark space create a unique scene that's romantic, if not downright seductive. While you can buy a pack of foreign cigarettes from their vast selection (The Shepherd's Hotel, from Germany, is spicy and rich), there's appeal for the non-smoker as

32 Watts St
(near Canal St)
212-941-1781
Sun-Mon 5pm-2am,
Tues-Sat 5pm-4am
Ⓐ Ⓒ Ⓔ to Canal St,
❶ to Canal St
$$

well. The cocktails, like the elegant Rio, with coconut rum and Chambord, are fantastic. Patrons also benefit from a fantastic ventilation system, which leaves no remnant of smoke except for a faint and altogether pleasant musk.

Sway

Lounge, Nightclub

305 Spring St (btwn Hudson & Greenwich St)
212-620-5220
Thurs-Mon 10pm-4am
❶ to Houston,
Ⓒ Ⓔ to Spring St

The weekend only ends when the sun rises on Monday morning, so why spend Sunday night at home? Spend it at Sway, a Moroccan-themed lounge and club, where every Sunday is Smiths/Morrisey Night—one of the craziest long-running dance parties in Manhattan. Hip, young, beautiful souls from all five boroughs make their way to Spring St to sing along to "This Charming Man" and "Everyday is Like Sunday," a song well-suited to the party. Of course, other evenings in this three-roomed space can be just as fun. Come for '80s Night on Thursdays or on a slower night to have a drink in the candlelit room in the back. Door policy can be strict, so try and keep your girl-to-guy ratio in mind.

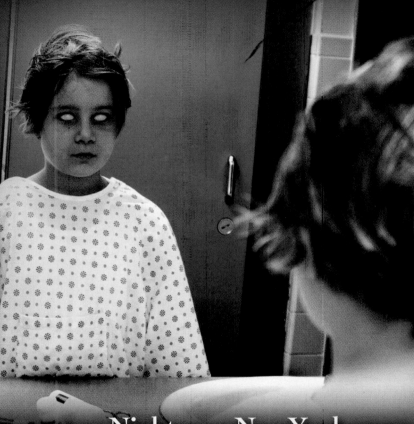

FYING HAUNTED HOUSE

NightmareNewYork.com
TICKETS: 212-352-3101
GROUPS 10+ 212-929-2963

CHINA

Chinatown has been famous for a long time, for reasons ranging from the justifiable to the ludicrous. The neighborhood is not, as many starry-eyed visitors conclude, an American-born, miniaturized Hong Kong with all the comfort and industry of that national capital. Chinatown is outstanding for its flawless transference of native customs to the streets of modern New York, but it remains cramped, and in some places extremely poor. To truly appreciate it is to celebrate its vividness.

Cantonese flurries over the sidewalk, where plump trash bags squat and yesterday's newspapers stick to sidewalk gum. Daylight finds peddlers hawking counterfeits, turtles, children's toys, jewelry, pashminas, and junk that wouldn't be appealing if the prices weren't so low or the items so outlandish. Parking is always an issue, and the constant deadlock means that pedestrians overrun the streets. Students set up inside bubble tea shops after school, chattering in English, FuZhounese, Cantonese, and Mandarin. Canal St swells with tourists hunting deals, while Mott and Bowery welcome foodies on a quest for authentic Chinese fare. All visitors would do well to collect a smattering of knowledge of Chinese—many shopkeepers and waiters can only grasp at English, despite spending generations in lower Manhattan. At night the neighborhood closes early: ribbed metal doors fall and lock away the flashy storefronts,

TOWN

shopkeepers retreat to the apartments above, straggler teenagers loiter, cars with tinted windows glide through the streets, and an older set gossips behind closed doors to the strains of 1430 AM, one of the few Cantonese radio stations on the dial. Rent an apartment here and you might see at your neighbor folding up zhong, a sticky rice snack, in piles two feet tall to peddle on the street.

The neighborhood formed over 130 years ago, though its roughly hewn bones are sometimes lost in the day-tripper clamor. Discrimination, as well as self-segregation, may have shaped Chinatown's individuality, but it also prevented the neighborhood's growth from 1943, when the ban on Chinese immigration was lifted, to 1965, when immigration laws stopped favoring Europeans. Despite recent luxury apartments, the area remains tinged with decay. Parks open to fanfare, then dissolve into littered grounds, deemed acceptable only by those who wipe down grimy benches in order to enjoy the pungent durian fruit outdoors. Walking to the subway, locals are often surprised to see a familiar hair salon closed on charges of prostitution, or that old noodle shop shut due to rats or roaches. Nevertheless, Chinatown has bustled for more than a century, and has even made valiant recent attempts to expand into the Lower East Side and SoHo—the neighborhood is far from giving up.

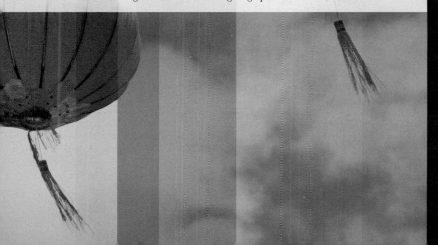

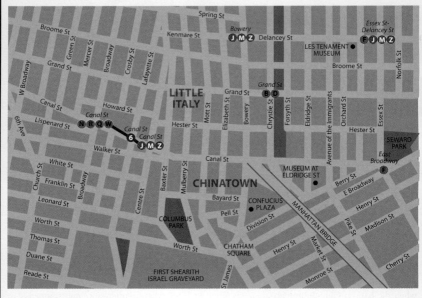

EXPLORE

Chatham Square

This small green space, also known as Kimlau Square, lies at the confluence of seven streets and feels like it. Tired pedestrians on well-deserved breaks dot the park

Intersection of Bowery, East Broadway, St. James Pl, Mott St, Oliver St, Worth St, and Park Row **V** to East Broadway, **N R Q W J M Z 6** to Canal St

in ones and twos, sitting under the contemplative gaze of a sculpted Lin Zexu, a Qing dynasty scholar. Skateboarders occasionally deign to take advantage of the garden plots' sloping banks. Along Oliver St towers the Kimlau Memorial Arch, erected in honor of Chinese-American soldiers and named for Lt Benjamin Ralph Kimlau, a Chinese-American bomber who perished in WWII. This small section of what used to be part of Five Points, the deadly territory for 19th-century Irish gangs, is the

perfect place for reflecting on the ever-changing face of the city.

Columbus Park

In the late 18th century, the area now occupied by Columbus Park was the most dangerous in town, averaging 15 mur-

67 Mulberry St (from Bayard to Worth St) Daily 8am-dusk **N R Q J M Z 6** to Canal St

ders a night. First-time visitors may recognize "Five Points" as Leonardo Di Caprio's dueling grounds in Martin Scorsese's Gangs of New York. Today the once-Dickenesian square offers security of mind to Chinatown residents. Clusters of Xiangqi and Mahjong players crowd the tables while elderly locals practice martial arts and tai chi. Bounded by Zhe "Zack" Zeng way, named for a 9/11 victim, the hum of conversation and erhu players carries to the other side of the street, where you can find a soccer field, basketball courts, and a playground.

Hua Mei Bird Garden

At any other time here, you wouldn't find anything exceptional: a basketball court, trash caught in dry bushes, and a skeletal network of wires strung from the trees. But in the mornings, caged birds alight on the delicate web, charming passersby and their owners with their ceaseless chirping. The members of the Hua Mei Bird Club are the only guests allowed into the Hua Mei Bird Garden, but pedestrians are welcome to eavesdrop on their earnest, competitive chatter. The owners, many of them male Chinese retirees, spend their mornings debating the various merits of the handmade cages and birds. It makes for a tranquil few hours, filled not with the incessant honking of Chinatown traffic, but with the light conversation of a few feathered friends and their owners.

Delancey St btwn Forsyth and Chrystie St
Mornings only, usually 7am-12pm
B **D** to Grand St,
V **J** **M** **Z** **6** to Delancey St-Essex St
Free

Museum of Chinese in America

One would be forgiven for mistaking this museum for a trendy restaurant, as the minimalist "MOCA" signboard is all that indicates what awaits within. Slick bronze and wood covers nearly every surface of the interior, designed by Maya Lin, the elegant hand behind the Vietnam Memorial. In addition to displaying sepia-toned photographs, traditional costumes, newspapers, and manuscripts, the museum celebrates individuals like writer Maxine Hong Kingston and Joseph L. Pierce, the only Chinese in the Army of the Potomac. Take the free walking tour and learn about the first Chinese laborers that set foot on American shores in the 1840s. MOCA keeps itself relevant to present-day Asian America

215 Centre St (btwn Howard & Grand St)
212-619-4785
Mon, Fri 11am-5pm, Thurs 11am-9pm, Sat-Sun 10am-5pm
N **R** **Q** **J** **M** **Z** **6** to Canal St
Adults $7, Students $4, Free on Thursdays

Pay only twenty dollars round-trip to Boston or DC via the immensely popular "Chinatown Bus," which travels from one city's Chinatown to another's.

LITTLE ITALY

Little Italy used to be a teeming enclave of Italian transplants—the Sicilians lived on Elizabeth St, the Geonese took over Baxter St, and the Northern Italians overran Bleeker. But today the entire neighborhood is little more than Mulberry St, and the few Italians who remain—most of the population has been siphoned off to the Bronx's Little Italy—are practically outnumbered by bright-eyed tourists who mistake the neighborhood for what it once was.

But Little Italy still offers something to New Yorkers who shed fears of inauthenticity and being mistaken for out-of-towners. The Feast of San Gennaro draws crowds who parade the statue of San Gennaro through the streets. Tourists pour in for the Summer in Little Italy Festival, which closes Mulberry to traffic. Restaurants take over the entire sidewalk, waiters idly watching for day-trippers who take the bait. **Ferrara Bakery & Cafe** *(195 Grand St)* is the country's oldest pasticceria and draws in first-time visitors, like President Reagan, with its cannolis. Or try the aranciata (fried rice balls) a few yards away at **Alleva Dairy** *(188 Grand St)*, the unsung, less expensive alternative to the nearby **DiPalo's** *(200 Grand St)*.

by hosting the Asian American ComiCon, the Asian American International Film Festival, and regular dumpling nights. You can even cheer for the MOCA team at the annual Hong Kong Dragon Boat Festival.

SHOP

Aji Ichiban

At first glance a mere downtown sister of Dylan's Candy Bar, Aji Ichiban is a tidy candy shop lined with bins of sweets to be scooped and sold by

37 Mott St (near Pell St)
212-233-7650
Daily 10am-8pm
N R Q J M Z 6 to
Canal St

the pound. But the differences will soon dawn on you when you hear the Chinese warbled in the background and examine the actual contents of those bins—dried plum, tamarind, ginger, and mango, as well as jerky and dried fish, all dubious addends to the definition of "candy." Find pocky and shrimp fries along the walls, and imported chewy treats in the center of the store, like lychee suckers and tea candy. Don't be surprised when the cashier rings up a steep price, as most of the snacks here cost $5 per lb. The wise take advantage of the abundant samples.

Asia Market

Chinatown is an obvious destination of the frugal grocery shopper, but the modest Asia Market's deals

71 1/2 Mulberry St
(at Bayard St)
Daily 8am-7pm
R Q J M Z 6 to
Canal St

are bound to prompt a stir frying craze among Lower East Siders. The storefront is straightforward, varying little from what the vegetable stands dotting the neighborhood offer—eggplant, yams, durian—and inside you'll find the familiar bins of rice and Vita tea six-packs. But the shop's specialty is Filipino, Thai, and Malaysian foods, each justly represented on the curry paste racks. Stock up on Kikoman soy sauce at a discount and explore the entire aisle devoted to canned baby corn, chili, and preserved ginseng. Toward the back you'll find ramen and Asian sweets. The Market's one-stop inventory rightly earns it the moniker "Chinatown's Pantry."

EAT

Banh Mi Saigon

Vietnamese, Sandwiches

In the last several years New Yorkers have fallen hard for banh mi, that venerable Vietnamese sandwich bred by the unlikely combination of French influence in Southeast Asia. The banh mi served at this bright, clean store on the border of Chinatown and Nolita is some of

CHINATOWN
best cheap asian eats

Great NY Noodletown- Take a seat off Bowery at this humble Cantonese shop to slurp up classic noodle specialties, especially the $7 Singapore Chow Fun, rarely found or done well in the city. *28 Bowery, 212-349-0923, Daily 9am-4am, B, D to Grand St, 6/J/M/N/Q/R/W/Z to Canal St, $*

Prosperity Dumpling- For two bucks and a few minutes, this hole-in-the-wall stirs up a filling and tasty meal—five chive and pork dumplings and a sesame pancake with beef. *46 Eldridge St, 212-343-0683, Daily 7:30am-9pm, B/D to Grand St, F to East Broadway, $*

Bo Ky Restaurant- This restaurant offers a refreshing break from the bombardment of garlic and brown sauce. Traditional Vietnamese Noodle Soup for traditional Chinatown prices. *82 Bayard St, 212-406-2292, Daily 8:00am-10pm, J/M/Z/N/Q/R/6 to Canal St, B/ D to Grand St, $*

Vegetarian Dim Sum House- While Dim Sum houses litter Chinatown offering a huge variety of tasty Chinese delicacies, this may be the only one that is purely vegetarian. *24 Pell St, 212-577-7176, Mon-Sun 10:30am-10:30pm, J/M/Z/N/Q/R/6 to Canal St, J/Z to Chambers-Brooklyn Bridge/City Hall, B/D to Grand St, $*

the best in town. The House Special consists of a crispy French baguette stuffed with sweet-glazed minced pork, Vietnamese salami, paté, cucumber, cilantro, pickled carrots and daikon, jalapenos, and hollandaise—tangy mouthwatering perfection. Step up to the counter and select from one of 11 other varieties on offer: the pork and water chestnut meatball banh mi (#4) is a warm, sweet mess not unlike a Vietnamese meatball sub. All of the unaccountably filling sandwiches come in at under $5. Who said globalization was a bad thing?

138 Mott St
(btwn Hester & Grand St)
212-941-1541
Tues-Sun 10am-7pm
B D to Grand St,
N R G J M Z G to
Canal St
$

Congee Village   *Chinese*

A veritable tiki palace on the border of the LES and Chinatown, Congee Village sprawls across several rooms and floors densely packed with plastic trees, bamboo, and large parties celebrating everything under the sun. Weekend

100 Allen St (btwn Delancey
& Broome St)
212-941-1818
Sun-Thurs 10:30am-12:30am,
Fri-Sat 10:30am-2am
F J M Z to
Essex-Delancey St,
B D to Grand St
$$
Additional location:
207 Bowery St

crowds sometimes necessitate long waits in the neon-lit bar, but half an hour is well worth the myriad Chinese specialties, both familiar and foreign. Start with a warming bowl of the namesake congee (the menu has some 30 varieties), and an order of the Small Juicy Buns. Then try the mildly spicy, curried Singapore mei fun noodles and the fried fresh squid with salted pepper. For the more adventurous, the menu also includes such delicacies as duck tongues, chicken feet, and goose intestines. Since most dishes are large enough to share, a satiating feast washed down with a Tsingtao should come to less than $20 a head.

Nice Green Bo

66 Bayard St (btwn
Mott & Elizabeth St)
212-625-2359
Daily 11am-11pm

to Canal St

$$

This unimposing room on Bayard St, painted hospital green and adorned with little more than one of those strangely glowing waterfall images so common to Chinatown restaurants, may not inspire much love in aesthetes, but once the food rolls out no one seems to mind. Order any number of Chinese favorites confident that they will be both familiar and better than any other local iterations. Steamed tiny buns filled with soup broth is the obligatory starting place for any meal here, while cold sesame noodles make a refreshing follow up. Even obvious choices like moo shoo pork and pan fried noodles—both in enormous, shareable portions—are striking in their simultaneous familiarity and high quality

Malaysian

Nyonya

Relocated from across the street, the date-friendly Nyonya boasts slick dark wood tables and dim, moody lighting that reveals a decorator's hand. The trendier accoutrements, however, have not altered the fact that the spacious restaurant serves Manhattan's best claim to Malaysian cuisine. Start off your meal with the Malay staple roti canai—a crisp puff of a pancake that you tear and dip into mild curry

MAHAYANA BUDDHIST TEMPLE
biggest buddha in town

At the entrance to the Manhattan Bridge, somehow impervious to the rumbling of trains and honking Brooklyn commuters, the Mahayana Buddhist Temple offers a chance at undisturbed meditation. The dark and cavernous space, trimmed in auspicious red and gold, contains a giant golden smiling Buddha surrounded by folding chairs and kneeling pads. Most signs are in Chinese, but "Noble Silence" and "Donations" is all that is entreated of English speakers. Walk upstairs to visit the gift store, where you can buy Buddha statues, tea sets, and children's books that chronicle the Chinese zodiac. If you balk at the $500 price tag that accompanies a few of the scrolls, donate a dollar to receive a small roll of paper with five nuggets of wisdom—some simply reading, "Probability of Success: Good."

133 Canal St
(at Manhattan Bridge Pl)
212-925-8787
Daily 8am-6pm
B/D to Grand St

sauce. The more gastronomically adventurous should try the Asam Laksa, though the menu suggests that you seek advice before ordering it. The sour and spicy soup bathes a heaping portion of thick rice noodles that

199 Grand St (btwn
Mulberry and Mott St)
212-334-3669
Daily 11am-11:30pm
 B D to Grand St,
J M to Bowery St
$$

leaves your mouth with a distinct fishy bouquet—an exciting and tasty dish, perhaps, but not the best way to end a date. Those looking to leave with better breath should try the Haianese Chicken, a straightforward steamed chicken with soy sauce that is done simply, but well.

PLAY

Lolita

Lounge

Stand by the bar, kick back in the main lounge area, marvel at the (purchasable) art by local artists displayed on the walls, or head downstairs for a private party—Lolita guarantees a laid-back

266 Broome St
(near Allen St)
212-966-7223
Daily 5pm-4am
F M B to
Essex-Delancey St,
B D to Grand St
$$

experience with a touch of class and no pretense. The touch of class comes from the bar's reputation as a low-key hideout for minor art

XI'AN FAMOUS FOODS
best place to singe off your taste buds

As SoHo and the LES close in on Chinatown, the prospect of losing the city's most authentic culinary imports looms ever larger. But the recently opened Xi'an Famous Foods, an outpost of the original Flushing-based Cantonese shop, proves the spirit of Chinatown is still alive. The restaurant—or, more accurately, the tiny storefront—offers a close view of wizened ladies making hand-pulled noodles. Hot dishes come coated in toasted cumin or caramelized lamb, while the liang pi cold noodles come in devilishly spicy sauce. This, of course, assumes you can snag one of two seats in the place; it's more likely you'll watch the noodle-making show from the line of

Chinese

88 E Broadway (btwn
Forsyth and Pike St)
212-786-2068
Daily 11am-8pm
B, D to Grand St
$
Additional Location:
Golden Shopping Mall in
Flushing
*Cash Only, Take Out

regulars snaking out of the storefront. Just grab a takeout bag of the astonishingly good and rarely seen Chinese lamb burgers, which taste like the sloppy joes in the elementary school cafeteria in Heaven.

stars on a break from the Lower East Side. Still, with a bar well-stocked with your favorite bottles, tap, wines, and spirits listed at reasonable prices, it's worth it to pass through for a drink or even camp out for the night. The recognizable tunes and prompt service from the bartenders ensure a reliable good time.

Santos Party House *Live Music, DJ*
Beneath a swirling haze of green, purple, and red lights hangs a neon sign that reads: "Party is our middle name." How fitting! Both levels of this music venue and nightclub are packed before midnight with a crowd of quirkily dressed and ready to dance partygoers, ranging in age from 18 to 40. It's no place to play the shy kid—waste more than a moment catching your breath and a friendly stranger will twirl you right back to the dance floor. If you must take a break from the shin-shaking bass, grab a stiff drink from the bar, where a sign wisely advises: "Keep on drinking." Otherwise, one of the candlelit alcoves makes for the perfect place to rest and watch the trippy projected videos of shapes that metamorphose to the rock, hip hop, and house played by DJs and live acts.

18
96 Lafayette St
(near Canal St)
212-584-5492
Hours vary by event,
doors open btwn
7pm- 11pm
ⓃⓇⓆ ⓦ ⓙ Ⓜ Ⓩ ⓺ to
Canal St
$$

LOWER EAST SIDE

A monumental diversity spans the decades since the founding of this neighborhood and still spins faster than a top. The first farms of the 17th century clustered around Delancey St. Then clumps of Europeans began settling in the area, coming to escape natural catastrophes and World Wars. The Irish left the Famine and boarded "coffin ships" to scour the Five Points for cheap rent, 170,000 Germans created their own "Kleindeutschland" complete with the motherland's beer halls, and able-bodied Italians arrived to work as ironmongers. But by the 1960s, the ethnic landscape had transformed again: Puerto Ricans flooded "The Loisiada" (a Spanglish adaptation of "the Lower East Side"), blasting salsa music and selling shaved ice in the East River Park. A handful of Bangladeshis and Dominicans also joined the scene, their presence today visible in the native grocery stores along Allen St.

The neighborhood's multicultural immigrant population continually replenishes itself, blending seamlessly with New Yorkers whose families have lived in the area for generations. Like Poles and Ukranians crammed next door to one another in its 18th-century tenements, denim-swathed Brooklynites now rub elbows with midtown bankers in packed bars. As SoHo types trickle into Prince St, sniffing out vintage skirts, Jewish families run the same 2nd Ave kosher delis their grandparents did, and attend the old Chasam Sopher Synagogue.

In recent years, investors have come up with all kinds of start-up business proposals specifically targeting the young and stylish. Once a hub for bargain shopping, Orchard St now glitters with stores dealing exclusively in designer belts and marked-up boutique hotels. Rustic cafes and poetry clubs have replaced the dirt cheap markets of Bowery St, enticing visitors with open mic nights and pistachio-filled pastries. Chelsea-like galleries have also sprung up, in ones and twos, ever-vigilant in chasing fresh ideas. Of course, nightlife is booming: world-famous DJs and bands looking to redefine "alternative" play along Ludlow St (particularly at Pianos, a bar with more scene than the Metropolitan Opera). Crowds of divas flock to R Bar for its stripper poles, while cubicle-dwellers who need to wind down head to Stanton Social for a top-notch combination of cocktails, dumplings, and comfy chairs.

And yet, with the help of residents and community organizations, the Lower East Side has not fully succumbed to the specter of gentrification. The Museum at Eldridge Street offers walking tours that showcase the Jewish and Chinese immigrant experiences. Similarly, the Tenement Museum has perfectly preserved six apartments, occupied by families over 100 years ago. As such, the Lower East Side bears more than one permanent stamp of its rich history as a melting pot within a melting pot—even in the face of its current hipness.

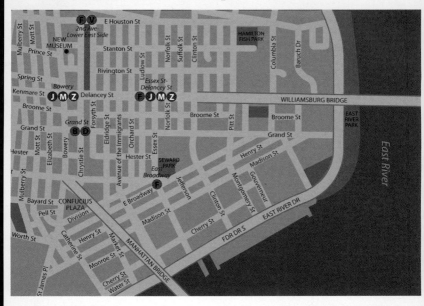

EXPLORE

East River Park

57 acres of jade fields, walking paths, sporting facilities, and heart-stopping views of the rolling river

Btwn Jackson & E 12th St
(along the East River)
🄵 🄹 🄼 🅉 to
Delancy-Essex St

make this park a popular destination for every New Yorker at leisure. Couples, families, and athletes crowd the area, which also boasts a limestone recreational building and a waterside promenade. Visitors are free to use the ball courts, playgrounds, and wild flower gardens, if they're not too busy fishing or playing basketball, baseball, tennis, and handball. East River Park is also a key community destination for public performances, with a monumental 1000-seat amphitheater that stages concerts, festivals, ceremonies, and a handful of Shakespeare plays throughout the year.

Museum at Eldridge Street

With its circular pillars, high rose windows, and plentiful Stars of David, this museum resembles a grand yet intimate place of worship—which it is. Placed

12 Eldridge St (btwn
Canal & Division St)
212-219-0302
Sun-Thurs 10am-5pm
🄵 to East Broadway
Adults $10, Students $8,
Free on Mondays

inside an 1887 synagogue, the Museum at Eldridge Street is a glimpse into the customs of the Lower East Side's famously resilient Jewish community. Visitors are required to take personalized tours, which leave on the half-hour and cover the museum and its environs. Guides walk the curious through the religious and social sites of Chinatown, expounding on a Chatham Square cemetery and a soapbox once used by politicians during both world wars. Inside, younger patrons create their own Yiddish newspapers while their parents peruse exhibits on Jewish courtship practices and traditional musical forms.

The New Museum

Like misshapen dominoes, six blocks of off-white steel are piled up on Bowery Street, the proclamation "Hell yes!" slapped on the façade like a rainbow name tag. Inside, the

253 Bowery (at Prince St)
212-219-1222
Wed 11am-6am,
Thurs 11am-9pm,
Fri-Sun 11am-6pm
🄵 to 2nd Ave,
🄹 to Bowery
Adults $12, Students $8

crowd quietly sifts into lime-colored freight elevators, eager to see if the Museum's offerings will stand by its name. And they do: every gallery on these seven bleach-white floors aims to display not just contemporary art, but also work that is completely new. Installations excel in inventiveness—in Rivane Neuenschwander's "I Wish Your Wish," museumgoers pluck hopeful messages written on ribbons out of cubbyholes. The Museum Store, tastefully obscured behind a crescent-shaped metal sheath, peddles pocket-sized knickknacks like a pair of salt and pepper shakers labeled Cocaine and Heroin.

SHOP

bio Emerging Designers

This boutique showcases local designer clothing and shoes for professional women— and yet there isn't a classic black pump in sight. Instead, bio seeks to transform the work-

29 Prince St (at Mott St)
212-334-3006
🄶 to Spring St,
🄽🄺 to Prince St
Sun 12pm-7pm,
Mon-Sat 12pm-8pm

place into an oasis of sophisticated trends. The racks are lined with green and yellow wraparound dresses, fit for both a Wall Street office and an after-work drink. Strappy orange heels and tunics with brown henna-style embroidery are also scattered around the store, amongst a few potted plants and distorted glass vases—one

TENEMENT MUSEUM

The Tenement Museum (97 Orchard St) is at first glance unexceptional, resembling any other Lower Manhattan apartment. Four wrought iron balconies and black emergency ladders hang from a classic brick façade, concealing the standard French windows. Still, the building is a rare historical treasure: from 1863 to 1988, it was home to 7000 immigrants from Eastern Europe. Since then, social activists Ruth Abram and Anita Jacobson have recovered six of its original apartments, which now appear as they did when occupied by their 19th-century inhabitants. Visitors can take guided tours through the latest restoration, a teal-green apartment clustered with copper pots that belonged to the Moores, an Irish Catholic family that resided there in 1869. Visitors can also participate in the Museum Shop's Tenement Talks, a series of discussions, readings, and performances that relate New York's rich immigrant experience. The Museum Shop stocks unusual New York-themed gifts: the $18 sizable ring watch in mauve is the summer's most popular item.

resembling a mustard yellow trumpet. These items can cost anywhere from $50 to $300, but guarantee a competitive edge in a homogeneous market of pinstriped blazers and stiff pants. The collection of costume jewelry near the register is also worth ogling. On a lucky day, a red ceramic ring with a Milky Way swirl can go for just $10.

OME

OME believes in glitter: shiny green flecks sweep the floor and dance on the purple curtain behind the register. The reigning credo at this boutique is "Life was meant to be adorned," and indeed, each piece of clothing has traces of sparkles, stones, or clusters of painted red flowers. The mannequin heads lining the ceiling are spray-painted gold and sport flapper-style bead-and-peacock-feather headbands. A glass cabinet showcases similarly styled jewelry made by local artists, where minimalists can inspect a cache of eclectic wire necklaces interspersed with crystal teardrop earrings. Prices fall along a wide spectrum, from a $15 turquoise bracelet to a $200 strapless silk dress. Fortunately, the sale rack can transform even the most frugal woman into a Manhattan showstopper.

259 Elizabeth St (btwn E Houston & Prince St)
212-343-4200
Daily 11:30am-8pm
B D F to Broadway-Lafayette St,
6 to Bleecker St

EAT

Bereket Turkish Kebab House   *Turkish*

Situated amongst many Lower East Side staples, this 24/7 haven for lovers of street meat managed to win the hearts of spoiled Houston Street diners. While success often brings a dip in quality, the buzz of Hebrew, Arabic, and Kurdish betrays this establishment's fidelity to authentic Turkish cuisine. The no-frills cafeteria décor prevents focus from straying beyond the amazing spreads of hummus, grape leaves, baklava, and, of course, kebabs. The meat selection extends far beyond the familiar chicken or beef, with many spiced variants lining the display case—waiting to be grilled on order, stuffed into a fluffy, fresh pita, and doused in a minty yogurt sauce. The grape leaves are an eye-opener, with a crisp outer leaf concealing a nutty mixture that truly awakens, like almost everything in store, with a squeeze of lemon.

187 E Houston St (near Orchard St)
212-475-7700
Daily 24 hours
F V to 2nd Ave,
F J M Z to Essex St-Delancey St
$$

Cheeky's Sandwiches   *New Orleans*

The stretch of Orchard between Canal and Hester encapsulates the neighborhoods that surround it, with a smattering of smart boutiques representing the LES, and Chinese

grocers going to bat for Chinatown. But Cheeky's Sandwiches, tucked into a simple, cozy storefront, radiates a casual, down home glow right where you'd least expect it.

35 Orchard St
(at Hester St)
Daily 8am-6pm
🅑 🅓 to Grand St,
🅕 🅙 🅜 🅩 to
Essex-Delancey St
$

Louisiana-style po' boys make up the majority of the menu and are not to be missed. The fried oyster sandwich is especially delicious, crisp and briny in a cushiony baguette. Stick around on one of the small stools lining the walls to enjoy the Southern bonhomie—it manages to avoid the theme-park feel accompanying the usual attempt to bring Southern comfort to the concrete, glass, and asphalt of Manhattan.

American,
Clinton Street Baking Company *Brunch*
Clinton Street Baking Company serves an eclectic American menu, focusing on classic foods and fresh ingredients. For the past nine years, people have been forming lines around the block to partake in its famous brunches, lured by the huevos rancheros, poached shrimp Cobb salad, and buttermilk biscuits. Try the

pancakes, served in fluffy towers of three, dripping with warm blueberry sauce and topped with fresh Maine blueberries and molten maple butter. The dinner menu is a stylized extension of brunch, offering a crisp, buttermilk fried chicken, given a bit

🍴 💲
4 Clinton St (btwn
Avenue B & Houston St)
646-602-6263
Sun 9am-6pm,
Mon-Fri 8am-4pm,
Mon-Sat 6pm-11pm,
Sat 9am-4pm
🅕 🅙 🅜 🅩 to Delancey
St-Essex St
$$

of tang by the honey Tabasco dipping sauce. If you're too full for dessert, the unbelievable baked goods—for which the restaurant is named—are all available to go. The chocolate chip cookie is pocked with more chips than most recipes would call for—a typical example of Clinton Street going overboard, in a good way.

Doughnut Plant *Doughnuts*
Cooped inside a small, rusty metal building, only one man stands behind the counter of doughnut glory. But that's just the tip of the iceberg: huge ovens line the back room, creating

UNDER $20

Make your morning sweet with a New Orleans-style breakfast at **Cheeky Sand-wiches** *(34 Orchard St)*. Be sure to order the 3 for $1 puffy beignets with flaky sugar and the ginger tea, which comes with honey.

Browse the dusty shelves of **St. Mark's Bookstore** *(31 3rd Ave)* for the latest in pop culture, history, and art design. Don't leave the sales section without a $5 Harry Matthews paperback.

When hunger bites again, head to **The Meatball Shop** *(84 Stanton St)*, where the options for ingredients go on for days. The $7 special is at the top of the menu: four meatballs served with hunks of focaccia. Stick to the classic beef and meat sauce, or get funkier with vegetable and parmesan cream.

A walk through the **Stephan Stoyanov Gallery** *(29 Orchard St)* will help burn some calories off. Admission is free, and the summer collection of photography and sculpture promises to be smoldering.

When the evening drifts in, kick off your shoes at **Welcome To the Johnsons** *(123 Rivington St)*, a dive bar that sells $2 PBRs after 9pm and manages to resemble your aunt's house at the same time.

---

aromas that are worth a visit alone. Doughnut Plant uses eggless recipes and makes everything from scratch, including jams, glazes, and peanut butter. They're as natural as doughnuts can get—no trans fat, preservatives, or artificial flavorings. The Plant has been making such irresistibly mouthwatering treats as creme, peanut butter and jelly, and tres leches doughnuts since it began operating out of a basement. A lot has changed since it's gained worldwide success—the website's "headlines" section includes the next TV show the plant will be featured on. Plump yourself on the multicol-ored doughnut bench and indulge, because it'll be hard not to.

379 Grand St
(at Norfolk St)
212-505-3700
Tues-Sun 6:30am-7pm
(or when sold out)
🅕 🅙 🅜 🅩 to
Essex-Delancey St
$

Falai

Italian

Compared to most of its Lower East Side neighbors, Falai has a distinctly uptown flavor—it serves delicate pasta dishes to an array of waspy patrons in white pants and boating shoes. But it also takes steps to pay homage to its downtown location. The restaurant is stuffed into a tiny space with an open kitchen, and reserves a single table overlooking the street in what

68 Clinton St
(at Rivington St)
212-253-1960
Sun 5:30pm-10:30pm,
Mon-Thurs 6pm-10:30pm,
Fri-Sat 6pm-11pm
🅕 🅙 🅜 🅩 to
Essex St-Delancey St
$$

LOWER EAST SIDE
best of the old jewish tradition

Katz's Delicatessen- The pinnacle of the NYC Deli. People come from all over the tri-state area to try the classic Jewish deli sandwich: a mountain of hot pastrami on mustard-slathered rye. *205 E Houston St, 212-254-2246, F/J/M/Z to Delancy-Essex St, Sun 8am-10:30pm, Mon-Tues 8am-9:30pm, Wed-Thurs, Fri-Sat 8am-2:30am $$*

Kossar's Bialys- Come here for the perfect bialy–a soft, steaming pouch of garlic flavor that would make bubby proud. Shmear sold separately. *367 Grand St, 212-473-4810, F/J/M/Z to Delancy-Essex St, B/D to Grand St, Sun 6am-8pm, Mon-Thurs 6am-8pm, Fri 6am-2pm $*

Yonah Shimmel's Knish Bakery- The best place to get the legendary densely packed pastry of baked potato puree and flaky, egg-brushed crust known as a knish. *137 E Houston St, 212-477-2858, F to 2nd Ave, 6 to Houston St $*

Russ and Daughters- An old-timey Jewish deli with 15 kinds of smoked salmon, 10 kinds of cream cheese, and fresh bagels. *179 E Houston St, 212-475-4880, F to 2nd Ave, F/J/M/Z to Delancy-Essex St, Mon-Fri 8am-8pm, Sat 9am-7pm, Sun 8am-5:30pm $$*

used to be a storefront in the space's former life. Head chef and owner Iacopo Falai's history as a pastry chef is evident in the beautifully crafted dishes, which can even look better than they taste—but that isn't true across the board. By sticking with the pastas and avoiding the crouton-like bread selection, one can leave with a truly authentic Florentine meal.

Georgia's Eastside BBQ   *BBQ*

More 'cue-shack than restaurant, Georgia's got that southern "charm" that wafts across the street. It's simply seven or eight tables with checkered tableclothes, one waitress, and all the classics of Southern barbecue, prepared in a uniquely tasty way. Chef Alan Natkiel serves down home cooking his own way by slow steaming the meat, resulting in unbelievably moist dishes. The pulled pork sandwich is succulent and juicy, but the ribs are divine—so meaty and tender that they can be eaten with a fork, falling apart with a gentle prod. Try the coleslaw or Georgia's sweet cornbread on the side, don't miss out on the tangy house-made barbecue sauce, and pray you get there on a day when they're serving banana pudding for dessert.

192 Orchard St
(near E Houston St)
212-252-6280
Sun-Mon 12am-10pm,
Tues-Sat 12am-11pm
F to 2nd Ave
$$

The Meatball Shop   *Italian*

Hardly kitschy, the Meatball Shop showcases the meatball in all its glory and all its variations. Don't be misled by the plain awning ("84 Stanton")—the interior is feverish and heats up as the night goes on. If you catch the lunch rush, it might be impossible to enjoy the bar, but you can more easily take in the retro and genial ambience that carries over from the kitchen fix-

84 Stanton St
(near Allen St)
212-982-8895
Daily 12pm-4am
F to Lower East Side,
F J M Z to Essex St
$

ture decorations to the '80s music overhead. All meat is ground in-house, losing none of its character in the process. Be sure to order chicken meatballs with a side of risotto, a lush and textured combination, and finish off with one of the housemade ice cream sandwiches. How to eat them neatly remains a mystery, but the mint smells and tastes exactly like a mint leaf, albeit one slightly melted between two crisp cookies.

Paladar   *Latin American*

With bright yellow doors framed by sky blue windows and topped with a red sign, Paladar has the jovial vibrance of a Mexican sunset. But don't be fooled: this chic restaurant offers more than just Sangria and a funky Latin feel. Chef Aaron Sanchez has trained the cooks in his cocina to serve a varied menu inspired by all of Latin America. Refresh your paladar (palate) with a tangy Guava Agua Fresca (guava juice, vodka, sugar, and tonic) or enjoy the sweet and spicy shrimp ceviche while reading the Spanish comic strips that hang above the bar. Complete the Latin American experience by treating yourself to a traditional Mexican coconut flan—topped with diced strawberries and a caramel drizzle, this dessert perfectly complements one of their signature sweet mojitos.

161 Ludlow St
(at Stanton St)
212-473-3535
Sun 11am-11pm,
Mon-Thurs 5:30pm-11pm,
Fri-Sat 5:30pm-2am
F to 2nd Ave
$$

ABC NO RIO

best communal-use silkscreen printer

One of the appallingly few remnants of CBGB-era downtown and an unmitigated rarity for Manhattan, ABC No Rio is among the the oldest and best-known artist collectives in the country. Since 1980, performers and activists have been meeting behind its aerosol-adorned storefront to brainstorm progressive political tactics, cook meals for Food Not Bombs, and stage weekly punk shows (featuring bands that have historically demonstrated openmindedness, of course). Whereas LIC galleries restlessly hunt the next innovator and the Chelsea art scene is money-driven, ABC No Rio has two almost quaint guiding principles: social awareness for all, and DIY is king. The proud keeper of a public darkroom, screen-printing studio, and a fantastically overstuffed zine library, the collective welcomes all and has a soft spot for those on the outskirts of society.

156 Rivington St (btwn
Suffolk & Clinton St)
212-254-3697
F to 2nd Ave, F, J, M, Z to
Essex-Delancey St

307

Shopsin's General Store

American, Global

120 Essex St (btwn Delancey & Rivington St)
Tues-Sat 9:30am-2pm
F **J** **M** **Z** to
Essex-Delancey St
$$

This family-owned general store gives diner a whole new name. It has a menu that looks like a Chinese newspaper, full of around 1,000 (yes, one thousand) all-out creative dishes that you'll wish your grandma had come up with. In fact, one trip to this market will make you wish Kenny Shopsin was your grandmother. Shopsin, the owner and head chef, is a bit of a character—a documentary was made showing him running his business at its former Greenwich Village location. The new spot is tiny, barely fitting the monstrous plates of classic diner dishes on steroids and crowds of Lower East Siders. Shopsin doesn't allow parties of more than four, so no one's left without trying his pomegranate maple walnut bread pudding french toast or the ever-popular mac and cheese pancakes: a concoction that epitomizes his deadly combinations.

Zucco Le French Diner

French

188 Orchard St
(at Houston St)
212-677-5200
Sun-Thurs 12pm-12am,
Fri-Sat 10am-2am
F to 2nd Ave
$$

The sign just inside the beaded doorway of this French diner declaring "No Bud, No Ketchup, No Zagat" prepares visitors for the simple dishes

RAYUELA
best ceviche-cocktail pairing

Freestyle Latin

165 Allen St (btwn Rivington & Stanton St)
212-253-8840
Sun 5pm-10pm, Mon-Thurs 5:30pm-11pm,
Fri-Sat 5:30pm-12am
F to 2nd Ave-Lower East Side, F,J,M,Z to Essex-Delancey St
$$$

Diners entering this popular "Freestyle Latin" eatery will undoubtedly marvel at the giant olive tree proudly planted in the middle of the restaurant. Connecting the two dining room floors, this elaborate tree represents the overall character of Rayuela: intriguing, fresh, and beautiful. With an eclectic menu of ceviches, tapas, and both traditional and non-traditional Spanish dishes, Rayuela offers an authentic and seafood-heavy menu. Its excellence is evident the moment your waiter offers you one of the signature Colombian cheese rolls, baked in-house every half-hour. The seafood certainly soaks up the limelight, with the lime-soaked ceviche taking front and center. For those looking to eat light and drink heavy, Rayuela's cocktails are as fresh with exotic Latin influence as the food—try the "Mezcal" for a spicier spin on the traditional margarita.

and low-key atmosphere. Inspired by a French truck stop, vintage posters of European advertisements and cartoons of cars line one wall and dated Polaroid photographs the other. The popular goat cheese salad, served with a square pastry filled with hot, soft goat cheese, doesn't even require the dressing for extra flavor. The burger, true to the sign, is served without ketchup or a bun or condiments of any kind—it's only topped by a sunny side up egg, but the beef, thick and slightly crunchy on the outside, satisfies on its own. Make sure to save room for dessert: the crème brulee is generously portioned and torched to perfection.

PLAY

169 Bar *Dive*

This century-old bar may as well have "dive" written on its red leather couches. It defines New Orleans kitsch, with fake palm trees and voodoo skulls littering the walls near a neon-lit Go

♪ ⚡
169 E Broadway
(near Rutgers St)
212-473-8866
Daily to 4am
F to East Broadway,
B D to Grand St
$

Go dancer stage. The bar's proximity to Chinatown inspires the rest of the vibe, as oriental light fixtures hang from the ceiling and dumplings are served all night. Fridays and Saturdays here tend to turn into dance parties, though live music is offered all week by performers ranging from jazz trios to DJs and funk bands. The selection of liquid courage is equally diverse, running the gamut from locally distilled liquor to every beer-pong-quality, step-above-seltzer beer you may have had in high school. But beer snobs despair not—there is a small but well-curated selection of draughts, including the all too rare Franziskaner.

Cake Shop *Dive, Café*

An anomaly of Ludlow's fast-paced bar crawl, Cake Shop is a chilled out combination of a

coffee shop, dive bar, and indie rock venue. This small basement/bunker books a ton of bands, both local and national, skewed strongly towards noise and experimental— the intimate, Christmas-lit stage has host-

♪ ❧
152 Ludlow St (btwn
Rivington & Stanton St)
212-253-0036
Sun-Thurs 5pm–2am,
Fri-Sat 5pm-4am
F to 2nd Ave
$

ed the likes of Ponytail, Vivian Girls, Chromeo, and Jangula. On street level, a coffee shop and full bar sit side by side, with a large selection of delicious, vegan-friendly cakes and cupcakes. The interior is 70s' basement chic, with fake wood paneling, comic illustrations, and drawings that look like they were done by fifth graders. On any given night, radicals sit around plotting revolutions, music junkies search for forgotten gems in the record collection (available for sale), and vegans dig into their desserts.

Home Sweet Home *Dance Club*

Home Sweet Home may seem like a funny name for a crowded, sweaty dance club decorated with taxidermy, but after years of playing the same role in the Lower East Side bar scene, home is exactly what it's become. Looking for a

⚡
131 Chrystie St
(at Delancey St)
212-226-5708
Sun-Mon 8pm-4am,
Tues-Sat 2pm-4am
F J M Z to Delancey-
Essex St,
B D to Grand St

place to dance where you know all the music, the people are in their twenties, and the drinks are typically priced? Well, you found it. On any weekend night, you can expect to hear Billy Idol and MGMT, groove with someone in flannel (plaid if it's summertime), and spend $5 on a Budweiser. All of this occurs under deep red lights and in the company of stuffed raccoons, beavers, rabbits, and peacocks—but nothing seems out of place. Home Sweet Home may not push the envelope, but it's reliable and totally fun.

The average age of a Lower East Side resident is 38.

Mason Dixon

Bar, Southwestern

133 Essex St
(near Rivington St)
212-260-4100
Sun, Tues-Wed 6pm-2am,
Thurs-Sat 6pm-4am
J M Z to Essex St
$$

With horseshoes on the wall, deer antler chandeliers, and a name like Mason Dixon, you can take a wild guess at what this bar is going for. Kitsch, however, takes a back seat to the extensive selection of bourbons, classic Southern and Cajun cooking, and spacious seating area this LES watering hole has to offer. Between its worn wooden walls, you can sip on a glass of Pappy Van Winkle, scarf down fried shrimp, and be sure that you'll have a seat, even on crowded Saturday nights. But don't drink or eat too much if you plan on getting the full experience—there's a fenced-off mechanical bull in the center that the brave, drunk, or both can ride for five bucks.

Mercury Lounge

Music Venue

217 E Houston St
(near Ludlow St)
212-260-4700
Hours vary by event
F J M Z to
Delancey-Essex St
Cover: $10-15

This is the best place in New York to catch bands just before they hit it big. Seen as a gateway to legitimacy by many East Coast acts, Merc has housed everyone from The Strokes to Lady Gaga, and we can only guess who's next. The space itself is simple—black and brick walls, a fairly big stage, and a bar area/break room in the front. It tends to get

MAX FISH
best place to drink like a fish

Bar, Lounge

178 Ludlow St (btwn
Houston & Stanton St)
212-529-3959
Daily 5:30pm-4am
F to 2nd Ave, F,J,M,Z to
Essex-Delancey St
$

One of Ludlow Street's oldest, largest, and brightest bars, Max Fish is a great place to kick off your night with $3 PBRs and some pool or pinball. It's also a notorious pick-up spot, so chances are strangers will try to strike up conversation with you about the skate videos playing on the projector or the local art on the walls. On a slow night, a drunk bartender might give you a free beer for guessing his favorite Lee Hazelwood song. On a crowded night—and there are many in the summertime—just getting to the counter can be a challenge. But on the best nights, you'll see Taylor Mead, the adorable 85-year-old Warhol filmstar, get treated to a beer in the corner before going off on his nightly walk around the LES to feed stray cats.

packed and sweaty like most general admission venues, but since the crowd comes specifically to see whoever's playing that night, they tend to go particularly wild. The bar room is rumored to be a common pickup spot, but that rumor isn't worth a $15 cover. If you're going to Mercury Lounge, go for the music.

Pianos — *Music Venue, Gastropub*

Still rocking the sign of the old piano shop it replaced, this combination music venue, club, bar, and restaurant has been king of the Ludlow crawl for nearly 10 years.

158 Ludlow St
(at Stanton St)
212-505-3733
Daily 2pm-4am
F J M Z to
Delancy-Essex St

By putting great care into the bands it books, Pianos maintains its status as a safe haven for Lower East Side cool. The subtle beach theme only amplifies the "cool"-ness, creating a calming vibe with photos of palm trees on the walls. Still, having housed bands as high-energy as HEALTH and Surfer Blood, this place can get pretty raucous. The upstairs dance floor is equally hot, with DJs spinning Tuesday through Sunday nights (Mondays are reserved for comedy and karaoke). The icing on the cake is the high-end bar food served in the front room, featuring a $5 burger and fries plate during happy hour that will ready you well for a night of drinking.

Sapphire Lounge — *Dance Club*

Despite its name, there's little space to lounge at this LES nightclub. While a few tables and chairs line one of the walls, they're usually deserted for the dance floor. A young crowd packs

249 Eldridge St (btwn
Houston & Stanton St)
212-777-5153
F to 2nd Ave
Sun 8pm-4am,
Mon-Sat 7pm-4am
$

this space on the weekends, when blaring top 40 hits make conversation impossible and leave no choice but to boogie. There's not much in the way of decor, but once you break a sweat dancing, you'll be thankful for the industrial grade fan facing the crowd. Do your best to avoid colliding with the gyrating bodies around you, since quarters are especially close. With no entrance fee before 10pm and a cheap $5 late night cover, you won't have to spend much dough to get down.

311

FINA

In the wake of the September 11 attacks, the Financial District—previously frequented by tourists and traders, but rarely by those who live above Worth St—carved out a sacred space in the hearts of mourning New Yorkers. But with the onslaught of the financial crisis in 2007, the city identified Wall Street as the scene of the crime and once again turned its back. Still, regardless of its wavering position, the neighborhood remains the hub of American finance and the nexus of city government: it's the engine that keeps New York running, if not always smoothly.

The oldest neighborhood in Manhattan, the Financial District was first established as a center for commerce by the Dutch West India Company in 1625. The area played an important role in the American Revolution: Federal Hall on Wall Street, for instance, saw the 1789 presidential inauguration of George Washington and the signing of the Bill of Rights to the Constitution. Three years later, Wall Street was born under a buttonwood tree, where 24 stockbrokers signed the Buttonwood Agreement to create the New York Stock Exchange. The NYSE would grow into the largest exchange group in the world, and Wall Street's skyscrapers became synonymous with American capitalism (and two centuries' worth of fat cat scandal).

Relics of colonial America still stand in the FiDi, the most famous of which is the 300-year-old Trinity Church, where Alexander Hamilton is interred. Nearby South Street Seaport, with

DIST

NCIAL

its cobblestone streets, Neoclassical facades, and harbor views, still evokes the lifestyle of the 19th-century merchant class that once inhabited its row houses. While today the port is more of a tourist attraction than a trading center, Manhattan's maritime history continues to surface— in July 2010, construction workers found the skeletal remains of an 18th-century ship 30 feet below street level at Ground Zero.

Conventional wisdom contends that the frenzied FiDi is abandoned after dark. It's true that the neighborhood, which has a residential population of less than 60,000, expands to accommodate a daytime population of about 300,000 tourists and stockbrokers, but it's hardly a ghost town. Financiers loosen their ties for an after-work drink on Stone St, a cobbled stretch of grills and taverns that welcome the same faithful crowds every weeknight. Arts and development initiatives like the River to River Festival bring free music and dance performances to the piers, Battery Park, and Bowling Green. Since the conversion of many office spaces to apartments and condos following September 11, the neighborhood's residential population has doubled. With its badge of historical significance, it's odd to think of the FiDi as an up-and-coming area in Manhattan, but it seems that the stroller crowd could make another new home below the glimmering Wall Street skyline.

RICT

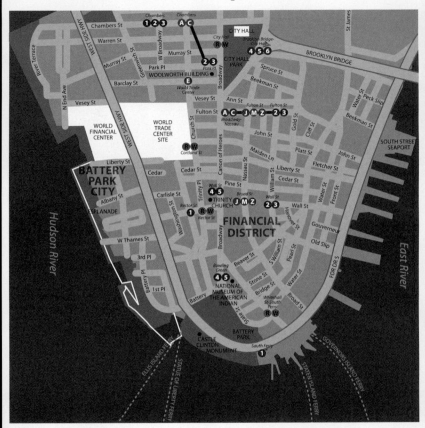

EXPLORE

Battery Park

Before Ellis Island became America's most celebrated doorstep, our ancestors arrived in Battery Park. Located on Manhattan's southern tip, the park now houses the Ellis Island and Statue of Lib-

South of Battery Place & State St
4 5 to Bowling Green, **1** to South Ferry

erty ferry. To buy tickets, visitors enter Castle Clinton, the circular sandstone fort that was the original immigration station. The waterfront promenade overlooking the docks has been popular with New Yorkers since the shore's use as an artillery fortification (hence the name Battery). In accordance with the park's long history, war memorials speckle the gardens. The bronze Sphere, the most recent addition, was moved from the World Trade Center following September 11th and remains in its damaged condition. Battery Park hosts events and performances year-round, all beneath the heat of Lady Liberty's flame.

Bowling Green

The oldest park in New York City, this wedge-shaped patch of green is perpetually filled with the office-bound seeking some lunchtime scenery.

Broadway & Whitehall St
Daily dawn-1am
4 **5** to Bowling Green,
1 to South Ferry,
R to Whitehall St,
J **M** **Z** to Broad St

Shady and well-maintained, it fits neatly into the space created by Broadway's splitting into two forks, a tiny strip that has played host to several iconic moments in American history. In 1776, after the reading of the Declaration of Independence, Washington's troops stormed the park to topple an equestrian statue of King George III. Bowling Green has been the traditional starting point for every ticker-tape parade since the very first, in 1886. Financiers talk shop on benches around the cobblestone perimeter and kids splash in the small pool, all under the gaze of the famous Di Modica-designed Charging Bull.

Irish Hunger Memorial

Just a block away from the World Trade Center lies another memorial, recalling an event that shaped New York in a drastically different manner. Constructed in 2002 to honor the million that

N End Ave (at Vesey St)
212-267-9700
Daily 8:30am-dusk
2 **3** **4** **5** **A** **C** **J** **M** **Z**
to Broadway-Nassau,
Free

perished during the seven-year potato famine of 1845, the Irish Hunger Memorial is designed to mimic Éire's postcard-perfect hills: native heather and foxglove spring from fields strewn with limestone, each boulder signifying one of Ireland's 32 counties. Designer Brian Tolle chose as his centerpiece a ruined 19th-century cottage from County Mayo—its fragmented stone walls narrate the hardship with engravings of poems, diary entries, and letters. While

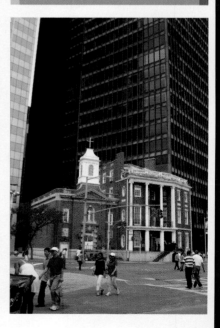

GROUND ZERO

In the aftermath of September 11, 2001, Mayor Rudy Giuliani proclaimed to his city, "We will rebuild…the skyline will be made whole again." However, during the following decade, plans to reconstruct and memorialize the **World Trade Center site** *(Church St at Barclay St)* have stalled due to city bureaucracy, competing design visions, and a dissatisfied public. The hotly debated and ever-fluctuating plan for redesign—not slated for completion until 2037—takes as its centerpiece One World Trade Center, the antennae of which will rise to the symbolic height of 1,776 feet. Work on the National September 11 Memorial and Museum commenced in 2006 and will feature a dense green forest, jarred by two pools in the hollow spaces where the towers once stood. Down the block, **St. Paul's Chapel** *(209 Broadway)* offers a permanent exhibit on the attacks, itself a part of history after providing a refuge for exhausted firefighters during the cleanup. Today, the best place to survey the progress is from the **Winter Garden** *(2 World Financial Center)*. Little construction is visible to visitors at the lookout points along Church St, which offer a view of the vast pit that now occupies the World Trade Center's 16 acres, the immensity of its negative space evoking a solemnity that perhaps no memorial could match.

the landscape recalls horrors from an era past, it also makes reference to today's ever-present hunger crisis and the ways in which history can threaten to repeat itself.

Poets House

Poets House began its public programming even before it had a home: while its new library was still a square-shaped hole, Bill Murray read poetry to construction workers on their lunch break. Founded in 1985 by former Poet Laureate Stanley Kunitz, the House moved to its current location in 2009, inaugurating one of the country's largest spaces for poetry appreciation. This is no dark and musty reading room—still sparkling new, the clean white walls, high ceilings, and sea-green armchairs are fresh but cozy (and sustainable—the building's insulation is made from recycled blue jeans). The library stores over 50,000 poetry collections, journals, chapbooks, and digital media. But the best reason to visit is to meet and greet with poets themselves: past readings have featured Billy Collins and Meena Alexander.

10 River Terrace (btwn Murray and Vesey St)
212-431-7920
Tues-Fri 11am-7pm,
Sat 11am-6pm
❶ ❷ ❸ to Chambers St
Admisssion:
Adults $10, Students $7

South Street Seaport

The walk from the ever-modernizing Financial District to the waterfront is a lesson in the convergence of old and new. Cobblestone paths are a reminder of New York City's old-world European beginnings, and their termination at Abercrombie & Fitch demonstrates the harmony between New Amsterdam architecture and Manhattan fashion. Pier 17's interior has been transformed into a top-shelf shopping mall, complete with a food court and over 100 retail options. The adjacent boardwalk is a leisurely spot to watch ships dock, join a tour of New York Harbor, or gawk at the dock's eight 19th and 20th century vessels, artifacts of the South Street Seaport Museum. As you unleash your shameful inner shopaholic, take comfort in the fact that the seaport is where New York's economy began.

Fulton & South St, Pier 17
212-732-7678
Sun 11am-8pm,
Mon-Sat 10am-9pm
❷ ❸ to Fulton St

Trinity Church

Sandwiched between downtown's giants of glass and steel, the spires of Trinity Church are made no less inspiring. Originally chartered by the Church of England in 1697, the church was rebuilt in classic Neo-Gothic style in 1846 af-

CHEAP EATS
best business lunch

Adrienne's Pizza Bar- The long lines at lunch act as this pizzeria's badge of honor in the financial district. Thin crust, perfect sauce, and aged mozzarella give its pies a distinct flavor. *54 Stone St, 212-248-3838, R to Whitehall St, Sun 11:30am-10pm, Mon-Sat 11:30am-11:30pm, 2/3 to Wall St, $*

Sandwich House- An ever-changing, never disappointing array of soups and very generous, creative sandwiches make this an ideal quick lunch. Try the Prosciutto di Parma for a well-executed classic. *17 Ann St, 212-566-6886, Mon-Fri 11am-10pm, Sat-Sun 12pm-9pm, 2/3/4/5/A/C/J/M/Z to Fulton St, $*

Zaitzeff- Burger and a coke is a classic lunch, but a juicy Kobe beef burger on muffin-style buns with a little bite to it makes it special. Don't forget the sweet potato fries. *72 Nassau St, 212-571-7272, Mon-Fri 10am-10pm, Sat-Sun 10am-6pm, 2,3,4,5,A,C,J,M,Z to Fulton St, $$*

ter two fires. Trinity's sacred grounds have attracted New York's most high-profile worshippers since 1789, when George Washington was a regular visitor to Trinity's St. Paul's Chapel, now

74 Trinity Pl
(at Broadway & Wall St)
212-602-0800
(tours 212-602-0872)
Sun 7am-4pm, Mon-Fri
7am-6pm, Sat 8am-4pm
❶ ❽ to Rector St,
❷ ❸ ❹ ❺ to Wall St,
❿ Ⓜ ❷ to Broad St

the city's oldest public building still in use. More recently, the gaping nave, drenched in ethereal blue from the altar's stained glass windows, served as a refuge for New Yorkers fleeing debris on September 11. Trinity continues to reach out to its surrounding community, hosting classical and contemporary music series and lectures by prominent theologians from around the country.

SHOP

Bowne & Company Stationers
In the face of countless blog posts foretelling the demise of print culture, Bowne & Co. Stationers holds out—and has been doing so since 1775. As part of the South Street Seaport Museum, this facsimile of a 19th-century print shop sits on the first floor of a red-brick Greek

FOLEY SQUARE

It's no accident that Francis Ford Coppola chose the steps of Foley Square as the setting for the Corleone family's murderous showdown with an agent of law and order. This is where practically every perp walk in the city goes down: the justice-wielding façades of the **New York County Supreme Court** *(60 Centre St)* and the **Thurgood Marshall Federal Courthouse** *(40 Centre St)* dominate the view from the park benches, while to the east stands the **New York County Municipal Building** *(1 Centre St)*. Just around the corner lies **Tweed Courthouse** *(52 Chambers St)*, funded by Tammany Hall's "Boss" Tweed. Bordered by Neoclassical colonnades, the grassy intersection of Duane and Centre Streets marks the seat of NYC government and is one of the most architecturally revered points in the city.

Trace the square's history by following the bronze medallions embedded in the sidewalk, which recount the area's political significance. One explains the creation of the **African Burial Ground National Monument** *(290 Broadway)*, built on an 18th-century African-American burial site discovered during the square's construction.

If possible, plan your visit on a Friday for the **Foley Square Greenmarket** *(Centre St btwn Worth and Pearl)*, and take a break from sightseeing with a cup of cider or a slice of pie.

Revival building on a riverside cobblestone street. Complete with functioning century-old treadle-powered letterpresses, Bowne & Co. is more than an inert museum exhibit: with over 1,200 typeface styles, the store still prints formal announcements, invitations, bookplates, and limited-edition volumes of Emily Dickinson's poetry. Hand-set invitations can cost up to $1,100 for a set of a hundred, but those who can only browse will enjoy examining Bowne's vintage maps, accounting books, wooden type, and rulers.

211 Water St (btwn Fulton & Beekman St)
212-748-8651
Wed-Sun 10am-5pm
❷❸❹❺Ⓐ❻Ⓙ❼Ⓩ
to Broadway-Nassau

EAT

Alfanoose

Middle Eastern

8 Maiden Lane (near Broadway)
212-528-4669
Mon-Sat
11:30am-9:30pm
❷❸❹❺Ⓐ❻Ⓙ❼Ⓩ
to Broadway-Nassau
$$

As falafel places become more common than pizza parlors in the city, it seems like the old question of "Who makes New York's best pizza?" is losing out to "What's the best place to get fried chickpeas around here?" Over the last decade, Alfanoose has garnered the reputation of a New York standby. However, this lunch joint truly merits

a visit with its authentic Lebanese and Syrian menu. Beyond the chickpeas, well-spiced and succulent meat platters and tubs of cold, creamy baba ghanoush are there to tempt as well. Meals can be taken out or eaten inside the mirrored, incense-scented restaurant. Whether you're a connoisseur of kabob or someone with an adventurous and potentially leathery palate, stop by for a quick lunch that's well-sized and well-priced.

PLAY

Beckett's Bar and Grill   *Outdoor Pub*
The rowdy after-work Wall St crowd descends nightly upon this large and convivial bar, where at least two sports games are always playing on TV and the music's on full-blast. Patrons talk shop or cheer their team over pints, sliders, and platters of blue corn nachos. In addition to drawing a devoted nightlife crowd, Beckett's is open for lunch daily and brunch on weekends, serving up pub fare and all-American standbys. Pull up a chair at the long bar downstairs or take a seat at one of the outdoor tables out back on Stone St. The first paved street in New York City, this charming

81 Pearl St (btwn Coenties Alley & Hanover Sq)
212-269-1001
Daily 11am-2am
❶ to Whitehall St,
❷ ❸ to Wall-William St,
❹ Ⓜ ❷ to Broad St
$$

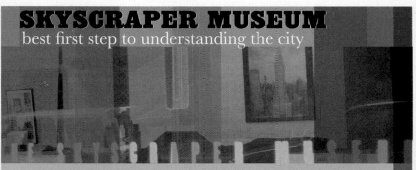

SKYSCRAPER MUSEUM
best first step to understanding the city

In the congested Financial District, it's easy to forget that the Lower Manhattan skyline is a paradigm of masterful engineering. Look up past the first floor façades concealed by bankers hauling briefcases toward the tops of these gleaming towers. The Skyscraper Museum, itself resourcefully designed, traces the history of New York's built environment through turn-of-the-century drawings and blueprints of the Empire State Building, the Flatiron Building, and other cloud-grazing landmarks. Exhibition space is limited to a mere 5,000 feet, but the way the museum emphasizes its own vertical character, creating the illusion of height with a mirrored floor and ceiling, is a show in itself. Decorate your apartment with one of the gift shop's posters of classic high-rises, and pretend you live there instead.

39 Battery Pl (at 1st Pl)
212-968-1961
Wed-Sun 12pm-6pm
R to Rector St,
4/5 to Bowling Green
Adults $5, Students
$2.50

Renowned director Michael Moore filmed a music video for the rock band Rage Against the Machine's "Sleep Now in the Fire" on Wall St.

and boisterous one-block cobblestone promenade is open seasonally and houses outdoor communal seating for Beckett's and the handful of neighboring taverns and grub hubs, including The Dubliner, Beckett's new sister pub.

Patriot Saloon — *Dive Bar*

This gloriously skeezy bar revels in its trashiness: the mascot is an enormous surfboarding alligator hanging from the ceiling with multicolored bras dangling from its limbs. In addition to this spectacular centerpiece, the bar has all the hallmarks of a good southern dive. The beer is dirt cheap (and well drinks are served with disdain), the loud country music's pumped out of two jukeboxes, and the hot bartenders dressed in conveniently low-cut tank tops could probably kick your ass. The two levels house arcade games and a pool table—welcome distractions to rampant pitcher guzzling. The Patriot is the perfect place to start a night, so long as you're not looking for too much intellectual stimulation.

18

110 Chambers St
(at Church St)
212-748-1162
Sun 12pm-4am,
Mon-Sat 11:30am-4am
1 2 3 A C to
Chambers St
$

BRIDGE CAFE
best restaurant older than the brooklyn bridge

Displaying such relics as its 19th-century liquors permit, this little riverside brothel-turned-restaurant knows the value of permanence. Dishes here may not take many risks, but why risk a standard that has been perfected over an illustrious 200+ year run? The famous soft shell crab in a refreshing and bright citrus sauce is reason enough to go, and the same can be said for the myriad of American classics. Bridge Café's persevering entrepreneurial spirit proves its worth, as the owner and the chef frequently wander out to chat with guests about the menu and local hotspots, gently encouraging visitors to keep this New York landmark thriving.

Seafood, American

279 Water St (at Dover St)
212 227-3344
Sun-Mon 11:45am-10pm,
Tues-Thurs 11:45am-11pm,
Fri 11:45am-12am,
Sat 5pm-12am
4/5/6 to City Hall,
2/3/4/ 5/A/C/J/M/Z to
Fulton St
$$$

BROO

GREEN

It may not seem far from Manhattan on the map, but Greenpoint maintains a mellow charm inconceivable on the opposite shores of the East River. Characterized by its chronic geographic isolation, Greenpoint's three occupational phases have corresponded with the slow evolution of transit through the region. Before the rise of the infrequent G train, the peninsula was the center of the lucrative 19th-century shipbuilding industry. During this time, the sole means of travel to and from these parts was by ferry, which had replaced the private skiffs that had transported both people and produce when the region was mostly pastureland.

When the Dutch snatched the last of these acres from Native Americans, the verdant farmland of Greenpoint was dotted with craggy bluffs and the blue crabs of Newton Creek. Families raised fowl and cattle, the women scoured their clothes in rivulets, and men built houses atop prime knolls. This insular community was separated from the rest of Brooklyn by dense marshes and from Manhattan by the East River. Makeshift boats were built to convey foodstuffs across the river, to be sold in the booming markets of downtown Manhattan.

Neziah Bliss was the visionary whose loping footfalls transformed this picturesque landscape into an industrial hub. After surveying the region's southern expanse, Bliss planned the construction of the Ravenswood, Green-Point and Hallet's Cove turnpike. Its completion was a momentous feat, facilitating access to this long-sequestered community. In 1832, a spell of

POINT

cholera and financial woes sent swarms of Manhattan's German, Irish, and Polish immigrants into Greenpoint. These families settled off the turnpike, which later became Frankin Street, the area's vibrant commercial artery.

With droves of newcomers, the neighborhood entered into a vigorous shipbuilding age. Along the buoyant waterfronts, shipyards sprouted faster than seedlings. Although this robust industry fizzled out after the Civil War, other trades, including printing, pottery, and iron manufacturing, continued to bolster Greenpoint's economy.

To this day, small but vital businesses cluster along the main thoroughfare, Manhattan Avenue—dubbed "Little Poland" for the multigenerational Polish bakers, butchers, cobblers, and grocers nested in its environs. Although scrappy smokestacks linger along neglected waterfronts and oil factories dominate the embankments of Newton Creek, the core of the neighborhood's activity has shifted to its eclectic shopping scene. Cramped meat markets, bakeries, thrift holes, and high-priced vintage boutiques cater to the locals' every need. Native Polski, young commuters, and the unfettered hipsters migrating north from congested Williamsburg live side-by-side. Local real estate shows promise of development in this culturally distinctive neighborhood, where redbrick brownstones, squat storefronts, angular intersections, and church steeples constitute a quaint and unassuming streetscape.

EXPLORE

Monsignor McGolrick Park

While overshadowed in size by the nearby McCarren Park, this compact playground—well shaded

Enclosed by Nassau Ave, Monitor St, Driggs Ave & Russell St
Ⓖ to Nassau Ave

beneath tall canopies—is favored by Greenpointers who prefer a cool summertime refuge to a spot in the sun. The colonnaded Shelter Pavilion lies at its center, flanked on the north and south by bronze war monuments. In contrast to this ceremonious centerpiece, the usual visitors are a laid-back and variegated bunch—babushkas idle in pairs as kids scramble wildly up the slides of the jungle gym. A dog run attracts local Fidos and their masters while drunkards swigging from flasks occupy their favorite benches all day long. Surrounding the park are rows of neat brownstones and the architectural charm of St. Stanislaus church.

Newtown Creek Nature Walk

Nature literally meets industry along this quarter-mile walkway—and the union is not in the least unpleasant. Constructed by the City's Depart-

84 Paidge Ave
(at Provost St)
718-389-2002
Daily dawn-dusk
Ⓖ to Greenpoint Ave

ment of Environmental Protection around the perimeter of a wastewater treatment plant, the Walk dynamically showcases the creek's evolution through time and how the area in general has culturally and environmentally developed. Ascend the steps of the stainless steel entry gate to arrive at a 170-foot long concrete path with high bowed walls, aptly named the "vessel"— but don't expect any greenery when you peep through the portholes. The "nature" aspect of the walk kicks in on the other side of the widening path, past the granite slab steps leading down to the water. It's a little odd to see such verdure so close to a sewage facility and mountains of scrap metal, but in a city like New York, the juxtaposition actually works.

SHOP

The Thing

Even die-hard garage sale junkies will be discombobulated by the pandemonium within this secondhand shop: haphazardly-arranged shelves, bins, and crates exploding with all manner of, well,

1001 Manhattan Ave
(btwn Huron & Green St)
718-349-8234
Thurs-Tues
9:30am-7:30pm,
Wed 9:30am-7pm
G to Greenpoint Ave

things. Apart from your standard thrift shop fare—books, CDs, DVDs, clothes, furniture, kitchenware, household appliances—there's an extensive collection of vintage porn magazines, a nude photo of Katie Holmes, and the odd mountain bike, piano, birdcage, and African mask. Plow through the impossibly narrow aisles to reach the store's real treasure: vinyl. Over 130,000 in number, at $2 each, and from every genre imaginable. Famous DJs from all over the world have flown to the city just to spend days in the florescently-lit basement, where the records are stacked from the floor to the ceiling. They aren't organized in any way, of course, so roll up your sleeves and prepare to dig—you just might unearth that Bobby Bland single you've always coveted.

Slodycze Wedel

This corner candy store's eye-popping supply of foil-wrapped bonbons imported from Poland would give Willy Wonka a run for his money. Customers young

772 Manhattan Ave
(at Meserole Ave)
718-349-3933
Sun 10am-6pm,
Mon-Fri 10am-8pm,
Sat 10am-8:30pm
G to Greenpoint Ave

and old rub their eyes to behold warm wooden shelves stocked with boxed confections bearing shiny letters they only wish they could decipher.

HISTORIC DISTRICT

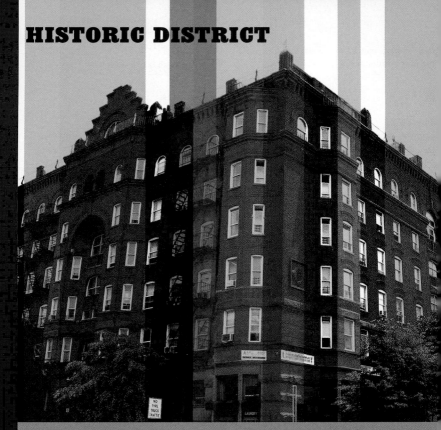

A charming piece of 19th-century Greenpoint is preserved in the distinctive architecture of this six-block area, wedged into the bosom of the neighborhood. Roughly bounded by Kent St on the north, Calyer St on the south, Franklin St on the west, and Manhattan Ave on the east, its tree-lined thoroughfares are primarily residential, but exquisite churches are interspersed amidst the houses (none of which, unfortunately, are for sale). Standing against the Manhattan skyline, the Neo-Renaissance-style brick façades along Kent St are accented with cast-iron lintels and Corinthian-columned porches. Greenpoint's oldest house of worship, the **Church of the Ascension** *(127 Kent St)*, is here as well, looking like it was plucked straight from the English countryside. Turn onto Franklin St to ogle the **Eberhard-Faber Pencil Factory** *(61 Greenpoint Ave)*, and the stunning brownstone arches of the **Astral Apartments** *(184 Franklin St)*, which once housed the workers at Charles Pratt's kerosene refinery. Even more captivating architecture can be found on Milton St, a motley of well-kept brick and limestone buildings enlivened by bay windows, elegant archivolts, and sweeping cornices. The pinnacle of them all is **St. Anthony's Church** *(862 Manhattan Ave)*, the neighborhood's own Willis Tower—its 240-foot spire can easily be seen from any point on Manhattan Ave.

Popular picks include sliwa—chewy plum cores encrusted in chocolate ($7.99 a pound)—and tin box Chopin samplers, which make for exquisite holiday gifts. As old as some of the local Polish meat markets and bakeries, Słodycze Wedel is a guilty staple for neighborhood kids with spare change. Figure-conscious fashionistas on Franklin Street try to avoid its toothsome goodies, but the prices are irresistible.

Word

Yuppies and hipster mothers (and their kids) are regular patrons of this cozy corner bookstore— Word's primary aim is to cater to the community, and it caters well. The orange-curtained storefront encloses a mere 1000 square feet of space, but the blond oak shelves house an extensive and well-groomed selection of literary classics, contemporary fiction, non-fiction, and cookbooks. In the back, there's a section dedicated entirely to children's books, puzzles, and gifts. Word's devilishly creative events further demonstrate its determination to be whatever the neighborhood needs it to be: there are readings with local authors, storytimes at Gym Park,

126 Franklin St
(at Milton St)
718-383-0096
Sun 12pm-8pm, Mon-Thurs 11am-8pm, Fri-Sat 11am-9pm
Ⓖ to Greenpoint Ave

literary mixers at The Diamond, the occasional potluck, and even a basketball league and a running group for the more athletically-inclined bibliophile. Among the most recent additions is a card brandishing the bookstore's modus operandi in Gothic wood type: "Eat. Sleep. Read."

EAT

Eat

New American, Organic

Eat's philosophy is as simple as its name: Mother Nature is a chef and you should eat what she gives you. Jordan Colon, the chef and owner, claims that he is only delivering what Nature herself offers. His dedication

124 Meserole Ave
(near Leonard St)
718-389-8083
Mon-Thurs 5pm-10pm,
Fri 12pm-10pm,
Sat-Sun 10am-10pm
Ⓖ to Nassau Ave
$$

to local business is admirable: everything from the cast iron sign above the door to the whimsical light fixtures are handcrafted by artisans in the area. Even the picnic tables—placed to encourage communal seating—are made by the owner's brother. The food is simple and beautiful. All organic and locally grown produce are prepared in dishes that highlight rather than hide the ingredients' incredible freshness. The

brooklyn.greenpoint.eat

menu changes daily to reflect the morning's harvest, so each dish is a unique vegetarian creation that is sure to delight and surprise.

Five Leaves

New American

This nautically themed grub house lulls diners into repose with rustic worn wood decor, smooth reggae, and unpretentious mason jar glassware.

18 Bedford Ave
(at Nassau Ave)
718-383-5345
Daily 8am-1am
Ⓖ to Nassau Ave
$$

The food is just as simple: begin with the cheese board or the flash fried oysters, which possess a salty crisp exterior that delicately balances the silky tenderness of their insides. The main course selection has something for seafood lovers and landlubbers alike. The yellowtail hamachi features both a traditional rare sushi-like interior and a delicate pan-seared crust. The grilled marinated flatiron steak comes with an elegant garnish of watercress and horseradish that delicately covers the boulangère potatoes, scalloped au gratin, hiding beneath. For an nice finishing touch, order the meringue-textured rosewater pavlova, a delectable medley of passion fruit curd, whipped cream, and kiwi.

Lomzynianka

Polish

Offering generous portions and uncommonly low prices, Lomzynianka is the eatery of choice for local pierogi connoisseurs. The tiny dining room is delightfully gaudy, sporting vibrant party ribbons

646 Manhattan Ave
(btwn Norman &
Nassau Ave)
718-389-9439
Daily 12pm-9pm
Ⓖ to Nassau Ave
$

and two mounted stag heads, and manages to fit two rows of wall side tables. Through the narrow aisle, a lone waiter buses bowls of steaming goulash while patrons converse quietly, mostly in Polish. The Hungarian pie—a Polish comfort food—surrounds a braised beef goulash with a pan-fried blanket of puréed potatoes. Another staple is the kielbasa, an unbelievably crispy pork sausage that is greased like the prize-winning pig it is. For the full experience try the Polish platter, a sampler with three different types of glistening light brown pierogi. Conclude your immersive evening with the blueberry blintz, a perfect arrangement of pastry layers spun around sweet farmer's cheese and oozing blueberry filling.

Peter Pan Donut & Pastry Shop
Bakery, Dessert

727 Manhattan Ave
(btwn Meserole &
Norman Ave)
718-389-3676
Mon-Fri 4:30am-8pm,
Sat-Sun 5:30am-8pm
Ⓖ to Nassau Ave
$

Among the plethora of Polish bakeries along Manhattan Ave—and the doughnut shops in all of New York City, as locals attest—Peter Pan Donuts reigns supreme. For 60 years, it's been delivering handmade doughnuts in a variety of old-fashioned flavors: vanilla, chocolate, cinnamon, sour cream, red velvet, whole wheat, white cream, apple, and coconut. They're done simple, cheap (at 95 cents a pop, $9.99 a dozen), and damn well: perfectly crispy crusts yield to light-as-air insides, lightly accented with vanilla and butter. The recipes haven't changed since Peter Pan's establishment, and it seems that the store hasn't either: the waitresses are clad in pink-collared pastel green smocks, '70s swivel stools flank a soda shop-style counter, and Sanka is even for sale. They also make an incredible bacon, egg, and cheese sandwich, and if you're feeling particularly indulgent, turn your doughnut into an ice cream sandwich for $3.50.

PLAY

Brouwerij Lane
Beer Bar

Lucky Greenpointers know Brouwerij Lane is one of the best-stocked beer bars in the city. With 19 brews on tap and another 150+ bottles to choose from in the fridge, there's sure to be

GREENPOINT
best cheap polish places

Karczma- Full of old country farmhouse charm and costumed waitresses, Karczyma proffers prime pierogies with Polish beer for under $10. *136 Greenpoint Ave, 718-349-1744, Sun 12pm-10pm, Mon-Thurs 12pm-10:30pm, Fri-Sat 12pm-11:30pm, G to Greenpoint Ave $*

Krolewskie Jadlo- On weekdays, this regal restaurant offers a feast fit for a king-rusted knights in armor included-with the $9 three-course lunch special. *694 Manhattan Ave, 718-383-8993, Sun-Wed 12pm-9pm, Thurs-Sat 12pm-10pm, G to Nassau Ave $*

Christina's Restaurant- Polish staples are flanked by American diner fare on the menu of this homey restaurant, yet the blintzes emerge victorious. *853 Manhattan Ave, 718-383-4382, Sun-Wed 8am-9pm, Thurs-Sat 8am-10pm, G to Greenpoint Ave $*

Restaurant Pyza- You'll look up the Polish word for bargain after scarfing a massive entrée surrounded by complimentary sides for cheaper-than-dirt prices at Pyza. *118 Nassau Ave, 718-349-8829, Daily 9am-9pm, G to Nassau Ave $*

FRANKLIN ST FASHION

Running parallel to the essential emporiums on Manhattan Ave, Franklin St boasts some of the neighborhood's classiest restaurants, vintage shops, and women's boutiques. In recent years, young entrepreneurs have transformed this street into a trend-conscious artery, a mini 5th Ave without the airs of age-old affectation. Grapevine opinion has it that the well-to-do's in Williamsburg are flocking north and fueling the market for innovative, off-beat designers.

Forget about H&M, the household name in Greenpoint is HH. Hailed as one of the first women's boutiques in the area, **Hayden-Harnett** *(211 Franklin St, 718-349-2247)* designs its own leather handbags and jewelry. Prices may be steep, but they're well-compensated by a generous repair and refund policy.

The aptly-named **Dalaga** *(150 Franklin St, 718-389-4049)*, Filipino for "a quintessential young woman in her prime," wows with its surprisingly affordable selection of chic dresses and accessories by local designers. Antique wall mirrors, deep velvet drapery, and ivory vanity sets create the feel of a Victorian boudoir, keeping the casual browser trapped for hours in this fashion fairyland.

Flaunting a collection of savvy streetwear, **Alter** *(men's: 109 Franklin St, women's: 140 Franklin St, 718-349-0203)* specializes in leather shoes and bags, zippered jumpsuits, and the battered urban look of torn jerseys. Rebelling against the vintage goddess assemblage, this closet-size shop glamorizes the bold black-and-white stripes of modern youth at competitive prices.

A wave-making newcomer, **Petit Boudoir** *(135 Franklin St, 718-383-3424)* channels a southern Provence vibe even in the cold of winter. Its maize yellow walls and decorative flourishes—straw hat, tennis rackets, and rowboat paddles—furnish the private dressing room of a sporty lady with a vulnerability for lace and flower print. The ever-helpful owners of this summer sanctuary will tailor shoppers' findings at no additional cost.

a beer to suit every customer's taste. For the less barley-savvy, the staff of locals is happy to offer suggestions for any occasion, be it a sweltering summer day, a breezy winter evening, or

78 Greenpoint Ave
(at Franklin St)
347-529-6133
Mon-Thurs 2pm-10pm,
Fri-Sun 12pm-10pm
Ⓖ to Greenpoint Ave
$$

just a search for something special. And here's the best part: since Brouwerij doubles as a full-fledged beer store, you can take the drinks with you! Sip a pint as you browse the aisles of domestic craft beers, international ales, and lagers. The smartest shoppers order the 32 or 64 oz growlers for $10-18, which allows them to sample all 19 beers on tap as they decide which one to take home. Brouwerij also offers the non-alcoholic alternative of Kombucha on tap, which is popular among health-conscious Brooklynites.

CoCo66 *Bar, Performance Space*

66 Greenpoint Ave
(btwn Franklin & West St)
718-389-7392
Daily 4pm-4am
Ⓖ to Greenpoint Ave
$$

Is it a bar? A restaurant? A music venue? The answer is yes(!), and it functions as all three with equal excellence. It's no wonder this converted woodshop is Greenpoint's pride and joy—it's the neighborhood's best bet for a cheap beer, tasty tacos, and great bands, a trifecta that is emphasized by the venue's three spacious rooms. Sit at a table and drink a Magic Hat on tap in one room, play a game of pool or foosball in another, and dance like a maniac to live tunes in the third. It's a cool place, and the people that come here are cool enough to suit it, so don't expect your usual keep-to-yourself dive feel. There's nothing wrong with talking or dancing with strangers at CoCo, because the crowd here is laid back in a Brooklyn-but-not-Bedford, G train sort of way.

Night of Joy *Cocktails, Bar*

667 Lorimer St
(at Meeker Ave)
718-388-8693
Mon-Thurs 5pm-2:30am,
Fri-Sat 12pm-4am
Ⓖ to Metropolitan Ave-
Lorimer St
$$

Night of Joy pairs a Victorian aesthetic with creatively crafted cocktails on the border of Williamsburg and Greenpoint. It shares much in common with its West Village sister bar, The Dove Parlour, but is afforded a lot more space by its Brooklyn location. This extra room is taken up by a marble fireplace, a pool table, and—you guessed it—a rooftop deck! Still, the number one priority in this libation lounge is cocktails. With names like rosemary bourbon, jalepeno tequila, and lavender gin, you can rely on every drink being as innovative as it is delicious. For this reason, the prices can get a little high, but happy hour every day from 5 to 8 pm makes Night of Joy the perfect place for an after-work drink. The only issue is having to decide between the mango margarita and the

cilantro Bloody Mary.

T.B.D.

With a 2,500-square foot garden that is the largest outdoor drinking space in Brooklyn, T.B.D. is big enough and simple enough to appeal to just about anybody. The spacious interior is minimally but tastefully decorated

Bar

224 Franklin St
(at Green St)
718-349-6737
Sun 12pm-2am,
Mon-Thurs 3pm-2am,
Fri 3pm-4am,
Sat 12pm-4am
Ⓖ to Greenpoint Ave
$

with framed photography of urban life, blue suede cube seats, and leather-bound armless couches. The even more spacious exterior is lined with picnic tables, where groups of friends share pitchers of beer and packs of cigarettes. As the hours pass, separate cliques tend to congregate for raucous, multi-table conversations. Their late night appetites are tested by woodsy barbecue smoke that swirls over from T.B.D's Garden Grill: options on the ten-item menu range from cheeseburgers with side salads to quesadillas with jalapeños and salsa.

ENID'S
best place to hit on the hip

Enid's is a well-established meeting place for young, stylish L-trainers from Williamsburg to Bushwick. The bar is decorated with white Christmas lights and vintage knickknacks surrounding old-school leather booths and wooden tables, creating a best friend's basement vibe to suit any occasion. A DJ in a booth above the bar spins underground hits at a volume for scream-free conversation. Drink specials are typical

Lounge, Bar Food

560 Manhattan Ave
(at Driggs Ave)
718-349-3859
Daily 12pm-4am
L to Bedford Ave,
G to Nassau Ave

of Brooklyn—five bucks will land you a beer and a shot of tequila or whiskey—but seven-dollar house cocktails like "The Harrison" (tequila, grapefruit, cranberry, fresh lime, and triple sec) are super strong and worth the Manhattan price tag. If you're hungry, be sure to check out the food menu, full of southern comfort specialties like mac and cheese or collard greens, or come by on Wednesdays for "Bean Day," when all food specials are bean-oriented—a tradition that earned the bar its lengthy nickname "Eat the Beanid's."

WILLIAI

When the Village of Williamsburg was founded in 1827, it had a little over 1,000 inhabitants, a post office and a fire department. But with its advantageous location on the East River, the town began to acquire somewhat of an international role. Raw materials came to its docks while finished products were shipped out, and in only a few decades, Williamsburg became as wealthy as the capitalists who built its shipyards. In 1903, the opening of the Williamsburg Bridge further precipitated the area's growth. Lured by commercial prospects, immigrants escaped insufferable upheaval in their native countries and chose Williamsburg over the crowded tenements of the Lower East Side.

Williamsburg thrived until the mid-20th century. As drug and crime problems increased, the area deteriorated and most of the factories and refineries became vacant, concrete skeletons. But this period only briefly tainted the area's rich and deep history. Like the industrialists years before, a group of developers saw an opportunity in Williamsburg and overhauled the crumbling infrastructure. A rezoning effort transformed the area, and by 2005, the neighborhood had shed a sketchy reputation and embraced its hip rebranding.

&BUSI

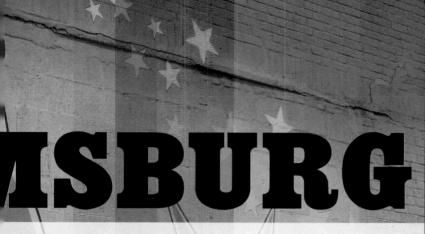

ISBURG

Today, many dormant factories have been converted into flourishing businesses and fancy lofts with sky-high rents. As evidence of its popularity, Williamsburg continues to attract investors as well as a number of celebrities—but it also remains an artist's enclave. With over 10,000 writers, artists, and performers calling it home, the neighborhood boasts New York's largest art community. An impressive underground music scene, thrift store subculture, and thriving nightlife, however, attract everyone else, from rich hippies to happy skateboarders. Once again, Williamsburg is back on the map.

Like Williamsburg, the neighboring Bushwick saw many struggles with drugs, crime, and poverty in the late 20th century. But the future looks hopeful for the neighborhood—the Bushwick Initiative was launched in 2005 to improve the lives of local tenants and the conditions of the area through necessary changes and developments, including over 200 fire alarm installations and job training programs. In a matter of a few years, the initiative succeeded in reducing crime, improving housing and sanitation, and increasing the overall commercial attraction of the neighborhood, making it an equally alluring, fun, and marginally cheaper extension of Williamsburg.

WICK

EXPLORE

Brooklyn Brewery

Home of the Brooklyn Lager since 1987, the no-nonsense Brooklyn Brewery is Williamsburg's modern answer to the traditional village green. Behind the formidable oak doors you'll find a boisterous scene, amidst Willy Wonka-esque machinery and the occasional stray cat. Every Friday, swarms of neighborhood regulars and adventurous Manhattanites arrive to taste its famous seasonal beers and staple brands. By the end of the night, the tables scattered throughout are covered in take-out containers (ordering in food is not only allowed, but encouraged) and plastic

79 N 11th St
(at Wythe Ave)
718-486-7422
Fri 6pm-11pm,
Sat-Sun 12pm-6pm
🄻 to Bedford Ave
Tours every hour
Sat & Sun 1pm-5pm

beer cups. On weekends tour groups can visit the brewery floor, which produces 20% of all inventory on-site at full capacity. Tastings are only available on Fridays, but given the fresh brews and the rough-and-tumble atmosphere, it's worth the wait.

Music Hall of Williamsburg

Prior to a 2007 corporate takeover, this concert hall was a singular outpost of independent and undiscovered music in

♫
66 N 6th St
(near Kent Ave)
718-486-5400

Brooklyn, a scrappy venue to match its scrappy environs, complete with bleachers imported straight from your high school gym. Then the Bowery Presents people got their hands on the Music Hall (née Northsix), adding a second balcony, swanky art deco neon, and a lineup of somewhat more established acts. For all the suspicion they've (predictably) garnered, the suits have managed to improve acoustics and aesthetics markedly inside. Today the Music Hall is mentioned in the same breath as Terminal 5, the Knitting Factory, and the Beacon Theater: a central stage for alt-rock enthusiasts whose slightly out-of-the-way location is totally worth the trip.

Pierogi 2000

Although pierogi and vodka are served in this snug exhibition space on opening nights, its name actually pays homage to Williamsburg's sizeable Polish population. Opened in 1994 by artist Joe Armhein for solo and two-person shows, Pierogi 2000 hit the art scene before Williamsburg earned its top spot in the gallery network. It has garnered international acclaim for its most important project: a trove of continually updated flat files that travels the globe periodically. Comprising over 700 portfolios, the collection is a bounty of pensive watercolors, abstract lithographs, acrylic figure studies, and minutely detailed collages. A satellite exhibition space called The Boiler, as well as the literary and art publication Pierogi Press, help preserve its status as a mainstay of the artistic community.

> 177 N 9th St (btwn Bedford & Driggs Ave)
> 718-599-2144
> Tues-Sun 11am-6pm, or by appointment
> ◐ to Bedford Ave

Williamsburg Art and Historical Center

Since 1996, this former Kings County Savings Bank (and National Historic Landmark) has been the epicenter of Williamsburg's ever-expanding art community. In addition to rotating exhibits of old-world New York artifacts and the most inventive contemporary art, the not-for-profit hosts a mélange of concerts, theatrical productions, poetry readings,

> 135 Broadway (at Bedford Ave)
> 718-486-7372
> Sat-Sun 12pm-6pm or by appointment
> ❶ Ⓜ ❷ to Marcy Ave, ◐ to Bedford Ave
> Free

lectures, and symposia. Most contributors are local artists, but WAHC maintains its international appeal with shows like the Japanese Mini Film Series. The Center also sponsors year-round events, including the Williamsburg Fashion Festival and "Musical Meltdown," where more than 20 bands rock from 4pm to 6am the next morning. In keeping with the preponderance of young folk in the neighborhood, much of the art opines on up-to-the-minute social and environmental issues.

HASIDIC WILLIAMSBURG

In the face of Williamsburg's ongoing hipsterification, a Hasidic enclave preserves the pre-Holocaust Askenazi way of life. The influx of secular and often scantily-clad young folk in the area has prompted clashing between the trendy and the traditional, especially over the Bedford Avenue bike lane, which the Hasids see as a danger to schoolchildren. Still, **Lee Ave** *(btwn Division and Flushing)* remains entirely Jewish: join the masses walking to temple on the Sabbath to listen in on Yiddish conversations and read Hebrew menus (all Kosher, of course). The community was settled by Jewish immigrants fleeing a devastated Europe after World War II. Now the Satmars, one of the largest Hasidic sects, have their world headquarters in Williamsburg, home to 70,000 adherents. The neighborhood celebrates between 300 and 400 weddings a year and remains one of the fastest-growing communities in the world. In a sure sign of cultural authenticity, Al Pacino visited South Williamsburg to prepare for his role as Shylock for the 2010 Shakespeare in the Park summer series. Neighborhood landmark congregation **Yetev Lev D'Satmar** *(at Kent Ave and Hooper St)*, which seats 4,350, earned the moniker "miracle synagogue" for being built in less than three weeks. On a Friday morning, follow the smell of freshly baked challah to **Lee Avenue Kosher Bakery** *(73 Lee Ave)* and treat yourself to another miracle, the spectacular cinnamon rugelach.

SHOP

Beacon's Closet

This legendary clothing exchange emporium is a Brooklyn institution and the front runner of the thrift store circuit. Unlike the posh and pricey boutiques along Bedford Avenue, Beacon's Closet sells used and vintage clothing and accessories at prices that won't break the bank, and it stocks everything from LaRok to Marc Jacobs. The "closet" takes up a daunting 5,500 square feet of space, and color-coordinated racks don't make the hunting process much easier, as they aren't organized by size—but chancing upon a perfect fitting tee or a bargain Betsy Johnson dress makes the experience worth the hassle. You'll find especially delectable steals in the shoe collection—keep an eye out for $75 Proenza Schouler pumps and $45 Jill Stuart slingbacks. Beacon's offers 35% cash or 55% store credit of an item's selling price, so bring your own shirt and make money before you turn around and spend it.

88 N 11th St (btwn Wythe & Berry St)
718-486-0816
Mon-Fri 11am-9pm,
Sat-Sun 11am-8pm
🕒 to Bedford Ave
Additional location:
92 5th Ave, Brooklyn

KCDC

Brooklyn's own Amy Gunther and Nevett Steele opened this roomy store in 2001 with one goal in mind: to keep skating alive and thriving in a gentrifying Brooklyn. KCDC has since become a hub for the city's oldest and most devoted skaters, who come for decks, gear, shoes, board tuneups, and a whirl on the in-store halfpipe. Local brands share shelf space with old corporate standbys, and the work of as-of-yet undiscovered artists from the area dangle from the walls. With frequent parties and video screenings, the shop is a pocket of unpretentiousness within this continually glamorizing

90 N 11th St (btwn Wythe Ave & Berry St)
718-387-9006
Daily 12am-8pm
🕒 to Bedford Ave

borough. Beginners are welcome to browse or take a basic skating lesson—all off-beat subcultures need someone to carry on the torch.

Peach Frog

Housed in a converted egg roll factory, this store advertises designer goods at up to 90% off—and, amazingly, it's good for its word. Against the exposed brick walls lean stacks of super soft tanks and tees by Mark and Estel for just over $15 and Diego Binetti runway dresses for $45. Peach Frog won't stay under the radar for long, so grab that discounted Vivienne Westwood bag before it makes its way onto the homepage of every fashion blog in Brooklyn. But camera shy shoppers beware: professional photographers and make-up artists turn random customers into models for in-store fashion shows—and then reward them with $100 gift certificates. If strutting the runway doesn't interest you, hit up a Peach Frog block party, where bands like the Asteroids Galaxy Tour keep customers dancing in their chic threads to psychedelic beats.

136 N 10th St (btwn Berry St & Bedford Ave)
718-387-3224
Mon-Fri 12pm-9pm,
Sat-Sun 11am-8pm
🕒 to Bedford Ave

Red Pearl

A welcome break from Williamsburg's hipster kitsch, this endearing boutique is upscale but entirely unpretentious. Shoppers can rifle through piles of sorbet-colored hobo bags, racks of garden party dresses from MK2K and Hype, and an impressive collection of undergarments in every shade of red. But it's the curious tabletop tchotchkas that distinguish Red Pearl from its countless trendy counterparts. Adorn your office space with old-fashioned feather pens and baby-Buddha paperweights or freshen your kitchen with heirloom tomato- and celery-scented candles. The shelf of urban gardening tools, which fea-

123 Wythe Ave (btwn 8th & 9th St)
718-388-6396
Tues-Fri 2pm-9:30pm,
Sat 12pm-10pm
🕒 to Bedford Ave

Williamsburg claimed the most densely populated blocks in New York City by 1917.

tures eggshell flower pots and "grow a garden in a bag" kits, is particularly nifty. Prices can be steep, so stock up on birthday gifts for your girlfriends during a seasonal sale, announced at redredpearl.com.

Pop Fuzz

Sean Powers and Alison Doshner began selling movies and music on eBay as a hobby before moving their operation to the sidewalk, and then to a home basement. The opening of PopFuzz in 2009 transformed their vocation into a full-time profession. Be prepared to spend a little money and a lot of time rummaging through the boxes and shelves of graphic novels, more than 7,000 books (many of which are only $1), an incredible 2.5 tons of records, and several thousand DVDs. The merchandise changes with the owners' latest obsessions, so don't expect neat genre categories: old-school trading cards like Pokemon and Garbage Pail Kids lie in stacks near Powers and Doshner's art toy creations. This is the perfect place to complete a collection or start a new one.

> 202 Bedford Ave
> (at 6th St)
> 718-599-0023
> Sun 12pm-7pm,
> Mon-Sat 11am-8:30pm
> 🚇 to Bedford Ave

Sound Fix

Loyal Pitchfork readers can feed their indie addictions at Sound Fix Records, a favorite outlet for new releases and old vinyl. After the six-year-old Williamsburg fixture, originally located on Bedford Avenue, was shut down in 2008 for a series of noise violations, owner James Bradley relocated to Berry Street so he could continue to offer live performances. The store keeps in step with the latest in underground music, so you won't find classic rock or Lite FM fare alongside The Dirty Projectors. Distinctive neon red shelves stock independent bestsellers like Animal Collective

> ♫
> 44 Berry St (at 11th St)
> 718-388-8090
> Sun 12pm-8pm,
> Mon-Sat 12pm-9pm,
> 🚇 to Bedford Ave

and lesser-known artists like Ty Segall, as well as rare vinyl LPs. As far as corner music shops go, Sound Fix is the well-groomed Goliath of the neighborhood. Don't leave the register without an events calendar—past shows have featured the likes of Bon Iver and Patton Oswalt.

Whisk

Kitchen Aid blenders are displayed alongside zebra-print spatulas, waffle makers are paired with rainbow egg cups, martini glasses are garnished with edible glitter: with its kooky twists on basic kitchen appliances, Whisk is no Williams-Sonoma. Amateur chefs will appreciate the personal touches found throughout this locally-owned store, such as the collection of cookbooks handpicked by the staff. Shoppers never suffer from a lack of individual attention, whether they want help mixing and matching designs, or desperately need to know the difference between German and Japanese knives. Come in for regular tasting samples and check the blog for cookie decorating parties and Thanksgiving Day turkey basting. And don't forget to browse the dazzling selection of bartending equipment near the coffeemakers and tea presses: it includes everything you'll need for a homemade martini.

> 231 Bedford Ave
> (at 4th St)
> 718-218-7230
> Sun 11pm-7pm,
> Mon-Fri 10:30am-8pm,
> Sat 10am-8pm
> 🚇 to Bedford Ave

EAT

Egg   *Brunch, American*

Egg lives up to its name—clean, streamlined, and white. The front of this southern-style restaurant is almost entirely open on a nice day, leading into the high-raftered, white-walled breakfast room. Egg also represents the highest evolution of the recent turn to local ingredients, as many come from their own farm near the Catskills. Likewise, unless you rise with the sun, be prepared for a wait—lines get mighty long after 10am. Yet the food, classic American breakfast fare made farm fresh, is deserving. The Country Ham Biscuit—flaky salty chips of country ham smothered in rich fig preserves—captures that down-home

135 N 5th St
(at Bedford Ave)
718-302-5151
Sun 9am-9pm,
Mon-Wed 7am-6pm,
Thurs-Fri 7am-11pm
to Bedford Ave
$

Kentucky taste (and price). Vegetarians will love the fluffy Graton Cheddar Omelet. Don't forget the side of creamy Anson Mills grits, a Yankee approved taste of Americana.

Fette Sau *BBQ*

Williamsburg's dedication to locavore organophiles has translated into excellence in the art of barbecue. Fette Sau only uses small family-farmed organic meat, a dry, never sauced, rub, and

354 Metropolitan Ave
(at Havemeyer St)
718-963-3404
Mon-Fri 5pm-11pm,
Sat-Sun 12pm-11pm
to Bedford Ave
$$

a smoker burning a variety of locally-sourced wood. From a distance, the neon red sign might be the only indication that Fette Sau is an eatery and not a driveway. The fenced-in entrance is lined with wooden picnic tables seating customers overwhelmed by the metal-trayed monster slabs of barbecue in front of them, including a flavor-exploding pork belly and classics such as ribs and a succulent pulled pork—all purchased by the pound. The inside resembles a rigid wild west saloon, with walls tattooed by charts that break down each cut of beef, pork, and lamb. Check out the knife-handled draughts on tap or wash down your meat feast with a great selection of bourbons.

La Superior *Mexican*

The drastically understated façade of this local Williamsburg taco shack makes the neighborhood's most beloved Mexican restaurant look average, but after several tortillas and a

WILLIAMSBURG
late-night munchies

Pies N' Thighs- It may be hip, but the food is old-school, offering the best dishes of Southern cuisine like crispy fried chicken, barbecue pork sandwiches, and fresh pies. *166 S 4th St, 347-529-6090, Mon-Fri 8am-12am, Sat-Sun 10am-12am, J/M/Z to Marcy Ave $$*

Vinnie's Pizza- Possibly the only late night pizzeria with several vegan options, Vinnie's makes tasty innovative pies like Black Bean Taco and Avocado Insalata, but also does the classics well—try the perfectly crisp Margherita. *148 Bedford Ave, 718-782-7078, Sun, Mon-Thurs 10am-12am, Fri-Sat 10am-3am, L to Bedford Ave $$*

Oasis- While cheap falafel sandwiches are what makes this Middle Eastern eatery perfect for after-dark cravings, the variety of other specialties like sumac spiced Spinach pies and homemade Mousaka set it apart from the average falafel stand. *161 N 7th St, 718-218-7607, Daily 11am-11pm, L to Bedford Ave $*

Noodle Shop- Serving heaping portions of various noodle soups, fried chive dumplings, and sliced pork belly over rice, the Noodle Shop has insanely late hours that make it every insomniac's dream. *549 Metropolitan Ave, 718-384-8008, Daily 12pm-6am, L/G to Lorimer St- Metropolitan Ave, $$*

El Diablo Taco Truck- Authentic Mexican fare like spicy Shrimp tacos, pork cheek sandwiches, and corn on the cob smothered in Queso fresco is what this food truck does best, satisfying customers into the early hours of the morning. *484 Union Ave, Mon-Fri 7pm-3:30am, Sat-Sun 1pm-3:30am, L/G to Lorimer St- Metropolitan Ave, $*

margarita it will be obvious that La Superior is an honest title. Each night, dinnertime crowds spill from the 30-seat interior onto wooden benches out front that look as though they've been imported straight from Tijuana. The straightforward fare is loyal to any bona fide taco shop's formula: carne asada, tinga de pollo, daily pescado, and a refreshing guacamole are served with only the freshest of ingredients. Every item on the slightly worn overhead menu is worth trying, but be sure to snag a few palm-sized tacos for a meager $2.50 apiece. The Torta Ahogada is the mouth-watering signature dish—there is nothing understated about this pile of juicy carnitas topped with beans, tucked between crispy sourdough bread, and smothered with a chile-tomato sauce.

295 Berry St
(btwn 2nd & 3rd St)
718-388-5988
Sun-Thurs
12:30pm-12am,
Fri-Sat 12:30am-2am
Ⓛ to Bedford Ave
$

Motorino — *Pizzeria*

The Williamsburg location of this up-and-coming pizzeria, the latest project of Belgian chef Matthieu Palombino, sits on a much more residential street than its East Village counterpart. Nonetheless, Motorino always seems to be crowded, with its spacious dining room and open kitchen. The dishes, while innovative, draw from rustic Italian ingredients: try the octopus salad with potatoes, celery, and capers or the refreshing fennel salad with red onion, orange slices, and lemon juice. The pizzas, thin with a pillowy crust, are just as impressive, pairing toppings like brussel sprouts, pancetta, and percorino cheese. More classic offerings include a plate of thinly sliced prosciutto with a loaf of homemade bread, brushed with thyme-infused olive oil, or the classic pizza Marguerita garnished with leaves of fresh basil.

319 Graham Ave
(at Devoe St)
718-599-8899
Sun 11am-12am, Mon-Thurs 10am-12am, Fri 10am-1am, Sat 11am-1am
Ⓛ to Graham Ave
$$

Peter Luger — *Steakhouse*

This steakhouse, established in 1887, has an unmistakably old-fashioned aura. But while the wooden tables and the waiters' white aprons and black bow ties certainly enhance the dining experience, nothing defines Peter Luger more than its dry-aged, perfectly marbled beef and signature horseradish-infused steak sauce. Though the food may be decadent, everything is prepared in the simplest manner, like the sliced beefsteak tomato and vidalia onion salad, or the extra thick slabs of bacon. Peter Luger also serves all the regular fixins of a traditional steakhouse: onion rolls and butter, jumbo shrimp cocktail, double thick lamb chops. And of course, there's the steak itself, served sizzling off the cast-iron pan with sides like creamy spinach or French fried potatoes. If there's any room for dessert, a generous portion of New York style cheesecake is the perfect indulgence.

178 Broadway
(at Driggs Ave)
718-387-7400
Sun 12:45pm-9:45pm,
Mon-Thurs
11:45am-9:45pm,
Fri-Sat 11:45am-10:45pm
Ⓙ Ⓜ Ⓩ to Marcy Ave
$$$$

Radegast Hall and Biergarten — *Gastropub, Eastern European*

In the forbidding hipster enclave of Williamsburg, friendliness and warmth may seem in short supply—but at Radegast Hall, the Slovak god of hospitality reigns supreme. Two equally appealing choices greet the lone (or accompanied) traveler upon entry: to the right, an open-air hall where office workers in shirtsleeves and artists in tattoo sleeves confer at heavy wooden tables; to the left, a bar for the more determined drinkers. Highlights from the extensive menu include the light and tangy German potato salad and the Spatzle, a German gnocchi blanketed with bubbling emmental cheese, hunter's bacon, and chives. This

113 N 3rd St (at Berry St)
718-963-3973
Mon-Fri 4pm-4am,
Sat-Sun 12pm-4am
Ⓛ to Bedford Ave
$$

being a biergarten, however, the beer is just as important as the food. Rely on the expert staff to set you up for drunken excess with brews from Germany, Austria, Holland, Belgium, and the Czech Republic. After enough Krusovice Imperial, you may find yourself face to face with old Radegast himself.

Saltie · *Sandwiches*

It may look like a grub shack on an old trawler, but this small, white-walled shop will surprise you with its salty-sweet sandwiches and breezy, by-the-beach character. A bright blue signboard

378 Metropolitan Ave
(at Havermeyer St)
718-387-4777
Tues-Sun 10am-6pm
🅛 to Bedford Ave
$

lists the signature options, all of which derive their names from the café's marine aesthetic: Scuttlebutt and Spanish Armada are particularly noteworthy. The Romaine Dinghy, listed on a separate, handwritten menu, is a delightfully plush concoction of thick foccacia, romaine leaves, radishes, and a generous drizzle of anchovy and mango sauce. A lighter option is the $6 summer special: long baby carrots dressed in a cool, almond mint paste. For a post-meal treat, be sure to check out the white showcase of eclectic pastries—among the brioches, tur-

quoise cups and *Diner Special* magazines, there resides a plate of chocolate pistachio cookies just waiting to satisfy your sweet-and-salty tooth.

Rabbithole · *American, Brunch, Café*

Friendly warmth collides with unprecedented dishes at this enchanting coffee shop, which transforms into a quaint dining spot after the sun goes down. Walk through the door into

352 Bedford Ave
(btwn 3rd & 4th St)
718-782-0910
Sun-Thurs 9am-11pm,
Fri-Sat 9am-1am
🅛 to Bedford Ave
$$

a dimly lit café, past the long full bar and into the open-air garden where ivy-draped walls surround a few tables, charmingly illuminated by twinkling tea lights. While superlative pastries and breads—all baked on the premises—are Rabbithole's calling cards, a down-to-earth collection of well-done American dishes defines the menu. The inconceivably soft black bean burger is a must-try for any veggie burger connoisseur. Wash it down with a signature cocktail, such as the sweet but tangy Strawberry Rum Fizz. Dessert, however, still reigns supreme: the Earl Grey Crème Brûlée will leave your sugar-craving taste buds vibrating long after the last bite.

347

PLAY

Barcade

Games, Beer Bar

This hybrid bar and arcade might be a safe zone for nerds who like to party, but the nerds of Williamsburg are as stylish, good-looking and outgoing as they come. Step inside the cavernous loft-like space to find over 20 classic 80's arcade games (all of which run entirely on wind power) complemented by a full bar and a pool table. If you're an expert gamer, try to snag a spot on the all-time high score chalkboard across the ceiling. Running out of quarters or frustrated with your Q*bert skills? One of the 24 specialty microbrews on tap is guaranteed to nurse away your disappointment. The marriage of old school gaming and savory beers is even conducive to a little romance—couples can often be found canoodling on the plastic elementary school chairs and holding hands across the anime-graffitied tables.

388 Union Ave (btwn Ainslie & Powers St)
718-302-6464
Mon-Thurs 5pm-4am,
Fri-Sun 2pm-4am
Ⓛ Ⓖ to Lorimer St-Metropolitan Ave
$$

Cyn Lounge

Dive Bar

Duck the Bedford-bound influx of NYC's hippest at this cozy corner dive. Never crowded but always lively, Cyn Lounge is no-nonsense about cheap drinks and good music. Five bucks will score a generous shot of whiskey with a PBR, and you can croon to the Rolling Stones or Jay-Z on the internet jukebox for 50 cents. Cyn Lounge is just as no-nonsense about décor, but the graffiti-coated cement walls, exposed aluminum roof, pleather couches, and haphazardly-scattered small tables have a grungy charm—which is only enhanced by faint red light emanating from the disco ball on the ceiling. If weather permits, take your drink outside to one of the four wooden booths of the spacious garden. An iron fence separates this smoker-friendly area from the sidewalk, but makes people-watching all too easy.

216 Bedford Ave
(at 5th St)
718-384-0100
Mon-Thurs 4pm-4am,
Fri-Sun 2pm-4am
Ⓛ to Bedford Ave
$

Death by Audio

Music Venue

"Rock and Roll Grandma," reads the otherwise unmarked door of Death by Audio. The sign reflects the underground rock club's all ages policy, though the crowd is often on the younger side. With inexpensive

ALL AGES $ 🍾
49 S 2nd St (btwn Kent & Wythe Ave)
Open Thurs-Sat
🄻 to Bedford Ave,
🄶 to Driggs Ave-S 2nd St
$$

beers for those over 21 and a cheap cover to see several performances in a night, DBA is accessible to anyone who can find it. As with most DIY music venues, the acoustics aren't great, the bathrooms are grimy, and clouds of cigarette smoke permeate the space. But DBA makes up for what some deem as drawbacks by booking awesome bands: the graffitied cement walls have played host to acts like Thurston Moore, Dirty Projectors, Japanther, Dan Deacon, and Movement.

Glasslands Gallery

Music Venue, Bar

🎵 🕺

289 Kent Ave (btwn 1st & 2nd St)
718-599-1450
Doors open Tues-Fri 8pm,
Sat-Sun 9 or 10pm
🄻 to Bedford Ave
$$

This intimate gallery space, known for its blaring music and unusually enthusiastic crowds, has played host to some of Brooklyn's finest underground acts since its opening in 2006. With DIY art, including an ethereal cloud-like light installation, adorning its walls, Glasslands caters to those who appreciate some aesthetic stimulation with their party.

williamsburg & bushwick
UNDER $20

Pick up some bold coffee and a homemade muffin at **New York Muffins** *(198 Bedford Ave)* and head up Bedford to enjoy breakfast in **McCarren Park** *(entrance at Bedford Ave and 12th St)*, where the young and the trendy of Williamsburg spend their summer days.

See the up-and-comers at **Pierogi 2000** *(177 N 9th St)*, a hole-in-the wall modern art gallery, then window shop on Bedford until you're ready to hit one of its intriguing cafés.

Get the best lunch deal at **Tai Thai Café** *(206 Bedford Ave)*—the food is spicy, the portions are filling, and the price is $5.55 from noon to 4:30pm. Choose from an assortment of curry, noodle, rice and meat entrées served with white rice and a spring roll.

Cross the street to **Earwax Records** *(218 Bedford Ave)* and browse vintage vinyls and an eclectic selection of CDs.

Take a digital photography class or learn the art of silversmithing at **3rd Ward** *(195 Morgan Ave)*, the Renaissance Man's arts venue.

Get a free personal pizza with your beer at the miraculous **Alligator Lounge** *(600 Metropolitan Ave)*, the most generous tavern in New York.

Seize the night at the LGBT club **Sugarland** *(221 N 9th St)*, where revelers turn a blind eye to indoor smoking and live drag reigns.

An elevated, kitsch-embellished bar serves the classic selection of Brooklyn brews, which you can savor away from the debauchery in a lofted seating area. The live music generally runs the gamut from electronic rock to metal—past performers include Dirty Projectors, Yeasayer, and Light Asylum, though most nights feature less-established local acts. Glasslands also frequently hosts dance parties and off-kilter game nights, so come get your groove on while playing bingo with your favorite Brooklyn bands.

Goodbye Blue Monday *Music Venue, Bar*
Entering this coffee shop cum music venue cum bar is like stepping into a bohemian *I Spy* book. The walls, decked out in everything from china dolls to umbrella lamps, hold infi-nite surprise for any observant visitor. A small stage, scattered tables, and crammed bookshelves consume the rest of the eclectic space. Goodbye Blue Monday's nightly live music, which is almost always free, is just as surprising as its furnishings: acts range widely in quality and genre, so keep an open mind. The friendly crowd leans further towards La Vie Boheme than Williamsburg-chic (while still sipping tall boy PBRs). But since Goodbye's quirks are its merits, forgo the Brooklyn favorite and try one of the homemade, seasonal specials, like Sangria Lemonade. If you're hungry, opt for

♫ 🥘
1087 Broadway (btwn Dodworth & Lawton St)
718-453-6343
Daily 11am-2am
Ⓙ to Kosciuszko St
$$

ZEBULON
best place to snack and dance

Zebulon is an anomaly of a modern day New York City mu-sic venue: they never charge a cover, serve affordable drinks, and house some of the most sophisticated yet accessible live music in town. Run by a team of European musicians looking to breathe new life into the W-burg scene, this cozy cafe and concert hall has become a safe haven for showgoers looking to appreciate some truly authentic tunes. Come join the crowd and dance, sway, or simply listen to the music while enjoying your beverage and a bite to eat—with snacks like pate and chorizo and bottles of wine as cheap as $22, the music isn't the venue's only appeal.

Music Venue, Bar, Cafe
258 Wythe Ave (btwn Metropolitan Ave & 3rd St)
718-218-6934
Sun-Thurs 4pm-3am, Fri-Sat 4pm-4am
L to Bedford Ave
$

the delicious, non-alcoholic carrot cake, as it may serve you well to have your wits about you in this coolly ungentrified neighborhood.

House of Yes

Performance Space

342 Maujer St
(near Morgan Ave)
Open Mon-Sat
🕐 to Grand St
$

Operated by the small group of performance artists who call it home, House of Yes is a DIY venue that throws weekly parties and events in East Williamsburg. The space is designed specifically for musical and acrobatic acts, with a big stage and long velvet ropes hanging from high ceilings. Velvet, in fact, covers most of the House's furniture, and for good reason: most of the performances are hedonistic dance parties or burlesque-themed shows. The themes change from week to week, according to the whims of their creative conceptualists, so visitors can always expect the unexpected. Swing by to pair cheap drinks with stilt walking, arts and crafts, tasteful striptease, death-defying acrobatics, and cool local bands.

Metropolitan   *LGBT*

This gay bar is Williamsburg's haven for those looking for a laid-back conversation. Its more intellectual and less entrepreneurial vibe, coupled with cheap drinks and free summer Sunday BBQs, draws in a pro bono, post-graduate crowd. Visitors gather around the pool table but rarely hit the dance floor, establishing the bar

as more of a pre-game and pick-up spot than a late night destination. This, however, is a major part of Metropolitan's charm. It provides a place for gay and straight girls and boys to mingle in a cozy environment

559 Lorimer St (btwn
Devoe St &
Metropolitan Ave)
718-599-4444
L G to Lorimer St-
Metropolitan Ave
$

without music blaring and lots of skin showing. In the summer months, the party tends to migrate outdoors to the vine-coated backyard garden, but when it's cold, the two fireplaces inside make for great places to warm up over a beer or two.

Spike Hill

With 80 different whiskeys, 50 Belgian beers, live music, and upscale bar food, Spike Hill is Williamsburg's jack of all trades. The main room resembles a warm English pub, with a long bar

Whiskey Bar

184-186 Bedford Ave
(at N 7th St)
718-218-9737
Sun-Thurs 11:30am-2am,
Fri-Sat 11:30am-4am
L to Bedford Ave
$

that runs parallel to secluded booths separated by floor-to-ceiling dividers. In the adjacent side room, local bands play every night of the week on an intimate, red-curtained stage. Weeknights reel in regulars for dinner, dates, and stiff drinks in the main room, while Fridays and Saturdays

attract partygoers looking to bust their moves. Regardless of the crowd, the savvy bartenders maintain the classy, whiskey tavern rep by pairing you with the single-malt that suits you best. And no matter when you visit, the ternary effect of food, drink, and dance lets you have three nights in one.

Spuyten Duyvil   *Beer Bar*

Slip inside the gated red entrance to discover one of the most highly specialized beer gardens in NYC. The menu showcases both local and international brews, with selections from Japan, Sweden, Finland, Germany, Belgium, and more. The seemingly endless list is scrawled across five chalkboards in near-illegible small print and constantly rotates. Need something potent? The Trappistes Rochefort (9.3% alcohol) might set your head spinning, so soak it up with some of the fine meats and cheeses sold at the bar. Although sophisticated drinking is clearly the top priority here, Spuyten Duyvil maintains a visual aesthetic as wildly eclectic as its beer selection. Random thrift store finds, including Chinese checker sets and a rusty old bicycle, are scattered throughout the narrow main room, which leads to a mas-

359 Metropolitan Ave
(near 4th St)
718-963-4140
Opens Mon-Fri 5pm,
Sat-Sun 1pm
🄻 to Bedford Ave
$$

JUNK
best grab-bag for the brave

Junk is exactly what its name evokes: a dark and musty basement teeming with worn suitcases, defunct typewriters, cheap CDs, century-old photos and postcards, and some eccentric curiosities that will be sure to ignite a conversation. The obscure merchandise comes from auctions throughout the Northeast: an hour or two of disciplined digging will uncover a record-playing end table or retro Happy Meal toys. If amassing useless knick-knacks lacks appeal, hit the racks of worn clothes (keep an eye out for '70s-era wedding dresses) or browse the vinyl collection. Although employees strictly enforce the "no haggling" rule, the treasures are generally well-priced—some records are as cheap as 49 cents. Junk's controlled chaos certainly demands patience, but oftentimes you'll find just what you were looking for—or, if you're lucky, something you weren't.

197 N 9th St (btwn
Bedford & Driggs Ave)
718-640-6299
Mon-Fri 9am-11pm,
Sat-Sun 9am-9pm
L to Bedford Ave

sive outdoor garden that attracts smokers in the summertime.

Trophy Bar

Dive, Dance Bar

351 Broadway
(at Keap St)
347-227-8515
Daily 5pm-4am
J M Z to Marcy Ave,
J M to Hewes St
$

Trophy is one of those shape-shifting bars that can provide all sorts of good times. Whether you're seeking a quiet drink out front with a friend, a BBQ on the patio, or a full on dance party under the disco ball, this bar rarely disappoints. Located in South Williamsburg off the beaten path of Bedford Ave, it never gets too crowded, but manages to attract some of the city's best DJs. Still, the bar maintains a laid-back vibe, with sparse decoration (the shelf of trophies behind the DJ booth being the most notable) and drink specials every night. Come by for Tac-colada Tuesday evenings with cheap tacos on the patio, and be sure to linger around for a Joy Division/New Order rager.

Union Pool

Bar

484 Union Ave
(at Skillman Ave)
718-609-0484
Mon-Fri 5pm-4am,
Sat-Sun 1pm-4am
G L to Lorimer St
or Metropolitan Ave
$

You won't find swimmers at Union Pool, but signs from the former pool supply and pest control store adorn its bright, Las Vegas-style interior, explaining the namesake. Woodford Reserve Bourbon Whiskey, the official bourbon of the Kentucky Derby, is poured generously for the good-looking twenty somethings that surround the concrete bar. Less eager patrons gather in the blue, half-moon shaped booths that line the shiny tin walls, but in summer months, it's best to push past the crowd and join the backyard party. Beneath a red awning, Cabana chairs provide some respite from the line for the photo booth and the ever-popular taco truck. Don't miss Monday nights at 11, when Reverend Vince Anderson and his Love Choir throw down gospel in the back room.

FORT G

Purchased by the United States along with the land for Brooklyn Navy Yard in 1801, the area today called Fort Greene developed under the guiding hand of the military during its first 50 or so years on American soil. It served as the site of the strategically vital (and later renamed) Fort Putnam during the Revolutionary War, which was maintained until the War of 1812. When the structure became obsolete, the adjacent navy shipyard kept both money and people flowing through the region. Still, like many outer borough neighborhoods, Fort Greene remained fairly remote until industrialization hit Manhattan like a freight train at the end of the century, sending Brooklyn strange bedfellows: the richest, seeking a "country" respite from the island's smog, and the poorest, who were simply crowded out of even tenement buildings.

This disjointed demographic set the stage for Fort Greene's unmatched outpouring of social activism and creativity over the next century. It was home to New York's first African-American school, built in 1847 on the iconic poet Walt Whitman's property. It housed Richard Wright while he was writing Native Son and Spike Lee while he pieced together Do The Right Thing—both works of politically charged African-American art that exemplify residents' habit of testing limits. Today, Fort Greene's BAM Cultural District stands at the helm of Brooklyn's artistic community. Establishments like the Museum of Contemporary African Diaspora Arts and the Irondale Theater, an experimental playhouse with a mission for social

& CLINT

REENE

change, challenge and inspire visitors. Calling Fort Greene a "black neighborhood" would be an oversimplification; well-to-do young professionals of every race have been migrating at a steady rate to the area for over a hundred years. The day-to-day interaction between professionals and artists of different ethnicities is what makes Fort Greene such a haven for creative wealth and unusually peaceful race relations.

To the east of Fort Greene is the smaller Clinton Hill, a more geographically dispersed region that shares much in common with its coastal neighbor. Clinton Hill was a very wealthy and fashionable neighborhood in the mid-1800s, accounting for the old mansions that line Clinton Ave today. An impressive handful of these gaudy buildings belonged to Charles Pratt, an oil industry pioneer who went on to found Pratt Institute, one of the leading art colleges in the country. Pratt's beautiful 25-acre main campus comprises a good chunk of Clinton Hill real estate, bringing a strong youth presence and a companion creative scene to Fort Greene's more established artistic denizens. The tiny area also competes with Fort Greene with regard to diversity—for all the wealth of Pratt and historic Clinton Hill, locals remain just as likely to come from the lowest economic bracket as the highest. Less gentrified than nearly all its riverside surroundings but definitely considered "up-and-coming," the neighborhood is diverting flocks of twenty-somethings from the more hectic Williamsburg. Lack of easy subway access to Manhattan has kept rents low so far, but the word is out.

ON HILL

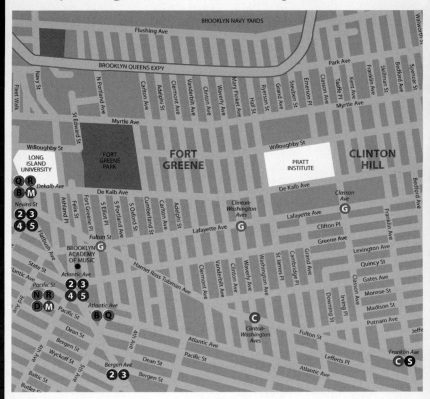

EXPLORE

Brooklyn Masonic Temple

This century-old building serves as a meeting place for the ever-mysterious Freemasons. Fitting the masons' biblical and allegorical tradition, the cornerstone is even said to replicate the relative dimensions of King Solomon's Temple. For the public, however, the temple plays host to concerts, weddings, and other private events.

317 Clermont Ave
(at Lafayette Ave)
718-638-1256
Ⓖ to Clinton-Washington Ave
Hours & prices vary

Every month or two, boomBOOM production company brings in musicians and performance artists—Brooklyn favorites like Poisson Rouge have performed among the colorful masonic murals, marble staircases, and imposing chandeliers. If none of the events spark your interest, come by just to marvel at the structure's neoclassical architecture.

Fort Greene Park

Designed in 1847 by Frederick Law Olmstead and Calvert Vuax, Fort Greene Park may not be as spectacular as its architects' masterpiece, Central Park, but it has its fair share of historical and literary glamour. The 30 acres form the oldest park in Brooklyn and today enclose a butterfly garden, tennis courts, bike paths, and basketball courts. A playground modeled after army fortresses commemorates the site's role in the Revolutionary War: the Continental Army established Fort Putnam there in 1776. Nearby looms the Prison Ships Martyrs Monument, a crypt built for American POWs who died aboard British ships during the Revolution. Poet Walt Whitman lived in a brick row house overlooking the park and was instrumental in its founding. The shady hills that so inspired him are now a focal point of Fort Greene's cultural life, playing host to live music, weekly Dusk Bat Tours, and a Summer Literary Festival.

Btwn DeKalb Ave, Myrtle Ave, Washington Park & Saint Edward St
718-222-1461
Ⓑ Ⓜ Ⓠ Ⓡ to DeKalb Ave, ❷ ❸ ❹ ❺ to Nevins St, Ⓖ to Fulton St

Museum of Contemporary African Diaspora Arts

MoCADA is somewhat of an elder statesman of the Fort Greene art scene, if such a term can be applied to an 11-year-old institution. Quartered in a rambling red brick building in the BAM Cultural District, the museum is dedicated to putting today's urban conflicts in the context of the African diaspora. In examining the art of the diaspora period, MoCADA seeks to reverse the marginalization of African descendants in world history. A wide array of multimedia exhibitions, including installations, film festivals, dance performances, and lectures, are put on every year. The most recent exhibition, "The Gentrification of Brooklyn: The Pink Elephant Speaks," was a particularly relevant collaboration between over 20 Brooklyn artists. City politics and African

80 Hanson Pl
(at S Portland Ave)
718-230-0492
Wed-Sun 11am-6pm
❷ ❸ ❹ ❺ Ⓑ Ⓓ Ⓜ Ⓠ Ⓡ
to Atlantic Ave-Pacific St,
Ⓖ to Lafayette Ave, Ⓖ
to Fulton St
Suggested Donation $4

neighborhhood
NECESSITIES

SUBWAYS 2, 3, 4, 5, B, C, D, M, N, Q, R

BUS B25, B26, B38, B52, B54, B57, B62, B67, B69

MARKETS Brooklyn Flea *(176 Lafayette Ave)*, Fort Greene Park Farmers Market *(Washington Park btwn DeKalb & Willoughby)*

LIBRARIES Brooklyn Public Library Central Branch *(10 Grand Army Plaza, 718-230-2100)*

MEDIA Clintonhillblog.com, *Fort Greene-Clinton Hill Courier*

FITNESS Crunch Fitness *(691 Fulton St, 718-797-9464)*, Lucky Lotus Yoga *(184 Dekalb Ave, 718-522-7119)*

BIKES Bicycle Station *(171 Park Ave, 718-638-0300)*

VICTORIAN BROWNSTONES

Once neglected housing in a pre-gentrified Fort Greene, the neighborhood's coveted brownstones remain nearly unchanged since the Victorian era—and today, you can't buy one for less than $1.5 million. Car horns and sirens blare down Lafayette Avenue, but on the more-than-pleasant side streets the buzz gives way to children riding bicycles and residents walking dachshunds. Scattered around Fort Greene Park, a masterpiece in itself, the broad façades with floor-to-ceiling windows are a major factor in the recent influx of well-off young families and artists. These Victorian relics and their new inhabitants live in tandem with Fort Greene's less developed areas, leaving the neighborhood to teeter on the threshold of gentrification and deterioration. Whatever Fort Greene's future, its signature brownstones will continue to demand the respect—and arrest the attention—of those who pass by.

achievement are MoCADA's specialty, from the local to the global level.

UrbanGlass

The oldest and largest open-access glass studio in the United States, UrbanGlass has played a crucial part in promoting its namesake as a creative medium since 1977. This altogether

647 Fulton St #1
(at Rockwell Pl)
718-625-3685
Tues-Thurs 10am-9pm,
Fri-Sun 10am-5pm
❷❸❹❺ to Nevins St,
Ⓑ Ⓜ Ⓠ Ⓡ to Dekalb Ave
Ⓖ to Fulton St,
Ⓒ to Lafayette Ave

unique resource for artists sans personal sand-blaster is housed in a solitary warehouse in the BAM Cultural District, where glass masters labor over blazing furnaces and mold neon flatware. Amateurs and practiced artists take classes in everything from hot casting and lamp-making to stained glass and mosaics. The studio displays and sells students' and visiting artists' work, and the Robert Lehman Gallery mounts exhibitions throughout the year. The fiscally minded will approve of the 20% students' discount, and the daily free tours of the glassmaking floor.

SHOP

Brooklyn Flea

Every Saturday, discerning New Yorkers from every borough converge at Fort Greene for one of the most rewarding yet affordable shopping experiences the city has

357 Clermont Ave
(near Greene Ave)
Sat 10am-5pm
Ⓐ Ⓒ to Lafayette, Ⓖ to
Clinton-Washington Ave,
❷❸❹❺ Ⓑ Ⓓ Ⓝ Ⓠ Ⓡ
Ⓜ to Atlantic Ave

to offer. Rain or shine, the basketball court at Bishop Loughlin Memorial High School hosts 150 vendors selling vintage clothing, furniture, records, and accessories. DJs and gourmet food stands (think coconut cupcakes and plum fried chicken) maintain the high energy level while fleasters search for mango wood coffee tables,

necklaces made from clothespins, and 19th-century round-frame spectacles. With masses of devotees and a fierce allegiance to the atypical, the Flea is a scene in itself—it might just be the best pick-up spot in New York among Ray Ban-clad hoarders.

Dope Jams

Specializing in underground dance music, this record store is committed to maintaining the spirit of NYC's hedonistic past with a carefully com-

580 Myrtle Ave
(at Classon Ave)
718-622-7977
Sun 12pm-7pm,
Mon-Sat 12pm-9pm
Ⓖ to Classon Ave

piled selection of vinyl, CDs, and sound equipment. It's known for throwing raucous parties, but if house music isn't your thing, Dope Jams offers another nighttime activity: it doubles as a magic store fit to rival Diagon Alley. The shelves along the dark wood interior are stocked with intricate amulets, copper wands, and tea leaves, and the pungent aroma of incense pervades the air. If your idea of a good Friday night involves either techno or tarot cards, Dope Jams has got what you need.

Greenlight Bookstore

Local literati line up around the block to get a signed copy of the latest it-book from Greenlight Bookstore. Although the sunny

686 Fulton St
(at S Portland Ave)
718-246-0200
Daily 10am-10pm
Ⓒ to Lafayette Ave

space is small, owners Jessica Bagnulo and Rebecca Fitting keep their floor-to-ceiling shelves impeccably organized and stocked with both classics and contemporary critical hits. Almost half the store is devoted to children's books—you'll find many a Brooklyn dad with Dr. Seuss in hand—and the travel corner carries some of the best coffee-table reads around. Greenlight's real accomplishment, however, has been to attract writers as prominent as Jhumpa Lahiri, David Mitchell, and Gary Shteyngart to its weekly author readings. The only downside is a

Walt Whitman grew up in Fort Greene.

lack of comfortable seating—the faux-industrial chairs built from shovels may be whimsical, but they don't allow for more than a chapter of pleasant reading.

EAT

67 Burger

American

67 Lafayette Ave
(at Fulton St)
718-797-7150
Sun-Thurs 11:30am-
10pm, Fri-Sat 11:30-11pm
Ⓖ to Fulton St, Ⓒ to
Lafayette Ave, ❷❸❹
❺ⒷⒹ❿❹Ⓜ to
Atlantic Ave

It's impossible to put down a 67 burger after your first bite, on account of both the taste and the fact that your plate will be covered with red flavory juice. A well-sized, sturdy bun and precisely arranged toppings make this wonderfully cooked burger one of the best in Brooklyn. The restaurant's dining area consists of mostly two-person tables, lending it a coffee-shop vibe—some customers bring their laptops—and also setting the scene for a perfect lunch date. While the burger is certainly the star of the menu, the normal trappings of fries, onion rings, and salads beat the curve. For those too hot to take their food outdoors, there are really solid milkshakes, which come in traditional kiddy options, along with the adult leaning beer flavor.

Bittersweet Café

Cafe, Sandwiches, Bakery

Ⓢ 📶

180 Dekalb Ave
(btwn Carlton Ave &
Cumberland St)
718-852-2556
Mon-Fri 7am-8pm, Sat-
Sun 7:30am-8pm
ⒷⓂ❸❹ to Dekalb
Ave, Ⓖ to Fulton St, Ⓒ
to Lafayette Ave
$

Planted on a small sliver of Dekalb Avenue without a Starbucks in sight, this easily overlooked coffee and pastry shop has become a neighborhood staple. Equipped with all the necessary trappings of a mom-and-pop brew house—handwritten chalkboard menus, worn wooden floors, and an affable staff—Bittersweet Café exudes small-town charm. Beyond the exceptional cup of high-octane coffee (injected with two shots of espresso), homemade ice cream is the darling of the store. Its funky flavors entice overheated Brooklynites of all ages: the delightfully crunchy Jamaican Grapenut, Vegan Coconut, and a special Espresso Float are particularly alluring. The extended weekend menu, which includes creamy bread pudding and toffee loaf, complicates an already difficult choice.

Caffe e' Vino
Italian

112 DeKalb Ave (btwn Ashland Pl & St Felix St)
718-855-6222
Sun 10am-10:30pm,
Mon-Thurs 10am-11pm,
Fri-Sat 10am-11:30pm
Ⓑ Ⓜ Ⓠ Ⓡ to DeKalb Ave, ❷ ❸ ❹ ❺ to Nevins St, Ⓖ to Fulton St
$$$

Caffe e' Vino is a common destination for BAM-goers and handlocked couples, and for good reason: everything about it is low-key and inviting. The dining area is small and intimate without being claustrophobic. A large open garden in the back is well-suited for groups, while the quieter front area is a perfect date spot. Giovanni, the chef and owner, greets everybody, jovially circulating the tables and making recommendations. The pastas, all of which are hand-rolled and homemade daily, are especially popular and endure as the best red sauce fare of the area. The secondi offer a little ingenuity in the filling with ricotta-stuffed veal meatballs, and chicken doubled over a cheesy spinach concoction. Finish your meal with the torte della nonna, Caffe e' Vino's take on traditional ricotta cheesecake: it is utterly transcendent.

Madiba
South African

New York City's first South African restaurant, Madiba offers the hodgepodge of Indian curries, Dutch sausages, and indigenous African specialties that defines South African cuisine.

BROOKLYN ACADEMY OF MUSIC
biggest avant-guarde authority

The Brooklyn Academy of Music is the oldest continually-operating performing arts center in the country. Since 1861, it has served as the nucleus of Brooklyn's artistic community and has evolved into a small district of establishments. The largest of the three seats over 2,100 people and has hosted performances from the likes of Isadora Duncan, Steve Reich, and Nirvana. Film buffs can catch a mix of independent, big budget, and classic flicks every night of the week at BAM Rose Cinemas. At BAMcafé, a younger crowd gathers to eat, sip cocktails, watch a live show, and mingle with Pratt students. For plays, musicals, and vaudeville shows, walk a few blocks from the Sharp Building to BAM Harvey Theater. Along with daily events, this multifaceted institution hosts educational programs and festivals like DanceAfrica, Next Wave, and BAMcinemaFEST.

30 Lafayette Ave
(near Ashland Pl)
718-636-4100
Hours vary by venue
2,3,4,5,B,D,N,Q,R,M
to Atlantic Ave
Prices vary by event

The broadcasting antenna of Brooklyn Technical High School is the tallest structure in Brooklyn.

CHEAP EATS
best cheap slices

Pizzamoto- Every Saturday, this mobile brick-oven sets up shop at the Brooklyn Flea, selling super cheap personal size classics like Margherita and White Pizza: they're always thin and crispy, and slightly burnt around the edges like they should be. *176 Lafayette Ave, 718-935-1052, Sat 10am-5pm, G to Clinton-Washington Aves, C to Lafayette Ave $*

Luigi's Pizzeria- With everything that a typical New York pizzeria should have—thin slices, garlic knots, calzones—Luigi's comes across as generic, but the pies are perfectly done, thin with a sweet tomato sauce. *326 Dekalb Ave, 718-783-2430, Sun 12pm-9pm, Mon-Sat 11am-10pm, G to Clinton-Washington Aves $$*

Nice Pizza- Although Nice specializes in the Italian-influenced pizzas and sandwiches of southern France, the menu, an endless list of gourmet pizzas, includes thin crust classics such as La Marguerite and La Pepperoni. *340 Franklin Ave, 718-230-3933, Daily 12pm-11pm, G to Classon Ave $*

195 Dekalb Ave
(near Carlton Ave)
718-855-9190
Daily 10am-12pm
Ⓖ to Clinton-Washington Ave,
Ⓒ to Lafayette Ave
$$

It takes its name from an honorary title given to Nelson Mandela, and many colorful portraits of Madiba himself hang on the walls among rustic Zulu masks, African drums, and cowskins. Go for the Durban Bunny Chow—a lamb curry served in a hollowed out bread loaf—or the Prawns Peri Peri, tiger prawns served over rice and flavored with a spicy red oil made from roasted chili peppers. Everything on the menu is made from native recipes, and is perfectly complemented by an $8 glass of the house South African Indaba Shiraz. Be sure to leave room for what Oprah called her favorite dessert, Malva pudding—a caramel-crusted cake with apricot jam, hot custard, and ice cream.

The General Greene   *New American*
Amidst the countless mom-and-pop-and-grossly-inadequate-square-footage cafés along Dekalb, the General Greene gives Brooklyn's younger eateries something to aspire to. With a minimalist aesthetic and a suitably eco-friendly devotion to local ingredients, the General serves up organic scrambled eggs and spicy crab legs as light and airy as its window-lined corner dining room. Some dishes aren't yet culinary standards—the red quinoa, doused with lime juice and bulked up with walnuts, is more refreshing than a walk through a sprinkler—and some are

merely the freshest incarnation imaginable of old recipes—herbed chicken liver toast with a salty kickback, and a crisp beet and blue cheese salad that still smells like Schenectady. The in-house grocer at the back sells choice dishes from the menu, as well as seasonal produce and spices from farther-flung locales.

🛥
229 Dekalb Ave
(at Claremont Ave)
718-222-1510
Sun 9am-10pm, Mon-Fri
8am-11pm, Sat 9am-11pm
Ⓑ Ⓜ Ⓠ Ⓡ to Dekalb Ave
Ⓖ to Clinton-
Washington St
$$

The Smoke Joint

BBQ, Hot Dog

🛥
87 S Elliott Place
(at Lafayette Ave)
718-797-1011
Sun-Thurs 12pm-10pm,
Fri-Sat 12pm-11pm
Ⓒ to Lafayette Ave, Ⓖ
to Fulton St, Ⓔ Ⓒ Ⓓ Ⓕ
Ⓖ Ⓜ Ⓑ Ⓓ Ⓝ Ⓡ to
Atlantic Ave
$$

From the co-chef-owners that brought you Picholine, Smoke Joint is a Brooklyn-born barbecue spot that doesn't look back. The restaurant prides itself on not attempting to replicate old-school Southern recipes, choosing instead to pave its way past obvious regional influence. Although many of the dishes were of course born in Texas and South Carolina, such as the beef short ribs or pulled pork, Smoke Joint adds its own kick with original spices and marinades called "jointrub" and "jointsmoke." If you're passing through, be sure to try the $3 black angus hot dog, as it's rumored to be one of the best franks in New York. All of this BBQ brilliance is brought to you in a warm, roadhouse setting in beautiful Fort Greene. For an after dinner drink, stop by next door at The Pig Bar, Smoke Joint's specialty whiskey tavern.

PLAY

Der Schwarze Kolner

Beer Bar

Der Schwarze Kolner translates to "The Black Cologner," a reference to Dale Hall, the owner of this German-inspired beer garden that opened just two years ago. As Fort Greene's only beer garden, it has quickly become one of the most popular places to drink in the neighborhood. With 18 German microbrews on draught and 29 in bottles, Der Schwarze's selection speaks for itself. Each draught is poured into its brewery's custom glass, which is designed to bring out the beer's full flavor. Pair your Köstritzer or Weihenstephaner with a no-nonsense paper plate of Berlin-style Currywurst—bratwurst on a roll covered with a sweet curry ketchup sauce and sprinkled with cumin. For now, choose between the big-windowed, black-and-white-tiled interior and the blue tables that line the sidewalk for your beer guzzling. Rumor has it that the real "garden" is opening in the back very soon.

Diamante's Brooklyn Cigar Lounge

Smoking Lounge

🍾
108 S Oxford St
(btwn Fulton St and
Lafayette Ave)
646-462-3876
Sun 1pm-12am, Mon-
Thurs 5pm-12am; Fri
5pm-2am; Sat 1pm-2am
Ⓒ to Lafayette Ave,
Ⓖ to Fulton St
$$

The Diamante family has been living and smoking cigars in Fort Greene for five generations. In 2009, David Diamante opened this lounge as a testament to his family's love for cigars. Located a stone's throw of four blocks from his childhood home, the lounge is small, circular, and rustic-looking, with antique furniture and a makeshift bar built from tattered wooden doors. At the bar, you can buy cigars from all over the world as well as housemade cigars that are rolled on site. You can also buy drinks, or you can bring your own bottle for a corkage fee of $8. Cigarette smokers

🛥
710 Fulton St
(near S Oxford St)
347-841-4495
Mon-Fri 2pm-2am, Sat-
Sun 12pm-2am
Ⓒ to Lafayette Ave, Ⓖ
to Fulton St, Ⓔ Ⓒ Ⓓ
Ⓔ Ⓜ Ⓑ Ⓓ Ⓝ Ⓡ to
Atlantic Ave
$$

The Richard Wright Bench in Fort Greene commemorates the spot where he spent many hours writing his masterpiece Native Son.

365

are equally welcome at Diamante's, one of the few indoor establishments in Brooklyn where smoking is legal. It's a great place to sink into a lush leather couch, puff away, and pretend it's the 1930s. Pretty soon you'll be saving up for a pinstripe suit.

Rope
Bar

Don't be afraid: the rats are only a decoration. With a rusted metal entrance, gray wallpaper covering exposed brick, and wooden frames of pin-up girls straddling beer bottles, Rope feels like

415 Myrtle Ave
(near Clinton Ave)
718-522-2899
Daily 5:30pm-4am
G G to Clinton-
Washington Ave
$

an old-world factory. The one dollar PBRs on Monday nights attract a loyal flock of Pratt students, but a young artsy crowd frequents the bar throughout the week. Patrons pile into the cozy gravel backyard, lit by strings of tiki lights—there's ample seating for both a gathering of friends and a one-on-one date. Stay for less than an hour and chances are you'll already find yourself taking shots with a friendly and talkative stranger. If the crowd doesn't keep you entertained, the selection on the jukebox will.

Sweet Revenge
Lounge

348 Franklin Ave
(btwn Greene and
Lexington Ave)
718-398-2472
Daily 4pm-4am
G to Classon Ave
$

Though you wouldn't want to bring your beach towel or even take off your shoes, the sand in the backyard of Sweet Revenge evokes a tropical oasis right in the heart of Clinton Hill. It's lit by tiki-torches and decorated with bamboo, and on warm nights, the bar is even set up outside. Sitting on one of the sandy benches, you're bound to strike up a conversation with one of the local or Pratt student regulars. Inside, live DJs spin vinyl all night, and there's plenty of room to dance, since the bar rarely gets too packed. Try one of the specialty drinks, like the Salty Poodle or the Hemingway Daiquiri. With two dollar beers on Mondays, and a five dollar beer-and-a-shot deal all day, every day, your wallet won't mind you paying a visit to Sweet Revenge.

BROOK HEIGH

What was once a blighted landscape of abandoned factories and parking lots is now home to upscale apartment buildings and trendy studios of up-and-coming artists. In the 1970s, an influx of craftspeople transformed the industrial district of DUMBO (Down Under the Manhattan Bridge Overpass) into a new center of culture. Home to innovative art venues and the annual Art Under the Bridge Festival, modern DUMBO is a hotbed of cutting-edge visual and performance art. Boutiques and artisan workshops make the neighborhood a popular daytime destination, while its posh clubs and avant-garde theater seduce Manhattanites to visit at night.

DUMBO's narrow cobblestone streets lead to an entirely different scene only blocks away. Brooklyn Heights is a largely residential neighborhood with beautiful architecture and significant history. The original "Town of Brooklyn," Brooklyn Heights was one of the first suburbs that housed the Wall Street crowd in the early 1800s. In 1814, Robert Fulton created the Fulton

&DU

LYN
S

Ferry, providing quick, convenient means of transportation for the daily commute between Lower Manhattan and Brooklyn Heights.

Today the neighborhood is home to picturesque brownstones, friendly eateries, Borough Hall (New York City's original City Hall), and the Promenade, a clean and open public space lined with gardens and scenic views of Lower Manhattan. Families walk along the path, bicyclists peddle over from Manhattan, and young couples eat picnics on benches overlooking the water. Taking a page from Union Square's events calendar, Borough Hall hosts a Farmer's Market at Cadman Plaza, where residents flock for fresh, locally-grown treats.

Walk along the Promenade back into DUMBO and head to the brand new Pier 1 and 6 parks for iconic views of the skyline. In the summer, you may even catch a free outdoor movie or join crowds in walking across the historic Brooklyn Bridge.

MBO

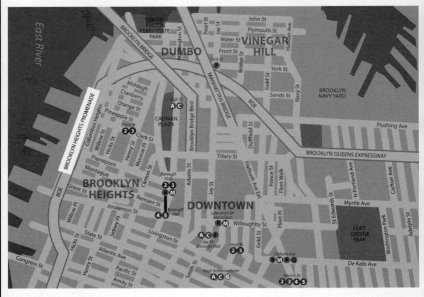

EXPLORE

famous greenmarkets on Thursdays and Saturdays, offering fresh local produce, meat, and baked goods for the peckish politically-minded.

Brooklyn Borough Hall

Built in 1846, the home of Brooklyn Borough President Marty Markowitz is a historical landmark and the oldest public building

209 Joralemon St
(at Court St)
718-802-3700
❷❸❹❺ to Borough Hall,
Ⓜ❸ to Court St,
Ⓐ Ⓒ Ⓕ to Jay St

in Brooklyn, having originally served as New York's first city hall. With its stately ionic columns, looming staircase, and intricate cupola casting a shadow over passersby, the edifice is as prominent and monumental as the business inside. Visit during the day for tours and to admire the architecture—a remarkable golden "Statue of Justice" stands atop the crowning dome—or at night to see the building illuminated in neon glory. As a bonus for the community, the Borough Hall courtyard hosts one of GrowNYC's

Brooklyn Bridge Park

We're not exaggerating: Brooklyn Bridge Park affords the best views of the lower Manhattan skyline. A million postcard shots

1 Main St (at Water St)
Ⓐ Ⓒ to High St,
❷❸ to Clark St,
Ⓕ to York St

have been taken (along with a million commercials filmed and ad campaigns photographed) from its grounds of the bridge arching into the Financial District's pillars of steel and concrete. The 85-acre park is still under construction, but 2010 saw the openings of grassy Pier 1 and Pier 6, which connect to the Brooklyn Heights waterfront in a stretch of picnic tables and playgrounds along the East River. Every summer, the wildly popular "Movies with a View" series screens new and old classics against the glittering backdrop of Manhattan. Lunch on a Brooklyn Bridge Park bench is the hands-down best way to absorb downtown New York in all its incandescence.

Brooklyn Heights Promenade

Columbia Heights (at Middagh St)
Ⓐ Ⓒ to High St, ❷ ❸ to Clark St, ❷ ❸ ❹ ❺ to Borough Hall, Ⓡ to Court St

If the Brooklyn Bridge Park is for sitting and marveling at what are undeniably the best views in New York, then the Brooklyn Heights Promenade is for sauntering alongside them. Spanning nearly ten blocks above the downtown Brooklyn waterfront, the spacious cement pathway is lined with playgrounds, gardens, and some of the borough's loveliest brownstones. Locals and tourists alike flock to the river's edge for tender hand-holding, uncompromisingly spicy Brooklyn sandwiches, and a front row seat at the Fourth of July fireworks. Come for a stroll on foot, scooter, or rollerblades (no bikes allowed) or have a bite on a bench overlooking the city's most definitive icons: Governor's Island, Ellis Island, New Jersey, the Statue of Liberty, the Brooklyn Bridge, and Wall Street.

New York Transit Museum

Boerum Pl (at Schermerhorn)
718-694-1600
Tue-Fri 10am-4pm
Sat-Sun 12pm-5pm
❷ ❸ ❹ ❺ to Borough Hall, Ⓜ Ⓡ to Court St, Ⓐ Ⓒ Ⓕ to Jay St
$5 Admission

Trudge down the stairs leading to an old metro station, purchase tickets at a wooden kiosk, and push through the heavy turnstiles to reach this awesome converted museum. Built into the now defunct Brooklyn Court Street station, the New York Transit Museum offers displays, historic photographs, artifacts, and numerous hands-on activities about the transformation of public transportation in the greater New York City region. Without a doubt, the museum's 20 vintage train cars are the highlight of the visit. Walk through

DUMBO A

Low rent and spacious apartments are bygone hallmarks of DUMBO—hallmarks that induced a sizable starving artist crowd from Manhattan to settle down across the bridge in the 1970s. The local art scene has flourished ever since, and although rent isn't what it used to be, a 21st-century crowd of paint-flingers and their coteries have lately taken up residence. Chelsea's galleries get more respect from big-name institutions, but DUMBO retains the air of an artists' outpost—the sculptor showing on Washington Street is more likely to live down the block than on Park Avenue. While day-trippers and natives linger in line for a taste of **Grimaldi's** *(19 Old Fulton St)* legendary pizza, art-lovers slip in and out of the galleries peppering the cobblestone streets. **Dumbo Arts Center** *(30 Washington St)* is famous for hosting the annual DUMBO Art Under the Bridge Festival, but small galleries like **Rabbit Hole Studio** *(33 Washington St)* and **Mighty Tanaka** *(68 Jay St)* deserve a look. Several offer free admission—and wine!—on the first Thursday of every month. DUMBO is also home to many talented and prolific street artists, whose vibrant masterpieces are displayed at no cost on old brick walls around the neighborhood.

cars with checkered floors, neon green ceilings, and striped yellow seats. All of them have the original floor plans, color schemes, and advertisements intact—and some even have tables. Visitors can also stop by the museum's gift shop for t-shirts boasting their favorite line.

SHOP

Blueberi

The DUMBO offshoot of the larger Prospect Heights boutique Redberi, Blueberi displays artfully constructed designs that are the fashion complement to the experimental work of the neighborhood's galleries. The spic-and-span white space, ornamented only by a simple Tiffany chandelier and plastic mannequins, flaunts sleekly modern cocktail dresses, lighter-than-air chiffon blouses, and high-quality, quirky vintage. Owner Suewayne Brown pairs a space-age cowl neck coat with a wispy pink frock, and black calfskin boots with a cherry-red vintage pancake hat. Prices are not surprising for a designer boutique, but much of Brown's inventory consists of little-known gems: she culls from art schools and foreign designers, so her pieces are more daring than most. Cap an outfit with a

143A Front St
(near Pearl St)
718-422-7724
Sun 11am-7pm,
Mon-Fri 12pm-8pm,
Sat 11am-8pm
🚇 to York St

Victorian umbrella or an electric-blue '60s-era wig.

Dewey's Candy Store

Think Charlie's Chocolate Factory with a lot more class. Among DUMBO's upscale clothing and jewelry stores, Dewey's blends the sophisticated with the saccharine. Designed to look more like Fred Segal than the neighborhood taffy shop, the store displays candy canes of every color on mock Victorian end tables underneath lollipops dangling from the ceiling like sugary chandeliers. Nostalgic shoppers can count on finding classic Hershey bars, gummy worms, ring pops, and Pez dispensers, but the more adventurous sweet tooth can sample Australian Cherry Ripe bars, Danish nutmeg suckers, and candy teeth grillz. At Dewey's, you're more likely to see customers carrying Louis Vuitton than a Jansport backpack—this sweets shop is where adults indulge in style.

141 Front St
(btwn Pearl & Jay St)
718-422-1333
Sun 12pm-6pm,
Mon-Wed, Fri-Sat
11:30am-7pm,
Thurs 11:30am-8pm
🚇 to York St

Jacques Torres

Renowned chocolatier Jacques Torres opened this eponymous chocolate factory and shop in 2000, and has since expanded the space to include a surprising variety of beverages, ice

cream, and pastries. The store exemplifies all that is characteristic of a classic French café: patrons indulge in café au lait, pain au chocolat, and dainty cocoa bonbons while enjoying the elegant tables' view of the factory next door, separated from the shop by huge panes of glass. The chocolates themselves are works of art—dozens of different, beautifully crafted truffles with colorful and festive designs. Remember that Jacques Torres traffics in delicacies, and the highly enjoyable shopping experience reflects this commitment to the refined palate right down to the price tag.

66 Water St
(btwn Main & Old Dock St)
718-875-9772
Sun 10am-6pm,
Mon-Sat 9am-7pm
🄵 to York St,
🄰 🄲 to High St

Neighborhoodies

Customize a hoodie, backpack, or even a pair of underwear at this boldness-inducing "make your own clothing" store and factory. Emblazon a crappy tee with your favorite quote or inside joke, or proudly sport your team, your town, or just your own name, Carrie Bradshaw-style, on one of the many garments for sale in-house, like zip-ups and other pieces from American Apparel. Orders take only 10 minutes to be filled and are made on the spot, so they're ready-to-wear within the hour. Prices vary depending on the article of clothing and whether the letters and logos are stitched or pressed (adding between $10-$30 to the initial cost)—but since when did individuality have a price?

26 Jay St (at Plymouth St)
718-243-2265
Mon-Fri 10am-6pm,
Sat 10am-5pm
🄵 to York St

Jay East

The warehouse storefront of this Asian furniture and antiques retailer seems dangerously close to spilling over with merchandise. Inside, the walls are just barely visible behind the beautiful deep red benches, trunks embellished with hand-painted images of China

and Tibet, looming mahogany bookcases, and intricately-paneled wooden screens. Some of the original items have only been touched up, but others have been wholly transformed by the skilled hands of the staff. An opium bed-turned-coffee table waits in the corner, refurbished with a stainless steel table top. Prices may stretch into the triple digits and beyond, but the singularity of a Jay East piece is well worth the tag.

67 Jay St
(btwn Water & Front St)
718-237-8430
Mon-Fri by appointment,
Sat-Sun 11am-6pm
F to York St

its reputation as one of New York's most high-brow booksellers. The tall wooden shelves are jammed with not only fiction and non-fiction of all genres, but also a vast assortment of used and rare volumes, reprints, galley proofs, and foreign language titles. The art and architecture and children's book collections are particularly comprehensive in scope and size. If the wide windows are letting in generous amounts of light, curl up with one of your discoveries on a well-positioned comfy sofa. You can also bring in used books to sell: parting with your dog-eared copy of The Catcher in the Rye won't be too hard when you realize all that P.S. Books has to offer in exchange.

P.S. Bookshop

P.S. Bookshop is as spacious, bright, and meticulously organized as your neighborhood Borders—but the persistent aroma of gently weathered pages belies

76 Front St (btwn
York & Washington St)
718-222-3340
Daily 10am-8pm
F to York St,
A **C** to High St

powerHouse Arena

DUMBO's intelligentsia convene here by day to browse the truly edgy coffee table reads, by night to load up on free wine and

37 Main St (at Water St)
718-666-3049
Mon-Fri 10am-7pm,
Sat-Sun 11am-7pm
F to York St,
A **C** to High St

cheese. The exposed piping and lone crystal chandelier of this cavernous waterfront warehouse frame the offices of renowned art book publishing company powerHouse Books. PowerHouse titles, known for their unorthodox image-essays, fashion and celebrity photography, and photojournalism, constitute most of the store's inventory, but customers also covet their graphic t-shirts, cheeky greeting cards, extensive children's section, and original artwork (displayed on the whitewashed walls). At night, the space hosts readings, launch parties, gallery openings, and panel discussions with local leaders of the alternative art world, including grafitti writers and offbeat performance artists.

Recycle-a-Bicycle

This deceptively tiny store is two organizations in one: a used bike shop and a youth-oriented non-profit. Like any good bike shop, RAB's primary goal is to promote greener transportation, and it spreads the word through environmental education programs and courses in bicycle mechanics. True to its name, the store saves 1,200 bicycles a year on average, recycling what would be 36,000 pounds of waste. Prices are a little loftier than at other repair shops, but RAB makes up the difference with its activism: internships, summer jobs, and the Ride Club

155 Plymouth St
(at Jay St)
718-801-8037
Daily 12pm-7pm
🄵 to York St

brooklyn heights & dumbo
UNDER $20

Breakfast on a one-dollar macaroon (or five) at **Almondine Bakery** *(85 Water St)*, or head across the street to the **Jacques Torres** chocolate shop *(66 Water St)* if you're one for cocoa.

Go a little out of your way to **P.S. Bookshop** *(76 Front St)* to rummage for a cheap used title. The musically inclined will appreciate the stellar vinyl selection at **Halcyon** *(57 Pearl St)*.

Most galleries, like **A.I.R. Gallery** *(111 Front St)* and **Caption Gallery** *(55 Washington St)*, offer suggested admission prices à la the Met.

Pause for a $5.50 salad (with six toppings!) at **Jimi's Market Inc.** *(52 Jay St)*. Satisfy your sweet tooth with penny candy at **Dewey's Candy** *(141 Front St)*.

Walk off the calories at **Brooklyn Bridge Park** *(1 Main St)* and meander over to the gorgeous mansions and brownstones on Cranberry, Pineapple, and Orange Streets for a photo op.

Browse for free events like the **Floating Kabarette** at **Galapagos Art Space** *(16 Main St)* or the **1st Thursday DUMBO Gallery Walk** for evening fun, or split a $14 hookah with a few friends at **Kapadoyka** *(142 Montague St)*.

are all available to young Brooklynites, as well as the opportunity to earn a bike by volunteering. The staff replaces your broken pedal one day, and turns it into a sculpture the next in a community class on making art from aluminum scraps. It's the cycle of life.

Zakka

The energy and creativity of Japan come alive at this unique half-gallery, half-retailer specializing in Japanese art and tchotchkes. With a stated mission to introduce budding artistic trends in Japan to receptive New Yorkers, the store invites all to indulge in one exceptional aspect of Japanese culture. Scan their exotic collection of rare anime figurines, elaborate posters, raucously graphic t-shirts, and, most notably, art books— Zakka proudly boasts an extensive library that carries books and magazines in all artistic genres. The clientele is just about evenly split between curious marathon shoppers and professionals of the art world. But naturally, what's

35 Pearl St (btwn John & Plymouth St)
718-858-2972
Mon-Sat 12pm-7pm
F to York St,
A C to High St

most distinctive about Zakka is the gallery—or rather, its "Creator's Market"—which invites emerging artists from all nooks of the industry to exhibit their work.

Zoe

High-end fashion meets warm and welcoming service at this cozy, one of a kind neighborhood boutique. With a carefully selected collection of the hippest apparel, shoes, and accessories for both men and women, Zoe offers what most large and crowded department stores can't: a relaxing shopping experience. The staff is a uniformly friendly group of stylish women who will not only suggest the most flattering items for your body type, but also politely persuade you to strut in the Chloe or Lanvin outfit, fashion-show style. It may be expensive, but there is almost always a sale going on, so you can snag that inexplicably expensive Diane Von Furstenberg dress at a magically affordable price. Just don't tear the hem while you're hamming it up.

68 Washington St (btwn York & Front St)
718-237-4002
Sun 11am-6pm,
Mon 11am-7pm,
Tues-Sat 11am-8pm
F to York St,

CHEAP EATS
distinctive delis

Lassen & Hennigs- This gourmet delicatessen offers a wide selection of soups, salads, baked goods, and prepared dishes, as well as a number of made-to-eat sandwiches that are named after the neighborhood streets. *114 Montague St, 718-875-6272, Mon-Fri 7am-9:30pm, Sat-Sun 7am-9pm, R to Court St, 2/3 to Clark St, 2/3/4/5 to Borough Hall $*

DUMBO General Store- Enjoy a coffee, cocktail, or one of the signature pressed sandwiches while lounging on the classy Victorian couches at this trendy sandwich shop. *111 Front St, 718-855-5288, Mon-Wed 8am-6pm, Thurs-Sun 8am-12am, F to York St, A/C to High St $*

Montague Street Bagels- Neighborhood locals flock to this deli for the freshest bagels in the borough. Be sure to try their specialty "French Toast Bagel." *108 Montague St, 718-237-2512, Daily 24 hours, R to Court St, 2/3 to Clark St or Borough Hall $*

Tazza- A combination of high-end and creative sandwiches, rich and delectable pastries, and an extensive selection of wine makes this upscale sandwich shop and café a must for breakfast, lunch, and dinner. *Two locations: 311 Henry St, 718-243-0487, N/R to Court St, 2/3/4/5 to Borough Hall. 72 Clark St, 718-855-2700, Mon-Fri 7am-10pm, Sat-Sun 8am-10pm, 2/3 to Clark St $*

Fast & Fresh Deli- Have a beer in the garden with friends while indulging in some classic Mexican dishes at this authentic Mexican deli. *84 Hoyt St, 718-802-1661, Sun 7am-6:30pm, Mon-Sat 6am-6:30pm, A/C/G to Hoyt-Schermerhorn Sts, F/G to Bergen St, 2/3 to Hoyt St $*

EAT

Almondine — *Bakery*

85 Water St (near Main St)
718-797-5026
Sun 10am-6pm, Mon-Sat 7am-7pm
Ⓐ Ⓒ to High St,
Ⓕ to York St
$

This small bakery looks—and smells—like it was plucked straight off the streets of Paris, with its mouth-watering assortment of pastries and epic selection of croissants: plain, chocolate, almond, almond-raspberry, chocolate-almond, and chocolate-almond-raspberry. From strawberry shortcake to chocolate fondant to passion fruit mousse, each brightly colored and beautifully crafted pastry can be enlarged to the size of a cake upon request. If you're desirous of something salty, try one of the classic French sandwiches packed with butter and tasty deli meats. Locals can order the "Almondine Room Service," a Sunday morning croissant, baguette, and coffee delivery service. Stay in the café, however, to enjoy the fragrance of freshly made baguettes while getting a clear view of the baking in the kitchen.

The Kitchen at Brooklyn Fare — *New American*

200 Schermerhorn St (btwn Hoyt & Bond St)
718-243-0050
Sun 8am-8pm, Mon-Fri 7am-9pm, Sat 8am-9pm
Ⓐ Ⓒ Ⓖ to Hoyt-Schermerhorn
$$$$

Twelve diners sit around a stainless steel island in an amply equipped kitchen where chef César Ramirez and his crew whip up 20 courses, tweaking and improvising nightly. The chef announces the scintillating ingredients in each bite-size creation to the twinkly-eyed looks of his captive diners. Watermelon radish lingers on the tongue with relish, while a gelatinous parfait of avocado, caviar, basil, trout roe, cured salmon, maple syrup, and mustard mousse concludes only the amuse-bouches chapter of an extravagant evening. Always willing to answer questions about particular ingredients, César is a stranger to the "secret recipe" notion of others. Service pace slows to a simmer, as his practiced team prepares the even more intricate main courses. At the end of a three-hour feast, the food dandies and young Brooklynites with wine-loosened tongues stick around to hobnob with the chef before slowly making their way out the kitchen door.

PLAY

Galapagos Art Space *Performance Space*
Eschew traditional bars and clubs to cluster around cocktail tables at this multidisciplinary performance art venue, tucked neatly between the Manhattan and Brooklyn bridges. Beneath the shimmer of a silver disco ball, diverse crowds watch

16 Main St (near Water St)
718-222-8500
Hours vary by event
F to York St, **2 3** to Clark St, **A C** to High St
$$

big-vision performances from island seats on a 1,600-square foot indoor pond—the space itself is an environmentally-friendly work of art. One Friday a month, Galapagos hosts a "Nite" for self-proclaimed nerds to listen to musings on pi and watch powerpoint presentations on the history of illegal pinball. A free Saturday night "Floating Kabarette" features short acts that vary from aerial acrobatics to a slumber party

VINEGAR HILL HOUSE
best place to meet the owners

This little restaurant is tucked away in cobblestoned Vinegar Hill, a neighborhood bordering the perennially hip DUMBO and Navy Yard. Upon entering, you'll find the accouterments of post-industrial Brooklyn: a bare, peeling concrete wall, worn wooden tables, and bits of farmhouse America, which all surprisingly add up to create a warm and inviting ambiance. The wine selection is extensive, but the moderately-priced and well-made cocktails are the focal point of the drinks list. Summer menu highlights include the zucchini tart and the cast-iron chicken. Served on a wooden cutting board, the former balances its creaminess with a side of white anchovy salad while the latter harmonizes a crispy skin with a juicy interior. Whether you're coming for dinner or brunch, Vinegar Hill House won't leave you with a bitter taste in your mouth.

Performance Space

72 Hudson Ave
(btwn Front & Water St)
718-522-1018
Sun 11am-3:30pm,
5:30pm-11pm,
Mon-Thurs 6pm-11pm,
Fri 6pm-11:30pm,
Sat 11am-3:30pm,
6pm-11:30pm
F to York St
$$$

turned strip tease, all emceed by a duo dressed like Greek goddess-ballerinas. No matter what day of the week, the spectacle is sure to be titillating, and nothing is supported by government grants or public funding—Galapagos truly encapsulates the strength (and eccentricity) of NYC's artistic community.

reBar

Gastropub

147 Front St
(at Maiden Ln)
718-797-2322
Sun 11am-2am,
Mon-Tues 11:30am-2am,
Wed-Sat 11:30am-4am
Ⓕ to York St

If the specialty beer and wine list doesn't seduce you, the juicy reBurger sure as hell will. This DUMBO hangout has quickly become one of the most popular spots in the neighborhood, and for good reason—gourmet food and ob-scure drinks are placed here in a setting that marries rustic authenticity with art deco indulgence. With room for up to 200 people in its former factory space, you can bring all your friends to try one of the 100 beers available (including the notorious 18% alc. Dogfishead 120 min. IPA), or sip on a Biodynamic, organic wine. The food is equally tantalizing: lavish New American dishes like oxtail with rhubarb chutney and truffle oil polenta are served alongside the usual classics. As if all this isn't enough, there's a pool table in the back where you can prove just how drunk or sober you really are.

St. Ann's Warehouse

Performance Space

For over 30 years now, St. Ann's Warehouse has been a preeminent force in New York's arts and performance scene. Originally a venue for

BARGEMUSIC
best floating flautists

There's nothing more characteristically New York than Gershwin against the backdrop of the Manhattan skyline. Welcome to Bargemusic, a renovated coffee barge docked near the Brooklyn Bridge—and one of the most unique venues in the world for classical, jazz, and contemporary orchestra concerts. The small, wood-paneled chamber makes for perfect acoustics, as the audience and the performers are literally placed on the same level, while its panoramic windows get the most out of its singular location. Bargemusic's repertoire includes the classical standards (Vivaldi, Beethoven, Haydn), experimental composers Steve Reich and Philip Glass, jazz ensembles, and renditions of rock opera ballads by The Who. Children are admitted for free on Tuesdays, Wednesday and Thursday afternoons for family-friendly "Music in Motion" concerts. While tickets can be pricey—$35 for adults and $15 for students—look out for free admission shows once a month. Check bargemusic.org for performance schedule.

Fulton Ferry Landing
(near Brooklyn Bridge)
718-624-2083
A/C to High St,
2/3 to Clark St,
F to York St
Adults $35, Students $15

mainly classical performances, it has since expanded into the go-to space for puppet operas and rock reunions alike. Housed in a former spice milling factory, the warehouse

ALL
AGES

38 Water St.
718-254-8779
🅕 to York St,
🅐 🅒 to High St
$$

has space for up to 1500 people, and its aesthetic changes to suit each event. The stage has welcomed musical legends such as Lou Reed, David Bowie, Emmylou Harris, and Jackson Browne, along with famous theatrical shows like The Seven Deadly Sins and The Barber of Seville. Many of the performances are started off with cocktail hour and finished with dinner, so be prepared to make a full evening out of your visit.

GREATER CARROLL

There's a reason why MTV chose to film the 2008 season of The Real World: Brooklyn in Greater Carroll Gardens. The tequila-fed group descended upon Red Hook's Pier 41, designating it Brooklyn's top spot for bar crawls (and, as the season went on, bar fights). With MTV's blessing, Red Hook and its surroundings have replaced Williamsburg and DUMBO as the go-to destination for young urbanites seeking an easy commute into lower Manhattan.

Greater Carroll Gardens today comprises the neighboring areas of Boerum Hill, Cobble Hill, and Carroll Gardens (collectively referred to as BoCoCa), as well as Red Hook and nearby Gowanus. Recent years have seen a spike in real estate prices, yet the area still heavily exhibits the influence of the Italian-American immigrants that began coming to northwest Brooklyn in the 1950s, making for a charming neighborhood with many culinary, shopping, and recreational options.

Before the Italians settled, Red Hook was home to an influx of Norwegians, and even hosted a visit from the King of Norway himself. In the mid-20th century the Brooklyn-Queens Expressway bisected Red Hook, separating it from the area that is now Carroll Gardens. At the same time, Italian-Americans became a significant presence in the area, working in the docks

and industrial yards. Arthur Miller famously depicted working-class Italian immigrants in Red Hook in his 1955 play A View From the Bridge (the title refers to the Brooklyn Bridge, visible from the waterfront, along with the Manhattan skyline and the Statue of Liberty).

Just across the BQE and Gowanus expressway, Carroll Gardens and the adjoining Cobble Hill and Boerum Hill, roughly bordered by 4th and Atlantic Avenues, have developed spectacularly in the last 20 years. BoCoCa has the beautiful parks, historic brownstones, and churches of Brooklyn Heights and the idyllic atmosphere and good schools of Park Slope for less—a irresistible environment for stroller-wielding young couples. The neighborhood is a newfound culinary destination, as the expanding urban professional population has created a demand for many new bars, cafés, and gourmet restaurants—although longstanding Italian family-owned pastry shops and pizzerias still dominate its tree-lined streets.

BoCoCa is the place to see New York gentrification in action. While Smith Street, the neighborhood's trendiest artery, offers new residents critically-acclaimed restaurants and antique shops, the area still maintains its very middle-class character. But it may not for long: make your visit before the Williamsburg crowd makes a mark on its crumbling charm.

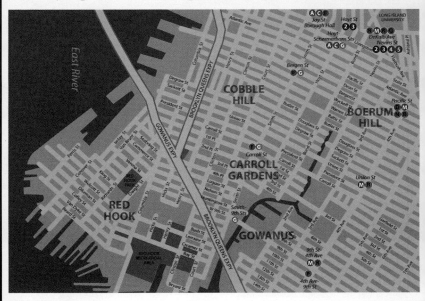

EXPLORE

Carroll Park

One block long and encompassing a mere 1.9 acres, Carroll Park is unusual in its unfailing ability to draw a crowd despite barely being big enough to show up on a map. Conceived as a private garden in the 1840s for the original neighborhood elite, the teeny plot was acquired by the city in 1853 and given a facelift, with new paths and a playground installed. Now the park is an important community meeting point for a neighborhood in flux—the landscaping fits basketball courts, several playgrounds, summer sprinklers, a baseball diamond, picnic tables, and a bocce court together like puzzle pieces, giving everyone something to do. A summer kids' music concert series also goes a long way to filling the park with the sound of wholesomeness.

Carroll St btwn
Court & Smith St
F **G** to Carroll St

Cobble Hill Park

Although only stretching half a block, Cobble Hill Park (or Verandah Park, as the locals call it) does much with its limited trapezoidal space. Surrounded by stately townhouses and the old-fashioned, narrow alley Verandah Place, this charming patch of greenery draws a diverse crowd around the dais of flowers in its center. On a typical day, the park is populated by lounging sunbathers, old men engrossed in heated checkers matches, and mommies chattering quietly while watching their children at the playground on the northern end. Built in 1989 on a long-disputed plot of land, the area is now a peaceful spot to munch on delicacies from one of the many nearby cafés or to catch a free concert in the summer.

Bordered by Congress, Verandah, and Clinton
F **G** to Bergen St

Gowanus Canal

A visit to the paved "banks" of the Gowanus Canal is a peek into Brooklyn's pre-organic farmers' market past. Stagnant since the main intake pump broke in the '60s, the canal was the prime dumping ground of the borough's corner-cutters for 40 years. The canal amassed enough sludge and body parts to earn the federal "Superfund" designation—it's officially one of the country's most dangerous waste sites—and the adjacent blocks constitute the one Brooklyn neighborhood to remain undeveloped in recent years. But slowly, Brooklynites have been trying to clean and reclaim it. Today visitors amble along the Carroll Street Bridge (one of the last retractable bridges in the nation), observe grizzled fishermen reeling in shrimp and blue crabs, and take canoes onto the revived waters.

Bond St at Douglass St
🅕 🅖 to Carroll St or
Smith-9th St

Micro Museum

While its name might suggest a collection of delicate doll houses or computer chips, the Micro Museum attracts the borough's most highbrow with its eccentric modern art installations, many of which are interactive or performance pieces. Constantly updated, the museum's exhibits feature a wide range of artistic mediums—particularly quirky highlights are the AC/DC Window, a kinetic sculpture that has been running since 1994, a virtual tour of the Louvre, and a couch with built-in phones. The owners are often there on Saturdays and have been known to give personal tours, and from 5pm to 7pm visitors can strike up a conversation with artists while sipping on complimentary refreshments. All works are also available for purchase, in case you're partial to one of the talking sofa cushions.

123 Smith St
(btwn Pacific & Dean St)
718-797-3116
Sat 12pm-7pm
🅕 🅖 to Bergen St
Admission $2.00

RED HOOK

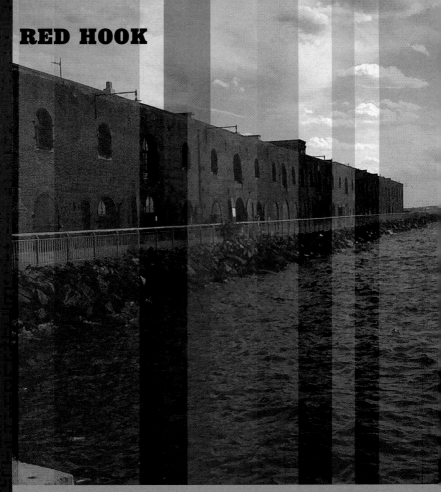

Although Red Hook is just across the East River from downtown Manhattan, it has been slower to develop than the rest of Greater Carroll Gardens. Its dusty industrial yards and relative distance from major subway lines have made it less attractive to new residents. In recent years, however, the neighborhood has begun to capitalize on its waterfront location, with a burgeoning artist community drawn in by the chic and comparatively affordable property, a huge **Fairway Market** *(480 Van Brunt St)* housed in a beautiful warehouse, and New York City's first and only **Ikea** *(1 Beard St)*. The present scene in Red Hook is quite different from what LIFE magazine saw when they named it "the crack capital of America" in the nineties, with an increase in awesome hidden dives like **Bait and Tackle** *(320 Van Brunt St)* and **Sunny's** *(253 Conover St)*. The coming years certainly look bright and promising for this peninsula.

Red Hook Recreation Center

Surrounded by housing projects, the Red Hook Park and Recreation Center is alive with playful screams of children and hip hop blaring from passing cars. The center is a sprawling complex of baseball pitches, soccer fields, basketball courts, picnic areas, a playground, and the 330-foot by 130-foot Sol Goldman Pool. The park's facilities attract people of all ages—mothers chatter into cell phones in Spanish, children on soccer teams kick up dust, and teens compete intensely in basketball. The indoor center offers fitness and cardio, arcade games, computer resources, and capoeira classes for members. Between swimmers doing break-of-dawn laps and night owls playing midnight pickup, the Red Hook Rec Area is a hub for fitness and neighborhood socializing at all hours of the day.

155 Bay St (at Henry St)
718-722-3211
Mon-Sat 7am-9pm
F G to Smith-9th Sts
$50 a year

St. Paul's Episcopal Church

Situated on a quiet residential street, this Anglo-Catholic church rises up from stoops cluttered with bicycles and barbecues, sticking out like a Gothic thumb. St. Paul's was founded on Christmas Day of 1849, and construction continued as the congregation grew until it reached its present state in 1860. Today the church attracts many an architecture buff, who admire the intricately carved columns, slated roofs, and immense stained glass windows. Perhaps its most impressive feature is the huge pipe organ in the back—the not-so-architecturally savvy can sit in the pews to listen to the choir or nod along at the monthly "Jazz at Mass" programs.

199 Carroll St
(at Clinton St)
718-625-4126
Sat 2pm-4pm
F G to Carroll St

Valentino Pier

Like Red Hook itself, Valentino Pier began life as an industrial shipping hotspot in the 1600s. The miniscule park was not added until 1996, and in fact is still somewhere in the adolescence of its transformation: the pier is part of the 14-mile stretch destined to be planted and polished by the Brooklyn Greenway project, a municipal effort at greening that has resisted naming a deadline for over a decade. But the pier is plenty enjoyable in its raw state, playing host to Civil-War era buildings, free kayaking, and the summer Red Hook Films series. Valentino Pier isn't the traditional green space—actually, it's mostly paved along the water—but it's astonishing for its survival and downright popularity among the surrounding dingy offices and warehouses.

Coffey St at Ferris St
(on the water)
F G to Smith-9th St
Free

Waterfront Museum and Showboat Barge

A Hudson River spice barge at its inception in 1914, this restored wooden hulk of a vessel is today the only covered barge of its time still floating, and an offshore exhibition of merchant life on the water. The inside is permanently adorned with accoutrements of the no-frills trade, including tools, the inner workings of the barge, a dingy, and a recreation of the captain's quarters. Layered on top of this history are seasonal installations of contemporary art, summer acoustic sets, and frequent presentations, for some reason, from circus performers who often tailor their acts to align with the spectacles of 1920s "showboats." The barge is docked at Pier 44, a peaceable bit of parkland open from sunrise to sunset.

290 Conover St
(at Pier 44)
718-624-4719
Thurs 4pm-8pm,
Sat 1pm-5pm
F G to Smith-9th St
Suggested admission $7

SHOP

BookCourt

Probably the biggest corner bookshop you'll ever visit. BookCourt prides itself on its family-owned independence, but

163 Court St (at Dean St)
718-875-3677
Sun 10am-9pm, Mon-Sat
9am-10:45pm
F G to Bergen St

its neighborhood presence is decidedly bright-lights-big-city, with a double storefront, periodic book signings featuring the likes of Rick Moody, Frank McCourt, and local fixture Jonathan Franzen, and a thoughtful, opinionated literary blog maintained on the store's slick website. BookCourt also partners in a reading series and has its own discerning publishing imprint and book club, all endeavors that place it in a nebulous space between a Border's-style chain, a university press, and your pushy cousin who keeps insisting that you read Paul Greenberg. But the

mixture works, and the store is comfortable and low-key enough for a few hours of afternoon perusal.

Brooklyn Bead Box

As burnished as its sterling silver spacers, the Brooklyn Bead Box is a perfect case study of Brooklyn's gentrification: the

244 Smith St
(at Douglass St)
866-504-2702
Daily 12pm-7pm
F G to Bergen St or
Carroll St

borough's old DIY creativity meets the slickness of many moneyed interlopers. But it's not an unholy union. The Bead Box, painted merry yellow and stuffed with worktables, is an extremely pleasant place to spend an afternoon picking out Peru opals, taking a class on wire wrapping, or renting the in-house tool kits to perfect your own creation. The selection covers all bases, from basic glass seed beads to Swarovski crystals to pewter charms for kids. BBB also holds a monthly themed contest, the

greater carroll gardens
UNDER $20

Start on Smith St, the commercial core of Carroll Gardens, with coffee and some zucchini bread at the unpretentious **Fall Café** *(307 Smith St)*.

Then stroll down Smith for early-morning bargain hunting at **Bird** *(220 Smith St)* and **Stinky Brooklyn** *(261 Smith St)*. Clothes and cheese: one needs nothing else in this life.

Take a ride to the 1920s on the **Waterfront Museum and Riverfront Barge** *(290 Conover St)*, your local floating solution to a normal day.

Then pause on **Pier 44** just outside to enjoy the view of the harbor. Otherwise take a walk to **Coffey Park** *(at King and Richards St)* for Red Hook's own little slice of grass and dogs catching Frisbees.

Feast on $7.50 schawarma "pitza"—pizza baked on pita bread—at **Zaytoons** *(283 Smith St)*.

End the day doing shots with a crowd of genuine Brooklyn 25-going-on-45-year-olds (the ones with money and real jobs) at **Abilene** *(442 Court St)*, the most clean-cut bar around.

winner of which receives a $100 gift certificate to the store.

One Girl Cookies

The only place in town where you can plunk down money for Sadie, Lana, and Cecilia and take them home with you, One Girl Cookies special-

68 Dean St (at Smith St)
212-675-4996
Sun 10am-7pm,
Mon-Fri 8am-7pm,
Sat 9am-8pm
Ⓕ Ⓖ to Bergen St

izes in careful craftsmanship accented with unexpected flavors. Each cookie, cupcake, and bonbon recipe is unique—both a departure from the traditional chocolate chip and a wholly different concoction from the other treats sharing its case. One Girl delivers throughout the United States, but it's much better to pick up Penelope (apricot, almond, and walnut in a butter cookie) and Juliette (chocolate cinnamon ganache, in hazelnut) in person, along with for a coffee at the too-charming counter bar. You can also pick up a dozen artisan whoopie pies for your Amish buddies.

Red Hook Lobster Pound

The Red Hook Lobster Pound aims to please, promising only the freshest and meatiest lobsters from the coasts of Maine—the workers themselves commute a few times a week to bring back boxes upon boxes of

284 Van Brunt St
(btwn Verona St &
Visitation Pl)
646-326-7650
Wed-Sun 12pm-7pm
Ⓕ Ⓖ to Smith-9th Sts
B61 to Verona St
$$

shellfish. In addition to whole live lobsters, the Pound also offers Jonah crab claws and their NYC-famous specialty lobster rolls—enjoy a cold "Maine-Style" with mayonnaise or a warm "Connecticut-Style" with butter. Limited picnic seating is available for those who wish to dine among the lobster tanks that crowd the store, but if weather permits, the Red Hook Recreational Area and Piers are only a few blocks away. To truly eat like a "Mainer" for the day, indulge in some dessert and order a classic Pine Tree State treat, the Whoopie Pie—a rich, cake rendition of the Oreo cookie.

389

JALOPY THEATRE
best bluegrass under the BQE

Swing over to the Jalopy for the most consistently and notoriously amazing bluegrass, folk, and blues in New York City. On the night of a show, audiences can expect to see a number of great acts hit the theater's intimate, red-curtained stage for a modest cover. Music lovers of all ages fill the church pew seats and dance in adjacent aisles as they sip wine, beer, and coffee. For those inspired by what they hear, the Jalopy also offers music lessons and instrument rentals and sales throughout the day. It's good vibes all over at this old-time American treasure chest, and a paper-mâché bust of Thomas Jefferson watches from on stage to make sure it stays that way. Come on down for the Roots & Ruckus party on Wednesdays or a clawhammer banjo workshop in the afternoon. Memphis never felt so close!

Music Venue

315 Columbia St
(near Woodhull St)
718-395-3214
Mon, Wed-Fri
2pm-12am,
Sat-Sun 12pm-12am
F,G to Carroll St
Cover $10-15
*All Ages

Steve's Authentic Key Lime Pies

The yellow, somewhat hidden door of this ramshackle warehouse on the Red Hook waterfront screams "PIES HERE." These aren't just any pies—they're exclusively key lime, and they're the best in the city (and maybe even the whole Northeast). Steve's Authentic Key Lime Pies sells only the homemade Real McCoy, baked daily with what they call "the element that sets our product apart": fresh-squeezed key limes. As an added bonus, the fruit supplies a pleasantly pungent aroma to the otherwise dark, uninviting room (or rather, a counter flooded

204 Van Dyke St (btwn Conover & Van Brunt St)
718-858-5333
Open daily, hours vary (updated on website)
F G to Carroll St

with limes and gewgaws) where the confections are sold. The pies come in three sizes: 10", 8", and a 4" tart, to be devoured straight from the dish at one of the outdoor picnic tables with a glass of fresh key-lemonade.

Store 518

Founded by dancer-turned-designer Nadia Tarr, this boutique offers a mix of eccentric apparel and outlandish, old-school houseware items. Marble door handles, creepy vintage dolls, funky lamps, and the kind of exotic feather duster French maids use in old mov-

518 Court St
(near Nelson St)
646-256-5041
Sun 11am-7pm,
Thurs-Sat, 12pm-8pm
F to Smith-9th Sts

ies are only a few of the knick-knacks you'll find in the antique hardwood chests lining the floors. There's both vintage and contemporary clothing, the latter featuring the bright-hued, elegantly draped dresses from Tarr's own collection, Butter by Nadia. Vintage accessories include fun-and-feathered hairpieces, "jellies" sandals, beaded jewelry, and glamorous lacy (never worn) bras. There's also an enticing selection of classic candy, like Necco Wafers, Sugar Daddies, and Candy Buttons, to nosh on while you browse.

EAT

Buttermilk Channel *American, Brunch*

The narrow strait between Governor's Island and Brooklyn—known as the Buttermilk Channel—was known to have waters so choppy that milkmen who tried to brave the passage would invariably

524 Court St
(at Huntington St)
718-852-8590
Sun 10am-3pm, 5pm-11pm, Mon-Thurs 5pm-11pm, Sat 10am-3pm, 5pm-12am
🄵 🄶 to Smith St
$$

have their milk churned to butter. The Buttermilk Channel restaurant honors this legacy by cooking up the most delectable buttermilk-battered fried chicken. While the restaurant is best known for its sublime brunch, the Monday prix fixe dinner is a fantastic find. For $25, the three-course meal features their signature fried chicken and waffles, served with a heavenly

CHEAP EATS
places to bring your parents

Saul- The lively ambiance and seasonal menu of this upscale restaurant will surely impress even the sternest parents, especially with specialties like duck confit over cheesy grits and caramelized scallops with white bean purée and chorizo. *140 Smith St, 718-935-9844, Sun-Thurs 5:30pm-10:30pm, Fri-Sat 5:30pm-11pm, F, G to Bergen St $$$$*

Prime Meats- Traditional rustic European specialties—beef Sauerbraten and red cabbage, pork Gulyas and spatzle, black angus steak frites—are prepared with quality meats in a sophisticated fashion at this elegant yet trendy Brooklyn eatery. *465 Court St, 718-254-0327, Sun-Wed 7am-1am, Thurs-Sat 7am-2am, F, G to Smith-9th Sts $$*

Char No. 4- With over 300 different kinds of bourbon, and a delicious mélange of comfort food like Jambalaya, smoked pork sausage, and housemade brisket sandwich, this bustling whiskey bar is a formidable homage to the South. *196 Smith St, 718-643-2106, Sun-Thurs 6pm-12am, Fri-Sat 6pm-1am, F, G to Bergen St $$*

combination of balsamic vinaigrette and maple syrup. The Pecan Pie Sundae offers a sugary culmination: pecan pie filling served in a glass, sandwiched between vanilla ice cream and whipped cream. If the subway ever happens to shut down, you may find yourself willing to risk crossing the strait on your own to reach this wonderful deal.

Frankies 457 Spuntino   *Italian*

If you are going to have one Italian meal in New York, put Frankies 457 Spuntino on your shortlist. This classic and stylish restaurant-cum-bar in Carroll Gardens doesn't play around when it comes to food—the owners go to Sicily every year to oversee the production of their own olive oil. After trying it, buttery and flavorful, you won't be surprised. The philosophy extends to their other purveyors, all of whom are wellvetted "friends" who own longstanding family-run shops. Frankies' minimal interior is an interplay of cream-colored tiles and dark wooden tables, rough brick walls, and exposed fixtures. The menu is simple and honest, with most dishes focused on the proper preparation of a few fresh, local, high-quality ingredients: one of the sandwiches combines salty, delicate

457 Court St
(near Luquer St)
718-403-0033
Sun-Thurs 11am-11pm,
Fri-Sat 11am-12am
F **G** to Carroll St
$$

WATERFRONT ARTISTS COALITION
most weirdly charming warehouse

Opened in 1902, Luna Park was a wildly popular entertainment spot featuring thousands of electric lamps, performing monkeys, and rides on domesticated elephants. Fire damage forced its closure in 1944, but after massive renovation, the grounds were reopened in May 2010 with a fresh array of rides, games, and spectacles. Lunatics can swing up to 50 feet on the Eclipse Pendulum, brave switchback curves on the Tickler, or attempt to keep down their cotton candy on the Electro Spin half pipe. Sandwiched between the notorious Cyclone roller coaster and Deno's Wonder Wheel Amusement Park, the revamped park has muscled its way back into Islanders' hearts. When you're sick of feeling your stomach drop, head next door to get your fortune told or take a picture with a live snake.

499 Van Brundt St
(near Reed St)
718-596-2507
Sat-Sun 1pm-6pm
F,G to Smith-9th St
Free

sausage with the bitterness of broccoli rabe and sweet, thin-sliced rosemary bread. During the pleasant months, enjoy your meal on the large shaded patio out back.

Mile End — *Deli*

97A Hoyt St
(btwn Atlantic Ave &
Pacific St)
718-853-7510
Mon-Tues 8am-4:30pm,
Wed-Fri 8am-10pm,
Sat-Sun 10am-10pm
Ⓐ Ⓒ Ⓖ to Hoyt-
Schermerhorn St
$$

If it seems unlikely that a law school drop-out could re-invent the Jewish deli, prepare to be shocked. With his Montreal upbring-ing in tote, Noah Bermanoff taught himself to cook in his Park Slope apart-ment and directed his newfound talent into Mile End. Seats at the counter may be dif-ficult to come by, but they grant a view of the open kitchen, replete with sizzling fresh smoked meat—a more flavorful Montreal derivative of pastrami—half-used heirloom tomatoes, and house-pickled cabbage. Further evidence of the deli's dedication to exceptional local ingredients is the house-made salami (beef short rib mixed with brisket), which constitutes the stunning Ruth Wilensky—a masterpiece of mustard, fried salami, and a pressed onion roll. While not necessarily traditional, it doesn't seem to mat-ter when the old man next to you breaks into a craggy grin at the mere sight of his sandwich.

Petite Crevette — *Seafood*

Ⓢ 🍶 🍦
144 Union St (at Hicks St)
718-855-2632
Mon-Sat 12pm-3pm,
5pm-11pm,
Sun 5pm-11pm
Ⓕ Ⓖ to Carroll St
$$

With barely a dozen small tables, Petite Crevette, or "Little Shrimp," is an aptly-named bastion of seafood located in the newly named Colum-bia Waterfront Dis-trict. Its walls are art-fully strewn with the owner's family photos and antique maritime art, though the true standout is the handwrit-ten menu posted on brown paper. Ingredients, coming from as far as Norway and as close as the Italian dairy across the street, are all impec-cably prepared and flavorful. Standouts include creamy seafood chowder with sizable chunks of scallops, cod, and shrimp, and the mustard-seed encrusted salmon, served alongside fresh vegetables and velvety mashed potatoes. A meal here is one of simple enjoyment—Johnny Cash and jazz play in the background, soft candles light up the room, and portions satisfy but don't overwhelm.

PLAY

Gowanus Yacht Club — *Beer Pub*

Ⓢ 🥡
323 Smith St
à(at President St)
Mon-Fri 4pm-closing,
Sat-Sun 2pm-closing
Ⓕ Ⓖ to Carroll St

This nautically-themed seasonal bar pops up in a vacant lot next to the Carroll Street station every May and disappears every October. Dur-ing the months in between, South Brooklyn's hippest youths congregate for beer, wine, and burgers in the sun. Named after the nearby ca-nal, Gowanus is far from a "Yacht Club": it's actually an assortment of picnic tables, church pews, and fold-out chairs where often unkempt patrons enjoy cheap-as-hell drinks among hang-ing buoy and oar decorations. With a rotating eight beers on tap, along with bottles, cans, and two house wines, the selection ain't bad con-sidering a lack of hard liquor. There's even a grill, where chefs cook up burgers, kielbasa, and vegan patties alike. It's the perfect summertime hangout, and if it gets too hot, the trusty misting system is always there to cool things down.

PA

Today, Park Slope is more famous for its demanding, relentlessly politically correct, bloody-fanged soccer moms than anything else—but describing it as such is akin to dismissing Manhattan as a noisy rats' den. It's true that this verdant bit of Brooklyn is awash in new wealth and newer babies, but the neighborhood's character has little to do with the nightmarish yuppie of myth. Named after its location just west of Prospect Park, the area was quietly farmed by the Dutch for two hundred years. There was little to distinguish it from the rest of Brooklyn, which was still largely pastoral.

After streetcars arrived in the 1870s and the Brooklyn Bridge opened in 1883, Park Slope met the outside world. Brownstones and grand Victorian mansions sprang up like weeds, built by members of the commuting upper crust. When the newly-minted Brooklyn Dodgers chose the neighborhood as its first home in 1879, it became a shining star of the borough. The team later moved on, but Park Slope's status as a power player remained.

Like many outer borough enclaves, Park Slope was profoundly changed when the rich staged an urban exodus in the 1950s. The area became home to working-class Italians, blacks, and Latinos, who were duly edged out over the next decade, when long-haired children of the '60s took over. And so it went: upper-middle class professionals came to vanquish the bohemi-

SLO

ans in the 1970s, followed by lesbian couples and young families, who worked to establish a strong sense of local community. Eventually, Park Slope regained its turn-of-the-century title as one of New York City's most well-to-do neighborhoods. Throughout the rapid-fire transformations, preservationists worked to save local historic houses and mansions, giving us the landmarks we know today.

A tumultuous background of settling and re-settling has worked to Park Slope's advantage, and these days it maintains a welcoming and unassuming vibe. Brooklyn celebrates its annual Gay Pride day in front of organic coffee houses and upscale specialty boutiques. Hippies still ponder progressive social resistance, only now they do it while sitting next to a busy playground, trust fund withdrawal requests in hand. There's plenty of classic self-starter enthusiasm to be found amidst the fancier new scene; Slopers can generally be counted on to come out in droves for anything arts-related, be it a dance performance in Prospect Park or a miniscule gallery opening by an unknown talent. Park Slope is the closest you can get to laid-back Northern California without leaving New York City. Depending on what street you're on, you'll also see glimpses of the Upper West Side, South Carolina's shady avenues, and the moneyed hedges of Alpine, New Jersey.

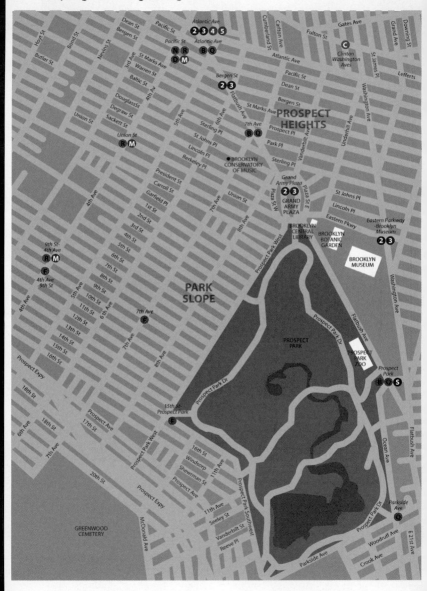